MEASURING POVERTY
AROUND THE WORLD

MEASURING
POVERTY
AROUND
THE WORLD

Anthony B. Atkinson

Edited by John Micklewright and Andrea Brandolini

With Afterwords
by François Bourguignon and Nicholas Stern

PRINCETON UNIVERSITY PRESS

PRINCETON AND OXFORD

LCCN 2019936797

ISBN 978-0-691-19122-5

British Library Cataloging-in-Publication Data is available

Editorial: Sarah Caro & Hannah Paul

Production Editorial: Ali Parrington

Text Design: Leslie Flis

Jacket Design: Lorraine Doneker

Jacket/Cover Credit: From "The Poverty Line," a typology of photographs examining the daily food choices made by people across the world living at the poverty line. Courtesy of Chow and Lin. www.thepovertyline.net

Production: Erin Suydam

Publicity: James Schneider, Caroline Priday & Nathalie Levine

Copyeditor: Cynthia Buck

This book has been composed in Minion Pro with Gotham Display

Printed on acid-free paper. ∞

Printed in the United States of America

10 9 8 7 6 5 4 3 2 1

For our grandchildren,
in the hope that they will see progress towards
the elimination of world poverty

CONTENTS

DETAILED CHAPTER CONTENTS

LIST OF FIGURES, TABLES, AND BOXES

FIGURES

TABLES

BOXES

FOREWORD

I am not sure that I will be able to finish, but it is quite interesting to read all the different country studies for places that I scarcely knew existed (like the Solomon Islands!). I keep an atlas on my desk! I am very impressed with the overall quality of the work being produced in statistical offices around the world, and feel that there is a lot of scope for mutual learning.

This is an excerpt from the last email that Tony Atkinson sent one of us before his death on 1 January 2017. The words are telling of his personality. They illustrate the intellectual curiosity that drove him to find and understand data. They show his respect for craftsmanship—be that of the official statisticians of the Solomon Islands (a country ranked 156 out of 188 countries according to the 2017 Human Development Index) or the carpenter who had fixed his bookshelves. They reveal an enthusiasm and a commitment to research that his illness could not restrain.

Sadly, Tony was indeed unable to finish. But before his death he asked us to take his manuscript forward to publication. He left an incomplete first draft. We quickly decided that completion of the book was impossible. We were unsure of how Tony planned to develop his lines of argument in the second half of the book and the details of his intentions for the large amount of data that he had collected. We might have imposed our own ideas, but we were clear that the book should remain Tony's rather than become a book coauthored by us.

With the agreement of Tony's family, we decided to bring the book to a state where it could be published while remaining incomplete. We have added a significant amount of material in chapters 3 and 4 with the aim of finishing Tony's discussion in the first half of the book of conceptual and practical issues in measuring poverty. (Here, and elsewhere, the section and subsection titles are those that Tony had already planned, with very few changes.) In part we drew on his earlier writings and on our knowledge of his views from our joint work with him over the years. Some additions are straightforward updates for developments that Tony would have definitely included, such as those relating to the EU social indicators or the Global Multidimensional Poverty Index. We added smaller amounts of text elsewhere, but much of what Tony planned to cover in several chapters in the second half of the book is still missing. (He had drafted most of the book's concluding chapter, however.) We also edited the sixty "national reports" at the end of the book that Tony had planned to draw on in chapters 6 to 9, adding and updating text and data, writing reports for several countries, and drawing graphs for others, although nineteen of the reports remain largely skeletons without the flesh that Tony would have supplied. Our edits and additions to the main text and to the national reports are not visible to the reader, but on occasion we have added notes in which we comment explicitly as editors. We have also written a longer explanatory note at the start of the national reports. In places there is cross-referencing from one chapter to another that Tony had drafted, but the passage to which the reader is referred is missing; we have retained these statements, as they indicate the links that Tony was aiming to incorporate.

We decided not to make an extensive search of relevant literature in order to fill any gaps in the main text. In particular, we have not consulted Martin Ravallion's 2016 book *The Economics of Poverty*, referred to by Tony in chapter 1, or the 2015 book *Multidimensional Poverty Measurement and Analysis* by Sabina Alkire, James Foster, Suman Seth, Maria Emma Santos, José Manuel Roche, and Paola Ballon, which Tony cites in a number of places. We have only partially updated references to the growing literature on multidimensional poverty, in particular that inspired by the Alkire-Foster measures of nonmonetary poverty discussed by Tony in chapters 3 and 5. (Tony includes estimates of poverty based on these methods in his national reports.) We have not completed chapter 9's discussion of rich countries, despite being familiar with the material. Our purpose has been to carry out the necessary editorial work to allow readers to appreciate the many insights contained in the draft left by Tony without nurturing an illusion that the book was almost finished. This is a book worth reading, but readers must be aware that it is an unfinished book.

The book grew out of Tony's work chairing the Commission on Global Poverty, set up by the World Bank in 2015, and his work on the Commission's report, *Monitoring Global Poverty*, published in 2017. He wrote this report single-handedly, taking sole responsibility for its contents, while acknowledging the contributions of the members of the Commission's advisory board (listed in World Bank 2017, pp. xi–xii). The experience led Tony to the decision to write a book for a broader audience about the nature and extent of poverty across the world. He drew substantially on material in the Commission's report in the draft that he left, and the World Bank has kindly agreed to this use of the material. We are convinced that with time he would have made more changes to some of the text concerned, in part to make the more demanding sections even more accessible to a general readership, and in part to recognise where the World Bank had accepted his report's recommendations. The Bank's response to the recommendations is detailed in World Bank (2016b), and its implementation of those that it accepted is indeed taking place. The first of the Bank's flagship *Poverty and Shared Prosperity* biennial reports, published around the same time as *Monitoring Global Poverty*, had already clarified that "the countries classified as industrialized . . . are assumed to have zero poverty at the $1.90-a-day poverty line, an assumption that may change in the future because of the World Bank's implementation of the report of the Commission on Global Poverty on global poverty estimation" (World Bank 2016, p. 19). This revolutionary change in the traditional World Bank approach at last closes the gulf between the rich, or "high-income," countries and the rest of the world, making the measurement of global poverty truly global. The 2018 edition of *Poverty and Shared Prosperity*, published after this book went to press, further responds to the Commission's recommendations. It includes: analysis of nonmonetary measures of deprivation (and their use with a monetary measure in a multidimensional poverty index); consideration of differences in poverty within the household; and estimates of poverty based on a "societal" poverty line that combines absolute and relative elements. The Bank has also now started to publish on its website short country "poverty briefs," following another of the recommendations made by the Commission.

However, Tony's book goes well beyond the Commission's report.

First, the report started from the World Bank's current measurement of "extreme poverty" and then broadened out to consider other measures, while in this book Tony starts from first principles of measuring world poverty. The Commission report was written to advise the Bank on two specific issues about its future measurement of poverty: how to update its methods based on households' consumption given that prices change over time and new rounds of international price comparisons become available, and whether and how to incorporate other dimensions of poverty and deprivation into its measurement. While the Commission report was largely restricted to considering methods, Tony wrote this book to address how one should measure poverty across the world starting from scratch and then to discuss what the available data actually reveal. The book is an example of the "principled" approach followed by Tony throughout his research: there is no measurement without theory, and conversely the theoretical developments are valuable only to the extent that they are liable to being used in practice. And behind the whole exercise, researchers have the duty to make explicit the ethical judgements embedded in the measurement—the enduring intuition of his landmark paper on the measurement of inequality in the *Journal of Economic Theory* in 1970.

Second, the book seeks to integrate international organisations' measurement of poverty with national analyses produced within each country. The existing literature tends to take one or other of these approaches without reconciling the two. To do this Tony set out to document the measurement done at the national level by national statistical offices and ministries and the trends shown by these national data, comparing them with what is shown by data published by international organisations. He planned to do this for sixty countries, the raw material forming the national reports at the end of the book. His intention was to use this material in the second half of the book, in chapters 6 to 9, to answer a standard set of "key questions" about poverty levels and trends for each of four regions or groups of countries—Asia and the Pacific, Africa,

Latin America and the Caribbean, and high-income countries. Of course, for many countries there exist exercises comparing poverty estimates elaborated at both the international and national levels, but the novelty of Tony's approach is to call for their systematic integration. In his view, this would serve to cross-check the conclusions on the structure and changes in poverty shown by different methods or sources, sounding a warning bell for users of the data where inconsistencies could not be explained. National measures are grounded in some kind of political process within each country, whereas the measures worked out by international organisations have a different origin. The integration of these two measurement exercises provides legitimacy to both, and eventually to the policy decisions that are taken based on them. The book is concerned both with the measurement of poverty in individual countries and with how to arrive at a global total for poverty. The "around" in the title has these two senses.

Third, Tony planned to address in chapters 6 to 9 a series of "general issues"—two per chapter—about the causes and correlates of poverty or about its measurement. These include, for example, the extent of the "trickle-down" to the poor from economic growth, the legacy from the colonial period to poverty today in former colonies, the poverty suffered by indigenous peoples, and the persistence of poverty in rich countries. This would have been a bold attempt to use the historical trends and structural patterns of poverty drawn from his national reports to illuminate fundamental questions about poverty.

In the event, the second half of the book remained largely unfinished. But Tony's broad plans for the use of the national reports to address the key questions and general issues are clear, if not in the detail that might have allowed us to go further in our work. (The reports also allowed him to make numerous references to national practices in the first half of the book.) The general issues are plainly spelt out even if most of the analysis is missing. These unfinished chapters offer a foundation on which other researchers can build and a challenge to them to do so.

Tony was ambitious in planning his book, in terms of both structure and content. The discussion in chapters 6 to 9 was not to be restricted to the countries that made up the region or group with which the chapter was principally concerned. He intended extensive cross-referencing to countries in other parts of the world. As he describes his intention in chapter 5, Tony saw chapters 6 to 9 as "building horizontal bridges between the measurement of poverty at a national level in different countries," referring also there to the "mutual learning" that he wrote about in the excerpt from the email at the start of this foreword. Tony notes in chapter 1 that the sixty countries for which he planned national reports represent nearly one-third of the world's total, and they include countries at all levels of development, as befits a book on global poverty. He of course does not mention the effort required to get to grips with national estimates and studies of poverty for that many countries, to tease out the right messages, and to compare intelligently the national figures with those from international organisations. And both the key questions and the general issues treated in chapters 6 to 9 are not just about measurement, belying the title of the book: Tony was concerned too with major issues of substance, underlining again his ambition for the work.

He also sought to give prominence to nonmonetary measures of poverty alongside the monetary measures that he had worked with for much of his career. We believe that Tony would have devoted considerable space to analysis of the nonmonetary measures if he had completed the book, in particular the short time series of data (often only two data points) available for many of the countries covered in his sixty national reports. Many of these data come from the work of the Oxford Poverty and Human Development Initiative (OPHI) and for several years have been published in the annual *Human Development Report* of the United Nations Development Programme (UNDP). Other data come from Eurostat's measurement of material deprivation for the European Union. Drawing on his notes and files, we have included some limited analysis of the data in chapter 5 but not in later chapters, and the unfinished state of this work is another challenge to other researchers. We also think that if Tony had completed his book, he would have continued to look for a middle ground in the debate that has surrounded these measures, pointing to the arguments on both sides (see chapter 3) while recognising that they have been adopted by many national statistical offices.

These observations should help the reader to appreciate why we have resisted both the temptation to go further in completing the manuscript and the suggestions by people who helped us that we refer to issues that Tony certainly considered important but were not covered in his draft. On the one hand, the structure that Tony had conceived for this book was unconventional and unusually complex, based on different intertwined layers. (It brought to mind for one of us the structure of Georges Perec's 1978 masterpiece *La Vie mode d'emploi*, despite obvious differences.) On the other hand, Tony's writings, while invariably elegant, were always succinct, with limited citation of his own work and rare concessions to unnecessary references. This was an important reason to refrain from filling the manuscript with even more editors' notes. We made only two major exceptions in our resistance to filling the gaps beyond the interventions described earlier. The two general issues to be covered in chapter 6 were the relation between growth, inequality, and poverty reduction and the relation between poverty reduction and action on climate change. Tony saw these issues as fundamental in the fight against poverty, but he ran out of time to address them. To fill these gaps, we asked two leading scholars in these areas, François Bourguignon and Nicholas Stern, long-standing co-authors and friends of Tony and both former chief economists of the World Bank, to deal with these subjects, which they have done in two extensive afterwords.

Where does the book fit within Tony's career and his huge research output? Tony is often thought of principally as a scholar of inequality, with his 2015 book *Inequality: What Can Be Done?* seen as a culmination of his life's work. But it is with poverty that he began his long line of books. This book appears exactly fifty years after Tony's first, published in 1969, *Poverty in Britain and the Reform of Social Security.* His many fundamental contributions to the study of poverty, both theoretical and empirical, are detailed, for example, in the article by us and fifteen other authors on "Tony Atkinson and His Legacy" in the September 2017 issue of the *Review of Income and Wealth.* (The article covers the wide range of Tony's output, including his foundational work on the study of public economics as well as his research on poverty and inequality and, for example, on official statistics.)

Tony's empirical work on poverty, inequality, and related subjects became increasingly international in coverage over those fifty years. The 1969 book was firmly focussed on Britain. There is passing reference to Sweden and to the United States, where he had spent a year earlier in the 1960s, but none, for example, to France—a country to which Tony devoted much attention in later years. (As François Bourguignon has noted, Tony was a Francophile as well as a Francophone.) However, he quickly engaged with the then European Communities in the early 1970s (recounted in Atkinson and Stern 2017), including with emerging debates on poverty and its measurement. His work on Europe in the 1980s included thinking through national versus supranational measures of poverty and led to his 1998 book *Poverty in Europe.*

His analysis of European poverty then moved towards the "principled" elaboration of a wider set of nonmonetary indicators of well-being in research with Bea Cantillon, Brian Nolan, and Eric Marlier, described in their influential 2002 book *Social Indicators: The EU and Social Inclusion.* This work on the European Union was extended onto a global field at the request of the United Nations in Atkinson and Marlier (2010). By then, Tony had also edited a United Nations University World Institute for Development Economics Research (UNU-WIDER) volume on *New Sources of Development Finance,* which was concerned with the funding of the Millennium Development Goals (Atkinson 2005), and he had written important papers with François Bourguignon on their ideas for the measurement of global poverty (Atkinson and Bourguignon 2000 and 2001), drawn on in this book in chapters 2 and 9 and a key influence on the 2018 edition of the World Bank's *Poverty and Shared Prosperity* report.

Tony's concern for cross-national comparisons of income inequality and poverty characterises much of his research. In the mid-1990s he coauthored with Lee Rainwater and Tim Smeeding a much-cited report on income distribution in OECD countries (Atkinson, Rainwater, and Smeeding 1995). His research in the 2000s on top incomes began again by covering OECD countries but then broadened out to other parts of the world—compare the two volumes that he edited with Thomas Piketty (Atkinson and Piketty 2007 and 2010)—

and in his final years he wrote a series of papers on top incomes in Africa in the colonial period and beyond (for example, Atkinson 2014; Alvaredo and Atkinson 2016). The unwritten section on the colonial legacy in chapter 7 in this book echoes this work. Tony had shown an early interest in measuring the world distribution of income in *The Economics of Inequality*, published in 1975; he dropped the chapter concerned from the 1983 second edition on grounds of space (we doubt that he would have made the same decision again now), but returned to the subject with one of us in an article many years later (Atkinson and Brandolini 2010).

Tony's chairing of the Commission on Global Poverty, his writing of the Commission's report, and now this book can be seen as the logical end of a lifelong process of engaging with the measurement and understanding of living standards across the world.

The book also fits into Tony's pattern of providing as much of the detail as possible about the data and sources that he used in his research. In this sense, the sixty national reports in this book are a successor to the mass of evidence that he gathered in 2005 on earnings distributions for each of twenty countries in the last part of *The Changing Distribution of Earnings in OECD Countries* (Atkinson 2008), or to the extensive appendices providing the raw tabulated data and a description of how ministries and national statistics offices had collected them in his 1992 book with one of us on *Economic Transformation in Eastern Europe and the Distribution of Income* (a book mistitled, much to Tony's amusement, by a University of Oxford magazine as "Economic Transfiguration . . ."). We should also mention *The Chartbook on Economic Inequality* (2017), which he coauthored with Joe Hasell, Salvatore Morelli, and Max Roser, as another recent example of compiling data and scrupulously documenting their sources. Tony was exceptionally careful with data, always insistent on reading footnotes and getting to the bottom of the matter on definitions, always hesitating over "joining up the dots" if he was not convinced that a series of data was consistent over time. We know that he did not have the time to check and check again all his material in this book. We have done our best to do so in his place, but we ask the reader to absolve him of any errors that may remain.

We are grateful to the Atkinson family—to Judith, Richard (Tony's literary executor), Sarah, and Charles—for their encouragement and their patience. We thank François Bourguignon and Nick Stern for enthusiastically agreeing to write their afterwords and for responding to our comments on drafts. Other friends and colleagues of Tony have helped us generously in various ways: Sabina Alkire, Chico Ferreira, Tina Gericke, Joe Hasell, Stephen Jenkins, Christoph Lakner, Eric Marlier, Luisa Minghetti, Brian Nolan, Max Roser, Yangyang Shen, Tim Smeeding, and Chloe Zeng. We want in particular to thank Joe Hasell for his invaluable assistance in updating Tony's use of international databases, his suggestions for revision of graphs, his careful input to the national reports at the end of the book (including to our introductory note), and his organisation of the resulting data; and Yangyang Shen for her help with data and methods in China, which she also worked on with Tony in his final months—without that work and her repeated efforts to respond to our queries, the information on China in the book would have been much weaker. Our work would have been nigh impossible without the resources of the University College London library. We thank Sarah Caro and her colleagues at Princeton University Press, including Charlie Allen, Cynthia Buck, Fred Kameny, Dimitri Karetnikov, Ali Parrington, Hannah Paul, and others with whom we have not had direct contact, for their enthusiasm and care throughout the publication process. We also thank the Press's anonymous readers for their comments.

Last, we are grateful of course to Tony for his trust in asking us to prepare his manuscript for publication, enabling a small part of our lifetime debts to be repaid. Trust in his coauthors was a hallmark of Tony's career, and in the last eighteen months we have tried not to be chased too much by the recurrent question: What would Tony have done here?

John Micklewright, University College London
Andrea Brandolini, Banca d'Italia

August 2018

PREFACE

This book owes much to other people. There are, first and foremost, my coauthors in the fields of poverty and income distribution, with whom it has been a great pleasure to work over five decades, including, in alphabetical order, Rolf Aaberge, Facundo Alvaredo, François Bourguignon, Andrea Brandolini, Andrew Leigh, Eric Marlier, John Micklewright, Salvatore Morelli, Brian Nolan, Max Roser, Thomas Piketty, Emmanuel Saez, Tim Smeeding, and Holly Sutherland. In particular, I have built on the collections of data on income distribution that I have assembled together with Andrea Brandolini and John Micklewright over the years, and together with Salvatore Morelli and Max Roser in *The Chartbook of Economic Inequality*.

The book would not have been possible without the work of the staff members of the World Bank. There had been earlier studies of international inequality, but the modern study of poverty on a global scale begins with the work of Martin Ravallion in the early 1990s. Together with Shaohua Chen and colleagues in the Development Research Group at the World Bank, he developed the estimates of global poverty that were the foundation for the monitoring of the Millennium Development Goals (MDGs) agreed in 2000 and their continuation as Goal 1.1 of the Sustainable Development Goals (SDGs) in 2015. The World Bank research has had many critics. One of the most prominent is Sir Angus Deaton, recipient in 2015 of the Sveriges Riksbank Prize in Economic Sciences in Memory of Alfred Nobel. His rigorous and painstaking research has been of fundamental significance. One important line of departure has been the extension to nonmonetary indicators of poverty and indices of multidimensional poverty. While my first book on poverty was concerned with income poverty, I have always been open to the application of nonmonetary measures, and I have moved further in this direction much influenced by the work of Amartya Sen on the capability approach and of Sabina Alkire, James Foster, and colleagues at the Oxford Poverty and Human Development Initiative (OPHI). Multidimensionality has been at the heart of the work of the United Nations Development Programme (UNDP) and its *Human Development Reports* originated by Mahbub ul Haq. Moving from global institutions to those concerned with particular regions of the globe, I should acknowledge the valuable assemblies of data by the Asian Development Bank (whose analysis is employed in chapter 6), the African Development Bank (chapter 7), the Caribbean Development Bank and the Socio-Economic Database for Latin America and the Caribbean (SEDLAC) (chapter 8), and Eurostat and the Organisation for Economic Co-operation and Development (OECD) (chapter 9 on poverty in rich countries). In each case, they in turn were drawing on the work of statistical agencies at the national level, which has provided a significant part of the evidence on which the book is based. The quality and depth of national studies has greatly impressed me. Finally, I have drawn extensively on the Key Statistics produced by the LIS Cross-National Data Center (formerly Luxembourg Income Study), now covering more than 60 per cent of the world population, and of which I have had the honour of being president in recent years.

The aim of this book is to present the evidence assembled from these sources in a way that is accessible to the general reader. This is a challenge, since the issues are technical and technicalities matter. Changing the period over which consumer expenditure information is collected from a week to a month may seem like no big deal, but it can make a sizeable difference to the number of people reported as living in poverty. Comparing living standards across countries may seem straightforward—one simply has to compare the price of a range of items like bread, burgers, and milk—but if the mix of spending differs across countries, you may get a different answer when comparing country A with country B directly from that if you first compare A with another country C and then compare C with B. Or, to take another example, a new census of population for a country may yield different estimates of the total population from those on which the poverty estimates have been based, leading to a major rethinking of the number of people living in poverty (a reduction of no less than 6 million in the case of Bangladesh). I would be doing the reader no service if issues of this kind were simply swept under the carpet.

The purpose of the book is indeed to raise questions as much as to provide definite answers. To this end, the analysis in chapters 2 to 4 takes the form of raising questions that the reader should have in mind when looking at the numbers. The reader should be asking all the time, just what is being measured here? If it is claimed that global poverty is falling, is this true for other definitions of poverty? Is a fall in those below the International Poverty Line masking a worsening of other nonmonetary dimensions of poverty? Is there growing inequality within households, so that women are being let behind? How are the conclusions affected by the move from an expenditure basis to an income basis, as we cross the Atlantic from Africa to Latin America? The conclusion of these chapters is a checklist that the user of poverty statistics may find a useful guide when puzzling over the numbers.

The first chapter introduces the key issues. It takes a first look at the numbers, for the book is about statistics. There are inevitably many graphs and tables. I appreciate that these are not to everyone's taste, but I have tried to ease the reader's path. I have followed the maxim, which I was taught by Brian Reddaway when I was a student in Cambridge, that a table or a graph should be intelligible to the reader without recourse to searching through the text for an explanation. To realise this ambition, I have in each case followed the excellent French practice of attaching to each table or graph a reading note that guides the reader through the material.

One of the aims of the book is to describe the state of poverty in a wide range of contexts. There are reports, assembled in the last part of the book, summarising the evidence for sixty individual countries. At the same time, the coverage of the world is only partial. The Irish mathematician Sir William Hamilton boasted at the age of thirteen that he had mastered one language for each year that he had lived (Bell 1953, p. 375). I can make no such boast. My language range is strictly limited. This means that the coverage here of the literature on poverty is biased towards sources that are in European languages. I should also say that, while the national case studies cover sixty countries, I have visited only a third of them, and few of those are outside Europe. The book has been written sitting in Oxford, not in airport lounges.

I began writing the book in October 2016, after completing the report for the Commission on Global Poverty for the World Bank (2017). In preparing that report, I was on a steep learning curve, and while I have drawn on some of the same material, my learning has continued. I am grateful to the Bank for allowing me to use the material where there is overlap, but this turns out to be much smaller than I originally envisaged. This does not mean that I have changed my mind on the key recommendations made to the Bank, but that I have developed the substantive analysis (which was not the main concern of the report) and have presented the analysis in a different way.

The cover notes to *Blue and Lonesome* suggest that the reason why the Rolling Stones are in their current astonishing position is "that they also listened to some records" (*Guardian*, 2 December 2016). In the work that lies behind this book, I have tried to read the literature, but there is undoubtedly much that I have missed. I apologize in advance to the researchers whose work is not adequately reflected in what follows.

Tony Atkinson, Oxford

December 2016

MEASURING POVERTY
AROUND THE WORLD

CHAPTER 1

Introduction

Why did I write this book and why should you read it? The simple answer to the first question is to be found in my personal history. I became an economist in the 1960s on account of reading *The Poor and the Poorest*, a landmark study of poverty in the United Kingdom by Brian Abel-Smith and Peter Townsend (1965) published on Christmas Eve 1965, and of my earlier personal experience of working with deprived children in Hamburg. My first book (Atkinson 1969) was about poverty in Britain and the need for urgent action. Some half a century later, I remain deeply concerned that, in countries that are many times richer than in the 1960s, poverty has become more, rather than less, entrenched. One of the main aims of the book is to highlight the lack of progress in tackling poverty and to hold our governments to account for their failure. At the same time, I am encouraged by the wider ambition that underlies the global poverty goals that have now been agreed worldwide—unthinkable when I first started work—and believe that it is important that words agreed at the United Nations in New York should be translated into effective action.

The simple answer to the second question is indeed that poverty is one of the two great challenges facing the world as a whole today, along with climate change, with whose consequences poverty is intimately connected. Achieving the ambitious Sustainable Development Goals to which world leaders committed themselves in 2015 is challenging in the extreme, and the book does not pretend to offer a route map to success. Instead, it seeks to provide the evidence about the extent and nature of poverty that is necessary to spur action and to design effective policies. Greater understanding of what is meant by "poverty" and its relation to action worldwide is, I believe, essential to keep the challenge high on the agenda of governments and citizens at a time when there is a risk that we become inward-looking and dismissive of the urgent need to work together.

THE SALIENCE OF POVERTY STATISTICS AND THEIR IMPLICATIONS FOR ECONOMICS

Learning about the extent of poverty is important in terms of understanding the world in which we live, but it is the link with action that marks out this issue from many other subjects of study in the social sciences. Poverty statistics matter because they motivate people to tackle a key challenge. The "rediscovery" of poverty in rich countries helped in the past place poverty on the political agenda. Greater knowledge about uneven development has played an essential role in demonstrating the need for development policy to consider a wider set of objectives than economic growth.

Motivating political action

The history of poverty measurement contains many examples of the ways in which poverty statistics have raised awareness and led politicians to campaign, often reflecting voter concerns and the lobbying of pressure groups. In the United States, President John F. Kennedy, while campaigning in the Appalachian region of West Virginia, was made aware of the levels of deprivation there. Later, after reading Michael Harrington's influential book *The Other America* (1962), which detailed the extent of poverty, Kennedy asked his advisers to plan new measures to deal with the one-fifth of Americans who had incomes below the poverty line. After Kennedy's death, President Lyndon B. Johnson, immediately on taking office, moved to develop this idea, calling in his 1964 State of the Union address for "an unconditional war on poverty."

In the European Union in the early 1980s, the first European Action Programme to combat poverty made use of estimates of the number of poor people in the European Community (as it then was) to motivate the investment being made in antipoverty policies. Later, the European Commission president, Jacques Delors, publicized the estimates of two academics, Michael O'Higgins and Stephen Jenkins (1990), and their use was instrumental in developing the social dimension of the EU. This led to the regular monitoring of the extent of poverty in the EU and the adoption of the Europe 2020 Agenda, with a target of reducing the number in poverty by at least 20 million. (How successful this has been is considered in chapter 9.)

Meantime, many countries have adopted their own national poverty objectives. In Europe, following the 1995 UN Social Summit in Copenhagen, the Irish government launched a National Anti-Poverty Strategy that contained a poverty reduction target relating both to the numbers below the poverty line and to those experiencing basic deprivation. In Africa, as described by the minister of finance in Tanzania, "the fight against poverty is a long standing agenda in the history of Tanzania.... The Tanzania Development Vision 2025 designed in 1999, together with the National Poverty Eradication Strategy and the Poverty Reduction Strategy Paper, set the goal of eradicating abject poverty by 2025" (Tanzania National Bureau of Statistics 2014, preface). The wider implications of poverty eradication were set out clearly in a speech in 2011 by Chinese president Hu Jintao, who observed that poverty reduction "had contributed to promoting economic development, political stability, ethnic unity, border security and social harmony."[1]

---

[1] *Editors*: We could not find the source of this quote. It appears on a Wikileaks page under the heading "China raises poverty line by 80 pct to benefit over 100 mln," and similar wording is

At a global level, the research initiated by Hollis Chenery, chief economist of the World Bank in the 1970s, provided the basis for the president of the Bank, Robert McNamara, to write in the foreword to the first *World Development Report* in 1978 that "some 800 million individuals continue to be trapped in what I have termed absolute poverty: a condition of life so characterized by malnutrition, illiteracy, disease, squalid surroundings, high infant mortality, and low life expectancy as to be beneath any reasonable definition of human decency" (World Bank 1978, p. iii). Ahluwalia, Carter, and Chenery (1979) had made estimates from household survey data of the number of people living with incomes below a poverty line set on the basis of Indian experience, but McNamara's concerns clearly embraced a multidimensional approach, that is, one which considers more than people's incomes. Such an approach, and supporting statistical evidence, underlay the UN's Human Development Index (HDI) initiated by the Pakistani economist Mahbub ul Haq and introduced in the *Human Development Report 1990*, the opening sentence of which is "this Report is about people—and about how development enlarges their choices" (UNDP 1990, p. 11). A broader range of statistics served to widen the agenda.

The statistics on poverty, in all its dimensions, underlay the subsequent setting of ambitious global goals. In September 2000, the members of the UN agreed on the Millennium Development Goals (MDGs) that included halving the proportion of people living in extreme poverty between 1990 and 2015. Statistics on the extent of poverty were necessary to establish the baseline. They were necessary to assess progress. The Central Statistical Office of Zambia stressed the role played by household surveys in monitoring "whether the economic growth the country is experiencing is pro-poor. . . . The LCMS [Living Conditions Monitoring Survey] was partly designed to help evaluate the impact of the FNDP [Fifth National Development Programme] and . . . to help assess whether the country is on course in terms of achieving the Millennium Development Goals" (Zambia Central Statistical Office 2012, p. 172). In China, the household surveys allowed the government to establish that the country had reached the MDG goal five years ahead of time.

The MDGs have in turn been followed by the Sustainable Development Goals (SDGs). In September 2015, the heads of state and government and high representatives agreed on a new set of global goals and committed themselves to their achievement by 2030. The new goals, the SDGs, which are listed in box C in chapter 5, came into effect on 1 January 2016 and are to guide development effort over the subsequent fifteen years. Goal 1 is to "end poverty in all its forms everywhere," and specific targets have been adopted towards this and the other goals. The establishment of these global targets could not have taken place without the possibility of providing quantitative evidence about the

---

found in a *China Daily* (Europe) news story of 30 November 2011 ("China raises poverty line to benefit at least 100m").

extent of progress. If we cannot monitor poverty in all relevant dimensions, the political commitment has no force.

The design of effective action

The ability, just discussed, to monitor progress is the first prerequisite for effective action. The second requirement is for the statistical information to be appropriate to design effective policy actions, seeking to establish what works and what does not. This has been an important role for research on poverty measurement: for example, "poverty measurement in China is mainly related to policy design and programme evaluation" (Zhu 2015, p. 1). We are concerned both with the retrospective evaluation of policies already in effect and with the prospective analysis of policies that are contemplated for the future. The value of this information arises for a wide range of actors. One thinks naturally of national governments, and of regional or local governments. Aid donors and international agencies are other obvious users of this information. But it is also relevant to nongovernmental bodies, such as development charities, and individual citizens.

The significance of survey data was clearly recognised by the minister of finance of Tanzania in her preface to the 2011–2012 Household Budget Survey cited earlier: "The review of PRSP [the Poverty Reduction Strategy Paper] guided formulation of the National Strategy for Growth and Reduction of Poverty (NSGRP or MKUKUTA). . . . The MKUKUTA strategy has been the guiding frameworks for growth and poverty reduction in Tanzania. To monitor all these, information from Household Budget Survey (HBS) is very crucial" (Tanzania National Bureau of Statistics 2014, preface). In his analysis of the Poverty Eradication Action Plan (PEAP) in Uganda, Kenneth Mugambe stressed

> another feature of the revision process—the use of information on poverty in the revision of the PEAP. The 1999 Poverty Status Report was particularly influential. The Report drew from three main types and sources of data. The first source was the Uganda Bureau of Statistics surveys, particularly the Demographic and Health and Household Surveys, which allowed the monitoring of national progress against many poverty indicators. The second was the management information systems in sector ministries. . . . The third source was the PPAs [Participatory Poverty Assessments]. The Poverty Status Report provided a sound body of evidence for the revision of the PEAP. Crucially, MoFPED [Ministry of Finance, Planning, and Economic Development] leadership was willing to use the analysis and information in the Poverty Status Report in their decision making. (Mugambe 2009, p. 162)

Statistics are essential in the design of effective antipoverty programmes. In Trinidad and Tobago, the government commented that the information from the Survey of Living Conditions "was critical in identifying suitable locations for the Government's Early Childhood Care Centres. Information from this survey was used to help shape the ministry's other outreach programmes" (*Trinidad and Tobago Guardian*, 26 April 2014).

For this reason, the World Bank established in 2015 the Commission on Global Poverty, which reported in October 2016 (World Bank 2017) with recommendations as to how extreme poverty should be monitored and as to the complementary measures that should be implemented. As chair of the Commission, I felt that the issues raised were ones that should be brought to a wider audience and presented in a less technical form. The agreement on the SDGs recognised the crucial nature of the challenge posed by global poverty, and the aim of this book is to bring home the nature and extent of this challenge.

The establishment of targets for tackling poverty means that the statistical measures play an essential role in assessing performance. Our political leaders have been courageous in setting goals, and we should be equally courageous in holding their feet to the fire. The annual monitoring of the numbers for people living in poverty and for those suffering material deprivation should be the occasion for asking what progress has been made and what new actions are necessary. Indeed, one of the reasons I was attracted by the analysis of *The Poor and the Poorest* in the United Kingdom was that the authors asked how far the government was successfully guaranteeing the minimum income that was embedded in the social assistance scheme. They questioned the adequacy of that minimum, but argued: "Whatever may be said about the adequacy of the National Assistance Board level of living as a just or publicly approved measure of 'poverty,' it has at least the advantage of being in a sense the 'official' operational definition of the minimum level of living at a particular time" (Abel-Smith and Townsend 1965, p. 17). Today, too, we may question the adequacy of the poverty standards embedded in national or global targets, but they are the politically accepted criteria by which it is legitimate to judge the extent of progress. It is on this account that they receive particular attention in this book.

At the same time, questioning the officially agreed poverty standards is of critical importance because there is a reverse relation between poverty measurement and political decisions. In many countries, the poverty lines and other indicators of deprivation are used in the administration of social transfers and other government spending. In the United States, the official poverty line is the basis for determining eligibility for many federal and state government programmes. In China, the Accurate Development-Oriented Poverty Alleviation Project employs multidimensional poverty indicators to identify and register poor households and poor villages. In many countries, at a geographical level, the percentages in poverty are the basis for allocating spending between districts or regions. Massachusetts Institute of Technology professor Abhijit Banerjee has emphasised this crucial role of poverty measurement in India and suggested that we may need two different poverty lines: "an ethical poverty line to describe the standard we should aspire to . . . and an administrative poverty line, which tells us how to best target our limited resources. As we get richer, perhaps the latter will be raised till it is effectively the same as the former" (Banerjee 2011, p. 2). Globally, development assistance decisions by donors and multilateral agencies may take account of poverty measures. Understanding and refining the poverty statistics may therefore be of key significance for individuals and their benefits and for governments at all levels. Statistics matter.

Economics, framing, and the environmental challenge

Although I am an economist, this is not a book about economics. (An account of poverty measurement much more orientated towards economists is the 2016 volume by Martin Ravallion, *The Economics of Poverty*. It is an excellent account, but long—700 pages. Readers who have also read Thomas Piketty's *Capital in the Twenty-First Century* will know that economists write long books!) At the same time, economic thinking underlies important parts of the analysis. The reader should therefore be aware that this leads in places to a specific "framing" of key issues. Indeed, one of my objectives is to highlight the need to break out of the conventional framework so as to avoid becoming prisoners of a particular view of the world.

To be more concrete, the typical economist, when asked to consider the problem of poverty, has in mind the standard microeconomic theory of a household taking decisions about which goods and services to buy from a given income, where that income depends on how many hours are worked by people in the household as well as on other sources, such as savings income. The decisions about consumption and about work are assumed to be taken to maximize the welfare of the household. A household is in poverty where the best that the household can do, in terms of maximizing its welfare, still leaves the household at a welfare level below a specified poverty level. This approach points in the direction of measuring poverty in terms of achieved consumption. It would, for example, be no use to a household to have a generous savings account paying interest if, on account of racial or other discrimination, no one will rent accommodation to the household. The approach also gives primacy to the choices made by the household: "One should avoid making judgments that are inconsistent with the preferences that guide people's own choices" (Ravallion 2016, p. 132). On this approach, we should not be looking separately at food intake or the availability of medical care.[2]

---

[2] *Editors*: This follows the doctrine of "consumer sovereignty," which posits that the consumer knows best what serves his or her own well-being. Poverty measurement is prevented from focussing on the consumption of separate items because this would mean interfering with the consumer's preferences: it is for the consumer to choose whether to sacrifice some food for

The explanation just given relates to the standard "workhorse" of microeconomics, taught in introductory courses. As I argue in the next chapter, we need to move beyond this, to take on board richer accounts of economic behaviour and alternative ethical frameworks. Here I simply want to stress that the standard version imposes a particular framing, closing down important issues. The textbook story rules out of court certain key questions. I give two examples. The first concerns what happens within the household. The model of household consumer choice takes for granted that there is harmony of interest within the household; there is assumed to be agreement on preferences. It is assumed that poverty, measured in terms of consumption, is a property of the household as a whole. Either everyone is poor or no one is poor. But one of the crucial issues concerns the way in which resources are divided within the household. If, as seems commonly to be the case, women get less than their proportionate share, then the wife may be below the poverty line but the husband above. Within-household inequality is one of the issues discussed here.

The second example concerns the role of the household in the wider community. The standard model sees each household as existing in splendid isolation, with the total of the economy formed by simply adding up all the individuals. But people have extended families; people live in towns or villages; people share ecosystems. Each household may be a small part of the total, but individual decisions may affect other members of the shared group. Suppose that the breadwinner in the textbook household can either work in a factory or go fishing in the communal lake, which he or she is free to do. However, the latter choice affects the fishing possibilities for other members of the community and over time may lead to the exhaustion of fish stocks. The textbook account does not entertain this possibility. The model does not allow for the erosion of natural capital. The particular framing adopted rules out a key set of concerns. The introduction of environmental concerns widens the range of variables with which we should be concerned when measuring nonmonetary poverty. But it also builds an important bridge with the second great global challenge—taking action to meet climate change and environmental degradation.

What is the relation between tackling global poverty and sustainable development? The overview to the first *Human Development Report* stated categorically that "poverty is one of the greatest threats to the environment. In poor countries, poverty often causes deforestation, desertification, salination, poor sanitation, and polluted and unsafe water. And this environmental damage reinforces poverty" (UNDP 1990, p. 7). More recently, Nicholas Stern, the economist responsible for the *Stern Review on the Economics of Climate Change*, has written that "the two greatest problems of our times—overcoming poverty

---

some medical treatment or vice versa. What matters is only whether total expenditure is sufficient to achieve the threshold welfare level.

in the developing world and combating climate change—are inextricably linked. Failure to tackle one will undermine efforts to deal with the other" (Stern 2009, p. 8).

My focus is on poverty, but I attempt to bring together the two challenges. Such a bridge is made conceptually in the discussion of the dimensions of non-monetary poverty, where environmental quality is a potentially significant part of the story. This in turn raises the basic question of the unit of analysis. In my example earlier, a whole village would become environmentally deprived if the fish stocks were exhausted: it is a matter of poverty at the level of the community, not the individual.

WHY SHOULD WE BE CONCERNED?

I began to write this book towards the end of 2016. There cannot perhaps be a less promising time to embark on an enterprise designed to raise the priority attached to the concerns of the world as a whole and to urge people to look beyond national interests. As the United Nations Research Institute for Social Development (UNRISD) said, in launching its 2016 report, "There are signs that countries are starting to retreat into isolationism, which could threaten prospects for much-needed international cooperation. The President-elect in the US has signalled his intention to withdraw from the Paris climate deal, and the UK is retreating from over 40 years of European cooperation" (UNRISD 2016).

Globalization and freedom for foreign travel

I begin with a request, which is to urge you to forget, if only temporarily, the word "globalization." This word has become a portmanteau term for all that is wrong with the world today, and this obscures the fact that there are many different dimensions to the changes that have led to unhappiness with the state of the planet. There is no doubt in my view that freedom of movement of capital and the failure to properly regulate and tax the activities of multinational companies have led to the loss of employment and to the creation of a sense of insecurity among workers and their families in many countries. Our governments have lost sight of their obligation to act on behalf of all their citizens; they have allowed them to become subservient to economic forces. We need to return to a situation where "the economy" is a means of fulfilling the life hopes and ambitions of people, not vice versa. "Putting people first in macroeconomics" is the title of a report that I wrote some ten years ago for the European Commission, and I remain convinced that this should be our aim.

But there are other dimensions to freedom. An important freedom is that for individuals to travel. In this respect, the world has changed beyond recognition. When I was young, there were many countries that one could not visit, or could only do so armed with a great deal of paperwork. I can recall travelling on a night train from Germany to Paris, and the police taking one of my fellow passengers off the train because he had failed to notice that the train passed through Belgium and he lacked the necessary visa.

I give this example because I believe that the freedom to travel is one important reason why the citizens of rich countries have, in recent decades, become more aware of the extent and depth of poverty in the rest of the world. The rise in charitable giving for development in the United Kingdom as a proportion of household income is highly correlated with the rise in the increased share of spending on overseas travel. As a result, many more people appreciate that the residents of rich countries neither should, nor can, cut themselves off from global challenges. Indeed, a benign interpretation of the Brexit vote in the United Kingdom is a rejection of any present-day concept of "Fortress Europe," whereby the citizens of a rich continent seek to insulate themselves from poverty in the rest of the world. This is not a perspective of the EU that I share, and such an interpretation of the Brexit vote is scarcely consistent with the avowed policies on immigration advocated by many of its supporters. But to the extent that it sees the United Kingdom as playing a global, rather than a regional, role, then such an ethical stance would indeed lead people to be concerned with the issues addressed in this book. And it is not just ethics; it is also self-interest. Raising the drawbridge will become less and less feasible if it remains the case that more than 40 per cent of those living in Sub-Saharan Africa live below the International Poverty Line (to be defined later in this chapter).

What are our responsibilities? Instrumental reasons

The reader may well ask at this juncture, what are our responsibilities? As citizens of one of the world's richer countries, what can we be expected to do, if anything? The case for being concerned can be either *instrumental* or *intrinsic*. In his book *Should Rich Nations Help the Poor?*, David Hulme opens his first chapter, "Why Worry about the Distant Poor?," with a clear statement of the instrumental case: "Rich nations, and their citizens, are increasingly experiencing the consequences of living in a very unequal world" (2016, p. 1). The instrumental reasons have been to the fore in the globalization debate, where the interests of the rich nations are seen as bound up with measures to improve labour standards and abolish sweated workshops in poor countries. This approach has been highlighted in the Decent Work Agenda of the International Labour Organization (ILO), which is now embodied in SDG Goal 8 ("Decent work and economic growth"). Such measures may reduce, or halt, profit-driven firms transferring production to such low-cost locations. Thereby, jobs are saved in rich countries. It is not pure gain to the poor in rich countries, since they are losing the ability to buy ultra-cheap goods. Goods of low quality may cease to be available. But it can certainly be seen as an instrumental reason for concern in rich countries about the circumstances of the poor in poor countries.

The instrumental line of argument has received much publicity on account of the publication in 2009 of *The Spirit Level* by epidemiologists Richard Wilkinson and Kate Pickett, and of *The Price of Inequality* by economist Joseph Stiglitz in 2012. However, I have never been a great fan. Wilkinson and Pickett may be quite right in asserting the "pernicious effects that inequality has on societies" (Equality Trust 2016). But I am all too conscious of the difficulties of establishing a direct causal connection between inequality and poverty, on the one hand, and social problems, on the other.

The instrumental argument is attempting a harder statistical exercise than that with which this book is concerned. Consider, for example, the argument that poverty in poor countries leads to increased outward migration and hence pressures for entry on the borders of rich countries and illegal immigration. (I am taking an argument directly relevant to the present book, not one drawn from the two cited books.) Here in this book we are concerned with establishing a satisfactory estimate of the poverty rate. The instrumental argument in contrast depends on estimating the strength of the relationship between the poverty rate and another variable, in this case outward migration, and establishing the direction of causality. This is a tougher assignment and leaves one open to a much wider range of potential criticism. In the case of migration, there are many possible determinants other than poverty that have been investigated. It is not enough to plot two variables, one against the other in a scatter plot, where poverty is measured along the horizontal axis and migration on the vertical axis, and look at whether countries with higher poverty rates tend to have higher rates of out-migration. As summarised by Ian Goldin, Geoffrey Cameron, and Meera Balarajan:

> To the extent that the decision to migrate is a choice, it is one that is influenced and constrained by a variety of factors. The desire to move on account of wage differences between countries is not sufficient to turn a potential migrant into an actual migrant. Migration assumes different levels of cost and risk for each individual, depending on their level of education, their financial resource, social capital, access to information, social networks, and other endowments. (Goldin, Cameron, and Balarajan 2011, p. 120)

It is clearly challenging to try in a multivariable analysis to isolate the role played in determining migration flows by living standards in the out-migration country and, even more, to convince people that the relationship is causal. Poverty and out-migration may covary, but this covariance may arise because they are both governed by a third variable, such as ethnic or religious status. Pulling the lever for poverty reduction will not in this case lead to a reduction in the out-migration of a persecuted minority.

The second reason I attach less weight to the instrumental argument is that I would not change my view about the urgency of tackling poverty if I were to learn that the causal argument did not stand up. To take an example from *The Spirit Level*, it is concluded that "levels of obesity tend to be lower in countries where income differences are smaller" (Wilkinson and Pickett 2009, p. 91).[3] However, if I were to wake up one day and discover that the line in the scatter plot sloped the other way, and that reducing income differences would increase obesity, this would not cause me to change my concerns about poverty, which are based on intrinsic arguments. In the case of global poverty, I share the view of Hulme that "having so much poverty and inequality in an affluent world means that rich nations and their citizens have no choice but to think through how they relate to the distant poor" (Hulme 2016, p. 3). But I am concerned that if this is the sole driver of our sense of responsibility, then the degree of support is fragile and unpredictable. As Hulme rightly says, there has to be a moral dimension, and this depends on the intrinsic case.

What are our responsibilities? Intrinsic concerns

To explore the intrinsic argument, let us commence with a simple example. Suppose that there is an upstream village and an equal-sized, in terms of population, downstream village. A project is being considered to dam the river upstream, causing the inhabitants of the upstream village to lose fishing possibilities worth $1 each per month, in order to supply a fish farm in the downstream village.[4] The inhabitants of the upstream village are asked how large the benefits to the downstream village would have to be in order for them to agree to the $1 per capita loss. Their reply might be that no gain to the downstream village would compensate for their loss: they are concerned only with their own standard of living. This may be referred to as an "isolationist" position. At the other extreme, they may say that any gain for the downstream villagers in excess of $1 would be acceptable. (Remember that there are the same

---

[3] As a sidelight on the problems of obtaining international data in other fields, it may be noted that the International Obesity Task Force, on whose work *The Spirit Level* draws, notes that "few countries conduct systematic measured surveys to obtain reliable nationally representative data to assess the degree of overweight and obesity in their populations. Self-reported surveys tend to significantly underestimate the scale of the problem. For example, the annual Behavioral Risk Factor Surveillance System telephone survey in the USA produced a self-reported estimate of the prevalence of obesity of 20% of adults in the same year that the National Health and Nutrition Examination Survey, using measurements obtained by trained personnel conducting a comprehensive examination, provided an estimate of 28% of men and 34% of women with a BMI>30" (2005, p. 6).

[4] *Editors*: The figure of $1 per month means that the value of the lost fishing is only modest in relation to a household budget equal to the International Poverty Line, defined later in the chapter as $1.90 per person per day. In other words, the upstream village is not living primarily from fishing, so its loss would not threaten the villagers' livelihood.

number of people in each village, so that the total would also be larger.) This may be described as a "cosmopolitan" position, where everyone in the world gets the same weight as oneself and everyone believes that social judgements should be formed by adding up the welfare of everyone, equally weighted. In between come answers where upstream villagers agree to the project but only if the gain per person in the downstream village is sufficiently large, for instance, at least $5 per month. Such a judgement by upstream villagers would be like saying that they take account of the gain in the standard of living of the downstream villagers, but give it only a weight of one-fifth relative to their own consumption. If they had required that the gain be at least $10, then the implied weighting factor would be one-tenth. Such a "limited sympathy" ethical position was described by the Oxford economist Francis Edgeworth as that of a person "for whom . . . his neighbour's well-being compared with his own neither counts for nothing, nor 'counts for one,' but counts for a fraction" (Edgeworth 1881, p. 102; I have substituted "well-being" for "utility").

How is this example relevant? If your answer falls in the isolationist category, then this book is probably not for you. The intrinsic argument is based on some degree of empathy with one's fellow citizens. But if your answer falls in the limited sympathy category, and still more if you are a global cosmopolitan, then the book is designed to help you think further about the ethical implications. To begin with, what should the weighting factor be? Here it is helpful to distinguish two separate reasons for applying a weight less than one to the plight of others: the first is that they are not you, and the second is that they may be better or worse off than you. You may say that inhabitants of the downstream village should get only a weight of one-fifth, but that this should be scaled up or down according to how well-off they are. You may even be a global cosmopolitan, starting from a weight of one, but scale this down if you take the view that the recipients are well-off. If you believe that the fish farm operators will become plutocrats, then you may well reduce the weight to zero. On the other hand—and this brings us to the subject matter of the book—you may say that you are concerned if the downstream village is currently living below the poverty line, but not otherwise. So the project is justified in your eyes if the gain exceeds $5 *and* the downstream villagers are currently at least $5 below the poverty line. (I will not go into the complications where the villagers are currently below the poverty line, but by less than $5.)

We need also to consider geography. For some people, "isolationism" involves concern only for people who live in their own country. They attach zero weight to the poor in other countries. However, they should read on. Much of the book is about poverty at the national level, and chapter 9 deals specifically with poverty in rich countries. Isolationist US citizens should be concerned with whether there are people in their country living on less than $2 a day. At the other extreme, for global cosmopolitans geography is irrelevant. As it was put by philosopher Peter Singer, "It makes no moral difference whether the person I help is a neighbour's child ten yards away from me or a Bengali . . . ten thousand miles away" (1972, pp. 231–232). In between these two positions comes that held by those for whom the weight attached to the additional consumption of beneficiaries may be larger for members of their immediate community and may fall as we cross national boundaries, while remaining strictly positive. For instance, for a project that benefits people in another country, the hurdle may rise from $5 to $10.

There is, however, a further important consideration. The discussion so far has assumed that there can be transfers without leakages. Yet the constructors of the fish farm may extort part of the benefits; the fish farmers may have to pay protection money; the bank may make an excessive charge for loans; and where cash is involved, as with transfers from other countries, part may be siphoned off by local or national politicians before it ever reaches the intended beneficiaries. The leakages may themselves have negative consequences, such as maintaining in power corrupt governments and encouraging people to seek careers in illegal redistribution rather than productive activities, as has been argued by Dambisa Moyo in her 2010 book *Dead Aid*. All this concerns the potential donors. To reach a $5 net transfer, the gross amount allowing for leakages may have to be $8. The weighting factor on the consumption transfer falls to one-eighth from one-fifth on account of the leakages. This applies to the fish farm example. In reality, the weighting factor will depend on the nature of the policies pursued.

What does this all mean for the measurement of poverty around the world? Suppose that we reject the extreme of isolationism and note that the other extreme of complete global cosmopolitanism corresponds to the existing calculations by the World Bank and others. While complete global cosmopolitanism is the only valid approach for an international organisation that has to give all world citizens equal weight, we need also to explore the implications of limited sympathy. Placed in terms of the concerns of a national government for counting the number in poverty, it may give full weight to those within its borders and a weight less than one but greater than zero to the poor in other countries (building on the suggestion made for measuring inequality by Brandolini and Carta 2016). So that, in the case of the United States, the poverty total is the sum of the number in poverty in that country plus the sum of the weighted numbers in poverty in each of the other 196 countries. The determination of the weights to be applied (with values between zero and one) will be governed by the considerations that have been rehearsed above. Since the different influences vary across countries, the weights too may vary, with the poverty number for India being weighted differently, say, from that in Indonesia. It is also clear that the calculation will be different for each country: what is being constructed is a *nationally specific* count of world poverty. The magnitude of world poverty as seen from India will be different from that seen from the United States; the two world poverty counts may even be moving in opposite directions.

All this may seem complicated, and the reader may settle for the global cosmopolitan position—which does indeed underlie the global results presented in the next section and in chapter 5. But we have to recognise that sympathy may, in today's world, be less than complete, and that this needs to be reflected in the measures employed. How the limited sympathy measure works may become clearer when we return to its use in chapter 9.

Sharing the burden

I have suggested a way of thinking about an intrinsic justification for concern about poverty that recognises that people have a positive but limited degree of altruism and that takes account of the potential leakages. It does, however, raise a further question about how much responsibility we should bear. Why, you may ask, do the upstream villagers bear all the cost? Taking the example to the world stage, how much should the citizens of one country contribute to solving the problem of global poverty? One country like the United Kingdom, France, Germany, or even the United States cannot be expected to shoulder all the burden. How should the burden be shared?

Exactly the same issue arises when it comes to the costs of climate change mitigation. In this context, one of the arguments is that of historical responsibility. In their review *Burden Sharing in the Context of Global Climate Change: A North-South Perspective*, Ringius, Frederiksen, and Birr-Pedersen begin with the norm that "those who have caused the problem are responsible for solving it," which they describe as "undoubtedly a generally accepted norm in international environmental affairs" (2002, p. 17). In the context of world poverty, application of a principle of historical responsibility points to the costs being borne today by those countries that benefitted from exploitation in the past of today's poor countries: it would be restitution for the slave trade and for centuries of resource extraction. There can be little doubt that today's rich countries benefitted greatly. When, in the eighteenth century, George III of England inquired as to the owner of the carriage that had just passed them, a carriage that was much more splendid than his own, he was told that it belonged to a "sugar baron" (Parker 2011, p. 296). There can be equally no doubt that part, at least, of the historically acquired wealth continues to benefit individuals and institutions in rich countries today. At the same time, the links are opaque and may not be recognised by those involved. The historical responsibility argument may therefore be less easily prosecuted, if only because it appeals to negative feelings of guilt rather than to any positive commitment. In view of this, I limit myself to the other side of the account, asking in chapter 7 how far present poverty can be traced to colonial heritage.

A forward-looking, rather than backward-looking, approach to responsibility may be reached by framing the issue in a way that makes sense of, on the one hand, the concern of the citizens with the disadvantaged in other countries and, on the other hand, the capacity of a single country to have an impact. In just the same way as a single donor to charity is often encouraged to "identify" with single families of recipients, so, too, it is reasonable for a country to see itself as responsible, not for the whole problem, but for its proportionate share. What is meant by "proportionate share"? It does not mean literal proportionality to its national income, but rather a relation to its ability to contribute, taken to be the excess of its national income per head over an affluence threshold. Countries would be identified as potential donor nations when their national income per head passes this threshold, and their contribution would rise from zero at the threshold in proportion to the excess of their national income per head. The implications of this approach naturally depend on the world distribution of income. As more countries enter the "high-income" category (see box A), this expands the range of donor countries, but at present, in round figures, this means each person in a DAC (OECD Development Assistance Committee) donor country "taking responsibility" for one person living in extreme poverty according to the International Poverty Line defined below.

In sum, my answer to the question posed at the outset of this section is that any judgement about the degree of responsibility accepted is a personal matter. It is understandable that some people have no concern for the well-being of their fellow citizens at home or abroad, and that they are not convinced by the instrumental arguments for tackling poverty. They do not believe that their own well-being would be advanced by measures to reduce poverty either at home or abroad, and they abdicate from any responsibility. Others may be persuaded by the instrumental case for action, although I have noted the difficulty of establishing a direct causal connection between poverty, on the one hand, and social problems, on the other. At the other extreme is the position of global cosmopolitanism, which in effect underlies the total poverty counts produced by the World Bank and other bodies. It is not, however, clear that such a position, while appropriate for international organisations, is accepted in general at the national level. My own view is that an enduring source of motivation is provided by people having a positive but limited degree of concern for their fellow citizens on this planet. The extent to which we are concerned may be limited to those below the poverty line and may be attenuated as we leave our borders and as account is taken of potential leakages. Countries may reasonably restrict their contribution to their proportionate share of income in excess of the donor threshold. But to varying degrees, we are accepting that we have a responsibility.

A FIRST LOOK AT THE EVIDENCE ABOUT POVERTY AROUND THE WORLD

The media—to their credit—often report the latest estimates of the extent of global poverty. Following the title of Paul Collier's best-seller published in 2007, they often refer to "the bottom billion." Today the number given by the World Bank is less than a billion, and their estimates suggest that global poverty is falling. Let us look at this more closely.

The extent of global poverty

In seeking to understand the extent and nature of global poverty, it is natural to start by looking at *poor countries*, which are countries where on average living standards fall far below those for the world taken as a whole. The World Development Indicators (WDI) assembled by the World Bank provide estimates of the gross national income (GNI) of each country divided by the total population of that country, in each case adjusted to allow for differences in purchasing power. The latter adjustment converts the figure obtained in local currency units (i.e., in India, so many rupees per person) to purchasing power parity (PPP) dollars calculated so that each dollar has the same purchasing power in that country as one dollar would have in the United States. Such an adjustment is not straightforward—see chapter 3 for further discussion—but for the present is taken at face value, as is the fact that we are looking at income rather than consumption. The resulting estimates of per capita GNI in 2015 expressed in PPP dollars per day (per capita incomes, for short) are used to construct figure 1.1.

For the world as a whole, the average per capita income is PPP$42.20 per day, a level at which one finds countries such as Brazil, Thailand, and Botswana. At half the world average, one finds countries such as Bhutan and Morocco. But many countries have an average income less than a quarter of the world average (PPP$10.50 a day), a level close to what one finds in Mauritania, Ghana, and Zambia. Forty-five countries are below this level, of which two-thirds are in Africa. The twenty-five countries with the lowest average incomes are shown in figure 1.1. All but three are to be found in the African region, the exceptions being Afghanistan, Haiti, and the Solomon Islands. The average per capita income in every case is below PPP$6.00 a day.

People who live in poor countries are not necessarily poor, and poor people do not necessarily live in poor countries. Poverty is an attribute of individual households, and whether or not a household is poor depends on how total income is distributed within the country. A high level of inequality may mean that a country has a much greater level of poverty than another country with the same average income but less inequality. But other things equal, poverty

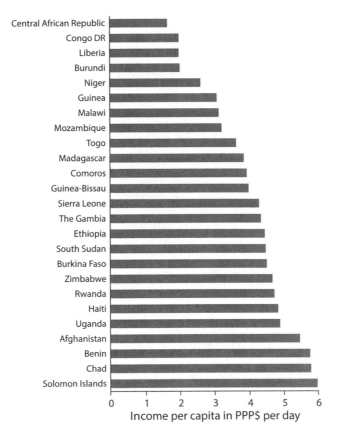

Figure 1.1. Twenty five poorest countries in 2015, measured by GNI per capita in PPP dollars

Source: World Bank, World Development Indicators, table 1.1 (downloaded 8 October 2016).
Reading note: In the Central African Republic, the GNI per capita in 2015 was $1.64 per day (in international PPP dollars).

measured in terms of a number of dollars per day, such as the PPP\$1.90 embodied in the first target under Sustainable Development Goal 1 of eradicating poverty by 2030, is likely to be lower the richer the country. In the extreme case where average income is below PPP\$1.90, as in the Central African Republic in 2015, it is arithmetically inevitable that some people fall short of the SDG threshold.

Let us now look within countries and investigate how many people are in fact poor. Using its PovcalNet database, the World Bank calculates the number of poor people by considering each country in turn and estimating (in a way described further in later chapters) the proportion living in households with consumption per head (or income in some countries) less than PPP$1.90 a day in 2011 prices. The Bank considers these people to be living in "extreme poverty." This threshold of PPP$1.90 is referred to as the International Poverty Line (IPL), following the practice used earlier in the literature for the predecessors of this threshold, endorsed by Recommendation 1 in the report of the Commission on Global Poverty (World Bank 2017), where "International" reflects the fact that it is the result of an international agreement. (The abbreviation IPL is not to be confused with the Indian Premier League!) The $1.90 standard is today's version of the original well-known "dollar a day" line and its successors (for example, $1.25). Figure 1.2 shows the resulting estimates of the number of people living in households below this latest version of the International Poverty Line and the percentage of the world population this represents for the period since 1990.[5]

The Millennium Development Goal target that preceded the one just described under Sustainable Development Goal 1 was to halve extreme poverty between 1990 and 2015. The data for the last two years of this twenty-five-year period are not yet available, but figure 1.2 shows that a halving of the total number in extreme poverty had already been achieved by 2012. The percentage of people in the world living below the International Poverty Line fell from more than a third (35 per cent) in 1990 to just over 10 per cent in 2013. This is a dramatic reduction. The proportionate fall in the absolute number was smaller, since over the period the world population had increased from 5.3 billion to 7.2 billion, but nonetheless the total number was more than halved, to 767 million.

The International Poverty Line plays a prominent part in this book. From this point on, for simplicity, the text referring to the $1.90 threshold or earlier values of this international line does not include "PPP" before the dollar sign. Nevertheless, the reader should keep in mind that the threshold to be applied in each country is one measured in international purchasing power dollars (a concept explained further in chapter 3) and not U.S. dollars converted at market rates. When the text refers to the $1.90 line, the reader should therefore understand this as $1.90 in international purchasing power dollars at 2011 prices.[6]

---

[5] *Editors*: Throughout the book, Tony refers to estimates published in the October 2016 release of PovcalNet and in World Bank (2016); we indicate where we have updated the figures. (Minor differences between these two sources are ignored.)

[6] *Editors*: The qualification that the $1.90 is in 2011 prices is also important to remember. In years other than 2011, whether earlier or later, the value in local currency of $1.90 at the PPP rate is "then converted to the prices prevailing at the time . . . using the best available Consumer Price Index (CPI). . . . All inter-temporal comparisons are real, as assessed using the country-specific CPI" (PovcalNet website, methodology page). Hence, the poverty rates shown in figures 1.2 and 1.3 are based on a $1.90 threshold adjusted in each country for changes in local prices.

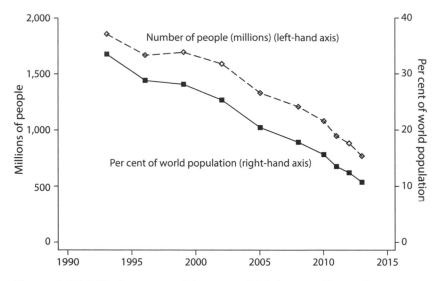

Figure 1.2. World Bank estimates of the extent of global poverty ($1.90 a day poverty line), 1990 to 2013

Source: World Bank (2016, annex 2A).

Reading note: In 1990 the number of people living in households below the International Poverty Line of $1.90 per person per day was 1,850 million (1.85 billion), or 35 per cent of the world population.

Where the poor live

Where do the poor live? Figure 1.3 shows the proportion of the population living below the International Poverty Line for four of the main regions where people are living below that threshold. Not shown are two further regions with substantial numbers in extreme poverty: Europe and Central Asia, and the Middle East and North Africa (for the latter of which the survey data coverage is too low).[7] Poverty fell in all four regions shown in figure 1.3, but there are striking differences. In 1981, the East Asia and Pacific region was bottom of

[7] *Editors*: The April 2018 release of PovcalNet includes figures for the two missing regions. The World Bank (2016, table 2.1 note) explained the absence of the Middle East and North Africa from the October 2016 version as follows: "Estimates . . . are omitted because of data coverage and quality problems. The population coverage of available household surveys is too low; the share of the total regional population represented by the available surveys is below 40 percent. There are also issues in the application of the 2011 PPP U.S. dollar to the region. These issues revolve around the quality of the data in several countries experiencing severe political instability, breaks in the consumer price index (CPI) series, and measurement or comparability problems in specific household surveys. These caveats suggest that more methodological analyses and the availability of new household survey data are needed before reliable and sufficiently precise estimates can be produced."

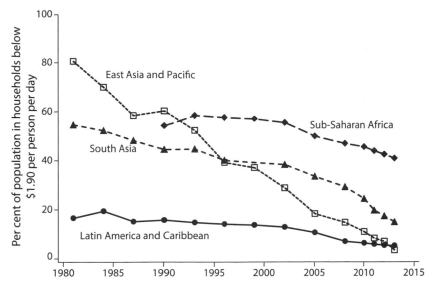

Figure 1.3. Poverty reduction by region ($1.90 a day line), 1981 to 2013
Source: World Bank, PovcalNet (downloaded 19 November 2016).
Reading note: In 1981, 80.5 per cent of the population of the East Asia and Pacific region were living in households with consumption below the International Poverty Line ($1.90 per person per day). The World Bank defines six geographic regions; the two not shown are the Europe and Central Asia region and the Middle East and North Africa region.

the class (at the top of the diagram); by 2013, it had the lowest percentage in poverty. Its line crosses that for South Asia in 1996. The reduction in South Asia is impressive: the poverty rate in 2013 is not much more than a quarter of the rate in 1981. But it is evident to the naked eye that the downward slope is much greater in East Asia and the Pacific. Latin America and the Caribbean began with a much lower rate in the 1980s, but in 2013 the region was level-pegging with East Asia and the Pacific. The series for Sub-Saharan Africa begins in 1990. Since then, the poverty rate has indeed fallen, but at a slower rate than in the other regions shown. In 1990, the proportion living below the International Poverty Line in Africa was ten percentage points higher than in South Asia; by 2013, the gap had widened to twenty-five percentage points. In this sense, Sub-Saharan Africa is being left behind.

Poverty in rich countries

In the World Bank global poverty count, high-income countries (defined below) are assumed to have zero extreme poverty, described as "a useful simplifying assumption that appears to closely approximate the correct estimate" (Ferreira

et al. 2016, p. 160).[8] At the same time, the adoption of a truly global approach to poverty measurement certainly implies that these countries should come within the scope of inquiry. A number of recent studies have suggested that there are significant numbers in the United States living on incomes below $2.00 a day (Shaefer and Edin 2013; Edin and Shaefer 2015; Chandy and Smith 2014; see the review by Jencks 2016). Chandy and Smith, for example, estimate that some 2 per cent of the US population had incomes below $2.00 a day in 2011 (Chandy and Smith 2014, table 1, p. 10, more extensive measure of income), although they demonstrate major differences according to the definition of income and the treatment of zero and negative responses to household surveys (for example, due to losses from self-employment). They also show that there are marked differences in the United States between low income and low consumption. "The range of consumption levels for those reporting zero or close to zero income is not only wide but indistinguishable from the equivalent range for those reporting income levels up to 20 dollars of income per person per day" (p. 14). Using consumption data from the US Consumer Expenditure Survey for the fourth quarter of 2011, they find that only 0.07 per cent (or 0.09 per cent when using a more selective definition of consumption) of the US population were below $2 a day.

High-income countries should be seen as within scope, and as raising significant issues that will be explored in later chapters. First, observation of the extreme bottom of the distribution in rich countries highlights the distinction between "consumption" and "income" and the choice between the two for the measurement of poverty.

Second, high-income countries illustrate the incomplete coverage of the data used to estimate poverty levels. These data typically exclude, for example, the homeless and may fail to capture adequately recent migrants to the country. As emphasised by the submission of the international movement ATD Fourth World to the Commission on Global Poverty, "Europe is confronted with an unprecedented flow of refugees fleeing war and destitution" (2016, p. 1), and many are suffering a high level of deprivation. Moreover, looking ahead to 2030 and the probable impact of climate change on the risks of weather disasters, it is likely that these will not be confined to developing countries.

Third, these countries underline the importance of monetary indicators of poverty being accompanied by nonmonetary indicators. To take just one example from the United States, there is evidence from the study of Case and Deaton (2015) of rising mortality among middle-aged white non-Hispanics between 1999 and 2013. As the authors say, "Concurrent declines in self-reported health, mental health, and ability to work, increased reports of pain, and dete-

---

[8] *Editors*: Following Tony's advice in the Commission on Global Poverty report (World Bank 2017, p. 47), the World Bank now includes high-income countries in its global poverty count and provides estimates for them in PovcalNet.

riorating measures of liver function all point to increasing midlife distress" (2015, p. 15078). Elsewhere, in his 2013 book *The Great Escape*, Angus Deaton has written that "it is easy to think of the escape from poverty as being about money—about having more and not having to live with the gnawing anxiety of not knowing whether there will be enough tomorrow" (p. xiii). But he goes on to argue that "the story of human wellbeing, of what makes life worth living, is not well served by looking at only a part of what is important." In Europe, the presentation of statistics on monetary poverty by the EU statistical agency Eurostat is now accompanied by measures of material deprivation that record households' lack of particular items such as a telephone or heating to keep the home sufficiently warm, and these measures contribute to the EU's monitoring of its 2020 poverty targets.

Relating the global to the national: Choice of countries for case studies

In studying the global poverty estimates, it became increasingly clear to me that there was a worrying gulf between the measures of global poverty—just discussed—and the measurement of poverty at the level of the individual country. The World Bank global estimates are built up from national data, but the loop does not seem to be closed by relating the country constituents of the global figure to the national studies of monetary poverty. Put bluntly, how do the poverty numbers for country X that appear in the World Bank database compare with those published by country X in its national poverty report for the same year? The figures may not be the same, but are they congruent? We need to "drill down" to the national level, and this is why the book contains case studies for sixty countries around the world and at very different levels of development.[9]

The gulf is worrying for two reasons. The first is because the country case studies provide a method of triangulation. Not only can the poverty estimates be compared, but the national data sources contain additional information that can be used to contextualize the World Bank numbers. Measures of nonmonetary deprivation, where available, may help us interpret the evidence. The second, and more important, reason is that it is largely at the country level that action to tackle poverty is realised. It is the national (and local) governments that use the statistics to plan policy interventions, in partnership with development agencies and other actors at the country level. For them, it is the national poverty figures that are paramount. Moreover, the issues that arise at the country level may well differ in different parts of the world and, indeed, be specific to a particular context.

[9] *Editors*: As explained in the foreword, completed national reports are present for fewer than sixty countries.

The book takes sixty countries for national case studies. What fraction is this of all the countries in the world? That is not a question that is easily answered. The UN had (in January 2016) 193 members and two permanent observers (the Vatican and Palestine). But this is not a complete list of countries. There are 249 country codes in the ISO 3166-1 list. The difference between 195 and 249 in the ISO list is explained in part by the latter's inclusion of two states with partial recognition, Kosovo and Taiwan, but most of the difference lies in the fact that the ISO list also includes Antarctica and forty-five inhabited (and six uninhabited) dependent territories. The modest, or zero, populations of these territories (which include Montserrat and St. Helena, both with populations under 5,000) suggest that we can take 197 (193 + 2 + 2) as the base figure and think of our sixty countries as nearly a third of the world's total. Indeed, in terms of population, while some large countries are not included, such as Nigeria, Pakistan, and Russia, the sixty are much more significant: they account for nearly three-quarters of the world's inhabitants.

How representative are they? Measured again in terms of counting countries, the sixty include nine of the twenty-five poorest counties as measured by per capita national income, as in figure 1.1—again around a third. They include some of the larger ones, such as Ethiopia with a population of 100 million. Are the countries biased towards those that are more or less successful? One test is provided by location of countries according to the World Bank groupings by GNI per head and their pattern of advance over time. Figure 1.4 shows the history of the sixty countries from 1987 to 2017. The World Bank method of classification is summarised in box A, and it should be noted that this is based on GNI valued at market exchange rates rather than using PPP dollars. This makes a big difference for many countries, as will be shown in chapter 3, where the PPP adjustment is examined further.

Thirteen of the countries were classified throughout the period as high-income. At the other end of the scale, ten countries were classified as low-income in 1987 and remained so classified in 2015, with no intervening change in their status. But there were an almost equal number (eleven) that were classified as low-income in 1987 but upwardly mobile, in the sense that their 2015 classification was higher: Bangladesh, Cambodia, China, Ghana, India, Indonesia, Kenya, Solomon Islands, Sri Lanka, Vietnam, and Zambia. It may be noted that all but one of the stationary groups are from the African region, and that this region supplies only two from the upwardly mobile group. There were twelve countries that began as lower-middle-income countries and ended with a higher classification, including countries from Africa (Botswana and South Africa) and Latin America and the Caribbean (Colombia, the Dominican Republic, Jamaica, Mexico, and Peru). Finally, mobility was not always upwards. Botswana, Brazil, the Côte d'Ivoire, Egypt, Georgia, Indonesia, Korea, Panama, Solomon Islands, South Africa, and Tunisia were all reclassified downwards at some point during the period. So that, while the selection was not made in such

---

Box A. The World Bank classification of countries

The World Bank classifies countries into four groups according to their gross national income (GNI), calculated using the World Bank Atlas method: low-income, lower-middle-income, upper-middle-income, and high-income.

The classification is revised each year, so countries may move between groups. For the 2017 fiscal year, the following cutoffs in US dollars apply:

Low-income economies: Annual GNI per capita of $1,025 or less in 2015
Lower-middle-income economies: Annual GNI per capita between $1,026 and $4,035
Upper-middle-income economies: Annual GNI per capita of between $4,036 and $12,475
High-income economies: Annual GNI per capita of $12,476 or more

The Atlas method of calculating GNI in US dollars uses a conversion factor that for any year is the average of a country's exchange rate for that year and its exchange rates for the two preceding years, adjusted for the difference between the rate of inflation in the country and international inflation; the objective of the adjustment is to reduce any changes to the exchange rate caused by inflation. The Atlas method aims to reduce the impact of exchange rate fluctuations in the cross-country comparison of national incomes.

---

a way as to be a representative sample of countries, the sixty national studies cover a range of differing development experience in recent years.

The discussion in chapters 6 to 9 of each country's experience is perforce brief and should be read in combination with the two-page (four-page in the case of China) standard reports at the end of the book. But I hope that they will together provide a flavour of what can be learned by drilling down to the level of individual countries.[10]

READING ON

Poverty is a concept with many potential meanings. Chapter 2 describes a range of different concepts, each legitimate in its own way, and each with different implications for the measurement of poverty. The discussion starts with "political" definitions—standards adopted by governments in order to classify a person as poor or not—which are then contrasted with subjective assessments

---

[10] *Editors*: Recommendation 2 in the report of the Commission on Global Poverty was that the World Bank should produce brief "National Poverty Statistics Reports" for each country (World Bank 2017, pp. 28–29), and the Bank accepted this advice. The national reports in this book reflect in part Tony's proposal, although his implementation differs from the World Bank's.

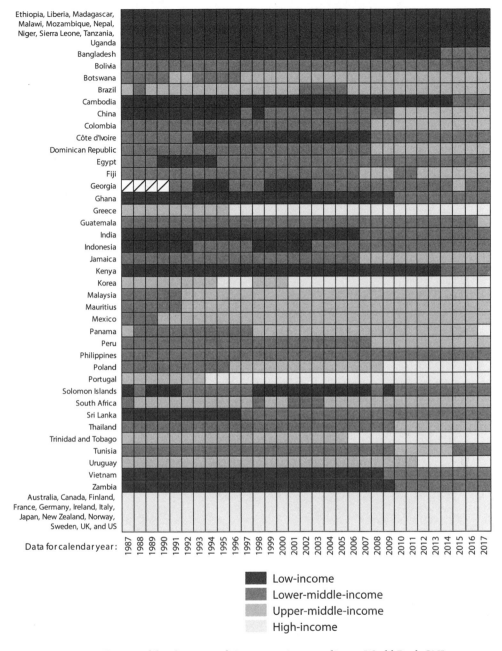

Figure 1.4. History of development of sixty countries according to World Bank GNI per capita (Atlas method) classification, 1987 to 2017

Source: World Bank website, "World Bank country and lending groups" page, historical classification by income (accessed August 2018). The graph presents the contemporaneous classification according to GNI thresholds that have changed in real terms over the period shown. (Box A shows the thresholds that applied to incomes in 2015.)

Reading note: Bangladesh was classified as a low-income country until 2013 and then as a lower-middle-income country.

based on individuals' own views of what constitutes poverty. Next come definitions based on calculations of what is needed to achieve a given minimum standard of living, such as the cost of the food required to reach a particular level of nutritional intake, an approach which has a long pedigree. The list is completed with the much more recent "capability" approach to assessing living standards of Amartya Sen and the assessment of poverty based on principles of human rights. The implications for measurement of the different concepts are taken up in the last section of this chapter with regard to the central debate between absolute and relative measures of poverty, and they are further developed in the next chapter, where the concepts of poverty are refined.

What are the key questions you should ask when faced with statistics about poverty? The purpose of chapters 3 and 4 is to provide a "checklist." Chapter 3 focusses on clarifying the concepts, dealing first with monetary measures of poverty defined in terms of levels of income or expenditure and then with nonmonetary indicators, for example, the absence of a particular item in the home or a lack of access to clean water. In both cases the user of poverty statistics needs to know what exactly is being measured and for whom it is measured—for an individual, for a family, or for a household. In the case of the monetary measures, what issues arise with the use of purchasing power parity exchange rates? How is the depth of poverty—its severity—being measured? Chapter 4 considers the data underlying the figures. To translate the concepts of poverty into concrete measures depends crucially on there being data that are fit for the purpose. What are the available data? Are they comparable over time so that trends in poverty can be measured adequately? How well measured within countries are price changes, which are vital to the updating of national poverty thresholds? And who is missing from the sources used to measure poverty? Comparability across countries is particularly important for any measure of global poverty—how comparable are the data sources? Great progress has been made in producing suitable data in recent years, but there remain major challenges.

Chapter 5 looks at the figures for poverty around the world produced by international organisations. It picks up where chapter 1 left off, with the monetary measures produced by the World Bank, after first reviewing the history of the Bank's measurement of global poverty. How rapidly is poverty falling on this basis? What is the relationship of poverty with inequality? Who is it that is living in poverty? The discussion then turns to the nonmonetary measures of poverty that are published by the United Nations Development Programme each year in the *Human Development Report*—do they tell the same story?

One of the principal aims of the book is to build bridges between the global estimates of poverty produced by international organisations and the national studies of poverty that are conducted within individual countries. Chapters 6 to 9 consider in turn the evidence about poverty in Asia, Africa, Latin America and the Caribbean, and the high-income countries, drawing on the material in the national poverty reports at the end of the book—the sixty national case studies described earlier. Each chapter does two things. First, I compare the evidence from the national studies with the global estimates of poverty from the international agencies. Second, I address two important issues in the battle against poverty, where these are different in each chapter and typically of global rather than just regional significance. Chapter 6 considers the relationships between poverty, inequality, and growth and between poverty reduction and action on climate change. Chapter 7 discusses whether there is a legacy from the past for poverty today in countries that previously formed the colonial empires of European countries, before looking at the correlates of success and failure in Africa where poverty has been successfully tackled or where it has stagnated. Chapter 8 returns to the issue of measuring monetary poverty with consumption or with income—the latter being common in Latin America and the Caribbean—and examines poverty among ethnic minorities and indigenous peoples. Chapter 9 investigates the persistence of poverty in rich countries and then returns to the global level to provide an estimate of world poverty based on a "societal" poverty line.

Chapter 10 concludes by drawing together the main messages of the book, emphasising that although our knowledge of poverty around the world is incomplete, we know enough to act.

CHAPTER 2

What Do We Mean by Poverty?

The "we" in the title of this chapter are the many people who have diverse concepts of poverty and apply the term in a variety of contexts. Poverty is interpreted in different ways in different countries and in different cultures. Poverty has been approached differently at different times in the past. Poverty is a contested concept, and readers of this book may hold a diversity of views about what they understand it to mean. The different concepts of poverty may each be legitimate and—what concerns me here—may have potentially different implications for how it is measured. There may not therefore be a single answer to the question, what is the extent of poverty? In this chapter, I describe a range of possible conceptual approaches: "political" definitions, subjective assessments, measures grounded in basic needs for consumption, measures derived from the capability approach, and measures based on minimum rights.

Which of these approaches should be adopted is a matter of personal judgement. I am seeking only to offer a menu of choice; there is no "chef's recommendation." But I should stress at the outset the importance of distinguishing between the judgements on which people base their own behaviour and the judgements that they would like to see applied in making decisions as a society as a whole. These may well be different. The former may give primacy to the standard of living of their own family, but the latter may lead them to support their local government implementing programmes of assistance to the homeless. There is nothing illogical in such a separation of judgements. Indeed, the separation is an essential feature of theories of justice, such as that of the Harvard philosopher John Rawls in his *Theory of Justice* of 1971. Rawls proposes that principles of justice should be established by people considering, not their actual circumstances, but how they would make judgements behind a "veil of ignorance," not knowing where they personally would end up. While I do not resort to such a rhetorical device, the discussion of different concepts of poverty is concerned with the way in which we would like to see our society—local, national, or global—approach the issue.

POLITICAL DEFINITIONS OF POVERTY AND SUBJECTIVE PERCEPTIONS

The distinction between the first concept considered—a "political definition"—and the remainder of the chapter is neatly illustrated by the contrast between the *Merriam-Webster Dictionary* definition of the "poverty line" as "a level of personal or family income below which one is classified as poor according to governmental standards" with that in the *Oxford English Dictionary*, according to which the poverty line is "the estimated minimum level of income needed to secure the necessities of life." In this section of the chapter, I begin by exploring the implications of defining poverty in terms of the standard adopted explicitly or implicitly by political authorities, whether at the local, regional, national, or global level.

Political action and assessing performance

Why should we pay attention to the political role of concepts of poverty? The first reason is that, as already observed in chapter 1, statements about the extent of poverty have served a significant function in motivating political action. A story from the early life of Sir Winston Churchill illustrates the political salience of statistical evidence about poverty in Britain. In 1901, Churchill reported that he had been studying Seebohm Rowntree's account of poverty in York: "I have been reading a book which has fairly made my hair stand on end [which] deals with poverty in the town of York. It is found that the poverty of the people of that city extends to nearly one-fifth of the population. . . . That I call a terrible and shocking thing" (reported in Jenkins 2001, p. 81). This account of British poverty contributed to Churchill leaving the Conservative Party and joining the 1906 Liberal government. As a Liberal minister, he introduced labour exchanges and unemployment insurance. As I shall demonstrate at a number of points, this is just an early example of how statistics have played an essential role in motivating action. The initiation of the War on Poverty in the United States by President Johnson following President Kennedy's concerns, described in chapter 1, is a second powerful example.

Statistical evidence about the extent and nature of poverty has been a major factor influencing political action in part because the existence of poverty reveals policy failure. The statistics are a performance indicator. The rediscovery of poverty in Europe was a wake-up call because it destroyed the comfortable belief that poverty had been eliminated in rich countries by a combination of economic growth, full employment, and the welfare state. The promise of an income floor, a guaranteed national minimum, was taken by those concerned with poverty as an implicit standard by which to judge performance. If people are living below this level, then this is a failure of the postwar welfare state. Coming to the present time, the minimum living standard guarantee, or *dibao*, programme introduced by China in urban areas in the 1990s and in the 2000s in rural areas provides a reference point when considering the official poverty lines.

The performance indicator role has been resisted by some statistical agencies. In Canada, it has been argued that "the low-income statistics are not intended to provide an indication of the success or failure of specific programs designed to assist the poor" (Murphy, Zhang, and Dionne 2012, p. 6n). The former chief statistician of Canada, Ivan Fellegi, has stated categorically that "the essentially political nature of such estimates render it inappropriate for a Statistical Agency to make such judgements" (Fellegi 1997). It is, however, not clear that other statistics produced by his agency are free from political judgements. Would anyone replace "low income statistics" with "national accounts" and claim that "the national accounts statistics are not intended to provide an indication of the success or failure of specific programs designed to raise the growth rate"? Yet anyone with experience of the construction of national accounts knows that apparently technical choices can have major political implications. When I reviewed the measurement of government output in the UK national accounts, the chief economist on my team was summoned to a meeting with members of the Cabinet to discuss the implications for the measured productivity of the government sector. I refused to attend because I wished to form my own independent view, but then, I had the luxury of being an academic, not an official statistician.

The role of performance monitoring has acquired much greater salience with the adoption, nationally and globally, of targets for the reduction or elimination of poverty. Statisticians are asked to report on the progress made towards the Millennium Development Goals and now the Sustainable Development Goals. Reports at the global level, such as the *Global Monitoring Report* prepared by the International Monetary Fund and the World Bank, assemble key data on progress towards the agreed targets. The foreword to the 2015–2016 report stated that "this is a pivotal year for global development. The Millennium Development Goals (MDGs) have guided countries and partners over the last 15 years in improving the living conditions of the poor. We are now transitioning to the Sustainable Development Goals (SDGs), a new set of global targets that embrace economic, social, and environmental priorities through 2030" (World Bank Group 2016, p. ix).

The findings are watched nervously at the national level. The 2015–2016 report, for instance, picked out Niger as the country with the highest rate of multidimensional poverty and identified Pakistan as a country where multidimensional poverty, at 44 per cent in 2013–2014, was much higher than the income-based poverty rate, which in 2010 was 13 per cent. At a regional level, the measurement of performance has in the past led to stark conclusions. The Australian Agency for International Development (AusAID) produced in 2009 a report "intended to help governments design policies and programs that hasten progress towards the MDGs," but its assessment was sombre: "The report finds that the Pacific as a whole is significantly off track to meet the MDGs by 2015. Some countries are translating economic growth into reducing poverty and meeting the MDGs. However, overall the Pacific is stalling and falling short of the goals" (AusAID 2009, p. 1). At a national level, the collection of household survey data is seen as a key to monitoring performance. The foreword by the vice chair of the National Planning Commission in Nepal to a report by the statistical office on poverty trends stated that the "wealth of information contained in this poverty report will greatly support in the monitoring and evaluation of the Tenth Plan/Poverty Reduction Strategy, MDGs and other development projects" (Nepal Central Bureau of Statistics 2005, p. i).

Monitoring is not, however, the preserve of governments: it should also be at the forefront of the activities of those who wish to hold governments to account. It can aid concerned individuals, and it can provide evidence to support the case being made by action groups. At a time when there were no statistics about poverty, critics of the government could refer to personal experience or to case studies. These are often telling, but they are much more persuasive if accompanied with statistical evidence about the extent and depth of the problem. As a member of the Child Poverty Action Group (CPAG) in the United Kingdom, I was involved in producing statistically based evidence that called into question the record of the 1964–1970 Labour government and called for more radical measures to tackle poverty. We were bitterly attacked and later blamed for Labour losing the subsequent general election. I doubt the latter, but the bitterness of the attack owed much to the fact that the evidence could not simply be dismissed.[1]

The political nature of poverty measurement is a theme that runs through the book, and it provides the immediate justification for studying poverty as defined by political concerns and agreements. But political influences themselves have more fundamental origins, to which we now turn.

Subjective views about poverty

Political views about the definition of poverty do not arrive simply out of the ether. As the example of Churchill illustrates, politicians are influenced by their experience, and much of that experience comes from talking to people. The views of their citizens—and particularly their voters—can sway them to give prominence to the issue and to consider the nature of poverty. For this reason alone, we should consider the subjective views of those exposed to the risk of poverty. But such views are themselves important in a society that aims at full participation of all its members.

---

[1] *Editors*: This episode is told in a report celebrating the fiftieth anniversary of the CPAG: "It [CPAG] began to campaign much more publicly than before, at the national level, with considerable impact. In May, it issued an election manifesto, *A War on Poverty: Poor Families and the Election*, with press releases headed 'Poor get poorer under Labour,' repeating its and other campaigners' demands. It got good radio, TV and press coverage which impressed politicians. Edward Heath, the Conservative leader, wrote a letter of support to CPAG and repeatedly quoted its claims in campaign speeches attacking Labour. CPAG's attacks on Labour increased its credibility among Conservatives and more widely, raising its national profile and that of poverty as a political issue, while some blamed it for helping to bring about Labour's election defeat" (Thane and Davidson 2016, p. 17).

A criticism commonly expressed in submissions to the World Bank's Commission on Global Poverty was that more should be done to solicit the views of the people living in extreme poverty. Such a participatory approach would learn from the experience of the poor in the countries where most of them are to be found. Why, it is asked, is the International Poverty Line designed in an institution based in a country where extreme poverty is assumed to be nonexistent? Why does the discussion seem to be dominated by the research of those who—like the present author—live in high-income countries?

The World Bank has indeed been alive to this criticism. A major feature of the *World Development Report 2000/2001* was the "Voices of the Poor" background study. This was based on a review of participatory studies involving some forty thousand poor people in fifty countries and on a comparative study in 1999 in twenty-three countries engaging about twenty thousand poor people (World Bank 2001, box 1, p. 3). There were a series of books (Narayan, Chambers, et al. 2000; Narayan, Patel et al. 2000; Narayan and Petesch 2002), the first of these recognising that "the development discourse about poverty has been dominated by the perspectives and expertise of those who are not poor" (2000, p. 2). More recent research has demonstrated the potential. Using household survey microdata from Benin (low-income), Mexico (upper-middle-income) and the United Kingdom (high-income), for example, Nandy and Gordon "show how, in each of the countries selected, there is a high degree of consensus about the necessaries of life, and that such consensus allows for the identification and establishment of social norms and those individuals/groups unable to meet such norms due to a lack of resources to be identified" (2015, abstract). As put by the Global Coalition to End Child Poverty, it is "only through a better representation and understanding of poverty—including who is poor . . . and how they experience poverty—[that] we can meet the urgent challenges of ending poverty in all its dimensions and reducing inequalities, leaving no one behind" (2015, para. 1.4).

The reference to "all its dimensions" is important. The findings of the "Voices of the Poor" study suggested that poverty was seen as consisting of many interlocking dimensions, where lack of food, poor health and illness, lack of access to public goods, and powerlessness were judged to be more important than monetary poverty. This underlines the significance of introducing nonmonetary poverty and of applying multidimensional indicators. As already signalled, these are an essential part of the book. The potential role of the participatory approach in identifying the relevant domains is discussed further in the next chapter.

Subjective views about poverty are undoubtedly a valuable ingredient, and more efforts should be made to develop the approach. For there are limits to what can be learned from "asking people," and not all views are equally valid. For instance, we may wish to ignore completely expressions of negative feelings towards others, such as the denial of the existence of poverty and hardship. Many years ago, in a more vigorous treatment of welfare economics than typically takes place today, Sir Dennis Robertson dismissed such elements, saying that our judgements should not "be eroded by the gnawings of the green-eyed monster" (1954, p. 678). He was referring to jealousy, but his warning would apply today to views based on religious bigotry and xenophobia.

There are in fact four ways in which subjective views can be applied:

1. Ask people to assess their own poverty status without any reference to a poverty line, and the total in poverty is then those who classify themselves as "living in poverty" (where the exact formulation of the question is clearly crucial).
2. Ask people about the minimum consumption they consider necessary to avoid poverty, and then ask whether or not their own consumption meets that standard.
3. Ask people about the minimum consumption they consider necessary to avoid poverty, and then obtain information about the household's consumption to determine whether or not their own consumption meets that standard.
4. Ask people where the poverty line, defined in terms of consumption, should be set, where this enters into the determination of the poverty line for the whole population (and no assessment is made of the status of the household interviewed).

These approaches are obviously different. The fourth is closest to the World Bank procedure for counting the poor (used for the estimates of global poverty in figures 1.2 and 1.3 in the last chapter) in that it leads to a population-wide poverty line.[2] It has indeed been extensively used. In the United Kingdom, the 1983 Breadline Britain study (Mack and Lansley 1985) identified the poor as those suffering from an enforced lack of socially perceived necessities. These necessities were identified by public opinion as possessions and "activities" that every family should be able to afford and that nobody should have to live without. (Only items considered a necessity by at least 50 per cent of the population were retained.)

The other three approaches lead to an assessment at the level of the responding household and no population-wide poverty line. The first makes no explicit reference to consumption but may be closest to the concerns of politicians. The finding that a substantial proportion of the population consider themselves "poor" may gird them for action, regardless of the basis for this subjective valuation. It is striking that in Uganda in the 2012–2013 Household

[2] *Editors*: The procedure used by the World Bank to arrive at the International Poverty Line of $1.90 a day is described in chapter 5 and does not draw on subjective views. Tony's comment here is merely intended to note that this way of applying subjective views does result in a poverty line that can be applied to the whole population, like the World Bank's.

Survey, 70 per cent of the population classified themselves as "very poor" or "poor," whereas the rate of monetary poverty according to the national poverty line was 19.7 per cent (Uganda Ministry of Finance 2014, table 2.4). The second approach is like the others in that it is mediated through consumption per head. The third approach differs in that, like the second approach, it is based on a subjective assessment of poverty status, but the subjective assessment is contrasted with *objective* measurement from survey information recorded by external observers. In all of the first three approaches, the poverty line being applied varies from one household to another because of their different subjective views. Any reported poverty line would be an average over respondents. It should equally be noted that both the first and second approaches can be applied to individuals within the household and may provide a source of evidence about within-household inequality, a subject considered further in the next chapter.

In interpreting the information obtained from participatory studies, the differences are important. As is well known (for example, from the literature on the use of reported happiness), the responses may reflect both adaptation and aspiration. Where people have adjusted to low levels of living, they may have adapted to these levels and regard mere survival as escaping poverty. In the opposite direction, responses may be influenced by rising aspirations, where people above the objective poverty line see themselves falling behind rising living standards elsewhere. In both cases, there is a potential bias, in the first case downward and in the second case upward. Moreover, the bias may differentially affect different groups. Remote rural communities, for instance, may be more likely to be affected by adaptation and their extreme poverty more likely to be understated.

In terms of concrete implementation, there are at least two possible roles for the collection of information by participatory input. The first application is to the choice of alternative poverty lines. For many years the World Bank has recognised multiple poverty lines. The 1990 *World Development Report* applied a line of $275 a year for the "extremely poor" and $370 a year for the "poor" (World Bank 1990, table 2.1). The 2000–2001 report, in addition to the $1 a day line (by then, strictly, $1.08 a day), showed the results of an upper poverty line of $2 a day, "reflecting poverty lines more commonly used in lower-middle-income countries" (World Bank 2001, p. 17).[3] Quite a number of countries make use of multiples of the International Poverty Line (now household consumption per head of PPP$1.90 a day—see chapter 1). Employment of mul-

---

[3] *Editors*: Alongside estimates of global and regional poverty totals based on the International Poverty Line of $1.90 a day, the World Bank's October 2017 release of the PovcalNet database provided figures for two additional poverty lines, $3.20 a day and $5.50 a day, where these lines are "based on the national poverty lines typically found in lower- and upper-middle income countries, respectively" (PovcalNet website, "What is new," 10 October 2017). We remind the reader that the dollars concerned are international purchasing power dollars.

tiple poverty lines provides one test of the sensitivity of the estimates. There can be greater confidence in the monitoring exercise if a range of poverty lines around the International Poverty Line all show a decline in the percentage of the population considered poor: there is then "dominance" (Atkinson 1987). However, simply taking a mechanical multiple does not seem to be the right course, in that there is no evident justification for taking a particular multiple. It would not satisfy those who are critical of the existing $1.90 a day line. It would adjust all country lines by the same percentage, whereas the relativities are open to question. As put to the Commission on Global Poverty by ATD Fourth World, "tracking poverty on other lines, such as $4 or $10, would just replicate the same problems and weaknesses" (2015, p. 5). One (although not the only) input into the choice of alternative lines should be information obtained by participatory studies. Do those living around the extreme poverty level consider that it is realistic? What is the view of those living in countries where there are many people in extreme poverty?

The second application is to learn more generally from participatory studies about the design of nonmonetary indicators of poverty. One aim of these indicators is to give voice to those individual circumstances that are not brought out by household-based measures, particularly the position of women and children. The Global Coalition to End Child Poverty has stressed that "participatory methods allow us to capture the views and perspectives of children, young people and other vulnerable groups providing valuable insight to better understand and contextualize poverty, vulnerability and exclusion" (2015, para. 1.1). Referring to the need for greater efforts "to ensure that all children are counted as part of poverty assessments, including children living outside of households and/or without parental care," the Coalition goes on to say that "nothing reveals this more clearly than listening to children themselves, about what they need and what they want." Or as Richard Jolly puts it, "Child poverty is . . . very different from adult poverty defined in terms of living below $1.25 a day [then the International Poverty Line]. . . . For a child, . . . adequacy must be assessed not just in terms of a child's immediate needs but in terms of what the child needs to grow in strength and capabilities so as to reach adulthood, with the basic capabilities needed for being a good citizen, within the community and beyond" (2012, p. xxxi). I discuss ways of taking more account of the position of women and children at greater length in chapter 3.

Conclusions

There is much that can be learned from participatory engagement, and poverty standards should be set after conversations all round the world, not just in Washington. However, subjective assessments cannot be the sole basis for monitoring trends in poverty. Otherwise, we would have to accept that a country can become poorer even though nothing has changed as far as an external observer is concerned. We need in addition measures of poverty based on objectively observed characteristics of households, to which I now turn.

CONSUMPTION AND BASIC NEEDS

What do we observe about households? The World Bank global poverty estimates are based on the level of household consumption as recorded in household surveys. (The concept of consumption is dealt with in chapter 3, and how it gets recorded is discussed in chapter 4.) This observed consumption is then compared with that deemed necessary to avoid poverty, but setting that poverty standard has been one of the central challenges to research in this field.

I start where much of the scientific study of poverty began: relating the poverty standard to a concept of *basic needs*. Such a concept has the apparent merit of providing a physiological foundation for the poverty measure. As I shall argue, this appeal to physiology is overdrawn, but the approach has long attracted investigators of poverty. At the beginning of the twentieth century in the United Kingdom, the chocolate manufacturer Seebohm Rowntree (1901) drew on the work of early nutritionists to determine minimum food requirements for a household, to which were added other "necessaries," consisting of clothing, fuel, and sundries, and an addition covering the rent paid. In the United States, an early application of linear programming was to the derivation of minimum cost diets that met specified nutritional requirements (Dorfman, Samuelson, and Solow 1958, p. 9n).[4] The official US poverty line developed from the work of Mollie Orshansky (1965), who took as her starting point the estimates of minimum food expenditure by the US Department of Agriculture, examined the proportion of income spent on food in households of different types and then multiplied up the food spending to allow for nonfood items. In India in 1962, the Planning Commission set a minimum consumption level as a target for the fifth Five Year Plan, based on the "minimal level" diet published by Sukhatme (1961), multiplied up to allow for nonfood spending.

Today a basic needs approach is widely employed in the derivation of national poverty lines, as shown by many examples in the national reports at the end of this book. In Jamaica, for example, the poverty line has been defined in terms of a food basket designed to provide a minimum nutritional requirement for a family of five, with an addition being made for nonfood items to cover the cost of clothing, footwear, transport, health and educational services, and

---

[4]Linear programming is a mathematical technique to obtain the minimum value of a linear function (in this case the cost of the diet) subject to linear inequality constraints (providing at least a specified level of each nutritional requirement). Stigler (1945) had previously solved the problem by a trial-and-error process that came close to the full linear programming solution. The application of linear programming in the definition of poverty lines for global poverty estimates has been revisited recently by Robert Allen (2017) in work discussed further in chapter 3.

other personal expenses (Planning Institute of Jamaica 2007). In Italy, the national statistical institute regularly produces poverty estimates based on baskets comprising food, clothing, housing, and other necessities which vary by age and number of household members and which are valued accounting for differences in prices across geographical districts and between urban and rural areas (Istat 2009).

The basic needs approach

What does the basic needs approach involve? There are three key steps in the method as typically practised:

1. Determination of nutritional requirements, here discussed in terms of individual food calorie requirements per day, which may vary with age and gender
2. Conversion of these requirements into a food budget, which involves the nutrition content of individual foods and their cost
3. Making an allowance for nonfood items

The first step draws on a large body of research by, among others, the World Health Organization (WHO) and the Food and Agriculture Organization (FAO) on calorie requirements. Calories are probably familiar to readers from information on the backs of cereal packets, but it may be helpful to spell out that they are a measure of energy requirements. I shall be referring to calories with an upper-case C (Cal.), which is the energy needed to increase 1 kilogram of water by 1°C at a pressure of 1 atmosphere. (You may also see references to calories with a lower-case c, which replaces 1 kilogram by 1 gram; thus, 1 Cal. = 1,000 cal.)

At the same time, the first step is not just a matter of looking up a number in a table. The Calorie levels required depend on the level of physical activity assumed. The FAO (2001, p. 36) provides estimates of energy requirements. These are defined relative to basal metabolism ("sleep") at 1.0 and range from 1.53 when the main daily activity is "sedentary or light" through 1.76 ("active or moderately active") to 2.15 ("vigorous or vigorously active lifestyle"). In more detail, "sitting on a bus or train" is scored at 1.2 for both males and females, whereas pulling a two-person rickshaw is scored for males at six times greater, 7.2 (FAO 2001, p. 92). Thus there is a range of choice for energy needs, and in practice different choices are made when constructing poverty standards. If we look at the Calorie requirements underlying national poverty lines in different countries, then we find that in Sri Lanka they are 2,030, in South Africa 2,261, in Pakistan 2,550, and in Uganda 3,000 (World Bank 2017, figure 2.1).[5]

---

[5] *Editors*: The figure for South Africa refers to 2001. The national report for South Africa at the end of the book cites a figure of 2,100 Calories being used in the official poverty line, which dates from 2012.

Such a range underscores the fact that judgement enters at each stage of the process. That the judgement may be questioned is illustrated by the World Bank's comment on the official poverty line in the former Soviet republic of Georgia, a line based, the Bank argued in 1999, "on the (unrealistically) high nutrition norms inherited from the pre-independence period" (World Bank 1999, p. 1).

The second step is the conversion of the nutritional requirements into food purchases, where the purchases are determined to secure the specified requirements of Calories and other nutrients at the lowest total cost given the price of each foodstuff. It follows that the composition of the food basket, and the total outlay, depend on the prevailing food prices and availability. If supermarkets in one country raise the price of flour, then this may tilt the basket away from flour, and it will certainly raise the total cost. It is also evident that the application of the second step necessitates the collection of detailed data on the cost of different foodstuffs.

This may sound like a mechanical process. However, the diet produced by the early linear programming calculations in the United States led to questions as to whether it was realistic to assume that it would be followed in practise. The application of mathematics took no account of whether people would actually eat the proposed diet. In his pioneering UK study, Rowntree (1901) drew on actual dietaries used to feed people in institutions, and so he included tea in the list of goods, even though it has no nutritional value. The minimum food expenditures used by Orshansky (1965) were based not solely on the intake of Calories and other nutrients, but also on views regarding an acceptable trade-off between nutritional standards and consumption patterns. These departures mean that the poverty line is set higher, to a degree that depends on judgement.

For this reason, an alternative approach may be followed, based on actual food consumption and the extent to which it generates the required nutritional intake. In simplified form, this means examining the nutrients contained in the foods consumed by different households (which requires information on the quantities and qualities of foods, such as in the case of Sri Lanka grams of basmati rice, as well as the amount spent) to see at what level of total food consumption the required intake is attained. Reading across from nutritional intake to total food consumption gives the food poverty line. The national reports at the back of the book show that many countries use the resulting figure as a threshold for what is often labelled as "extreme" poverty—the situation where total household expenditure on both food and other items is below the food poverty line, as in, for example, Ghana, Kenya, Zambia, Bolivia, Brazil, Colombia, and the Dominican Republic. In Kenya, the National Bureau of Statistics refers to this as "hard-core" poverty and in addition defines "food poverty" as a household's food expenditure alone coming below the food poverty line.

The third step involves the addition of nonfood items; here there is a choice of methods and considerable room for discretion. Following the approach in the previous paragraph, we could read across, not to total food consumption, but to total overall consumption, including nonfood. A total poverty line would be set by the amount of total consumption at which a household could be expected to spend just enough on food to satisfy the nutritional requirements. For the household just at the nutritional cutoff, this would be equivalent to multiplying the food consumption by the reciprocal of the food share—i.e., if the household spends half its consumption on food, then we would multiply by 2. Alternatively, as in the work of Orshansky in the United States, the food share may be estimated from another source; the value selected was 0.33, so the cost of the minimum food expenditure was multiplied by 3. The food share is taken as 0.5 in Brazil and as 0.7 in Georgia, leading to the cost of the food bundle being multiplied up by 2 and 1.43, respectively. Or nonfood needs may be estimated directly, specifying minimum requirements of clothing, shoes, heating, health care, and other items, as in the most recent poverty line used by the Planning Commission of the Government of India, although in this case the difficulty of setting norms led the Expert Group to recommend that in practise observed expenditure on these items by households in the middle of the distribution be taken instead. In the EU, there has been extensive research on consensual budget standards. (See, for example, Bradshaw and Mayhew 2011, which contains a synthesis report covering thirty-two European countries.) A major project has been the EU Reference Budgets Network (see Goedemé et al. 2015; Storms et al. 2013). While a "consensual" standard provides a line of justification, it is rather removed from the concept of the poverty line having a purely physiological basis. As Peter Townsend remarked in his critique of the basic needs approach in the United Kingdom, "A family might maintain its physical efficiency just as well in a caravan . . . as in a three-bedroom house. It could go to bed early and spend nothing on electricity" (1962, p. 215).

So far, I have discussed the calorie requirements as though everyone were identical, but the construction of the basic needs standard has to make judgements regarding its *structure*. An important example is provided by gender. Should the basic needs standard be the same for men and women? One consequence of the nutritional approach is that the requirements are usually set at a lower level for women than for men. Applying the basic needs approach as described above would mean setting a lower poverty line for women than for men (as used to be the case in the United States and is still the case in Jamaica but not in Italy, to use the examples given at the start of this section). Is this a feature that should be introduced into the global poverty calculations? Given concerns about the gender composition of the poor, such a move would spark definite reactions, and the application of the basic needs approach may have to be accompanied by an overriding condition that the resulting poverty standard be gender-neutral.

To put some flesh on this account, let me illustrate by the calculation made for Vietnam in constructing the basic needs–based poverty line for 1993. (The procedure has since been revised, but the earlier version conveys the essence more clearly.) As described, in setting the Calorie requirement at 2,100 per day based on WHO and other sources, "it is useful to take an average requirement over the entire population" (World Bank 1999a, p. 145): i.e., to take no gender differences into account. To identify a basket of food consumption that meets this calorie target and reflects Vietnamese food consumption patterns, households in the 1993 Vietnam Living Standards Survey were divided into five equal-sized "quintile" groups in order of their total expenditure per head.[6] For example, those households ranked from 40 per cent to 59 per cent made up the middle quintile group. It turned out that it was this group whose food consumption generated calories per capita closest to the 2,100 Calorie threshold, and it was their consumption that was used to identify the basic-needs basket of foodstuffs. So, if one looks into the entrails, one learns that the basket contains, among other things, 169.6 kilograms of ordinary rice per year, 11.4 kilograms of sweet potatoes, 5.9 kilograms of cabbage, and 6.6 kilograms of bananas (World Bank 1999a, p. 148, table A.2.2).

The household survey collected data by commune on the market prices of nearly all the relevant foodstuffs, and the median prices were used to make a calculation for Vietnam as a whole. The resulting total for January 1993 was 749,723 Dong, and this was the basis for the Vietnamese Food Poverty Line. To apply it to the measurement of poverty, the recorded household expenditure had to be adjusted to a national basis, adjusting for regional price differences, and to a January 1993 basis. To go from the Food Poverty Line to the General Poverty Line, a simple addition was made for nonfood based on the average nonfood expenditure of the third quintile group. This brought the total to 1,160,363 Dong per person per year in 1993—i.e., an increase of 55 per cent over the Food Poverty Line, reflecting the high share of food in total spending in Vietnam at that time (around two-thirds). It should be noted that the nonfood expenditure figure included both explicit spending and the imputed values of durable goods and owner-occupied housing. (I return to this issue in chapter 3.)

Basic needs as a moving target

The above description relates to the establishment of the basic needs–based poverty line at a particular point in time. But how should it change over time?

---

[6] A distinction should be made between quintiles and quintile groups. "Quintile" refers to the level marking the points in the distribution when we reach 20 per cent, 40 per cent, 60 per cent, and 80 per cent. The "quintile groups" consist of those between 0 and 19 per cent (first quintile group), between 20 and 39 per cent (second quintile group), and so on.

The simplest answer is that the line is increased in line with the general level of prices, as measured by the consumer price index (CPI). "Simple" is, however, a misnomer, since such price adjustments are often much debated. Does the CPI, designed for the general population, capture the effects of inflation on the poor? Is the CPI itself fit for purpose? Price indices have often been the subject of intense political disagreement. These questions are taken up later in chapter 4.

Even, however, if there is agreement on the price adjustment, experience with the basic needs approach has shown that in application it is subject to continual revision. The approach described above in the case of Vietnam in 1993 has since been revised, with a broader consumption aggregate and a different technique for obtaining the required total food spending. In Malaysia, the official poverty line was first formulated in terms of food needs in 1977 and was used until 2005 to monitor the country's progress in eradicating poverty, but in 2005 the line was substantially revised to make it more comprehensive and more generous than its 1977 predecessor. In Nepal, the poverty threshold was defined to satisfy minimum caloric requirements, but in 2010 it was replaced by one that was 35 per cent higher in real terms "to reflect changes in well being over time" (Nepal Central Bureau of Statistics 2011, p. 16). In Italy, the method used to estimate absolute poverty since 1997 was extensively revised in 2009 by an ad hoc commission which recommended reviewing periodically the consumption basket and the hypotheses adopted in its definition in order to reflect changes in "the socio-economic reference context" (Istat 2009, p. 24). Going back in the mists of time to the studies of poverty in the United Kingdom by Rowntree (1901), his later poverty lines applied in 1936 and 1950 allowed for additional nonfood items, such as a radio, that had not been included—or indeed contemplated—in his first study of 1899.

The official US poverty line provides an exception to the policy of revision. The poverty thresholds for different types of family are adjusted each year by changes in prices, but the thresholds themselves have been left unaltered (bar revisions in the case of farm households, for example). Poverty in the United States today is still assessed by the Census Bureau on the basis of a calculation made in the first half of the 1960s. The use of this line in the administration of benefits has contributed to curbing its updating, despite the steady erosion of its value relative to mean income (Blank 2008). The Census Bureau also presents figures that incorporate regular changes in the consumption basket taken to represent basic needs, but, significantly, they are labelled a "supplemental poverty measure." (The development of the US poverty line and its history in the following twenty-five years is described in Fisher 1992; the supplemental measure is explained in Renwick and Fox 2016 and followed on from the review of poverty measurement in the United States by Citro and Michael 1995.)

Adjustments to the basic needs standard may be expected to be upwards in the case of nonfood items, as in the examples just cited, but on what are they based? How do we decide on an extension of the list of items? One route is via subjective assessments, although, as noted earlier when discussing the level, this takes us away from a physiological basis; moreover, the specification of the poverty line is inevitably influenced by prevailing living standards and the possibilities of the technology of the time. Can this be avoided by the use of food requirements, multiplied up by the inverse of the food share? Not entirely, since the question then becomes, whose food share? One of the few empirical regularities in economics with a lengthy shelf life is Engel's Law, which states that the proportion of total spending going to food declines as total spending rises. (This was the work of the German statistician Ernst Engel, not to be confused with Friedrich Engels.) As a society gets richer and the food share falls, the reciprocal—the inverse of the food share—rises, and with it the implied allowance for nonfood items associated with any set of basic food needs.

The food needs themselves raise major questions when it comes to updating over time. The fact that energy requirements are greater for those undertaking heavy work means that the food requirements should vary with the level of activity. Put in reverse, a country where most workers are sitting looking at screens should have a lower nutrition requirement than one in which many people are pulling rickshaws. Allen (2013, table 2) shows a time budget for a labourer in mid-eighteenth-century London, whose activities required 2.16 times the intake of the basic (sleeping) requirement. If the worker had instead been seated at a desk, the requirement would have fallen to 1.41. The lower needs may be offset in part by the fact that nutritional requirements rise with the greater height and body mass in rich countries, but the possibility should be contemplated that a basic needs–based poverty line should fall the higher the level of development. Such an outcome would no doubt puzzle those unfamiliar with the construction of the poverty line and might cause political embarrassment. It would be possible to specify that adjustments should be "upward only," but that would be a flagrant departure from any physiological justification.

That this is a potentially serious matter is illustrated by the case of India. The pattern of calorie intake in India has been examined in depth by Deaton and Drèze, who find that "average calorie consumption in rural areas was about 10% lower in 2004–05 than in 1983. The proportionate decline was larger among better-off sections of the population, and close to zero for the bottom quartile of the per capita expenditure scale" (2009, p. 62). On the face of it, this evidence points to a lower level of basic needs associated with less demanding activity levels, although they conclude that "this hypothesis remains somewhat speculative." Even more importantly, they argue that "average calorie intake has serious limitations as a nutrition indicator [and] close attention needs to be paid to other aspects of food deprivation, such as the intake of vitamins and minerals, fat consumption, the diversity of diet, and breastfeeding practices" (2009, p. 62). I come back to this in chapter 3 when discussing the design of multidimensional measures and the use of outcome indicators such as stunting.

Inverting the telescope

Before leaving the basic needs approach, I should point out that we can "invert the telescope." The discussion so far has run from basic needs to the resulting poverty line, but the approach is also illuminating in the reverse direction. The question becomes, what does the International Poverty Line of $1.90 per person per day allow a household to buy? By relating the poverty standard to household budgets, light can be cast on its implications for household living standards. There was a famous occasion in the United Kingdom during an inquiry into dockworkers' pay in the 1920s, when the union leader appeared in court with a plate bearing a few scraps of bacon, fish, and bread and asked the statistician (Sir Arthur Bowley) whether this was sufficient breakfast.[7]

Today the basic needs calculations would allow different levels of total consumption to be mapped back to the level of nutritional intake that they permit. The calculations would allow scrutiny of the allowance for nonfood items. In the case of India, Drèze and Sen note that the Indian "reference budget associated with the urban poverty line includes . . . ten rupees per month for 'footwear' and forty rupees per month for health care. The former would just about make it possible to get a sandal strap repaired once a month, and the latter might buy something like the equivalent of an aspirin a day" (2013, p. 189). Subramanian has similarly commented that in urban Tamil Nadu the official poverty line for a family of four, after allowing for shelter and food, "would have left a good deal less than nothing to spend on education, clothing, and transport" (2009, p. 68). The reverse calculations provide a basis for engaging the wider public in a consultative process: "Such an approach would make more meaningful the otherwise arcane statistical procedures on which the risk-of-poverty indicator is based. It would be a good means by which Governments could engage those experiencing poverty and social exclusion" (Marlier et al. 2007, p. 156).

Conclusions

The basic needs approach has played a major role in the development of poverty lines around the world. Historically, it has been influential in the measurement of poverty in rich countries. It provides insight into the meaning of

---

[7] *Editors*: The work of artists Stefen Chow and Lin Huiyi provides contemporary examples of poverty-line diets. They have taken photos for some thirty countries of food that can be purchased on the budget provided by national poverty lines, photos drawn on for the cover of this book (see www.thepovertyline.net).

poverty lines derived by other means—illuminating what the International Poverty Line, for example, would buy. However, the claims for the basic needs approach should be stated carefully. It cannot be said to provide, even at a point in time, a purely physiological foundation for measuring poverty, since at each stage of the calculation a significant degree of judgement is being exercised. It can be implemented in a variety of ways. When it comes to up-rating over time, both the nonfood and the food components raise major issues, which is a serious obstacle to its use for monitoring progress.

POVERTY AS DEPRIVATION OF CAPABILITIES

If the basic needs approach is long-standing, the capability approach dates from recent decades. In a series of contributions, Amartya Sen (1985, 1992, 2009) has argued that well-being should be judged in terms of the *functionings* achieved by people and of the *capabilities* open to them. By functionings are meant the activities and states valued by a person, and capabilities are the various combinations of functionings that he or she can achieve: "the actual opportunities of living" (Sen 2009, p. 233). In the context of measuring poverty, Sen has argued that this should be seen as the deprivation of capabilities, where that deprivation limits the freedom of a person to pursue their goals in life: "Identifying a minimal combination of basic capabilities can be a good way of setting up the problem of diagnosing and measuring poverty" (1993, p. 41). In this section, I consider what this means and how it can be put into operation.

The capability approach

Reactions to the capability approach vary a great deal. On one side there is enthusiastic endorsement among those who see it as offering a new perspective to assessing well-being and as transforming the measurement of deprivation. On the other side, there are those who question whether the vocabulary of capabilities adds much that is new; they suggest that the implications for poverty measurement are of little significance. It is with the latter that I begin. What is meant by the capability approach, and how does it differ from that based on household consumption, as in the textbook account?

There are in fact several key ingredients. The first is a concern with *opportunities*, where these describe the scope for choice but are not confined to the actual choices made. The capability set is a description of the menu of possibilities. A young person may dream of playing for Barcelona or at Wimbledon when they grow up, but more realistically they may plan to become a teacher, or to set up their own business as a computer consultant, or to become an independent fisherman. If they know that their family cannot afford to send them to school, or that they have not the capital to buy a boat, then this is a restriction of the range of opportunities. Now, it may turn out that the person wants to be a teacher in any case, so the absence of capital to buy the boat is irrelevant. The achieved functioning is the sole concern, and we are back with an evaluation close to that applied in the standard approach. However, the essence of the capability approach is that we are in addition concerned with the roads not followed, and particularly with those that are not followed because they are blocked. As it was put clearly by Kenneth Arrow with the aid of some mild algebra, "The choices that are open to the person but that she or he does not make are also relevant. . . . The objects that should be ordered are not the outcomes x but the pairs (x, A), where A is the set from which the choice is to be made ['menu' in Sen's terminology] and x belongs to A" (2006, p. 54).

Evaluating the outcome is the meat and drink of what this book is about, but what about the set of opportunities? The chances, in the example, of entering different occupations are multiple valued, not immediately reducible to a single number. How do we combine the chance of being a teacher and that of being a fisherman? In a sense, economists are used to doing this. If we have multiple indicators of deprivation, then the same problem arises. One resolution is to look for comparisons that are unambiguous, where, for example, a country is doing better, or no worse, on all dimensions. In the case of a person, a new opportunity, such as the opening of a college for nurses, unambiguously expands the set of options. The new situation is said to "dominate" the previous one. But what it does not resolve is what happens when the opportunities for nursing improve but pollution means that fishing is a less viable option. We have then to combine the different elements via some procedure for aggregation to see whether the gain from one outweighs the loss from the other. This procedure will take into account the relative desirability of the different career paths, and this begins to sound like the kind of process lying behind the determination of the actual outcome. Is it not much the same as a household choosing its consumption to maximize its well-being? In fact, the process is different, since the implementation suggested by Arrow and others takes account of the value of flexibility where the valuation is made in advance of knowing the actual preferences and the valuation is not solely based on the actual outcome. There are differences, but they are of some subtlety. The capabilities theory does indeed illustrate the general point that the goal of securing equality of opportunity, while enjoying wide acceptance, is a concept whose precise definition is varied and often elusive, whereas the goal of tackling outcome deprivation, much more contested, is—relatively—easier to translate into agreed concrete measures.

It is to concrete measures that I turn below. First, however, there is a second major ingredient, one that links with other developments in consumer economics, notably those that see the household as akin to a small factory, engaged in household production. The household budget approach to poverty measurement has pinpointed the consumption of goods and services ("commodities"), but Sen, like a number of other economists, has argued that commodities are a means to an end and that we need to consider the ways in which they make possible the functionings which are the ultimate concern. He traces therefore the chain

Commodities → Characteristics → Capabilities → Well-being

So, to take Sen's example, possession of a bicycle has the characteristic of allowing you to travel; this characteristic ensures the capability to get to work, and that underpins your well-being. Where the capability approach differs is that it is concerned with the third, not the fourth, link in the chain. In contrast, the basic needs approach starts from a specified standard of living and works back to the necessary commodities, with little attention being paid to the intervening steps.

A focus on the intervening steps is a crucial contribution of the capability approach. To see what is involved, let us suppose that each unit of commodity—which may be food or nonfood—yields a specified amount of each of the relevant characteristics. The amounts per unit of a commodity are referred to as "output coefficients," and the whole array covering all commodities makes up a "matrix." In the case of foodstuffs, the coefficients tell us how many calories, proteins, vitamins, etc., are generated per unit purchased. A set of purchases will then provide a total, adding up across all the commodities, of each of the characteristics. Since the characteristics are what secures the desired level of capabilities, we want to reverse the process and find the necessary purchases of commodities. In mathematical terms, this requires us to invert the matrix, so we can read back from the desired level of capabilities.

In terms of foodstuffs, what has been described so far is not different from the linear programming exercise used in the early US calculations, but there are two distinct features that become apparent from the capability approach. The first is that the coefficients are not purely technical. The significance of such an approach is demonstrated by Sen in his analysis of "Gender and Cooperative Conflicts" (1990). He builds on the household production approach, but with the key difference that "technology is not only about equipment and its operational characteristics but also about the social arrangements that permit the technology to be used and the so-called productive processes to be carried on" (1990, p. 463). In terms of foodstuffs, the social arrangements clearly include such matters as dietary norms and religious restrictions, but for all commodities it is the case that the coefficients reflect the prevailing consumption practices in the society in which people are living. In his 1899 investigation, Rowntree recognised that the allowance for clothing for a worker should "not be so shabby as to injure his chances of obtaining respectable employment" (1902, p. 108). The allowance today would be rather different. The matrix of coefficients depends on the society and the date.

An immediate consequence is that the commodities required to achieve a specified level of functioning are influenced by the society in which a household lives and may change as the society develops. As it was put by Sen, "In a country that is generally rich, more income may be needed to buy enough commodities to achieve the *same social functioning* . . . to the capability of 'taking part in the life of the community'" (1992a, p. 115). If the level of consumption that is required to function within a society varies with the average level of consumption, then a standard that is *constant* in the space of functionings or capabilities would imply a standard in terms of consumption that varies over time and across countries.

There is a second dimension of poverty that has so far been missing from the story: the role played by suppliers and producers. In constructing the matrix of coefficients, account has to be taken of the extent to which goods and services are *available*. Households can only buy what is in the market, and this is decided by the suppliers. Potential consumers may be excluded from the market by the decisions of firms regarding which quality of product to supply. As overall living standards rise, shops may no longer offer cheaper cuts of meat, and small-sized packs of food may no longer be available. The cost of food may depend on the location of employment: a worker may have to purchase more expensive meals away from home on account of the increased concentration of production in distant urban locations. A worker dependent on public transport to get to this work may find the service withdrawn as the rest of society gets richer and can afford its own transport.

Capabilities and poverty measurement

The capability approach is in many respects congruent with other developments in the measurement of poverty in rich countries that have stressed its role in preventing people from participating fully in society. This is indeed the way in which poverty has been defined following the work of UK sociologist Townsend, who saw poverty in terms of ability to participate in society: "Individuals, families and groups in the population can be said to be in poverty when they lack the resources to obtain the types of diet, participate in the activities and have the living conditions and amenities which are customary, or at least widely encouraged or approved, in the societies to which they belong" (1979, p. 31). Such an approach was implemented in 1984 by the European Council of Ministers, who defined those in poverty as "persons whose resources (material, cultural and social) are so limited as to exclude them from the minimum acceptable way of life in the Member State in which they live" (decision of the Council of Ministers, 19 December 1984). The capability approach provides theoretical underpinnings for this essentially political definition of poverty, but there is clearly a gap between the idea that the necessary commodities should rise with living standards and the concrete implementation in terms of poverty measures. This gap is where, just as with the basic needs approach, the exercise of judgement plays an important role. The current form of the EU commonly agreed measure of "risk of poverty" draws a threshold at 60 per cent of the median disposable income (adjusted for household size and composition) in the country in question. But why 60 per cent? The 60 per cent of median threshold replaced an earlier line drawn at 50 per cent of the mean, but that simply pushes the search further back in time. The study underlying the design of the EU Social Indicators (Atkinson et al. 2002) referred to a range of percentages from 40 per cent to 70 per cent.

In seeking an answer to this question for the United Kingdom at the time (1968–1969), Townsend took an approach that at first seemed promising, which was to examine the relationship between observed income and the reported inability of a household to participate in a range of activities. The activities included such matters as having a week's holiday away from home, having a birthday party for the children, having sole use of a flush WC, sink, bath, or shower or gas/electric cooker, or having a cooked breakfast most mornings (remember it was the 1960s). The resulting deprivation score, formed by combining these indicators, when averaged over households in an income range showed a fall as incomes rose. What Townsend was seeking was a threshold, or a kink in the relationship, with the decline being steeper below the threshold. The findings turned out to be suggestive but "inconclusive" (1979, p. 255). While there was "no evidence . . . of a pronounced threshold . . . the increase in the proportion of households with high scores was particularly marked once income had fallen to a level of 60 to 69 per cent of the mean. This suggested that if a poverty line were to be drawn, it would seem justified to draw the line within this band" (p. 258).

I have spent some time on this classic study because it is a fine example of applying social science research to answer a very real policy question. Fastforwarding some thirty years, the EU-based study by Fusco, Guio, and Marlier (2010, figure 6.2) examined in a similar way the relation between the intensity of deprivation and household income in twenty-five European countries. The deprivation questions were not the same: ownership of a washing machine, colour TV, and a car were now entered. Some questions, on the other hand, were similar, such as a week's holiday away from home. Inspection of the graphs (by eye) suggests that there was a smooth downward curve and no threshold in a number of cases: Greece, Hungary, Latvia, Lithuania, Poland, Portugal, and Spain. But for others, a threshold is detectable (subject to more rigorous testing) at around 60 per cent of the median income (adjusted for household size and composition): Austria, Belgium, Cyprus, Germany, Estonia, Italy, Luxembourg, Slovakia, and Slovenia. These findings are suggestive, but not definitive. How this evidence is weighed is a matter of judgement.

The capability approach may provide only an incomplete answer to the level at which the poverty line should be set, but it does, however, go further. In particular, it provides a framework for thinking about the *structure* of the poverty standard. This is demonstrated by Sen's lead example of disability: "The relevance of disability in the understanding of deprivation in the world is often underestimated, and this can be one of the most important arguments for paying attention to the capability perspective. People with physical or mental disability are not only among the most deprived human beings in the world, they are also, frequently enough, the most neglected" (2009, p. 258). Here lies the value of separating the links in the chain from commodities to capabilities. In the example given above, it was taken for granted that possession of a bicycle supplied the capability of getting about, but for people with certain disabilities, this is not the case. At the very least, the bicycle would have to be specially adapted. The technological coefficients are different, and hence different amounts of goods and services are needed to ensure a specified level of functioning. (I return to this issue in the next chapter.)

Finally, capabilities are essentially multidimensional, and the construction of multidimensional indicators may be viewed as an operationalization of the capability approach, where the theoretical foundation provides guidance as to the dimensions to be included. At the same time, just making a list of dimensions is not sufficient, and—as we have seen in the case of income poverty—the setting of concrete thresholds requires other inputs and the exercise of judgement.

Conclusions

The capabilities model has undoubtedly enriched the way in which we approach the measurement of poverty and provides a framework for tackling difficult definitional issues—including the roles of absolute and relative poverty, to which I come in the final part of this chapter. At the same time, it does not eliminate the need for judgement: there is a gap between theory and application. It is an approach, not a resolution.

MINIMUM RIGHTS AND POVERTY

To this juncture, we have been concerned with a well-being approach to the measurement of poverty. I turn now to the alternative "rights-based" approach, an approach that has elements in common with those already discussed, but which may take us in some different directions. If you doubt this and are thinking of skipping, I should just note that the basic needs approach in the United States happily for many years set a poverty line that was lower for women than for men, whereas that would have been ruled out of court by a rights approach.

Human rights

I begin with a compact account of the rights approach. "Compact" may seem inconsistent with the vast literature on "rights," and indeed a necessary immediate step is to limit the field severely. First, I do not discuss the instrumental role of the right to freedom from poverty in underpinning a general catalogue of human rights. The abolition of poverty may be an essential precondition for the full enjoyment of other human rights, but it is with the intrinsic importance of attaining "poverty rights" that I am concerned here. Second, I return to a governmental view of the definition of poverty, as in the first section of this chapter, taking as given the way that rights are defined by national—and, more especially, international—bodies. Again, performance is being judged according to stated goals.

How can this be made concrete? Can the objective be formulated in terms that capture the essence? "Human rights always come to us in lists," according to Nickel (2014, p. 219), and he goes on to say that "international law uses a standard list that mainly comes to us from the Universal Declaration of Human Rights. This list consists of seven families of human rights, the first six of which are found in the Universal Declaration." (The Universal Declaration was adopted by the UN General Assembly in December 1948.) The sixth on the list is "social rights that require that people be provided with education and protected against starvation and severe poverty." The Universal Declaration itself has a more extensive list. Article 25 states that "everyone has the right to a standard of living adequate for the health and well-being of himself and of his family, including food, clothing, housing and medical care and necessary social services," and Article 26 adds that "everyone has the right to education," with a specific reference to elementary education.

This formulation in the Universal Declaration does not lead us directly to a poverty line, but it is informative in three respects. The first is that rights are defined on an individual basis. It is true that Article 16 says that "the family is the natural and fundamental group unit of society and is entitled to protection by society and the State," but there are no attached rights of families or households. In this book, I take rights as individual. It is, for example, concern with the individual rights of women that underpins the case I make for nonmonetary measures that allow gender inequality to be identified. It should, however, be recognised that, right from the start, the Universal Declaration was criticised as being too dominated by Western values with their individual focus. Eleanor Roosevelt, widow of American president Franklin D. Roosevelt and chair of the Declaration's drafting committee in 1947, recalled in her memoirs that some had argued for a more pluralist approach, with one Asian member suggesting that the Secretariat might well study the fundamentals of Confucianism (UN 2017). A starting point of society as a whole, or of distinct population subgroups (defined, for instance, by geography or ethnic composition or religion), may lead to a focus on the right to live harmoniously in such a society. As noted in the next chapter, this would lead to the extension of a portfolio of nonmonetary indicators of poverty to include dimensions of a different kind.

The second respect is that the list of rights in the Declaration makes frequent use of the word "everyone" and is explicit as to when rights are not neutral between individuals. Otherwise, the rights are universal. To reiterate a point made earlier, this means that there is no justification for the situation when, as was the case in the past, the US official poverty line, derived from a basic needs approach, was lower for women than for men. At the same time, there are exceptions. Article 25 goes on to say that "motherhood and childhood are entitled to special care and assistance. All children, whether born in or out of wedlock, shall enjoy the same social protection." Here particular attention should be paid to the rights of the child (Pemberton et al. 2007), as embodied in the UN Convention on the Rights of the Child, a document which, to quote the former UN high commissioner for human rights Mary Robinson (2002), "adds value because it provides a normative framework of obligations that has the legal power to render governments accountable."

The third contribution is that the lists identify key dimensions that are relevant when considering a multidimensional approach, as in the next chapter: education, food, clothing, housing, medical care, and necessary social security. Such a list is similar to that given by rights theorists, although with some interesting differences. For example, Shue cites "unpolluted air, unpolluted water, adequate food, adequate clothing, adequate shelter, and minimal preventative health care" (1996, p. 23). Here again the focus on the rights of the child is important. "Child mainstreaming" has been stressed in the development of nonmonetary indicators in the EU. Eric Marlier, Bea Cantillon, Brian Nolan, and I commented that the common social indicators were unsatisfactory when viewed from the child perspective; instead, "we need to approach the issue from the opposite direction: to start from the perspective of children and then consider the selection of indicators" (2007, p. 102). (For further discussion of child material deprivation, see Guio, Gordon, and Marlier 2017; see also Micklewright 2002.)

Rights and poverty measurement

[*Editors*: Tony left no notes on this subsection. We guess he would have developed further the concrete implications of the Universal Declaration for poverty measurement beyond the three general issues just discussed. For the UN special rapporteur on extreme poverty and human rights, extreme poverty "involves a lack of income, a lack of access to basic services and social exclusion" (website of the Office of the UN High Commissioner for Human Rights, January 2018). See also UN (2012). Tony might have discussed the approach taken in the reports of visits to countries in recent years by the UN special rapporteur. (These countries include Chile, China, Ghana, Mauritania, Romania, Saudi Arabia, the United Kingdom, and the United States.)]

Rights and diverse cultures[8]

The word "poverty" has different meanings in different cultures: "To write about the Japanese poor in English is an anomaly in itself, because whatever stands for 'poor' in the Japanese language has its unique flavour within the Japanese sociocultural context, lost when rendered into English" (Chūbachi and Taira 1976, p. 433).

A report by the Solomon Islands National Statistical Office and the UNDP puts it well:

> Traditional Solomon Island society, as well as Pacific societies generally, embraces caring for and sharing with family and clan. As a result, there is a continuing belief that poverty cannot and should not be a part of normal life in the Pacific region. The suggestion that there might be poverty in some form is not, therefore, something that many people have been prepared to readily accept. Indeed, the usual images of poverty (starving children, landless peasants, and men and women toiling with ox ploughs) do not immediately spring to mind in relation to the Pacific or Solomon Islands. (2008, p. 8)

The report goes on to say: "However, the increasing monetization of Pacific economies, the impact of television and internet, and increasing rural/urban migration leading to greater urbanization, have begun to undermine these traditional structures. . . . As a consequence poverty and hardship, as now defined and understood in the Pacific, . . . are being increasingly accepted as concerns which need greater attention" (p. 8).

Returning to the capability approach, Martha Nussbaum has proposed functional freedoms, or central human capabilities, as a rubric of social justice, paying especial attention to the unequal opportunities of women in different cultural settings (for example, Nussbaum and Glover 1995; Nussbaum 2000, 2000a).

ABSOLUTE AND RELATIVE POVERTY IN A GLOBAL POVERTY COUNT

The different concepts described in this chapter have differing implications for the measurement of poverty. These will become apparent in the next chapter

---

[8]*Editors*: We have only isolated paragraphs for this subsection. Tony seems to have intended to discuss what poverty means in different cultures, as his opening words show.

when I discuss the translation of concepts into measures. But there is one important issue where we need immediately to confront the differences: the long-standing debate contrasting absolute and relative poverty. This acquires particular salience here where we are concerned with poverty across the globe, with countries at very different levels of development.

Absolute and relative poverty

To begin with, we must define terms. "Absolute" can bear at least two different meanings. The first is that there is an inherent justification for a particular poverty standard, with scientific basis in physiological or other considerations. It may require measurement, but in this respect is like the speed of light. As we have seen when discussing the basic needs approach, such a line is not readily established, and the idea of a purely physiological basis is illusory. The term "absolute" has come therefore to assume a second meaning: a poverty line that is fixed in terms of consumption, adjusted over time in line only with changes in prices. To distinguish this version, we may refer to it as "anchored absolute," and we have seen several examples in this chapter. If we turn to a "relative" poverty line, then we find that the poverty status of a household is related to the prevailing living standards in the society in which the household lives. An example is where the poverty line is set as a percentage of the median consumption or income level of the country in question. There may be a mix of absolute and relative lines, where the initial poverty line is set as a percentage of the median, but the line is then adjusted over time according to the movement in prices, giving an "anchored relative" poverty line. This is the case with the lines used by the EU to estimate the "at-risk-of-poverty rate anchored at a point in time" (Eurostat 2017).[9]

Two features are apparent. First, an absolute measure, unlike a relative measure, can be applied to a single household in isolation. A person's ability to meet his or her basic needs can be judged independently of the situation of all other inhabitants of the planet. In contrast, a relative measure, as with the capability approach, is essentially concerned with the ability to function in a particular society. Second, while there are extremes of pure absolutism and pure relativism, there are also intermediate cases along the continuum:

---

[9]*Editors*: Another way of achieving the mix of absolute and relative concepts is when an absolute line is indexed to movements in nominal incomes rather than prices, as, for example, with the social and subsistence minima calculated for the former Czechoslovakia in the 1970s (Atkinson and Micklewright 1992, p. 211). For a treatment by Tony of the distinction between absolute and relative lines in the context of measuring poverty in Europe, see Atkinson (1998, pp. 18–28). See also Foster (1998) for a discussion of different meanings of the word "absolute" in the context of poverty measurement.

> Absolute line ↔ Anchored absolute line ↔
> Anchored relative line ↔ Relative line

It should be evident from the earlier discussion that the different concepts point to different places in this continuum.

A global poverty measure

Following the global scope of the Sustainable Development Goals, the measurement of poverty is seen in this book as a global exercise, encompassing rich as well as poor countries. The embracing of both developed and developing countries, however, is often represented as generating an inevitable conflict between "absolute" and "relative" approaches. But this is not necessarily the case. The shift in perspective to a capability approach provides one route to resolve any such tension, as François Bourguignon and I have argued (Atkinson and Bourguignon 2000, 2001). Not only does the approach provide an underlying theoretical framework for analysing deprivation, but it also shifts the standpoint from which ethical considerations are applied.

The application of the capability approach can indeed be seen as building on the earlier discussion of the energy requirements of different activities. "Bare survival" may be seen as requiring for an individual a level of food and other inputs, broadly independent of the overall standard of living. On the other hand, "work" does indeed have higher energy requirements (with the caveat about the shift away from heavy labour), but it is an activity where other requirements apart from nutrition are significantly socially determined and can be expected to rise with the overall standard of living. A linen shirt may have been sufficient at the time of Adam Smith, but today a job seeker requires internet at home.[10]

This provides a way of understanding the evidence about national poverty lines. Many years ago, using data from 1985, Ravallion, Datt, and van de Walle (1991, figure 1) plotted national poverty lines against mean household consumption for thirty-three countries. Observing that the national poverty lines tended to rise with the level of mean consumption in the country in question, they fitted a statistical model to describe the relationship between the two, involving the logarithm of the poverty line rising with mean household consumption and its square. The same data, however, suggested to François Bourguignon and me (Atkinson and Bourguignon 2000, figure 1) that the national poverty lines were better viewed as—at that time—the greater of $1 a day per

---

[10]*Editors*: The reference to the linen shirt is to Adam Smith's famous comment in his 1776 *Inquiry into the Nature and Causes of the Wealth of Nations* that, "in the present times, through the greater part of Europe, a creditable day-labourer would be ashamed to appear in public without a linen shirt, the want of which would be supposed to denote that disgraceful degree of poverty" (book V, chapter II, article IV).

person in international purchasing power dollars and 37 per cent of mean consumption per person. There was a switching point around the overall consumption per head in Morocco. We went on to argue that such a switching explanation corresponded to the theory of capabilities described in the previous paragraph. Below a certain level of overall consumption, the availability of individual consumption associated with basic needs is what limits capabilities, but once the switching point is reached, it is another set of consumptions that limits capabilities. What is more, the first constraint is governed by a fixed level of consumption, appropriately adjusted for differences in prices, but the second set varies with the overall level of consumption in a particular context. Typically, this relativity is expressed as a percentage of the mean consumption in the country at a particular date.

This way of viewing the global poverty situation is well described in the report on the 2005 Kenya Integrated Household Budget Survey: there is a

> hierarchy of basic needs which begins with survival food needs and is followed by basic non-food needs. Many activities that are deemed essential to escaping poverty cannot be performed without participation in society; for example, employment and schooling. That social participation is not possible without incurring the basic non-food expenditures on, for instance, shelter, clothing and hygiene. (Kenya National Bureau of Statistics 2007, p. 27)

The different possibilities are illustrated in figure 2.1, where countries' mean consumption per head is measured along the horizontal axis and an individual household's own consumption per head on the vertical axis. To determine whether a particular household is in poverty, it is necessary first to identify where their country is located along the horizontal axis—say, at the level X. The poverty status of the household is then governed by its own consumption per head: i.e., where the household is located on the vertical line going up from this point. For a country with mean consumption to the left of level A on the graph—the switching point—the applicable poverty line is the *absolute* threshold represented by the horizontal section of the poverty line, level B. In a country with mean consumption per head at the level of X, a household is in poverty if its consumption per head is below level B. For countries to the right of point A, the *relative* threshold, which is higher, is applicable, and this is represented by the upwards-sloping section of the poverty line. Among this group of countries we are concerned both with those households living below the absolute poverty threshold and with those above this threshold but below the relative poverty line. Thus, it is possible to identify three areas of poverty: areas I and II correspond to absolute poverty in poorer countries and richer countries, as identified by their positions relative to A; area III corresponds to relative poverty, a condition that occurs only in richer countries where escaping poverty requires satisfying needs that go beyond mere survival.

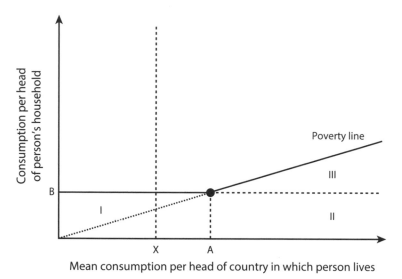

Figure 2.1. Absolute and relative poverty in global poverty measurement
Source: The graph draws on Atkinson and Bourguignon (2000).
Reading note: The poverty line has a fixed value, level B, until a country's mean consumption per head reaches level A, at which point the value of the line increases with the level of mean consumption per head.

This may sound complex, but the key constituents are familiar. The first is the absolute poverty threshold, level B, taken here for the purposes of discussion to be the International Poverty Line, $1.90 per person per day. The second is the slope of the section of the line showing the relative poverty threshold. Here too there is a degree of familiarity, in that relative poverty measures in high-income countries are typically expressed as percentages of the mean or median income. So, in 2001, the EU adopted as its official definition of relative poverty—as one of the Commonly Agreed Social Indicators referred to as "poverty risk" (Atkinson et al. 2002)—60 per cent of the median disposable income (adjusted for household size and composition). This is broadly the counterpart of 50 per cent of mean income.[11] In other countries, the figure taken is 50 per cent of the median (Morelli, Smeeding, and Thompson 2015, p. 609), or closer to 40 per cent of the mean. The level of the absolute poverty threshold and the slope of the section of the line showing the relative threshold together determine which

[11] *Editors*: The distribution of individuals' household consumption or income is asymmetric with a long upper tail. The mean value (the arithmetic average) is some way above the median (the value which splits the distribution into two, with half of individuals above this level and half below).

countries are to the left or right of the switching point, A. The level of country mean consumption at which the regime switches is equal to the reciprocal of the slope times the value of the International Poverty Line. In the case illustrated, with a slope of 0.3, or 30 per cent, the poverty line starts moving upwards when a country reaches a mean consumption of three and one-third times the International Poverty Line. In 2011 PPP terms, this is a mean consumption level equal to $6.33 a day. The figure of 30 per cent for the slope is close to the 37 per cent suggested by François Bourguignon and me (Atkinson and Bourguignon 2000). Question for the reader: how would the diagram have looked if the slope had been taken as 50 per cent?[12]

In chapter 9, I explore the implications of this application of the capability approach for the measurement of poverty in the world as a whole. In this way, we are making a reality of the goal of the SDGs to be inclusive of all societies—rich and poor.

Finally, it should be reiterated that the capability approach in the form adopted here misses much of the richness of the foundational work by Sen and Nussbaum, and that it involves a distinct shift in perspective. It is, for instance, possible that a rise in the income of a person below the poverty line leads to an increase in measured poverty. Seen in terms of income, this makes no sense (see Decerf 2015), but seen from the standpoint of capabilities, the consequent rise in mean income may have the consequence that people above but close to the poverty line are more challenged when they seek to participate in that society.

CONCLUSIONS

In this chapter, I have discussed different interpretations of the word "poverty," staying at a broad, conceptual level. While there is a range of different approaches, I have tried to show that there is common ground that is relevant to any attempt to measure global poverty, with the capability approach playing an important unifying role in thinking about countries at different levels of development. The focus has been on the implications of each approach for the measurement of poverty, and the next two chapters now consider measurement in more detail.

---

[12] *Editors*: The answer comes in chapter 9! Using a much larger database in terms of countries and years, Jolliffe and Prydz (2017) reconsider Atkinson and Bourguignon's approach together with alternative proposals by Ravallion and Chen (2011) and Garroway and de Laiglesia (2012). In the report of the Commission on Global Poverty, Tony discussed the possibility that the intercept implied from projecting back the sloping part of the poverty threshold is different from the value of zero shown in figure 2.1 (World Bank 2017, pp. 142–144), but here he went back to the original Atkinson-Bourguignon formulation.

CHAPTER 3

Clarifying Concepts

If you are told that 20 per cent of the population in a country is living in poverty, there are lots of questions that you should ask before reacting. In each case, one needs information about how the poverty line is established, how the circumstances of households are assessed, and how one arrives at the summary statistics. What is needed in fact is a *checklist*, and the purpose of this chapter and the one that follows is to provide such an aid to understanding poverty statistics.

WHAT IS BEING MEASURED?

Is it monetary poverty or nonmonetary poverty? Nonmonetary measures are considered later in the chapter. But if it is monetary poverty, then does "money" mean what comes in, as income, or what goes out, as spending?

A much-debated question: Consumption or income?

Suppose that poverty is defined as lack of resources. The first question on the checklist concerns the choice between measuring resources in terms of consumption and measuring them in terms of income. The two concepts now need to be defined—the words "consumption" and "income" have been used repeatedly in this book already, but definitions have yet to be given. Consumption is the *use* of resources, whether acquired through purchase (expenditure) or through household production—for instance, growing vegetables or keeping livestock for one's own use—or provided from outside the household, such as by relatives, charities, or the government. So that, in a given period, a person may buy food, clothing, and other goods, may eat food grown at home, may use a durable good bought some time before, may receive a gift from a relative, and may receive medical attention free from a publicly employed doctor. All of these sources of consumption should in principle be covered. Income, on the other hand, is the *flow* of resources that are received, where these include labour earnings, income from self-employment (for example, from a farm or a profession), investment income, government transfers (such as unemployment benefits, disability allowances, and state pensions), and private transfers (private pensions, remittances), net of taxes and social insurance contributions, but also the value of household production net of costs incurred and income in kind from the state. The concepts are considerably more complex than "money in" and "money out." And it is immediately clear that the implementation of such measures poses serious data problems. These are taken up in the next chapter, but we should recognise from the outset that in general neither concept is fully measured in practice.

On one basis a family may be judged poor, but on the other be regarded as above the poverty line. With the $1.90 a day per person poverty line, a family of four with an earned income of $7 a day is below the line on an income basis, but if they receive in-kind help valued at $1 a day from a relative, then this may allow their consumption to reach the $7.60 threshold.

Which should we choose? China's National Bureau of Statistics has used a criterion of both low income *and* low expenditure to measure rural poverty, in a way described in the national report for China at the end of the book. However, in general a choice between the two is made. The World Bank has a definite answer to the question: "consumption per capita is the preferred welfare indicator for the World Bank's analysis of global poverty" (World Bank 2015, p. 31). The Bank reasons that "policy makers are interested in capturing the living standards *achieved* by individuals. These are directly reflected in a well-constructed comprehensive consumption measure. Incomes, in contrast, reflect an *opportunity* to reach a given welfare [level] but may provide only an imperfect proxy of what welfare level was finally achieved" (p. 32, emphasis in the original). On this argument, the family of four had an opportunity with their own income measured by only $7 a day but were able to achieve a welfare level of $8 due to the help received.

However, income may be the preferred welfare indicator when we want to focus on potential spending power rather than actual expenditure. A miserly millionaire who lives on virtually nothing would from one point of view appear rich, and from the other poor. The choice of income is indeed recognition that the use of resources goes beyond consumption. This could bring us to be concerned with the right to a minimum level of resources, as in the human rights approach introduced in chapter 2. This approach has been interpreted as viewing poverty in terms of deprivation of a certain minimum right to resources: people are seen as entitled to a minimum income, which is a prerequisite for participation in a particular society. On this basis, if the poverty threshold for the family of four is $7.60 per day and the family has only $7 of its own earned income, it is classified as poor despite the help received from the relative. The family's own resources fell short of the threshold.

The choice may also be influenced by practical considerations of data availability. In the case of Malaysia, the UNDP reports that

> Household Income Surveys are conducted on a regular basis whereas expenditure surveys are conducted less frequently. Moreover, the Household Income Survey contains rich information about each member of the household, information

typically not available in expenditure surveys. Knowledge of each member's characteristics may help in analyzing the causes of poverty rather than simply measuring its incidence or severity. For these reasons, poverty analysis in Malaysia is based on household income. (UNDP 2007, p. 17)

Income is used to measure poverty in many Latin American and Caribbean countries, where, as in Malaysia, regular surveys of income are more readily available than are surveys of expenditure. The EU's measurement of monetary poverty is now based on income, although this has not always been the case, partly on grounds of the availability of comparable data for the member states (these data are described in chapter 4). The long-standing official measure of poverty in the United States also assesses families' income rather than their consumption. But most of the World Bank's measurement of global poverty does indeed use data on household consumption, which, it argues, "are typically more easily and more accurately collected in the developing country context. This is particularly the case when attention is focused on the poor" (World Bank 2015, p. 33). The World Bank's reasoning is considered further when the problems in measuring consumption and income in practice are addressed in the next chapter.

As a prelude, we can look here at an important conceptual issue of measurement. We have to be careful to distinguish between consumption and expenditure, despite the two words often being used interchangeably, both in this book and by other authors. The available data may refer only to the latter. The distinction is evident in the case of durable goods. A household derives benefit from the use of a durable good, such as a fridge or a car, which may be regular or even continuous, and not from the money spent on the good's initial purchase or replacement, which will only be very infrequent. The former is the consumption, which is the service provided by the fridge, and the latter is the expenditure, which is the money paid to buy the fridge. Expenditure on fridge purchase will be zero for most households in any given period for which data are typically collected—for example, a week or a month. One way to estimate the service of a durable good is to spread its cost over the years it is expected to be used.

An even larger problem arises with the consumption of owner-occupied housing. What is the value to a homeowner of the addition to their living standards that comes from being in their own property? The rent paid by tenants is included in total expenditure. Would ignoring the value of living in your own house not imply a difference in treatment between homeowners and tenants? The value to the owner may be taken as the rent they would receive were they to rent out their home—the "imputed rent." Is imputed rent in or out of the data used for poverty statistics? Of course, a figure for each household has always to be estimated, as it is never actually observed. In a number of countries there are moves to include imputed rent on owner-occupied housing. Imputed rent is estimated in household surveys in Uganda and Zambia, for example, and in the integrated nationwide survey introduced in China in 2013. This can make a major difference to the total reported household expenditure. The Solomon Islands 2012–2013 income and expenditure survey estimates total expenditure in the country as $SBD 6.9 billion, and of this $SBD 1.1 billion represented imputed rent, or 16 per cent of the total (Solomon Islands National Statistical Office 2015a, p. xii). Viewed from the income side, imputed rent represented slightly less: 15 per cent of the total (and home production accounted for 20 per cent). In Italy, the national statistical institute traditionally estimates poverty rates based on expenditure including imputed rent on owner-occupied dwellings. In its annual release of income-based estimates of household living conditions, it publishes statistics with and without imputed rent: in 2014 the income share of the bottom fifth of the distribution rises from 6.7 to 7.7 per cent after including imputed rent in the income definition (Istat 2016, p. 9). Törmälehto and Sauli (2017) provide estimates for the distributional impact of imputed income from rent for EU countries, noting that homeownership rates and the proportion of households holding mortgage debt vary widely across member states. (Interest payments on mortgages are subtracted from the imputed rents.) Relative income poverty rates fall modestly in most countries when allowance is made for imputed rent but increase a little in some (2017, table 7.3) The decreases are concentrated among the elderly, who tend to have the highest homeownership rates and lowest mortgage debt.

What difference does it make in practice whether we take income or consumption? In its 2016 report on *Poverty and Shared Prosperity*, the World Bank compares the extent of overall inequality in a number of countries in Eastern Europe and Central Asia for which data are available for the Gini coefficient, a widely used index of inequality ranging from zero to one, measured in terms both of income and of consumption expenditure. It finds that consumption-based Gini coefficients are considerably lower than income-based coefficients, but that the ranking of countries was similar and that, as far as trends over time over the period 2008 to 2013 are concerned, one measure does not produce a consistently smaller change in inequality than the other. The World Bank concludes that "the ranking of countries by the Gini index is somewhat robust to whether consumption or income is used, although there are some notable exceptions" (World Bank 2016, p. 79). This conclusion echoes the result of an earlier comparison: "In most countries, measured inequality based on income is higher than if it is based on consumption. But this is not inevitable, and the degree to which the two indicators disagree varies from country to country" (World Bank 2005, box 2.5). The need for caution is reinforced by recent evidence for the United States. On the one hand, Fisher, Johnson, and Smeeding (2015), using a data set where income and consumption are measured for the same set of individuals, the Consumer Expenditure Survey, estimate that consumption inequality increased almost as much as did income inequality from 1984 to 2011. On the other, Meyer and Sullivan (2017) find that the rise in overall consumption inequality was small relative to that of overall income inequality from the early 1960s to 2014, with patterns for the two measures differing by decade; their results use two different sources, the Consumer Expenditure Survey and the Current Population Survey, respectively.

These results refer to inequality—the extent of dispersion in the distribution of income or consumption as a whole—and our interest here is with poverty, that is, with the bottom of the distribution. The use of income data is likely to lead to a higher estimated poverty count. In the case of Mexico in 2012, for example, where both kinds of data are available, on an income basis, the proportion of the population below $1.90 a day is 5.9 per cent, but on a consumption basis, applying the same poverty line, the figure falls to 2.7 per cent (figures from the World Bank PovcalNet database).[1] The World Bank's global poverty estimate uses income data for countries where consumption data are not available and hence may appear an overstatement; moreover, the overstatement applies particularly to Latin America and the Caribbean, where, as noted, income surveys are more frequent, distorting the measured regional composition of the global poor. At the same time, the extent of the difference should not be overstated. Chen and Ravallion examined the poverty rates in surveys for twenty-seven countries where both consumption and income data were available and "found only . . . a statistically insignificant difference [for the average poverty rate] . . . consumption had a lower mean but also lower inequality" (2004, p. 13). Using the $1 a day line, the average proportion of poor people was 17.8 per cent for consumption and 21.2 per cent for income.

While these results appear to offer some comfort for the general picture across countries, the user of statistics for any individual country would do well to check figures on both bases when available and to be cautious if comparing a figure based on income for one year with one based on expenditure for another.

I return to this issue in chapter 8 when considering the measurement of poverty in Latin American and Caribbean countries, and then again in chapter 9 in the context of conceptual issues with income and consumption that are of particular importance when measuring poverty in rich countries.

Persistent poverty and the accounting period

Poverty measures calculated from household survey data typically provide "snapshots" of the extent of poverty at the time of the survey, since they are cross-section surveys. This means that when a new survey is mounted in a given

---

[1] *Editors*: These figures come from the October 2016 version of PovcalNet. In the April 2018 update, the difference between the two rates in 2012 is much smaller: 3.9 per cent when using income and 3.4 per cent when using consumption (see figure 8.3 in chapter 8.)

country, it comprises an entirely new sample of households. One is unable to track the circumstances of individual households over time, and one cannot therefore say anything about the duration, or persistence, of poverty. Thus, a comparison of the incidence of poverty in India between 2004 and 2009 is able to tell us how much overall poverty increased or decreased during this interval. What the comparison is unable to tell us is the proportion of the poor in 2004 who remained in poverty in 2009, or how many of the poor in 2009 were not in poverty five years earlier.

There are multiple reasons as to why information about the persistence of poverty might be of interest. There may be normative grounds to worry more about poverty if it is a "chronic" condition than if there is a high rate of turnover among the poor. Certainly, the nature and form of policy interventions are likely to be different when addressing "transient" versus "chronic" poverty. In the case of the former, policy-makers might focus on introducing or strengthening a safety net that aims to prevent households from falling into poverty as a result of some unforeseen event. In the case of chronic poverty, they will be generally more focussed on enhancing human and physical assets of the poor—in an effort to lift them, in a sustained way, out of poverty. To produce estimates of the persistence of poverty, cross-section surveys are not enough. Panel data are needed. Panel surveys follow the same households over time and are therefore able to observe directly whether households drop in or out of poverty, or remain in poverty over extended periods of time.

Panel surveys have been developed in a range of rich industrialised countries and used to analyse the dynamics of poverty—to go beyond the snapshot. There is a long record for the United States (Bane and Ellwood 1986 was an influential early study) and a substantial one in several European countries (see Jenkins 2011, for example, for the United Kingdom). The EU statistical office now publishes figures for poverty persistence for member states (Eurostat 2017). But despite these developments, panel data remain scarce in practice, particularly in the developing world. There are currently too few proper panel data sets to allow for a reliable estimate of the persistence of poverty at the global level. Such surveys are typically expensive, administratively and logistically complex, and associated with a variety of analytical challenges linked to measurement error (causing mobility in or out of poverty to be mismeasured) and attrition (the phenomenon of households dropping out of the survey). (Conceptual and measurement issues in the analysis of poverty dynamics are discussed by Bradbury, Jenkins, and Micklewright 2001, chapter 2, and Atkinson et al. 2002, chapter 6.) It is unlikely therefore that there will be a dramatic expansion of panel surveys in the near future.

What does all this imply for the poverty checklist? First, although the poverty rate for a particular country may be from a cross-section survey, it is important to probe for other sources. Do figures exist on movements in and out of poverty based on data from a panel survey to complement the picture from the snapshot? Second, even without such data, an awareness of the dynamics of poverty helps focus the mind on a related question: Over what period do we consider the circumstances of a household interviewed in a cross-section survey? Is the accounting period a week, a month, a year? The shorter the period the more likely that the circumstances observed are transitory in nature, that a household found below the poverty line has escaped by the next period, or that another household has become poor. A short period might register coincidental fluctuations in income or expenditure that would have been evened out over a longer period. But the longer the period the greater may be the potential for error in the measurement, with the household having to remember, or record in a diary, a greater volume of information. An exception in the case of income is where the household can use information from an annual tax declaration.

Focussing on income, the choice between, say, monthly and annual figures will depend in part on the assumptions made about the effect of short-term fluctuations on the economic well-being of individuals and households. This brings us back to the earlier discussion of income versus consumption: "The distinction . . . is more important the shorter the period of time over which the two are assessed. One reason, therefore, for looking at income assessed over longer periods is that long-term income is likely to provide a better indicator of consumption at each point in time (because of consumption smoothing)" (Bradbury, Jenkins, and Micklewright 2001, p. 35). That is, some households will be able to maintain their consumption during short spells of low income by using savings, by borrowing, by postponing some nonessential expenditure, or, as in the example used earlier, through the help of a relative. The extent to which this is possible is likely to vary across countries, depending on whether institutions and family structures help income smoothing.[2]

The mysteries of purchasing power comparisons

When data for different countries are brought together in estimates of poverty in the world as a whole, or in regions of the world, then it is necessary to compare the poverty standards across boundaries. This requires accounting for differences in the cost of living, which has typically been achieved by carrying out purchasing power parity (PPP) comparisons. In simple terms, this means that the International Poverty Line applied in India is not obtained by converting dollars into rupees at the market exchange rate. Rather, the conversion allows for the fact that the purchasing power of money in India is different. In 2011, for example, the market exchange rate was such that one obtained 46.67

---

[2] *Editors*: In the case of the United States, see, for example, Morduch and Schneider (2017), who draw on the information collected over the course of a year from 235 low- and moderate-income households by the US Financial Diaries project (www.usfinancialdiaries.org).

Indian rupees for a US dollar, but the results of the UN International Comparison Program (ICP) exercise for 2011 showed that just 14.98 rupees would have been sufficient to buy the same basket of goods and services as $1 in the United States. Such PPP exchange rates are based on the substantial investment that has been made in collecting and analysing the price data necessary to compare purchasing power in different countries. Since 1970, there have been eight rounds of ICP data collection, the most recent to date being that for 2011 (World Bank 2014).

The intuition underlying PPP indices can be grasped by considering the Big Mac index published by *The Economist*. In July 2011, the average price of a Big Mac, a burger that has characteristics roughly comparable across the world, was $4.07 in the United States and 84 rupees in India (*The Economist* 2017). With 168 rupees, someone could buy two burgers in India, but not even one in the United States, as 168 rupees would have been converted to $3.60 at market exchange rates. Thus, the purchasing power of a given amount of money in India was more than twice that in the United States using the price of a Big Mac as the metric. All this implies that in India the $1.90 a day threshold of the International Poverty Line would have been 39 rupees when converted with the Big Mac index instead of 89 rupees with market exchange rates. Measured poverty is clearly lower in the former than the latter case. The ICP exercise applies the same reasoning but uses a far larger basket of goods and services than a simple Big Mac. Based on the 2011 ICP, the actual threshold used in India for the count of global poverty is 28.46 rupees = 14.98 × 1.90, which is about three-quarters of the value suggested by the Big Mac index.

The reason for using PPP rather than market exchange rates derives from the fact that the latter are influenced by many factors, such as the flows of international trade or speculative capital movements, and need not reflect the price structures that prevail in the various countries. In poor countries, labour-intensive nontradable services are typically cheaper than in richer countries: since market exchange rates are unlikely to account for these price differences, their use leads to understating real incomes in poor countries. The PPP exchange rates obviate these problems, since they are the relative values, in national currencies, of a given basket of goods and services. They provide the conversion rates from national currencies to an artificial common currency, such as the "international dollars" used in the computation of global poverty. If you have ever thought that the price of a meal in a restaurant in another country seems either very cheap or very expensive after a mental calculation of the price in your own country's currency using the rate at which you changed your money, this may signal a departure of the PPP exchange rate from the market rate.

Of course, coming to a judgement on the basis of a single meal could be premature—no less so than looking at the price of just a Big Mac. The Big Mac index is an admirably simple way to illustrate the logic underlying international purchasing power comparisons. But it is revealing in a subtler sense. The astute reader may have been puzzled by the reference to the price of a Big Mac burger, which is typically made of beef, in a country like India where cattle are held sacred. The surprise is well founded, since no beef (or pork) is served in any McDonald's outlets in India—as confirmed by a glance at the menu posted on the company's Indian website. A closer look at the footnotes of the charts on *The Economist*'s Big Mac index webpage solves the mystery: "India's Maharaja Mac is made of chicken"! This story exposes the difficulties of international purchasing power comparisons: a supposedly "identical" product such as the Big Mac is not truly identical across the world. The comparisons must come to terms with local differences in product availability as well as in people's uses and beliefs, all of which affect consumption patterns and make the construction of an identical basket of goods and services a challenging task.

The difference made by use of PPP exchange rates to the comparison of incomes across the world is illustrated in figure 3.1. The graph compares countries' annual GNI per capita in 2015 when expressed in PPP dollars with the US dollar value of the same measure obtained using market exchange rates. The latter applies the Atlas method, described in box A in chapter 1, which averages the market rate over three years (adjusting for differential inflation rates). These GNI values obtained with the Atlas method are reported on the horizontal axis on a logarithmic scale, meaning that a given distance along the axis shows the same proportional difference rather than the same absolute difference in dollars. As explained in chapter 1, the World Bank classifies countries into four groups of level of development according to GNI per capita based on the Atlas method. The threshold levels for these groups are shown in the graph by vertical lines.

The vertical axis shows the ratio of GNI per capita measured in PPP dollars to that at market rates. India is one of the countries with the highest values: GNI per capita in PPP dollars is 3.8 times the value obtained using the Atlas method. This is second only to the figure for Myanmar (4.3) and just ahead of those for Pakistan and the Gambia (both 3.7). In ten other countries the ratio is over 3.0, including, among the countries covered by national poverty reports at the end of the book (and in descending order), Nepal, Madagascar, Malawi, Egypt, Indonesia, Cambodia, and Sri Lanka. (The other three countries are Iran, Afghanistan, and Bhutan.) In half of all countries, the figure is over 2.0. In only a dozen high-income countries on the right-hand side of the graph does the use of PPP reduce the valuation of GNI per capita beneath that at market exchange rates (i.e., values below 1.0), although there are other countries in the same group where the valuations are close. The four lowest values are for the Bahamas, Australia, Switzerland, and Norway. The ratio tends to fall as national income per head rises, so the use of PPPs tends to reduce the relative gap in GNI between lower- and higher-income countries (and may also reduce it in absolute terms, for example, when comparison is with those high-income countries where the ratio is less than 1.0).

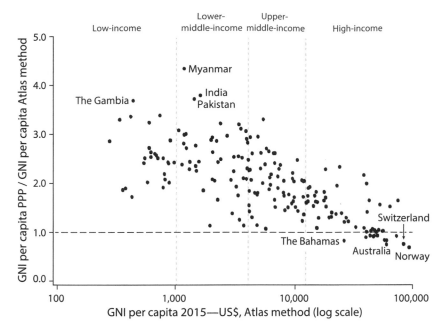

Figure 3.1. GNI per capita for the world's countries, 2015: PPP and Atlas method compared

Source: World Development Indicators series NY.GNP.PCAP.PP.CD and NY.GNP.PCAP.CD (downloaded April 2018).

Reading note: In the Gambia in 2015, GNI per capita valued using the PPP rate (from the 2011 ICP) was 3.7 times GNI per capita valued using the Atlas method (market exchange rates), as shown on the vertical axis; the horizontal axis shows that the level of GNI per capita with the Atlas method in the Gambia in 2015 was US$440.

What about the implications of using PPPs for the measurement of global poverty? Within each country, income and expenditure are measured in the national currency, so nothing changes by using PPPs. PPPs matter, however, when converting the International Poverty Line from dollars into national currency. Suppose the market exchange rate rather than the PPP rate were used for this conversion into rupees in India. As we have seen, the line would be much higher and many more people in India would be classified as poor; in fact, it is easy to show with the World Bank's PovcalNet database that only a small minority of the population would *not* be in households below the poverty line. Large impacts would also be found in many other low- and middle-income countries where the discrepancy between PPPs and market exchange rates is substantial, as shown in figure 3.1. But there is a second reason why PPPs matter. The $1.90 line itself was developed with the use of PPPs, as it was calculated by averaging the values of fifteen national poverty lines, which were made comparable by converting their values in local currency into international dollars by using the PPP rates (described in more detail in chapter 5). Thus, the story is more complex than it first appears.

The decision to use a PPP index is intuitively appealing, but it raises several problems.[3] First, the PPPs estimated by the 2011 ICP are typically now used in the analysis of global poverty, and unless otherwise stated, these are the PPPs used in this book. But the 2011 ICP is not the only source. The estimates available in Maddison (2001) and in several releases of the Penn World Table—for example, Feenstra, Inklaar, and Timmer (2015)—are often used in the economic literature. The underlying data generally come from one or more rounds of the ICP, but the final PPP rates may differ because of methodology: for instance, the EKS method, the GK method, and the IDB method are three alternative ways to summarise the bilateral price comparisons between all pairs of countries into a set of PPP indices.[4]

Second, PPP indices are estimated for various national accounts aggregates. In the case of the 2011 ICP, there are PPP indices for gross domestic product (GDP) and for individual consumption expenditure by households (ICEH) as well as for several other expenditure components. The Indian PPP of 14.98 rupees for a US dollar refers to ICEH; the conversion factor for GDP would be only slightly different—15.11 rupees for $1—but the one for, say, food and non-alcoholic beverages would rise to 20.87 rupees for $1. Focussing only on the main aggregates, the PPP for ICEH might be preferable to the one for GDP because it measures purchasing power in terms of consumption of goods and services, while GDP covers items which are generally not included in measures of disposable income or consumption expenditure gathered in household surveys, such as in-kind transfers for education and health care (Smeeding and Rainwater 2004).

Third, the use of standard PPP rates can be criticised as being based on a basket of goods that includes items not relevant in the measurement of absolute poverty because they are only used by the nonpoor or in rich countries (Reddy and Pogge 2010). The question of the weights used in constructing PPPs—the importance given to each item in the index—is investigated by Deaton and Dupriez (2011), who make use of data from household surveys from sixty-two countries to examine the expenditure pattern of households at or near the poverty line and calculate PPPPs—poverty-weighted purchasing power parities. They find that the PPPP rates do not differ much from the standard PPP rates and explain: "Although it is true that poor people have different consumption patterns from the aggregate patterns in the national accounts, the

---

[3] Deaton and Heston (2010) discuss several practical issues not dealt with here (see also Deaton 2010). These include taking account of differences across countries in the quality of goods and services, the treatment of urban and rural areas in large countries, and the estimation of prices for government services such as health and education.

[4] The EKS method is named after O. Éltető, P. Köves, and B. Szulc, the GK method after R. Geary and S. H. Khamis, and the IDB after D. M. Iklé, Y. Dikhanov, and B. M. Balk. See Deaton and Heston (2010) for discussion and references.

reweighting is similar in different countries, so that the price indexes between each pair do not usually change by much" (2011, p. 160). (They also underline that there are important differences between the expenditure shares in the surveys and those in the national accounts.) From this analysis, they conclude that the use of poverty weights "will not, in and of itself, make a large difference to global poverty counts" (p. 157). Deaton and Dupriez focus only on the weights of goods and services in the consumption basket and do not account for the different prices faced by the poor. This issue will be taken up in chapter 4.

A recent example of an approach that appears to play down the role of PPPs is the work of Allen (2016), who suggests using linear programming to calculate separately for each country the cheapest basket of goods that provides predefined levels of nutrient requirements; the poverty threshold for a country is then obtained by adding the cost of a few nonfood necessities (housing, fuel, clothing) to the cost of this basket. Allen argues that "comparability across countries and over time is guaranteed by using the same [food and nonfood] requirements everywhere—not by PPP" (2016, p. 17).[5]

The importance of the choice of the PPP index for the estimates of global poverty is shown in chapter 5, which illustrates the impact of the switch from the PPPs of the 2005 ICP to those from the 2011 exercise.

WHO IS BEING MEASURED?

Are we talking about individuals or about the families in which they live? How does the calculation take account of differences in needs? After all, a family of four has greater needs than a person living alone.

Individuals, families, and households[6]

A natural starting point for construction of any social indicator for a country is consideration of the position of its individual citizens. If our concern is with health status, then we may sample households for a survey but need to know about the health of all individual members, ranging from the newborn to the

---

[5]*Editors*: The published version of the paper (Allen 2017) is even more explicit in proposing to abandon PPPs and hence the World Bank's approach to measuring global poverty. Apart from refinements to the methodology, the main point of departure from the earlier version known to Tony is Allen's choice to rely entirely on the country-specific poverty lines obtained through linear programming (rather than, as implied in the earlier version, converting them into international purchasing power dollars, taking their average across poor countries, and then reconverting this average to local currencies). Allen's proposal has been criticised by Ferreira (2017) and Ravallion (2017).

[6]*Editors*: The first part of this discussion draws on Tony's work with Bea Cantillon, Eric Marlier, and Brian Nolan, reported in Atkinson et al. (2002) and Atkinson and Marlier (2010).

great-grandmother. However, in the case of a monetary measure of poverty, we will wish to examine the position of a wider unit than the individual. It would not make sense to consider the baby's income without regard to that of her parents and maybe others. Once we aggregate, however, a range of possible definitions opens up for the unit of analysis, making use of criteria such as the following:

1. Common dwelling, with a *household* comprising those residents in a dwelling who share some degree of common housekeeping but are not necessarily related by family ties
2. Common spending, where the *spending unit* is defined as those taking spending decisions to a significant degree in common, but who may be people who have no family relationship
3. Blood or marital relationship, where members of the *family unit* are related by marriage or cohabitation or by a blood relationship
4. Dependence, where the unit is defined to include a single person or couple plus any dependants (children and/or adults), this constituting the *inner family*

In practice, the issue is more complicated. For instance, the survey carried out in 2005–2006 in the Solomon Islands required "living together" but not a common dwelling: a private household was defined as "a group of people (related or unrelated) who live together (not necessarily living in one housing unit) and share a common cooking arrangement" (Solomon Islands Statistics Office 2006, p. 9). This example shows that the previous entities all broaden the unit beyond the individual, but we may wish to go further and consider wider groupings, including the extended family. In such cases, there may well be some commonality in the standards of living of its members. The grandmother may live around the corner but eat all her meals with the family; the son may be a student with a room in the city, but brings his laundry home each weekend; the breadwinner may be away, working in the city, but sends regular remittances. We may wish to consider wider kinship groupings, characterised perhaps by less regular sharing of resources but important support networks. The standard of living of a person cannot be judged independently of these networks. As Angus Deaton has noted, such wider groupings are important in developing countries:

> Several generations or the families of siblings may live in a single compound, sometimes eating together and sometimes not, and with the group breaking up and reforming in response to economic conditions. In some countries there are lineages to which groups of households belong, and the head of the lineage may have the power to command labor, to order migration, to tax and reward individuals, and to control communal assets. Even so, members of the lineage will typically live in separate households, which will nevertheless not be the appropriate units for the analysis of at least some decisions. (1997, p. 24)

The problems of defining households in such circumstances have been emphasised by Casley and Lury (1987) in their classic study *Data Collection in Developing Countries*. They give the example of a polygamous rural family in which "each wife (and her children) may live in a separate hut, cultivate her own piece of land, and prepare meals for herself and her children independently of the other wives." They then offer their own definition of a household "as a starting point," noting that the ties of kinship have to be specified in the particular cultural context: "A household comprises a person, or group of persons, generally bound by ties of kinship, who live together under a single roof or within a single compound, and who share a community of life in that they are answerable to the same head and share a common source of food" (p. 163). Casley and Lury warn that definitions that are adopted vary across countries and that within any country "the definition may change from one survey to another, resulting in incompatibility and consequent loss of analytical comparisons over time or between groups" (p. 161). Deaton provides an example from Thailand, where, he notes, compound living arrangements are common. The National Statistical Office changed its practice between surveys for 1975–1976 and 1981, counting subunits as separate households. Over this period, average household size recorded in the surveys fell from 5.5 persons to 4.5 persons, "and at least some of the change can be attributed to the change in procedure" (Deaton 1997, p. 24).

The use of a narrower definition tends to involve an increase in the measured poverty rate, since less income sharing is assumed to be taking place. (Note, however, that when the threshold is a relative line, the impact on measured poverty may be ambiguous depending on how the mean or the median vary by changing the definition of the reference unit.) Conversely, the student son may be below the poverty line if considered as a unit on his own, but when his income is added to that of his parents, the total may be enough to keep all of them out of poverty. The choice between different units involves assumptions about factual matters, such as the extent of support offered by other family members, including the extended family. The great-grandmother living with her family would probably share the household's standard of living, but a group of students living together could not be treated as a unit. This involves value judgements about the extent to which people should be dependent. A policy change that discouraged people in their twenties from leaving home might reduce measured (income) poverty but would not necessarily be regarded as effecting social improvement. The choice as far as global measurement of poverty is concerned may also be influenced by the differences across countries in household composition.[7]

[7]Some of these differences are shown in publications of the Population Division of the UN Department of Economic and Social Affairs. For example, households with both a child (aged under fifteen) and an older person (aged sixty or over) account for 14 and 13 per cent, respectively, of all households in Africa and Asia and 8 per cent in Latin America and the Caribbean, but only 2 per cent in Europe and the United States (UN 2017a, figure 4, data for 2010). Polygamy

Countries across the world have had to deal with this issue when producing their poverty estimates. Statistics Canada notes that, "when using the LICO [low income cut-off] or the MBM [market basket measure], the economic family is the appropriate unit. When using the LIM [low income measure], the household is the appropriate unit" (Statistics Canada 2016, p. 9). The agency explains that "an economic family refers to a group of two or more persons who live in the same dwelling and are related to each other by blood, marriage, common-law, adoption or a foster relationship," whereas a "household refers to a person or a group of persons who occupy the same dwelling and do not have a usual place of residence elsewhere in Canada. Thus, a household may comprise more than one economic family or a combination of economic families and persons not in an economic family."

More subtle differences can be found in definitions. In Finland, "a household is formed of all those persons who live together and have meals together or otherwise use their income together. . . . Excluded from the household population are those living permanently abroad and the institutional population (such as long-term residents of old-age homes, care institutions, prisons or hospitals)" (Statistics Finland website, October 2016). But the statistical office goes on to say that "the corresponding register-based information is household-dwelling unit. A household-dwelling unit is formed of persons living permanently in the same dwelling or address. More than one household may belong to the same household-dwelling unit. The concept of household-dwelling unit is used in register-based statistics in place of the household concept."

The importance of the distinction between different definitions of the reference unit depends of course on actual living arrangements on the ground. In the case of the economic family and the household in Canada, "practically, there is little difference in the definition, as 95% of households contain only one economic family and only 2.5% of individuals live in secondary economic families" (Murphy, Zhang, and Dionne 2010, p. 92). However, the choice of definition may still be important for the measurement of poverty, as household arrangements vary up and down the distribution of income or consumption. In the United Kingdom, it is possible to calculate the proportion of the population living in benefit units (inner families) below the poverty line of 60 per cent of the income of the median family and compare the results with the proportion of people living in households below 60 per cent of the corresponding median income. An interesting exercise was undertaken by one of my students, Jo Webb, in her thesis at Oxford (Webb 2002). She shows, as we knew from other studies (for example, Johnson and Webb 1989—no relation), that the

---

was legal or "generally accepted" in thirty-three countries in 2009 (twenty-five in Africa), and Demographic and Health Surveys in twenty-six countries over 2000 to 2010 show between 10 per cent and 53 per cent of women aged fifteen to forty-nine reporting that their husband had another wife (UN 2011, p. 4).

proportion below the poverty line in the United Kingdom is higher on a family unit basis. But she also shows that the proportion of households containing more than one family declined markedly from 1961 to 1999, from 34 per cent to 17 per cent. As a result, the gap between the two series narrowed. The rise in the poverty rate in the family unit series was less than that in the household-based series, so that by 1991 they were only two percentage points apart. In this sense, the choice of definition mattered: the official series tended to give the impression of a faster increase in poverty. In the developing country context, migration from rural to urban areas may change the importance over time of the choice of definition.

The fact that we may wish to consider the position of a household or a family as a whole does not imply that we should then count the number of poor households or families, weighting each of them as one regardless of the number of members. The issue of weighting is distinct from the choice of the unit of analysis. Our concern when measuring poverty is with the position of individuals, and this entails counting persons. The circumstances of the households or families in which individuals live are clearly major determinants of the level of their well-being. Hence, individuals should not be considered in isolation—but each person should count as one. (Unless otherwise stated, the figures in this book are on that basis.) The role of weighting is worth stressing because it is rarely given explicit attention; nor is it always evident from published tables what weighting has been applied. The national estimates for Kenya provide a good example of clarity, with separate figures given for the numbers of poor individuals, poor households, and poor "adult equivalents" (see the discussion below of equivalence scales) (Kenya National Bureau of Statistics 2007, table 4.1).

Inequality within the household

The statistic for global poverty is typically stated as x million people living in poverty, but the correct statement about the figures quoted in chapter 1 is that there are x million people living *in households* that are in poverty. What the World Bank statistics capture is the number of households in poverty, treating the household as a statistical unit (leaving aside here its exact definition). No account is taken of the unequal distribution within the household. (On within-household inequality, see, for example, Folbre 1986 and Woolley and Marshall 1994; Haddad and Kanbur 1990 and Jenkins 1991 focus specifically on its implications for the measurement of poverty.) Neither conceptually nor practically can the data used to calculate global poverty provide evidence about the intra-household distribution. Conceptually, there is the problem of allocating the benefits from shared purchases and home resources. Practically, there is the problem of collecting information on individually consumed goods, intensified when the survey is based on a single individual responding on behalf of the household, who may not know the answers, and where other household members may find the questions intrusive. In view of this, the statement in the *Global Monitoring Report 2015/2016*, for example, that "poverty remains unacceptably high, with an estimated 900 million people in 2012 living on less than $1.90 a day" (World Bank Group 2016, p. 1) should refer instead to the "900 million people in 2012 *who are in households* living on less than $1.90 a day per person."

How much does this matter? If the conceptual problems in defining individual consumption could be overcome, would the resulting figure for the number of people with individual consumption below the poverty line be higher? If, in a two-person household, one person consumes $1.80 and the other consumes $2.20, then the household as a whole has consumption per person above $1.90, thus missing the person who is actually below. On the other hand, the poverty head count may move the other way. While the household head count is an understatement in the two-person example just given, it would not be if the poorer person has $1.50, causing both to be counted as poor on a household basis, rather than just one of them on an individual basis. In such a case, switching to an individual basis would reduce the measured poverty head count. In passing, I should note that this possibility would not apply if we were to make use of the "poverty gap," a measure of the depth of poverty to be defined later in the chapter, which is definitely higher on an individual basis (Ravallion 1988).

Firm empirical evidence about what happens within the household is limited. In the case of income, it is possible to allocate certain categories of income, such as earnings, to individuals, but there remains the need to make assumptions about other sources, such as the profits from a family business—for example, a farm. Recent research on the EU (Corsi, Botti, and D'Ippolito 2016, table 3) reports that, measured in terms of individual income, the proportion below 60 per cent of the median was double (around 40 per cent) for women than men (around 20 per cent). On the side of consumption, studies have been made of variables such as individual calorific intake. In a survey of rural Philippines, Haddad and Kanbur find that measures of the adequacy of individual calorie intake, compared to assuming receipt of the average of individual adequacy, lead to a proportion of the population estimated to be poor that is in fact higher (for the reason given above) on a household basis, but that the poverty gap is understated by 18.4 per cent (1990, table 4).

It is not, however, easy to observe individual consumption within the household. This has been regarded as a challenge. Can we approach the question indirectly, inferring how consumption is allocated within the household from what we do observe? Can we, for instance, extrapolate from the observed household expenditure on women's clothing to her total share of expenditure? Such an indirect approach requires assumptions (see, for example, Browning, Chiappori, and Weiss 2014; Chiappori and Meghir 2015). The most commonly employed set of—strong—assumptions involves a model of collective decision-making, with efficient allocations and caring preferences,[8] which allow the implicit preferences and sharing rules to be identified. Based on such modelling of sharing rules, Lise and Seitz (2011), for instance, find for a subset of working-age households in the United Kingdom that consumption inequality was considerably understated, although to a declining extent, over the period 1970 to 2000, so that both level and trend would be affected. Using a sample of couples from the US Panel Study of Income Dynamics, 1999 to 2009, Cherchye and his coauthors estimate that "11% of our child-less couples have incomes below a two-person poverty line, but taking the individual allocations of resources within households into account, our bounds show that 15% to 18% of individuals are below the corresponding poverty line for individuals. Moreover, it turns out that poverty is more prevalent among women in childless couples than among men in childless couples" (Cherchye et al. 2015, p. 2005).

The analysis of within-household inequality exemplifies the way in which measurement and economic theory are intimately bound together. It is no accident that many of the pioneers of economic measurement were also known for their mastery of economic theory, Richard Stone, director of the Department of Applied Economics in Cambridge from 1945, being a prime example. (The first time I acted, rather nervously, as a final-year examiner in Cambridge, my co-examiner was Richard Stone, and I discovered to my surprise that it was his first time too!) In the present case, the measures of within-household inequality described in the previous paragraph depend essentially on a theoretical model where it is assumed that household decisions are efficient: no alternative would be preferred by all members of the household. Such an assumption allows for a variety of theoretical models that have been proposed. At the same time, it is open to criticism on at least two grounds.

To begin with, the framework of collective decision-making does not allow models of inefficient bargaining, and readers might not be surprised by the notion that households may get trapped in outcomes where at least one member could be better off without making the others worse off. One such model is that of Basu (2006), where, in a two-person household, the household maximizes the weighted average of their individual welfares, where the weights depend on the decisions taken. It is not just the potential wage of the wife that matters but also whether she actually has her own earnings. Basu shows how the dynamics of such a model may generate inefficient outcomes (in the sense of

---

[8] Efficiency here refers to the concept of "Pareto efficiency"—an "efficient allocation" is one in which no change can be made within the household without making at least one person worse off. "Caring preferences" mean that each household member values positively increases in the welfare of other household members.

"efficiency" used earlier). Secondly, the literature is largely based on the standard textbook model, whereas alternative approaches to household behaviour may yield different predictions. In particular, the capability approach, discussed in the previous chapter, is relevant not only to normative evaluation of outcomes but also to the positive explanation of household behaviour. The potential richness of such an approach is demonstrated by Sen in his analysis of "Gender and Cooperative Conflicts" (1990). He builds on the household production approach, but with the key difference that production is not a purely technical matter: "Technology is not only about equipment and its operational characteristics but also about the social arrangements that permit the technology to be used and the so-called productive processes to be carried on" (1990, p. 463). "The nature of 'social technology' has a profound effect on relating production and earnings to the distribution of that earning between men and women and to gender divisions of work and resources" (p. 465). He goes on to argue that the determination of the social technology is a balance between conflict and cooperation: "Although serious conflicts of interests may be involved . . . the nature of the family organization requires that these conflicts be molded in a general format of cooperation, with conflicts treated as aberrations or deviant behavior" (p. 481).

We should also take account of evidence from studies that have specifically sought details on how households manage their finances, where the evidence comes from direct questioning on the subject. There are problems with both the collection and interpretation of the data. Are the members of each household questioned in private, away from one another? (In the research reported in Pahl 1989, a well-known UK example, couples were interviewed both together and separately.) If pooling of income is reported as complete, does this imply equal command over the pooled resources? Early literature in this area for high-income countries drew on small samples (Jan Pahl's study was based on 102 couples), but there is recent evidence from large-scale surveys. Ponthieux (2013, 2017) uses information collected for twenty-one countries in 2010 in the surveys that lie behind the EU's harmonised Statistics on Income and Living Conditions (SILC). The proportion of men in couples where both partners have some personal income who report keeping at least some of it "separate from the common household budget" varies substantially, from 10 per cent in Spain to 76 per cent in Malta, with an average of 37 per cent (Ponthieux 2017, table 9.1; the figures for women differ only very slightly). Of course, the evidence from studies of high-income countries cannot be taken as representative of patterns of management of money elsewhere in the world.

Pursuit of this research is indeed promising as a route to learn more about inequality within the household, in high-, middle-, or low-income countries. But it is likely to be some time before the results can be applied to poverty measurement on a regular basis, and the presentation of the method would need to be transparent.

Allowing for differences in needs

A household's income means less if it has to provide for a couple with two children than if it accrues to a single person. This consideration is at the basis of an adjustment for differences in needs mentioned earlier. This means that an "equivalence scale" is typically applied to adjust total household income or consumption before it is assessed against the poverty threshold. Or, viewed another way, the threshold varies with the number and type of people in the household. One possibility is simply to divide household income by the number of household members, which is the per capita adjustment. But this ignores any economies of scale—two people living together may need less each than either of them living alone—and other equivalence scales allow for the fact that not all spending has to be increased per person and that needs may differ by age or gender.

Practice differs substantially around the world, as shown by examples from the national reports at the end of the book. In Kenya, a national equivalence scale is used for the country's poverty estimates: children aged zero to four are treated as equivalent to 0.24 adults (i.e., they need approximately one-quarter of what an adult person needs), children aged five to fourteen are treated as 0.65, and all people aged fifteen years and over are treated as 1.0. In Ghana and Tanzania, assumed needs differ between men, women, children of different ages, and the elderly. In Fiji, the scale is much simpler and does not distinguish between younger and older children: everyone aged under fifteen counts as 0.5, and everyone else counts as 1.0. The same simple scale is used in the Solomon Islands, but the switch comes at age seven.

In these cases, no allowance is made for any economies of scale—it is just the (assumed) differences in needs of different types of people that are taken into account. While there is only limited truth to the adage that "two can live as cheaply as one," many scales give a greater weight to the first adult in the household, including the widely used "modified OECD scale," which is 1.0 for the first adult, 0.5 for each additional person aged fourteen or over, and 0.3 for each child under fourteen. This is the scale used by Eurostat in its calculations of monetary poverty for the EU. The US official poverty line gives an even greater weight to the first adult, assuming larger economies of scale. In Mauritius, the number of adult equivalents in a household is taken as the number of adults plus 0.7 times the number of children (persons aged less than sixteen), with this total raised to the power 0.7. A family with two adults and two children therefore comprises 2.36 adult equivalents, similar to the figure with the modified OECD scale (2.1 if the children are both aged under fourteen and 2.5 if over fourteen). In the United States, the poverty threshold for such a family is just twice that for a single person living alone.

Two decades ago, in a report prepared for the OECD on income distribution in rich countries, Lee Rainwater, Tim Smeeding, and I gathered as many as fifty-four different equivalence scales then used by national authorities and academics in the countries covered by the study (Atkinson, Rainwater, and Smeeding 1995, table 2.2). The relationship between needs and size implicit in each equivalence scale was summarised by calculating the elasticity of the adjusted income (a measure of economic well-being) to the household size: the larger this elasticity the smaller the economies of scale.[9] The results of this exercise spanned "almost the entire range from no adjustment to per capita adjustment" (p. 20). This evidence illustrates the wide variability of the methods in use, possibly reduced in recent years owing to the adoption of the modified OECD scale in European statistics. But it also indicates that some adjustment has been carried out in high-income countries for a long time.

In contrast, outside this group of countries, many national statistical institutes and government agencies favour a per capita adjustment. This is the case in Brazil, China, India, Indonesia, Niger, and South Africa, for example. Likewise, the calculation of global poverty by the World Bank is made on a per capita basis. That is, total household consumption is divided by the number of members of the household and the household is deemed poor if the resulting figure falls below the International Poverty Line of $1.90. Or, put differently, the poverty line for the household of four considered at the start of this chapter is four times that of a single-person household—they are only poor if their total consumption falls short of $7.60. The authors of the World Bank estimates note that "the adoption of a per capita scale imposes cross-country comparability and is easy to explain." But they go on to warn that "it does not, however, address the deeper issue of what the 'best' equivalence scale might be in each country" (Ferreira et al. 2016, p. 149).

A great deal of effort has gone into trying to deduce the "best" equivalence scale in different settings. Part of the literature follows a similar path to the work described earlier on intra-household inequality, drawing on a blend of economic theory and data on households' consumption of different goods. Another strand draws on subjective evaluations of how much people think households of different types require for their needs. Ferreira and Ravallion argue that "there is no agreement on which particular scale to be used. There is likely to be more agreement, in fact, with the statement that different scales may be appropriate for different settings (such as, say, South Korea and Togo)" (Ferreira and Ravallion 2009, p. 608). Their conclusion is that a departure from the per capita scale in international comparisons "is, given the present state of knowledge, likely to contribute to less, not more, clarity" (p. 608).

This conclusion appears too conservative. With a basic needs foundation for the estimate of global poverty, it seems impossible to ignore the differing needs of households made up of different numbers and people of differing ages, even

---

[9] The elasticity between two variables is the percentage change in one that is associated with a percentage change in the other.

if we cannot agree on just how large those differing needs are. At least we need to know how the levels and patterns of poverty would vary with alternative assumptions to the per capita adjustment.

The implications for the number of poor people depend on the absolute level at which the poverty line is set when a particular equivalence scale is chosen. If one were to apply the International Poverty Line allowance of $1.90 a day as the amount for a single adult, then, with the modified OECD scale, the threshold for the household with two adults and two children would be reduced to $3.99 from $7.60 a day, and estimated poverty would be substantially lower. Batana, Bussolo, and Cockburn make calculations of this kind for seventy-three countries for the year 2000, with three alternative equivalence scales to the per capita adjustment. For example, the estimated poverty rate for Sub-Saharan Africa drops sharply from 54.6 per cent with the per capita scale to 22.6 per cent with the modified OECD scale (2013, table 1). The calculations differ somewhat, but the reader may like to refer back to the series for Sub-Saharan Africa shown in figure 1.3 in chapter 1, estimated using the per capita scale. The move away from the per capita adjustment also brings down the poverty rate for children closer to that for adults, as "children tend to live in households with more (discounted) children and larger household size (economies of scale)" (Batana, Bussolo, and Cockburn 2013, p. 407).

Batana, Bussolo, and Cockburn conclude that existing estimates of global poverty based on the per capita adjustment may be substantially overstated, as they ignore both differences in needs by age and economies of scale in consumption. However, caution is needed. The International Poverty Line was set with a per capita calculation in mind, and the introduction of a different equivalence scale would necessitate a reconsideration of the amount for the first adult (see Ravallion 2015 for discussion of this point). Nevertheless, the point is well taken that the composition of the poor can be sensitive to the choice of equivalence scale. (For a discussion of this issue for industrialised countries, see Buhmann et al. 1988; Coulter, Cowell, and Jenkins 1992; and Atkinson 1998. For developing countries, see Newhouse, Suarez-Becerra, and Evans 2016.) The consideration of the income adjustment (or lack thereof) for difference in needs and economies of scale must be on the poverty checklist.

One issue that should be better explored is the way in which equivalence scales can reflect the fact that people with disabilities face higher costs of living than other people to achieve the same quality of life. Accounting specifically for disability in the analysis of poverty is uncommon both in academic research and in official statistics (Morciano, Hancock, and Pudney 2015), possibly due to lack of appropriate data. Indeed, in the case of Canada, "low income statistics under the current practices in Canada may well under-estimate the hardship experienced by people with activity limitations. For any person dealing with health issues, it is reasonable to assume that the cost of living would be higher than for an otherwise identical person. But none of the three low-income lines takes this into consideration" (Murphy, Zhang, and Dionne 2012, p. 40). This point is emphasised in the capability approach. Amartya Sen remarks that "the extent of comparative deprivation of a physically handicapped person vis-à-vis others cannot be adequately judged by looking at his or her income, since the person may be greatly disadvantaged in converting income into the achievements he or she would value" (1992a, p. 28).

Kuklys (2005) and Mitra (2006) discuss how the capability approach can help deal with disabilities in poverty analysis. They observe that disabled people face a double disadvantage: on the one hand, the disability tends to impair their earning capacity; on the other, they need more money than an able-bodied person to achieve a comparable level of well-being. "For example," writes Kuklys, "an individual bound to a wheelchair may need a specially adjusted car to be mobile, compared to a standard car for a non-disabled. Other examples are special bathrooms, ramps, stair lifts, Braille books or computer hardware that need to be bought to perform certain activities non-disabled can do without additional help" (2005, p. 75). With Finnish data for 1987, Klavus (1999) calculates that a household with a chronically ill person needs an extra income from noncash transfers of 40 per cent to reach the same welfare level as a healthy household. Using British data for the late 1990s, Kuklys estimates that an adult with disabilities needs almost 60 per cent more income than an able-bodied adult to achieve the same level of income satisfaction: the poverty rate is higher for households with a disabled member, but it more than doubles when the equivalence scale is adjusted also for disability (2005, pp. 96–99).

Problems are possibly worse in developing countries, although no corresponding estimates for equivalence scales are available. Mitra, Posarac, and Vick (2013) use data for fifteen developing countries in Sub-Saharan Africa, Asia, and Latin America. They find that in only three countries are the poverty rates based on consumption significantly higher for households with persons with disabilities than for other households. However, deprivation is significantly higher for households with disabilities in all countries if assessed by means of the multidimensional poverty index calculated using the Alkire-Foster method (see below), covering education, employment, nonhealth and health private consumption expenditure, possession of consumer durables, and indicators of living conditions.

MULTIDIMENSIONAL POVERTY

Poverty has come, particularly in the Anglo-Saxon countries, to mean a low standard of living, measured in terms of consumption or income. But this is only part of the story. Poverty is also deprivation in a wider sense, encompassing many dimensions of a household's circumstances. It has indeed been increasingly recognised that we need to look beyond monetary poverty, and there has been a surge in recent years in both theoretical and empirical studies of nonmonetary measures.[10] When it comes to the national case studies, I shall be asking how far the evidence from the World Bank monetary poverty indicator—applying the International Poverty Line of $1.90—is coherent with the evidence regarding nonmonetary poverty, making use of national as well as international studies.

The argument for considering dimensions in addition to income or consumption follows naturally from the capability and minimum rights approaches considered in chapter 2. At the same time, neither provides an immediate step to a multidimensional set of indicators. Turning to the founders of the capability approach, Martha Nussbaum has drawn up a list of capabilities that can be applied generally (1988, p. 176; 2000; 2003), but Amartya Sen has resisted the adoption of a definite list and argued that any such specification of dimensions depends on the context.

Concern with a multidimensional approach did not, of course, originate with the theory of capabilities. The main poverty statistic adopted by a parliamentary commission of inquiry over destitution in Italy in the early 1950s was a weighted count of the number of households failing to achieve minimum levels of food consumption, clothing availability, and housing conditions (Aaberge and Brandolini 2015, p. 146). A multidimensional approach has long underpinned the measurement of well-being in Nordic countries, and these applications have developed lists of relevant dimensions. The Swedish Level of Living Survey conducted in 1968 was multidimensional, being influenced by the earlier UN expert group (UN 1954). There were nine domains: health and access to health care, employment and working conditions, economic resources, education and skills, family and social integration, housing, diet and nutrition, recreation and culture, and political resources (see Erikson 1993, p. 68). In the United Kingdom, the pioneering study of relative deprivation by Townsend (1979) made use of some sixty indicators covering, among other dimensions, diet, clothing, fuel and light, housing, conditions and security of work, recreation, health, and education. A lack of, or nonparticipation in, these dimensions was seen as an indicator of deprivation. Multidimensionality has been at the heart of the European concept of social inclusion, and when the member states of the EU came to agree on an overarching portfolio of indicators, it was multidimensional: in the portfolio revised in 2015, the outcome indicators included income poverty, material deprivation, access to health care, education, employment, housing, and participation in the labour force (Social Protection Committee Indicators Sub-Group 2015).

In the present context of measuring global poverty, multidimensionality is not only widely accepted but essential to the Sustainable Development Goals

[10]The economic literature on multidimensional poverty is summarised in Chakravarty (2009, chapters 5 and 6), Aaberge and Brandolini (2015), and Alkire et al. (2015).

listed in box C in chapter 5. The second target under Goal 1 ("no poverty") refers to the reduction "at least by half [of] the proportion of men, women and children of all ages living in poverty in *all its dimensions* according to national definitions" (UN Sustainable Development Goals website, emphasis added). Hunger (Goal 2), health (Goal 3), and education (Goal 4) are all aspects of living standards that feature in discussion of nonmonetary poverty. The "national definitions" of particular relevance are those in countries that have adopted at a national level Multidimensional Poverty Indices (MPIs), drawing on the methods developed by the Oxford Poverty and Human Development Initiative (OPHI). (These national indices should not be confused with OPHI's Global MPI included in the UNDP's *Human Development Report* for 2010 and later years and discussed further below.) The countries adopting an official national MPI include Armenia, Bhutan, Chile, Colombia, Costa Rica, the Dominican Republic, Ecuador, El Salvador, Honduras, Mexico, Mozambique, Nepal, Panama, and Pakistan. What are the implications of a multidimensional approach? And how are the indices calculated?

A dashboard of indicators

Consider a dashboard of outcome indicators, where the term "dashboard" refers to a set of dials, each associated with a specific dimension of deprivation. (The parallel with a car dashboard is not in fact exact, as explained below.) What, however, is the case for a multi-dial dashboard? As stressed by Aaberge and Brandolini, "acknowledging the multidimensional nature of well-being does not necessarily imply that the social evaluation must also be multidimensional" (2015, p. 142).

In considering the rationale for a dashboard, one has to begin with the fact that broad support for a multidimensional approach reflects a diversity of concerns, and that one has to distinguish a number of perspectives, since they can lead in different directions when it comes to implementation. In particular, a contrast may be drawn between the standard-of-living perspective, on one side, and the capabilities/minimum rights perspectives, on the other side. Moreover, the reasons for adopting a multidimensional approach may be either instrumental or intrinsic.

Where the concern is to deepen understanding of the standard of living, there are many reasons, as discussed elsewhere in the book, why household consumption as measured in the World Bank estimates and in other studies is less than a fully satisfactory indicator. There is incomplete coverage where consumption is not recorded from home production or the services of durable goods and other assets. There are issues of timing, where the observed consumption depends on the season or is affected by temporary fluctuations. Hence, the distinction drawn between observed "transitory" consumption/income and unobserved "permanent" consumption/income. The survey may not record individual consumption of publicly provided health care or education. Collection of information on other variables in these circumstances can improve the assessment of the standard of living of the household. But it does not follow that, for this purpose, multiple indicators are required. The additional information may be incorporated in an improved measure of "extended consumption" or "extended income."

The value of assets can be converted into a flow and added to the consumer expenditure or income, as suggested, for instance, by Weisbrod and Hansen (1968). A long-established strand of research accounts for the distributive impact of publicly provided education or health care by valuing these services at market prices or actual cost and, again, adding them to income or consumption to obtain an extended measure. The impact on measured poverty due to the imputation of public services may be substantial in high-income countries, where welfare states are more developed. For instance, according to Aaberge, Langørgen, and Lindgren's estimates for European countries, "by replacing cash income with extended income . . . poverty rates are reduced by 30–50 per cent" (2010, p. 339). The pattern is more diversified in developing countries. In her study covering Armenia, Bolivia, Brazil, Chile, Colombia, El Salvador, Ethiopia, Guatemala, Indonesia, Mexico, Peru, South Africa, and Uruguay, Nora Lustig (2015) concludes that spending on preschool and primary and secondary education is pro-poor in twelve countries and health spending is pro-poor in only five countries, while spending on tertiary education is never pro-poor.[11]

The construction of an extended measure clearly generates a richer representation of consumer well-being, but one that remains one-dimensioned. This formulation retains all advantages offered by remaining with a single dimension, but for several reasons it may not always be possible or acceptable. The market prices required to value different items may not exist or may be unrepresentative. The fees charged for private education may bear no relation to the value of a poorly maintained village school without a regular teacher. The value of health services depends on the circumstances of the individual and household. To these considerations should be added the intrinsic reasons why, on a standard-of-living approach, there may be a case for multiple indicators. As

---

[11] *Editors*: As emphasised earlier in this chapter, any extension of the definition of income or consumption should be accompanied by a reconsideration of the level of the poverty line: one cannot simply add to one side of the analysis. In the same vein, the equivalence scale also needs to be adjusted. See the discussion in Aaberge, Langørgen, and Lindgren (2010, pp. 334–337), who explain their allocation of education and health expenditures as "following standard practice . . . students in a given country that attend the same education level are assigned an equal amount of educational benefits, whilst health care expenditures are allocated to gender and age groups based on estimates of utilisation profiles made by national statistical agencies" (p. 330), the latter being described in an earlier study of high-income countries as a "risk-related insurance premia approach" (Smeeding et al. 1993, p. 230).

argued by Nobel laureate James Tobin (1970), in addition to an overall evaluation in terms of the standard of living, there may be scarce commodities whose distribution is a specific matter of concern. Under the heading of "specific egalitarianism"—the equivalising of the consumption of particular commodities—he maintained that there should be an express concern with the basic necessities of life, health, and citizenship, as "the social conscience is more offended by severe inequality in nutrition and basic shelter, or in access to medical care or to legal assistance, than by inequality in automobiles, books, clothes, furniture, boats" (1970, p. 265).[12] These dimensions should be kept separate in the social evaluation. A more general formulation is provided by Walzer (1983), whose book *Spheres of Justice* is subtitled *A Defense of Pluralism and Equality*. His approach requires that each dimension be kept distinct, and there can be no reduction to a single index of well-being. There are therefore both instrumental and intrinsic grounds for a standard-of-living perspective to lead to a dashboard.

The capabilities/minimum rights perspectives, in contrast, are intrinsically multidimensional. For Alkire and her coauthors (2015, p. 5), defining poverty in the space of capabilities implies, first of all, that the measurement must be multidimensional. They quote Sen: "The capability approach is concerned with a plurality of different features of our lives and concerns" (Sen 2009, p. 233). The lists relevant to human rights referred to in chapter 2 were not inputs into a general index of rights but identified distinct domains where there is no presumption of a possible trade-off.

Choice of dimensions

There are therefore a variety of perspectives that lead to the adoption of a multiple indicator approach. These perspectives may, however, have different implications for its design. Viewed in terms of a dashboard, the design includes both the specification of the individual dials and the composition of the portfolio of indicators as a whole. Which nonmonetary indicators should be selected, and how should they individually be designed?

The rationale for the multidimensional approach influences the choice of dimensions. If the aim is, instrumentally, to improve the evaluation of the standard of living, then an indicator highly correlated with observed household consumer expenditure may bring little added value to the measurement of that one dimension. In contrast, such a high correlation may be of considerable significance if there is an intrinsic concern for different functionings. A low score on both dimensions represents the cumulation of deprivations. As ex-

---

[12] Tobin defined specific egalitarianism in more detail as "the view that certain specific scarce commodities should be distributed less unequally than the ability to pay for them" (1970, p. 264).

plained by Alkire and her colleagues, "If indicators are very highly associated in a particular dataset, that is not sufficient grounds to mechanically drop either indicator; both may be retained for other reasons. . . . The normative decision may be to retain both indicators . . . but the analysis of redundancy will have clarified their justification" (2015, p. 229).

In considering how the dimensions of a dashboard can be determined, the first issue is that of process. A number of the considerations underlying the concern with multidimensional poverty arise from international standards, such as those based on the rights of the child. National governments have embodied their views in multidimensional indicators. There is also a role for consulting a country's citizens; the user of poverty statistics may ask what is the degree of general support for the dimensions that are chosen. The consultation may be direct, as with the World Bank's Voices of the Poor approach described in chapter 2, or it may operate through institutions, as illustrated by CONE-VAL, the National Council for the Evaluation of Social Development Policy, an independent institution established by the Mexican Congress to measure poverty and evaluate social policy. The approach adopted by CONEVAL to the choice of dimensions involved three criteria: (1) legal norms, where they existed, (2) criteria defined by experts or by specialized public institutions in each field, and (3) results derived from statistical analysis, with final decisions made by the Executive Committee (see CONEVAL 2010).

The participatory approach has played an important role in high-income countries too. In Germany, a broad public discussion led to the definition of the conceptual multidimensional framework, based on the capability approach, underlying the official *Poverty and Wealth Reports* regularly released by the government around midterm since 2001 (see, for example, Bundesregierung 2017). This process is described by Arndt and Volkert, who note that "the identification of main capability dimensions will necessarily stay heavily influenced by 'experts' and organized stakeholders. However, from a [capability approach] perspective, the public, notably the poor, deserve more attention" (2011, p. 316). Likewise, in Italy the national statistical institute (Istat) and the National Council for Economics and Labour (CNEL) launched in 2011 the Equitable and Sustainable Wellbeing (*benessere equo e sostenibile*, BES) project. An extensive public consultation involving representatives from social organisations as well as academic and professional experts identified over one hundred indicators, clustered into twelve domains, which are updated annually by Istat. In 2017 an ad hoc expert commission selected twelve of these BES indicators for regular inclusion and monitoring in the future official government budgetary documents (Ministero dell'Economia e delle Finanze 2018).

There is wide agreement in any discussion of nonmonetary poverty that the dimensions should, like the UNDP's Human Development Index (HDI), include education and health status, underlined by their prominent place among the SDGs. Tobin's "specific egalitarianism" implies giving priority to basic necessities of life and points to the inclusion of nutritional status. This also follows naturally from the basic needs approach. For adults, nutritional status is commonly measured in terms of the body mass index (BMI), defined as weight in kilograms divided by the square of height in metres. For children, there are measures of "stunting" (low height for age) and "wasting" (low weight relative to height). Further strong candidates for inclusion are variables measuring deprivation in terms of shelter (housing) and personal security. The strength of the case for these two dimensions is underlined by the fact that, in contrast to education and health status, there is a serious risk that outcomes may be worsening for significant fractions of the population. The adequacy of housing is threatened by population movement, on the one hand, and by climate change, on the other hand. Personal security is threatened by internal and external conflict.

The dimensions identified above find resonance in those present in the national Multidimensional Poverty Indices that have recently been adopted by governments. Table 3.1 summarises these for eight Latin American countries. As may be seen, there are differences. Mexico, for example, includes in its indicator list, with a weight of 50 per cent, a basic income indicator. But there is considerable common ground, with education, health, housing, and access to work appearing in all cases.

From dimensions to indicators

How are the dimensions represented by indicators? For each individual dimension, the construction of a dashboard of nonmonetary measures is a process of moving from the broad field to a specific indicator or set of indicators. This involves a series of steps, such as:

1. Identification of the possible set of indicator variables and consideration of the extent to which they potentially fulfil the desired objectives. Transparency and a clear normative interpretation are key factors.
2. Exploration of the availability of data that allow the establishment of a baseline and the monitoring of changes over time (see chapter 4). In the case of measurement of global poverty, the exploration involves both multi-topic household surveys with global or multi-regional coverage and national sources.
3. Choice among the potential candidates that satisfy the desiderata and for which empirical data are available for a sufficient range of years and—in the case of multi-country or global measurement—countries.
4. Determination of the cutoff(s) to be applied.
5. Validation of the robustness of the results for the selected indicator(s).

What concretely does this approach entail? Let us take SDG Goal 2, "zero hunger." This goal captures three related but distinct aspects: "End hunger,

Table 3.1. Dimensions in official Multidimensional Poverty Indices
in Latin America

Country	Dimensions
Chile	Education; health; work and social security; housing and local environment; networks and social cohesion
Costa Rica	Education; health; work; social security; housing
Colombia	Education; childhood and youth conditions; work; health care; housing and public services
Ecuador	Education; health, water, and nutrition; work and social security; housing and public services
El Salvador	Education and childhood; health and food security; work; housing; security and environment
Honduras	Education; health; work; housing
Panama	Education; health; work; housing; basic services and internet access; environment; local environment and sanitation
Mexico	Education; access to health care; access to food; access to social security; housing; basic home services; income

Source: World Bank (2017, table 2.2); Multidimensional Poverty Peer Network webpages from the OPHI website (accessed May 2018) for Chile, Costa Rica, Honduras, and Panama.
Reading note: The Chile MPI has five dimensions: education, health, work and social security, housing and local environment, and networks and social cohesion.

achieve food security and improved nutrition and promote sustainable agriculture." Under Goal 2, there are nine indicators relating to targets that have dates by which they should be achieved. The first point to note is that, of the nine indicators, five are concerned with food security and sustainable agriculture. For example, one is "the proportion of agricultural area under productive and sustainable agriculture." These five indicators tell us nothing directly about the achievement of zero hunger: they relate to inputs rather than nutritional outcomes. Table 3.2 focusses on the four indicators aimed at these outcomes. The second column summarises the information given about data availability (we are straying again into the topic of the next chapter): for these four indicators, data are available for a large number of countries, but by no means all.

The third and fourth indicators refer to child malnutrition. There are in fact two measures proposed under the fourth, but that concerned with overweight (weight for height above two standard deviations from the median) does not seem relevant to a goal of zero hunger, although it clearly matters for the susceptibility to developing chronic diseases. This leaves the wasting indicator (more than two standard deviations of weight for height below the median) and

Table 3.2. Nutrition indicators for Sustainable Development Goal 2 ("zero hunger")

Indicator	Data Availability
2.1.1 Prevalence of undernourishment	Data are available for 115 countries. No data are currently available for developed countries.
2.1.2 Prevalence of moderate or severe food insecurity in the population, based on the Food Insecurity Experience Scale	Data are available for over 141 countries from 2014.
2.2.1 Prevalence of stunting (height for age is more than two standard deviations below the median of the WHO Child Growth Standards) among children under five years of age	Data are available for more than 150 countries.
2.2.2 Prevalence of malnutrition (weight for height is more than two standard deviations above or below the median of the WHO Child Growth Standards) among children under five years of age, by type (overweight and wasting)	Data are available for more than 150 countries.

Source: United Nations (2018) and information on metadata for indicators available on the Sustainable Development Goal indicators webpage.
Reading note: Data are available for 115 developing countries on the prevalence of undernourishment.

the stunting indicator (below two standard deviations in terms of height for age). The UNICEF Child Nutrition website suggests two further possibilities: severe wasting (below three standard deviations of weight for height) and underweight (more than two standard deviations of weight for age below the median). There is therefore a choice. In figure 3.2, the four measures for Bangladesh are plotted from the mid-1980s onwards. It appears that the use of the stunting and underweight indicators would show a similar downward trend. However, the wasting indicators do not demonstrate a comparable improvement. There may therefore be a question of weighting different indicators even at this elementary level. The primary concern may well be with the direction of change—we wish to know if poverty is falling or not. But the difference in level raises the question of the cutoffs applied to determine nutritional deficiency. Is stunting much more prevalent than wasting, or is this an artefact of applying a two-standard-deviation criterion in both cases?

The case study just given illustrates the kind of detailed issue that needs to be addressed in creating the portfolio of indicators for multidimensional measurement of poverty. First, we must distinguish between outcome variables, on the one hand, and input or contextual variables, on the other hand. This

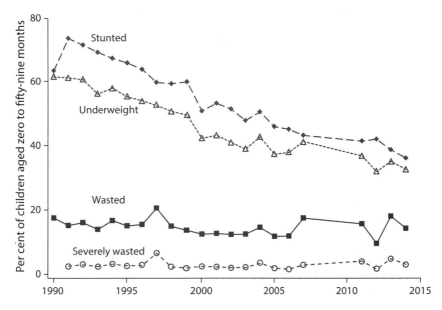

Figure 3.2. Child nutrition indicators in Bangladesh, 1990 to 2014
Source: WHO website, "Global database on child growth and malnutrition" (downloaded May 2016).
Reading note: In 2014, 36.1 per cent of children in Bangladesh were stunted, 32.6 per cent were underweight, 14.3 per cent were wasted, and 3.1 per cent were severely wasted.

was shown for the nine indicators under SDG Goal 2, but it shows up in any multidimensional exercise. While most of the indicators employed in the national MPIs fall into the outcome category, there are variables that are not strictly so. For example, the indicators for Mexico include "access to social security," which is better seen as an input variable. Social security transfers may prevent financial poverty, but their impact should be recorded as such. In the case of Italy, the BES indicators to be monitored in official government documents cover contextual aspects such as crime, illegal building activity, the efficiency of civil justice and CO_2 emissions, besides outcome variables for economic conditions, health, work, and education.

Unit of analysis and reference population

The second question raised by the example of SDG Goal 2 concerns the unit of analysis. The nutrition indicators relate to children aged under five, hence the unit of analysis is the individual child. Can they be incorporated into a dashboard alongside indicators, such as those for housing, that cover all members of the household? Or, in the case of education indicators, can use be made of school achievement among those currently of school age? There may also be indicators, such as the contextual ones, that relate to a larger group than the individual household. Personal security is a case in point. This dimension may have a wider scope, covering, for example, all inhabitants in a village exposed to the risk of flooding or located in a conflict zone.

One significant concern with the monetary measures is that they are household-based and take no account of individual circumstances within the household. An attraction of measures of nonmonetary poverty is that they can, in principle, provide an avenue for illuminating within-household inequality and hence the possible gender and generational fault lines. Take the case of nutritional status as assessed by anthropometry—measurement of the human body. Examples given earlier were the body mass index for adults and stunting and wasting for children. A large-scale study of thirty Sub-Saharan African countries has shown that about three-quarters of underweight women and undernourished children are not found in the poorest 20 per cent of households when judged by an index of household assets (Brown, Ravallion, and van de Walle 2017). Moreover, the authors go on to note that in the subset of countries where male BMI is also recorded in the data, "we have shown that the extent of intra-household inequality entails that the bulk of underweight women and undernourished children are found in households where the male head appears to be adequately nourished" (p. 22).[13]

Nonmonetary indicators can drill down further into the household than the usual monetary measures of poverty, provided that information is collected for all relevant individuals within the household. This is the case for the indicators for adults in the new EU measure described below (used to analyse gender differences in deprivation by Guio and Van den Bosch 2018), but not for the new child indicators adopted by the EU in 2018 (Guio et al. 2018). In terms of age groups, there are good reasons for considering children and young people, but the position of the elderly should not be overlooked. In this connection (and anticipating here the discussion of data in the next chapter), it should be noted that a number of the statistical sources do not interview older persons individually. For example, the focus of the Demographic and Health Surveys (which we will see are a key source for the Global MPI) on women of reproductive age (fifteen to forty-nine) who are the subject of the individual questionnaires limits their ability to shed light on differences between men and women. As this illustrates, breakdown by age or gender is not simply a matter of decomposi-

---

[13] Care is needed in the interpretation of anthropometry. For example, stunting provides imperfect information on individual living standards on account of genetically determined variation in height. Genes explain most of the variance in individual stature, although "genetic differences approximately cancel in comparisons of averages across most populations" (Steckel 1995, p. 1903), this providing the basis for comparing countries or particular groups in the population. (See also Micklewright and Ismail 2001, who argue that anthropometric status does not provide a ranking of well-being in the same sense as would an adequate measure of income.)

tion of a household measure; it also should influence the choice of indicators (and the cutoffs, as with nutritional requirements). One example of such an approach is the Youth Well-being Index proposed in Egypt's 2010 *Human Development Report*, where it is said that "while education, health and income indicators are included, the greater benefit will come from the ability to measure such qualitative indicators as leisure and satisfaction, the quality of jobs, and even social capital and cohesiveness" (UNDP and Institute of National Planning 2010, p. 12). This builds on earlier work, such as the Youth Well-being Index constructed for Brazil by Dell'Aglio and her coauthors (2007).

This advantage of observing the individual means that there needs to be clarity about the unit employed in practice in measures of multidimensional poverty. Does the information relate to the whole household (for example, the household has no electricity), to everyone in the household (no one has primary education), to a specified person within the household (the respondent or the head of household), or to any unspecified person in the household (for example, any child)? The Global MPI published in the *Human Development Report* has ten indicators covering three dimensions (described further below), of which six relate to the household and four to any member of the household. As this example illustrates, different units may apply to different indicators. This does, however, raise the question of to whom the dashboard relates. In the case of the Global MPI indicators, it is the household, as the four measures that relate to any member are, like the other six, defined at the household level (for example, no child in the household has died in the previous five years), even though they are based on individual characteristics. In this case, the potential for multidimensional measures to cast light on differences within the household is not exploited. Examples of multidimensional measurement that do use the individual as the unit of analysis are described in Alkire (2018).

A related definitional question concerns the reference population. With the monetary poverty indicator, the reference population is the entire population, but this is not evidently the case with a number of nonmonetary indicators. While the majority of the indicators in the Global MPI apply to the whole population—such as those for nutrition or access to safe drinking water—there are some indicators that apply only to a subset of the population. For example, in the case of the education domain, the indicator for school attendance applies only where there are school-aged children in the household.

Changing indicators

Then there is the problem that indicators may become dated. The analogy with the measurement of monetary poverty is the issue of updating a poverty line over time (discussed in chapter 2), although the analogy is not perfect— thresholds for nonmonetary indicators may not "age" so quickly. Reference was made earlier to Peter Townsend's landmark study of poverty in the United

Kingdom in which he used a wide range of items to measure household deprivation. From the list of sixty that he developed, he chose twelve with which to construct a summary index, albeit noting, which has sometimes been overlooked, that this was "for illustrative purposes" (1979, p. 251). Among the twelve was an indicator that the respondent had "not had a cooked breakfast most days of the week." But was the eating of a cooked breakfast going out of fashion, so that its absence for many people indicated choice rather than deprivation? As Townsend noted, "The point at which a custom is no longer practiced is debatable" (p. 249). In the 1968–1969 survey that Townsend carried out for his study, two-thirds of respondents did not eat cooked breakfasts, the highest figure for any of his twelve indicators.

A more recent example is provided by the EU's measurement of "material deprivation." This began in 2009, based on the self-reported inability to afford the following nine items:

- Mortgage or rent payments, utility bills, hire purchase instalments, or other loan payments (leading to arrears)
- One week's annual holiday away from home
- A meal with meat, chicken, fish, or vegetarian equivalent every second day
- Coping with unexpected financial expenses
- A telephone (including a cell phone)
- A colour TV
- A washing machine
- A car
- Heating to keep the home sufficiently warm

The measurement has now been revised (Guio and Marlier 2017; Guio, Gordon, Najera, and Pomati 2017; European Commission 2017, box 4), although statistics based on the existing measure will continue to be published. The new measure of "material and social deprivation" is based on thirteen items. It no longer includes indicators for the enforced lack of a washing machine, colour TV, and phone, as most EU countries are now saturated with these assets; in their place is the inability to afford the replacement of worn-out furniture. The revised measure also includes six new items collected for each adult in the household, such as the possession of two pairs of properly fitting shoes (including a pair of all-weather shoes) and a connection to the internet. (Again, deprivation is indicated by the enforced lack of the new items.) The household is classified as deprived on one of these indicators if the majority of adults are unable to afford them. But the data for the new items will also allow investigation of differences within the household, something not possible with the original nine-item measure.

A global reach

Some readers will be interested in national measurement, in quantifying poverty in a particular country. But if our concern is with global measurement, a dashboard of nonmonetary indicators should have global reach, covering all countries of the world.[14] This immediately brings us to the issue, raised in chapter 2 in relation to the UN Declaration of Human Rights, as to whether there can be global agreement on a single set of values underlying the choice of indicators. If, across the world as a whole, there is a plurality of values, then this may require a wider set of indicators than considered so far. In making the case for the dashboard, I have stressed the importance of individual measures, but these may need to be accompanied by indicators at the level of a society as a whole, such as the degree of peace, harmony, solidarity, cohesion, environmental integrity, or integration (to give just some of the possible alternatives).

At a more detailed level, the translation to specific indicators for a global measure and the application of cutoffs introduce a number of issues, as may be seen from the comparison made in table 3.3 between the indicators underlying the Global MPI as constructed by Alkire and her colleagues (2015) and some of the indicators that form part of the EU portfolio of Social Indicators (Social Protection Committee Indicators Sub-Group 2015). (The Global MPI now also takes child nutrition into account—see chapter 5.) This table does not contain all EU Social Indicators (for example, some relate to inputs or do not address poverty and social exclusion), but it encompasses those that are central to the target set in the Europe 2020 Agenda.[15] In 2010, the EU adopted the target for the year 2020 of lowering by at least 20 million the number of people at risk of poverty or social exclusion in the EU (see Frazer et al. 2014, for a discussion of the target). The target indicator of "risk of poverty or social exclusion" in fact combines three elements: risk of income poverty, (quasi-) joblessness, and severe material deprivation (measured with the nine items described earlier). Moreover, the EU Social Indicators are organised in layers: there are overarching indicators, and then primary and secondary indicators and context information. This distinction is ignored in the table.

To avoid confusion, we can note that the Global MPI developed by Sabina Alkire and her colleagues in Oxford at OPHI is not fully global, as it does not cover the high-income countries (more details of coverage are given in chapter 5). So, in making a comparison of the Global MPI and the EU Social Indicators, we have to bear in mind that we are comparing measurements applied to

---

[14] The issues that arise when indicators are applied globally are considered in Marlier and Atkinson (2010) and Atkinson and Marlier (2010, 2011).

[15] For further discussion of the EU Social Indicators, see, among others, Guio, Gordon, and Marlier (2012, 2017), Frazer et al. (2014), Guio and Marlier (2017), and Atkinson, Guio, and Marlier (2017).

Table 3.3. Indicators of deprivation contrasted: Global MPI and EU Social Indicators

	Global MPI	EU Social Indicators
Education	No household member has completed five years of schooling Any school-age child is not attending school up to class 8	Early school leavers (who are not in education or training)
Health	Any child in the household has died	Healthy life expectancy Self-reported unmet need for medical care
Shelter	Household has no electricity Sanitation facility shared or not improved No access to safe drinking water Dirt, sand, or dung floor Cooks with dung, wood, or charcoal	Overcrowding Housing deprivation (see material deprivation under "assets")
Nutrition	Anyone in the household is undernourished according to body mass index measurement	See material deprivation under "assets"
Monetary poverty		Risk of poverty (living below 60 per cent of median national household equivalised income, in current year and at real value in 2008) Persistent risk of poverty
Employment		People living in jobless or quasi-jobless households Long-term unemployment rate Employment gap of immigrants Employment rate of older workers In-work at-risk-of-poverty rate Activity rate
Assets (Global MPI)/material deprivation (EU Social Indicators)	Household does not own a car or lorry and owns at most one of the following: radio, telephone, TV, bike, motorbike, or refrigerator	Enforced lack of three (four in the case of severe deprivation) or more of: one-week annual holiday; adequately heated home; meal with protein once a day; no arrears; capacity to face unexpected expenses; washing machine; colour TV; phone; car

Source: Alkire et al. (2015, table 5.5) for the Global MPI; Social Protection Committee Indicators Sub-Group (2015) for the EU Social Indicators. (See the main text on the recent revision of the EU material deprivation indicators and chapter 5 on the September 2018 revision of the Global MPI indicators.)

Reading note: The Global MPI has two indicators relating to the education dimension, and the EU Social Indicators have one.

low-income to upper-middle-income countries, on the one hand, and to countries in the high-income category, on the other.[16]

Comparing the columns in table 3.3, it might appear that the gulf is too great. The dimensions may be the same, but the implementation is quite different. There is, however, a parallel with the different cutoffs applied in the societal measure of monetary poverty described at the end of chapter 2 (the discussion surrounding figure 2.1), and the same procedure can be adopted. Both education indicators refer to school completion. In the Global MPI case, the cutoff refers to primary education; in the EU case, it refers to secondary education. Provided that two variables can be employed, a common approach can be adopted, with primary education corresponding to the International Poverty Line and secondary education to the high-income country relative poverty line (the sloping segment of the poverty line in figure 2.1). As can be rationalized on a capability approach, the hierarchy of functionings leads to a staged set of indicators. Lack of access to safe drinking water is a clear case of a measure applicable at the first stage, that is, applicable globally. On the other hand, the lack of specified assets (for example, a radio, TV, phone, bike, motorcycle, or refrigerator) is a criterion influenced by the prevailing society. While the former may be identifiable according to physiological needs, the latter may be better approached by a consensual approach, based on the views expressed by the members of the society, including those below the poverty line, about what is required to have a decent life in the society in which they live.

Multidimensional poverty indices

Reference has now been made several times to the Global MPI, published in the *Human Development Report* since 2010, and to national MPIs that follow a similar methodology. These indices go beyond the dashboard, trying to bring together the information that each dial contains into one number. The desirability of a single summary measure combining the different dimensions is much debated. There are strong supporters, as is well summarised in the submission to the Commission on Global Poverty by the Global Coalition to End Child Poverty: "Multidimensional poverty measures that are aggregated into a single composite index can be particularly powerful in summarizing global and national data on poverty in many dimensions. This would allow the dissemination of new figures and findings to broad audiences and mobilize public support to end poverty in all its dimensions" (Global Coalition to End Child Poverty 2015, para. 2.3). "One number" inevitably gets a lot of attention. Amartya

---

[16] *Editors*: Alkire and Apablaza (2017) illustrate the extension of the Alkire-Foster methodology to measurement of multidimensional poverty in Europe (with dimensions and indicators that differ from those in the Global MPI). See also the application by Whelan, Nolan, and Maître (2014).

Sen recounts that he was originally a sceptic of the use of a composite index when confronted with the enthusiasm of the originator of the *Human Development Report*, Mahbub ul Haq, but was converted when he saw the power of the Human Development Index to channel public interest into the different dimensions of well-being covered by the report and away from the default of falling back on national income as a summary measure of development (UNDP 1999, p. 23). (I owe this observation to Micklewright 2001.)

In contrast, Ravallion is sceptical about the assumptions required to calculate the MPI: "It is one thing to agree that consumption of market commodities is an incomplete metric of welfare—and that for the purpose of assessing poverty one needs to also account for indicators of non-market goods and services—and quite another to say that a single 'poverty' measure should embrace all these things" (2011, p. 246). Elsewhere, he refers to "mashup" indices (Ravallion 2012). The development of social indicators for the EU stopped short of adopting an aggregate indicator: as I argued with Eric Marlier, Bea Cantillon, and Brian Nolan, "even though composite indicators, like the Human Development Index, undoubtedly can play a valuable role in certain contexts, we do not feel that they should be employed as part of the current EU Social Inclusion process" (Marlier et al. 2007, p. 185). Views for and against aggregate indicators differ widely and are strongly held. Such is the divergence that Aaberge and Brandolini end their survey with the statement that "there is little chance that we will ever settle the controversy between the dashboard approach and summary indices" (2015, p. 203). The form that the aggregation takes in the case of the Global MPI will be described below in general terms and then again in more detail in chapter 5.

WHAT IS BEING COUNTED?

The 20 per cent figure cited at the start of this chapter is a "head count" of how many people are living below the poverty line, but should we not also be interested in how far they fall below it? In the case of a multidimensional poverty measure, of particular interest is the extent to which the same people are deprived in different domains. How can overlap be measured?

Head counts and poverty gaps

When I wrote my first book on the number of people in Britain who were in poverty, I was taken to task by one of the (then-Labour) government's advisers for not considering how many were in fact very close to the poverty line. He felt that the simple head count exaggerated the problem, and he was clearly right: the depth, as well as the extent, of poverty is important. It should be taken into account when making comparisons—across countries and across time.

What is more, using the head count as a measure may lead to apparently perverse conclusions. Suppose that 5 rupees are given to a person who is 2 rupees below the poverty line, raising the recipient out of poverty, but that the 5 rupees are found by taking them away from another person who is 2 rupees below the poverty line. Poverty measured by the head count falls, but it is not evident that this should be chalked up as a policy success, since the second person has been left in more serious poverty. This is not just a theoretical concern. It may be tempting for policy-makers to concentrate help on those most easily raised above the poverty line. In the design of social security transfers, for instance, there is often a choice between raising universal benefits and targeting transfers to those with the lowest incomes. Income-tested transfers, however, commonly reach only a proportion of those entitled on grounds of incomplete take-up or lack of information (Atkinson 2015, pp. 210–211). This means that, while the targeted transfers may raise the recipients above the poverty line, they do not help the worst-off at the very bottom (those not reached). The poverty head count in this way can overstate the relative effectiveness of targeting.

This brings us to the "poverty gap," which, as the name immediately suggests, gauges the depth of poverty. It has the further attraction that it is a measure of how much income or consumption is needed, in an arithmetic sense (an important qualification, discussed further below), to bring everyone up to the poverty line. To be more precise, the poverty gap is defined as the mean shortfall in consumption or income from the poverty line, where the mean is measured over the whole population, counting the nonpoor as having zero shortfall, and where the mean is expressed as a percentage of the poverty line. If all those below the poverty line were to have no consumption, then the shortfall in every case would be equal to the poverty line, and the poverty gap would be equal to the head-count rate. In reality, the poor have some positive consumption, so that the shortfall is less than complete, and the poverty gap as a percentage is less than the head-count rate. The World Bank global estimates for 2013, with the $1.90 a day per person poverty line, show the poverty gap as 3.23 per cent and the head-count rate as 10.67 per cent. In aggregate terms, the 767 million in poverty had a total annual poverty gap of 161 billion international dollars:

$$3.23 \text{ per cent of } 7.18 \text{ billion} \times \$1.90 \times 365 = \$161 \text{ billion}$$

where 7.18 billion is the total world population. To put this figure in perspective, it is some 1 per cent of the 2013 gross national income of the United States. (The international dollars are normalized so that an international dollar is equal to a US dollar.) Or in more human terms, the globally poor were on average some 58 cents a day, or 31 per cent, below the $1.90 poverty line. (This percentage is referred to as the "income gap ratio," the gap being averaged over those in poverty, not over the whole population.)

At an aggregate level, the poverty gap provides a valuable gauge of the scale of the problem. Not only does 3.23 per cent seem more manageable than 10.67 per cent, but it also corresponds to the reality that most of the poor are not totally without resources. At the individual level, it underlines the perverse outcome of the rupee example given above: the total gap rises by 3 rupees (and hence the mean is increased). At the same time, it has been criticised on the grounds that it attaches the same weight to all shortfalls: the 10 cents needed to take a person to the poverty line is treated the same as the 10 cents going to someone with nothing. This led Amartya Sen (1976) to propose, but not christen, the Sen poverty index, which weights poverty gaps according to the rank of the household in the distribution of people below the poverty line, so that the very poorest household gets the highest rank and the household nearest the poverty line gets zero weight.[17] Alternatively, we could weight the poverty gap according to the distance from the poverty line, as in the poverty index proposed by James Foster, Joel Greer, and Erik Thorbecke (1984). The FGT (Foster-Greer-Thorbecke) index, as it has come to be known, in its simplest form squares the poverty gap, and the resulting FGT2 index thus gives more weight to larger gaps. The World Bank uses FGT2 as one of its summary poverty statistics. From this we can see that, between 1981 and 2013, the global head count was estimated to have been reduced by a factor of just under 4.0 (3.9), but the FGT2 index fell by a factor of more than 6.0 (and the poverty gap by a factor of 5.5). The greater decrease indicates that not only the extent but also the depth of individual poverty had been reduced, with those furthest from the poverty line gaining most.

Should we therefore replace the head count by the poverty gap or by the more nuanced FGT2 index? Use of the poverty gap, or of weighted gaps, as a representation of the depth of poverty is attractive, but there are several qualifications. The first is that—despite the excellent expositions that exist—it remains the case that these more complex measures are not easily explained to a wider audience. This applies to the indices: what "can a squared-poverty-gap index actually signify? And how to explain it to a government Minister" (Duclos and Araar 2006, p. 84). (Jean-Yves Duclos later became a minister in the Canadian government of Justin Trudeau.) Of poverty depth measures in general, Castleman, Foster, and Smith say that, while they capture "the intensity as well as the prevalence of poverty, they are often not central to policy discourse because they are perceived to be too 'unintuitive' to have traction" (2015, p. 2).

The second qualification concerns the sensitivity of the poverty gap, and of the weighted poverty indices, to errors of measurement (discussed more in the next chapter). Statisticians may be confident that a household is below the pov-

---

[17] In its use of rank as a weight, the Sen poverty index is the counterpart of the Gini coefficient of overall inequality, which is half the mean absolute deviation divided by the mean.

erty line of 30 rupees but less confident as to whether the shortfall is 10 or 15 rupees. This would not affect the head count but would change the poverty gap. Zero is quite frequently recorded for income, and indeed recorded income may be negative, almost certainly mismeasuring consumption. Grounds for believing that this is the case are provided by the countries in the World Bank's PovcalNet database, where results on both bases are quoted: in Mexico in 2012, the income-based survey reported a head-count poverty rate that was 2.2 times that in the consumption survey, but the poverty gap was 3.3 times that in the consumption survey.[18] When using measures of the depth of poverty, such as the poverty gap, it becomes even more problematic to amalgamate income and consumption measures.

The third qualification arises from consideration of the underlying judgements. Concern with the depth of poverty has been represented by the weighting of the poverty shortfall, but this needs closer scrutiny. With the version proposed by Sen, the weights in effect go from 1.0 for the poorest person to zero for a person just at the poverty line. It is not, however, evident that we should draw such a sharp distinction looking only at those in the poverty population. Should we instead, as argued by Shorrocks (1995), look at the position of people, not just within the poor population, but within the population in the country as a whole, rich as well as poor? Such a shift in perspective reduces the differences in the weights applied at different points below the poverty line. To take an example, if the head count is 20 per cent, then the weights go from 1.0 for the poorest person to 0.8 for a person just at the poverty line. In fact, where the distribution of consumption is hump-shaped with a single mode, the weights have, when viewed over the whole distribution of consumption, a slow-quick-slow property: initially the weights fall slowly with the level of consumption, but then the decline accelerates up to the mode (assuming a single mode), after which the fall slows down again as the top is reached (Atkinson and Brandolini 2010, p. 17). Seen this way, the rank-order weights appear to be steering us back towards the simple head-count rate. In the limit, the poverty line is so low that sharp distinctions are not drawn between people living at different levels below it. Such an "either/or" view is, moreover, the natural result of adopting the alternative "rights" view of poverty discussed in chapter 2.

Finally, the poverty gap has been taken as a measure of the "cost" of eliminating poverty. For example, the official Kenyan report on poverty refers to it as providing "the information required to compute the total resource trans-

[18] *Editors:* Tony used data from the October 2016 version of PovcalNet. The April 2018 version shows smaller differences: the head-count poverty rate and poverty gap for 2012 measured using income were 1.2 times and 1.4 times, respectively, the rate and gap measured using consumption. And the analogous figures for 2008 and 1998, for example, were 1.3 and 1.8 (in 2008) and 1.4 and 1.7 (in 1998), again showing a larger difference for the poverty gap. Time series for the two head-count rates in Mexico, one based on income and one on consumption, are shown in figure 8.3 in chapter 8, drawing on the April 2018 PovcalNet data.

fers required to eliminate poverty" (Kenya National Bureau of Statistics 2007, box 4.1). And the report for Mauritius uses a calculation of the poverty gap to conclude that, "for 2012, the amount of money that is required to move people out of poverty is estimated at Rs 1.3 bn" (Statistics Mauritius 2015, p. 5). However, this assumes that all that is required is a simple transfer, whereas in reality there are likely to be spillovers, and the cost to those financing the transfer may exceed the amount received by those in poverty. As it was expressed by the US economist Arthur Okun (1975), redistribution involves a "leaky bucket." To raise the consumption of the poor by X million, the cost may be considerably greater than X million. The poverty gap is therefore only a rough first approximation of the money required.[19]

The qualifications just outlined may explain why the head count remains the most widely employed indicator. Since I rely in this book on secondary sources, I have to make use of the statistics as published, and this means that the head count will be the main tool. The reader should, however, bear in mind that the point from which we started—the need to consider the depth of poverty, as well as its extent—remains an important consideration. The checklist includes a search for any available measures.[20]

Multidimensional poverty and the overlap of deprivations

The representation of the different dimensions has been described earlier in the chapter, following custom, as a "dashboard": just as in a car, there is a row of dials recording performance on different dimensions. The parallel, however, is inexact. There can be a dashboard for a single household, telling us how they are faring, but for the society what is recorded is a summary of the performance of all households. It would be as though the speedometer on our car told us how many drivers on all roads in the country were travelling at less than x miles per hour. This distinction is important since the move to a multidimensional concept of poverty involves two key elements: the extension of dimensions and the introduction of correlation between these dimensions across the popula-

---

[19]*Editors*: Tony is concerned here only with the cost associated with any transfer (for example, administrative costs, imperfect identification of entitled beneficiaries). From a broader perspective, transfers may modify people's behaviour (for example, labour supply, savings decisions) and their opportunities (such as allowing credit-constrained parents to invest in the education of their children). The concerns about changes in behaviour are typically raised to question the effectiveness of redistribution. Tony dealt extensively with these problems in chapter 9 of *Inequality: What Can Be Done?* and concluded: "The a priori view that there is an inevitable conflict between equity and efficiency is not borne out by an examination of the underlying assumptions" (2015, p. 262; see also Atkinson 2014, chapter 3).

[20]*Editors*: That search may often be fruitful. Although the national reports at the end of the book focus on the head count when describing national estimates, many countries (at all levels of development) do publish figures for the depth of poverty—Kenya and Mauritius are far from being the only examples.

tion. There is interest both in what is shown by each dial *and* in the relation between what is happening on different dials. It is not just how many people are deprived, but also how many households have a low score on all or several of the dimensions. Do those with low levels of education also suffer from poor health? From the standpoint of evaluating policy, the different dimensions have to be examined in conjunction. In their review of the Millennium Development Goals at midpoint, François Bourguignon and his colleagues noted that, "because MDGs are presented as independent goals, they tend to be evaluated independently" (2010, p. 28), but one needs to know how far—at the level of the individual household—progress is taking place across the board, and how far gains in one dimension are being accompanied by reverses elsewhere. We cannot just look at "marginal distributions"—the distribution of the population across the possible categories of each indicator when taking each indicator separately (Ferreira and Lugo 2013).

There are several possible ways of capturing the correlation. The most widely used procedure, and that recommended in the report of the Commission on Global Poverty, is based on counting the overlap of deprivations over the population. Once the threshold for each indicator has been determined (for example, no electricity = deprived), the only decision that has to be made concerns the critical number of overlaps. To be more concrete, the first step is to classify each person (or household) with respect to the thresholds for all n indicators, so that people are identified as being deprived or nondeprived for each indicator, and the second step is to count the number of indicators on which the person is deprived. The chosen cutoff, k, determines the number of indicators on which a person must be deprived in order to be considered multidimensionally poor. The proportion of the population with k or more deprivations is the head-count ratio, H, of multidimensional deprivation. The cutoff, k, is likely to be chosen to lie strictly between 1 and n. A cutoff of 1 would mean that anyone below *any* threshold is counted: this is the "union" approach to the counting. A cutoff of n means that people are only counted if they are below the threshold on *all* dimensions: this is the "intersection" approach. Counting is an easily explained way to proceed: "Counting the number of observable deprivations in core indicators has an intuitive appeal and simplicity that has attracted not only academics but also policy-makers and practitioners" (Alkire et al. 2015, p. 143).

In the case of the EU's measurement of household deprivation described in the previous section, as first introduced in 2009, n is equal to 9: there are nine indicators. Two different values of the cutoff, k, are used. For "material deprivation," k is equal to 3: a household (in this case the unit of analysis is not the person) is classified as suffering material deprivation if it has an enforced lack of at least three of the nine items. And "severe material deprivation" is the situation where the household is unable to afford at least four items. Following the recent revision of the measurement to cover more indicators ($n - 13$), the statistics for severe material deprivation based on the nine-item measure continue to be published but are now accompanied by those for the new indicator "material and social deprivation," which is defined as the situation where k is equal to 5 (out of 13).

Each of the nine indicators, or thirteen with revised measurement, is equally weighted in the EU's calculations of the deprivation head count. Things are a little more complicated in the case of the Global MPI. There are ten indicators ($n = 10$), which relate to three dimensions—education (two indicators), health (two indicators) and standard of living (six indicators). The three dimensions are equally weighted so that each of the four education and health indicators has a weight of one-sixth and each of the standard-of-living indicators has a weight of one-eighteenth. A household is classified as multidimensionally poor if it is deprived in one-third of the weighted indicators ($k = 3.333$)—for example, in one of the education and one of the health indicators, or in one of the health and three of the standard-of-living indicators. (More details of the Global MPI, including the threshold for each indicator, are given in chapter 5.) The issue of the selection of weights has been highlighted by Aaberge and Brandolini, who say that there is no getting away from the fact that "the choice of weights might have a significant effect on the results of multidimensional analyses of inequality and poverty" (2015, p. 153; see also Decancq and Lugo 2012). The testing of the robustness of results to the choice of weights has been an important part of the research programme underlying the construction of the Global MPI (see, for example, Alkire and Santos 2014). In considering robustness to changes in weighting, one needs to distinguish between "local" and "general" sensitivity. Ideally, the conclusions drawn—for example, about the change over time—should not be materially affected by modest (local) variations in weights. On the other hand, if the findings are not affected by a major reduction in the weight—a general change—then this would call into question the pertinence of the indicator in question.

If a household ceases to be deprived on any dimension, should a measure of multidimensional poverty always fall? The multidimensional head-count measure does not have this property. For example, if, on the EU measure, a household is deprived in six out of nine indicators, then because it now becomes able to afford a washing machine, the head count is unchanged. The household still meets the cutoff for "material deprivation." The head count therefore fails to satisfy what is known as "dimensional monotonicity," which requires a strict reduction in the poverty measure. This is not a surprise, given the arguments for the poverty gap and the FGT index rather than the head count when measuring poverty in the single dimension of income. But this shortcoming of the head count with multidimensional measurement has to be acknowledged, as should its vulnerability to manipulation by policy-makers. These considerations led Alkire and Foster to propose the "adjusted" head-count ratio, which multiplies the head-count rate by the average "breadth" of deprivation among the poor (Alkire and Foster 2011, p. 482). The adjusted head-count rate is used alongside the head count in the Global MPI constructed by OPHI and in a range of national MPIs based on the same methodology. In the example of the EU measure just given, the adjusted head-count rate shows a reduction as the circumstances of the household in question have improved, reducing the average breath of deprivation.

What about the overlap of nonmonetary with monetary poverty? I owe to Xiaolin Wang, Hexia Feng, Qingjie Xia, and Sabina Alkire the observation that the words employed in the Chinese definition of poverty help us understand the relationship between the two (Wang et al. 2016, p. 3). The ancient *Analytical Dictionary of Characters* defines "poverty" (贫困, *pin kun*) as "little wealth." The modern *Xinhua Dictionary* defines "poor" (贫, *pin*) as "little income and difficulties in life" and defines "predicament" (困, *kun*) as "falling into a harsh environment or any environment that one cannot shake off." Thus, in this interpretation, the "poor" aspect of poverty mainly refers to the lack of income and the "predicament" aspect of poverty emphasises the social environment and nonmonetary dimensions.

One possibility is simply to include income (or consumption) as one of the dimensions in the multidimensional measure. This is the practice adopted in the MPI in Mexico (see table 3.1). However, if the aim is to complement a monetary measure, then one should not to seek to combine the two different approaches.

The extent of overlap between monetary and nonmonetary measures of poverty has been examined in a number of countries. For example, in Uganda, of the 19.7 per cent of the population estimated to be below the national monetary poverty line using the 2012–2013 Household Survey, more than four out of five (16.4 per cent) were deprived on at least four of the twelve dimensions used to define nonmonetary multidimensional poverty (Uganda Ministry of Finance 2014, table 2.10). But of the 53.8 per cent who were deprived according to this criterion, two-thirds (37.4 per cent) were above the income poverty line. In Ireland, the official measure of poverty is actually defined as the overlap: it is the proportion of people living in households that are both suffering multiple deprivation (defined as the enforced lack of two or more items from a list of eleven) *and* below the monetary poverty line. This is labelled in the Irish statistics as "consistent poverty."[21]

[21] *Editors*: We think that Tony would have added to this discussion—for example, by comparing figures on the degree of overlap for a number of countries or by enlarging on the Irish experience (for example, by describing how the overlap has changed over time or how it varies for different groups in the population). The national report for Ireland at the end of the book shows that in 2014 the multiple deprivation rate for the population was estimated to be 29.0 per cent, the monetary poverty rate was 16.3 per cent, and the intersection of the two in the "consistent" poverty rate was 8.0 per cent.

CONCLUSIONS

[*Editors*: Tony had not yet drafted conclusions for this chapter. Besides summarising the key points, perhaps by brief reference to the top half of the poverty "checklist" in box B in chapter 4, he might have noted that measurement in practice is only as good as the data that are available for the job, the subject of the next chapter.]

The Key Role of Data

As it was put by the president of the World Bank, "We will not be able to reach our goal unless we have data to show whether or not people are actually lifting themselves out of poverty. Collecting good data is one of the most powerful tools to end extreme poverty" (World Bank 2015a). In this chapter, I describe the data that are needed and ask how far the existing sources are fit for purpose.

Since much of the discussion of existing sources is critical and emphasises the need for additional investment, I should begin by stressing the very considerable efforts that are already being made. The quantity and quality of household surveys have improved in recent years to a quite remarkable degree. This achievement has required significant resources and the cooperation of a wide range of people. The government statistician of Ghana, introducing the 2012–2013 Ghana Living Standards Survey (GLSS), brought this out clearly:

> The methodology of the survey is such that it required substantial human, material and financial resources to successfully implement it. The effort of the GSS [Ghana Statistical Service] was complemented by the substantial support and cooperation received from various stakeholders to make this report possible. The GSS would, therefore, like to acknowledge the varied stakeholder contributions that led to the successful completion of the survey. First, we would like to thank the selected households for their patience and cooperation and for devoting time to the field personnel during the numerous visits and questioning. Our appreciation also goes to the field personnel and data entry officers for the meticulous manner in which they discharged their duties. Many thanks go to the regional and district administrators as well as the traditional rulers and community leaders for the diverse ways in which they provided assistance to the field teams to ensure the success of the fieldwork. (Ghana Statistical Service 2014, p. ii)

It should be added that the Ghana survey received financial support from the UK Department for International Development (UK-DFID), UNICEF, UNDP, and the International Labour Office (ILO). If you ask, "Where does our aid money go?," then one answer is the improvement of the information basis for monitoring and designing development policy. Bilateral and multilateral aid has been important for the creation of several series of the multi-topic household surveys listed in table 4.1. The Living Standards Measurement Study (LSMS) surveys, an initiative of the World Bank, have been used to measure monetary poverty, although they are far from being the only sources employed

Table 4.1. Multi-topic household surveys with global or multi-regional coverage

Survey	Number of Countries Covered	Lead Agency	Brief Description
LSMS (Living Standards Measurement Study)	41 (111 surveys)	World Bank	Multi-purpose household survey data, including poverty measured in terms of consumption; launched in 1980; sample size ranges from 780 to 36,000 households, with a median of 3,600
DHS (Demographic and Health Survey)	90 (301 surveys)	USAID	National sample surveys of population and maternal/child health, at individual and household levels; surveys typically conducted about every five years; first held in 1984; sample size ranges from 1,381 to 609,120 households, with a median of 9,476
MICS (Multiple Indicator Cluster Survey)	113 (351 surveys, including those planned for 2018–2019)	UNICEF	Data on key indicators of the well-being of children and women, including health, education, and child protection; first round conducted in 1995; sixth round to run in 2018–2019; in the fifth wave (around 2014), sample size varied between 685 and 55,120 households, with a median of 9,179

Source: Author's elaboration based on information available on the survey websites (updated August 2018). For the DHS, only standard and continuous surveys are considered.
Reading note: There are 111 LSMS surveys covering 41 countries, carried out with the support of the World Bank.

for this purpose, whether by the World Bank or by governments and statistical offices of individual countries. (Deaton [1997] describes the rationale and early history of the LSMS programme.) The Demographic and Health Surveys (DHS) sponsored by the US Agency for International Development (USAID) and the Multiple Indicator Cluster Surveys (MICS) led by UNICEF provide the data for most of the estimates of nonmonetary poverty in the UNDP's *Human Development Reports*—i.e., the Global MPI estimates outlined in the previous chapter and described in more detail in chapter 5. The range of topics covered by the data that the DHS and MICS collect at the level of the individual or the household allows the extent of overlap of deprivation across dimensions to be assessed.

ARE THERE ANY DATA?

The first question under the "data" heading on the checklist is whether there *are* any data. Are there data on the circumstances of individuals and households obtained from household surveys or equivalent sources that allow us to estimate the extent of monetary and nonmonetary poverty and to monitor how it is changing over time? The addition "or equivalent sources" refers to the fact that a number of countries now make use of administrative sources, such as population registers, to obtain information about the circumstances of their citizens.

Bricks without straw?

I begin with the World Bank's PovcalNet database, which provides the basis for the global estimate of monetary poverty and is made freely available for use online by other researchers. The nonexistence of data in PovcalNet may be revealed by a blank in the relevant tables. For example, the 2013 estimates of global poverty by the World Bank were based on estimates for 155 countries out of the total of 197 identified in chapter 1. In some cases, the population of the missing countries is small, such as the Marshall Islands or St. Kitts and Nevis. At the risk of offending readers in those countries, we may conclude that their omission is unlikely to change the global picture. In the case of some larger countries, like New Zealand or Singapore, few people are likely to be below the International Poverty Line of $1.90 per day (at 2011 prices). But some of the missing countries are significant in terms both of their total population and of the risk of poverty. These include Afghanistan, Algeria, Cuba, Egypt, the Democratic Republic of Korea, Myanmar, Saudi Arabia, Syria, and Yemen. While one can perfectly understand the evident difficulties in making estimates for a number of these countries, there are good reasons for believing that, on account of conflict and forced migration, the citizens of these countries are particularly at risk.[1]

---

[1] *Editors*: Tony's comments in this section refer to the 2016 version of PovcalNet. The April 2018 version includes estimates for Algeria, Egypt, Myanmar, Syria (the data are for 2004 and hence predate the civil war), and Yemen (where the data are for 2014, predating the start of the current conflict).

When I say that the 2013 World Bank figures are based on estimates for 155 countries, the word "estimates" is deliberate; it does not imply that there are 2013 data for every one of these countries. The reader who follows up by downloading the PovcalNet data may be surprised to discover that only just over a quarter have data for 2013: forty-three out of 152 countries (three are not included in the PovcalNet current at the end of 2016). The coverage is quite varied but tilted towards Latin America, which accounts for fourteen of the forty-three countries, and towards Central Europe/Asia: urban Argentina, Armenia, Belarus, Bolivia, Brazil, Chile, China, Colombia, Costa Rica, Djibouti, the Dominican Republic, Ecuador, El Salvador, Georgia, Honduras, Indonesia, Iran, Kazakhstan, Kosovo, the Kyrgyz Republic, Laos, Micronesia, Moldova, Montenegro, Pakistan, Panama, Paraguay, Peru, Poland, Romania, Rwanda, Serbia, Seychelles, Sri Lanka, Tajikistan, Thailand, Turkey, Uganda, Ukraine, the United States, and Uruguay. In terms of population, they account for five of the six largest countries (the absentee being India) and around a third of the total world population. If we add those countries that have data for 2014 (but not 2013), then the number rises to forty-eight, or a third. If we bring in those with 2012 data, then the total rises to eighty-seven, or 57 per cent. It remains the case that for sixty-five countries the data are two years or more out of date, and that for nineteen countries they are more than five years out of date, including some from the 1990s, notably from the Caribbean (for example, Belize, 1999; Guyana, 1998; Suriname, 1999; and Trinidad and Tobago, 1992).

For the majority of countries, the World Bank estimate is based on updating data for an earlier year, where this updating is based on the assumption that all households have experienced a proportionate rise in their consumption per head equal to the proportionate rise in the mean consumption per head as derived from national accounts statistics. This is equivalent to adjusting the International Poverty Line backwards to the earlier year by dividing the proportionate growth since then in the mean consumption per head. If the mean in 2011 is 15 per cent higher than when the survey was conducted, then applying a poverty line of $1.65 to the survey data is equivalent to applying $1.90 in 2011. Filling the gap in this way does, however, raise problems when the aggregate national accounts statistics show different movement over time from the household surveys. What do we do if, at the time of the next survey, we find that the updating process based on national accounts is out of line with the increase shown in the surveys? The relation between household surveys and national accounts—a subject that has generated much controversy—is taken up below in the section on "Triangulation."

If we turn from PovcalNet to other data sources, we encounter the problem that the nonexistence of data may be less overt, particularly if one makes use of the secondary databases on inequality and poverty that have been assembled in recent years. In the same way that nature abhors a vacuum, so the constructors of databases tend to regard missing values as a challenge to be overcome. In some cases, this takes the form of imputing values. The Standardized Income Inequality Database (SWIID) constructed by Frederick Solt, for example, has developed a sophisticated approach to imputation that completes the gaps by using information from other variables and other countries. It remains limited, however, by the non-availability of data. As a consequence, "in the developing world . . . most SWIID estimates are based on ratios observed in other countries" (Solt 2016, p. 1277).[2] In other studies, the blanks are filled by using data for the country in question and adopting related but different calculations.

A good example of making bricks without much straw is provided by the series for the proportion in poverty in Kenya covering the period from 1914 to 1976, which shows poverty halving from 1914 to 1964, and then remaining stable from 1964 to 1976. The author of this series, Professor Arne Bigsten (1986, 1987) of the University of Gothenburg is quite clear about the nature of the exercise. There are no underlying household survey data; such data do not exist back to 1914. What Bigsten does is to analyse the mean income of different groups of income-earners, and then make the assumption that the distribution within each category has a particular form: the logarithm of income is assumed to follow the bell-shaped normal curve familiar from statistical textbooks. This assumption of a lognormal distribution cannot be tested against actual distributional data for Kenya, and Bigsten is careful to underline the approximate nature of the calculation, describing his estimates as "very crude" (1986, p. 1159). However, the reader may well not appreciate their limitations and be led to believe that Kenya is a leading contender for the world's longest series of data on poverty. (Kenyan estimates for income inequality back to 1914 appear in the UNU-WIDER World Income Inequality Database.)

A different and more recent illustration is provided by the example of Liberia. The Core Welfare Indicator Questionnaire (CWIQ) survey collected data in 2007 on household consumption and was used to estimate the extent of poverty. Another CWIQ survey was then carried out in 2010. "In 2007, nearly two-thirds [63.8 per cent] of Liberia's population were living below the poverty line," reports a World Bank note on tracking changes in poverty in the country. It continues: "However, based on data from the 2010 CWIQ, poverty is estimated to have fallen to 56.3 percent in 2010" (World Bank 2012, p. vii). Again, the key word is "estimated," since the 2010 survey contained no data on consumption. Rather, a statistical model was developed to relate consumption to other information collected in the 2007 survey, and this was used to impute a figure for consumption for each household in the 2010 data based on variables common to both surveys. A later paper giving details of the procedure reports that the results were sensitive to the choices made over the statis-

---

[2]*Editors:* For a critical discussion of the SWIID, see Jenkins (2015) and, with a focus on South Africa, Wittenberg (2015), as well as the reply by Solt (2015).

tical model fitted to the 2007 data: when ownership of mobile phones was included as a correlate of consumption, the estimated decline in poverty between 2007 and 2010 was some four percentage points larger (Dabalen et al. 2014, table 3). As the authors note, "Imputation relies on the assumption of the stability of the relationship between covariates and poverty over time, which can be a strong assumption in rapidly evolving economies" (p. 16). In Liberia, cell-phone ownership had risen from 30.5 per cent of households in 2007 to 56.6 per cent in 2010. Imputation has been used in other countries—the national report for Niger at the end of the book describes another example.

In the case of nonmonetary measures of poverty based on the Alkire-Foster methods, the 2016 *Human Development Report* contains head counts for 102 countries relating to a year in the period 2005–2015. In fifty-three cases, these are based on DHS data, in thirty-nine on MICS, and in ten on other sources. None of the estimates are for the high-income countries as classified by the World Bank. Of the forty-three countries covered by national reports in this book that are not in the high-income group, there are figures for thirty-five; the countries with no estimates are Fiji, Malaysia, the Solomon Islands, Sri Lanka, Botswana, Mauritius, Panama, and Uruguay. For the high-income countries, I draw in the national reports on Eurostat's estimates of "material deprivation" for European countries and on national sources elsewhere.

Data fit for purpose

What, then, do we have to do to obtain "real" data? In securing for a particular country the household survey data necessary to construct a global poverty measure, there are in fact four hurdles that have to be jumped (the last not being relevant if the interest is in just a single country rather than a global total):

1. A recent survey has to have been conducted.
2. The data from the survey have to be available to researchers.
3. The data have to be comparable with those from earlier surveys (in order to measure the trends over time).
4. The data have to be comparable with those for other countries, and in line with the checklist adopted for the global poverty measure.

Surveys are expensive and require scarce trained staff. It is not therefore surprising that in many developing countries they are only conducted at intervals. In Zambia, for example, Living Conditions Monitoring Surveys (LCMS) have been carried out since 1996, and the survey in 2015 was the seventh. In Mozambique, budget surveys were conducted in 1996–1997, 2002–2003, 2008–2009, and 2014–2015. In fact, these cases are reasonably good by the standards of many other countries. The gaps in coverage—specifically the countries without a single data point—were cited by the president of the World Bank in 2015 when he pledged "to work with developing countries and international partners to ensure that the 78 poorest nations have household-level surveys every three years, with the first round to be completed by 2020" (World Bank 2015a). The cost of implementing a multi-topic household survey every three years in these countries between 2016 and 2030, including the cost of providing technical assistance, has been estimated to be about $1 billion (Kilic et al. 2017). It is not only resources that limit the ability of governments to carry out household surveys: the civil war was a major reason why the 2014 national survey of household income and expenditure in Liberia was the first since 1964 (Liberia Institute of Statistics and Geo-Information Services 2016, p. 1). A fifty-year gap clearly limits what can be said about trends over time.

The nonmonetary measures of poverty now included in the *Human Development Reports* are a relatively recent advance, and as a consequence there is limited information on changes over time. Of the 102 countries with data on the incidence of nonmonetary poverty in the 2016 report, there is an estimate for a single year for sixty-five countries, and in only fifteen countries are there figures for more than two years.[3] The two main underlying surveys are only conducted at intervals. The DHS has taken place, on average, every five years; the MICS had a similar periodicity in the past but is now moving to a three-year cycle. This limits their applicability for annual monitoring.

Existence and availability of data

Survey data have to be not only in existence but also accessible to researchers. Access is a major issue not just for academic scholars but also for international organisations. In the case of Africa, the World Bank study *Poverty in a Rising Africa* (Beegle et al. 2016) identified 180 surveys over the period 1990 to 2012, but around a fifth were not available in the microdata library. It is not just developing countries that pose problems. In its 2015 report, the OECD notes that there are alternative data for Japan from the National Survey of Family Income and Expenditure, but that "the lack of data beyond 2009 is due to the fact that no recent estimates were provided by the Japanese authorities" (OECD 2015, p. 57). Overcoming this second hurdle depends crucially on collaboration with national statistical offices and other data suppliers. The achievement of better data on poverty rests on the resources available to these institutions and on their own organisation and priorities. It depends on the engagement of the national offices. Lack of data availability in the past may be due to other statistical operations taking precedence. Countries in receipt of development assistance may have been subject to conflicting donor preferences. It is to be

---

[3] *Editors*: The OPHI website provides data for years before 2005 for some countries, and in total there are data for more than one year for fifty countries in the Global MPI data tables for 2017.

hoped that the establishment of the SDGs will raise the priority attached to the supply of data and ensure that all surveys are accessible. In terms of making progress towards improving the statistical picture, such steps appear like low-hanging fruit.

COMPARABILITY

Comparability is a challenge, first of all at the level of the individual country. Are the data for different years comparable? A satisfactory answer to this question is necessary if we are to be able to monitor progress over time.

Comparability over time

The increase in quality of household surveys in recent years has been noted earlier. The improvements are clearly to be welcomed, but there is a tension between improving the statistical instrument and preserving comparability with the past.

Comparability is, of course, a matter of degree, so that judgements may differ, but the World Bank's study of *Poverty in a Rising Africa* set out three reasonable criteria: (1) the sample should in each case be nationally representative; (2) the surveys should have been carried out at periods of the year that are comparable in terms of seasonality; and (3) the instrument for recording (recall or diary, for instance) and the reporting period should remain consistent. Applying these criteria to the data for the African study from 1990 to 2012, the World Bank authors conclude that, of 113 surveys for which data were available, in only 78 cases were they comparable with at least one other survey for that country (Beegle et al. 2016, figure 1.4). For South Africa, there are two pairs of comparable years, but the pairs cannot be linked.[4] Guinea and Mali each carried out four surveys, but none were deemed comparable. When the criteria for comparability are applied, there were on average just 1.6 poverty estimates per country over the period 1990 to 2012 (Beegle et al. 2016, p. 33).

Concrete examples from national studies illustrate the problems that arise. In its report on the Kenya Integrated Household Budget Survey (KIHBS) for 2005–2006, the Kenya National Bureau of Statistics explained why the findings of poverty could not be directly compared with those from the earlier Welfare Monitoring Survey (WMS) in 1997. The KIHBS in 2005–2006 collected more extensive information covering more expenditure items and distinguished between food items purchased over a one-week period and those actually consumed during that period—a distinction that was found to be "criti-

---

[4] *Editors*: The first pair of years is 1995 and 2000. These appear in the World Bank series shown in figure ZAF in the national report for South Africa but not in the national estimates.

cal to correctly construct the food consumption aggregate" (Kenya National Bureau of Statistics 2007, p. 24). The KIHBS was one year long, whereas the WMS was conducted over a shorter period and could not readily be adjusted for seasonal effects. In 2005–2006 a different food basket was employed when calculating the poverty line, and the prices used were the median of those observed, rather than the mean, as in 1997. In 2005–2006 a different approach was adopted for the measurement of the nonfood component of the poverty line. The WMS for 1997 excluded certain northern districts, where the poverty rate could be expected to be higher. In view of these major differences, the 2005–2006 and 2015–2016 results are shown in figure KEN as a separate series in the national report for Kenya.

Shifting continents, we can learn from a second example of three surveys carried out in Cambodia in the 1990s:

> Despite this active investment in data gathering, all supported by international donors, each survey was inconsistent with previous and subsequent surveys so no firm evidence exists on whether poverty rose or fell. The initial 1993–94 survey had a very detailed consumption recall list (ca. 450 items). . . . The second survey in 1997 used only 33 broadly defined items in the consumption recall, and was fielded at a different time of the year. Consumption estimates from this survey were adjusted upwards (and poverty rates downwards) by up to 14 percent for rural households to correct for a perceived under reporting of medical expenses. . . . The apparent fall in the headcount poverty rate from 39 to 36 percent between 1993 and 1997 is reversed if this adjustment is not applied. The third survey in 1999 used 36 items in the consumption recall and was in conjunction with a detailed income and employment module. It was again conducted in different months than the earlier surveys. But this time, it was randomly split into two rounds, with half the sample in each. Greater efforts to reconcile consumption and income estimates at a household level in the second round led to dramatic changes in poverty estimates. In the first round, the headcount poverty rate was 64 percent, and in the second round it was only 36 percent. The dramatic fall in the poverty rate came from higher recorded expenditures and lower inequality in the second round. No robust poverty trend for the 1990s can be calculated from these irreconcilable data. (Gibson 2005, p. 137)

In the case of Nepal, the World Bank commented in 1999 that

> the few nation-wide surveys conducted over the past twenty years (in 1977, in 1984/85, and in 1995/96) all used different methodologies to collect data on incomes and consumption and to define measures of poverty. The estimates of poverty obtained on the basis of earlier surveys cannot be directly compared. . . . For example, it would be erroneous to compare the figure of 49 percent for the incidence of poverty in 1991 reported in the Eighth Plan (which was based on the 1984/85 data) with the 42 percent figure . . . for 1995/96, and conclude that

poverty has declined over the five-year period. The two figures are not comparable. (Prennushi 1999, p. 6)

In the case of the Solomon Islands, it is tempting to draw conclusions from the
fact that the estimated poverty rate for 2012–2013 (12.7 per cent) is around half
that found in 2005–2006 (23 per cent), but the statistical report states categorically that "a simple comparison of the two estimates at their face values must
be avoided because there are significant differences in data collection methods as well as in the method used in quantifying poverty" (Solomon Islands
National Statistics Office 2015a, p. xii). Differences in the poverty calculation
can be taken into account by applying the same method to both surveys, and
this exercise suggests that there had been a decline of eight percentage points.
However, that does not take account of the effect of differences in questionnaire design and survey implementation. As a result, the statistics office formed
the view that the poverty estimates are indicative of the direction of change,
but counsels caution in reaching any conclusion about the extent of the decline
in poverty. The two data points based on the same method are therefore shown
as two series in figure SLB in the national report for the Solomon Islands. The
"dots" are not joined up.

Each of the surveys may have been valuable on its own, but they could not
be used to study trends over time. They would not be useful for a monitoring
exercise. We should not lose sight of the breaks in continuity, even if it is tempting to elide them when drawing conclusions. In the case of Kenya, for example, despite the rehearsal of the reasons why the data are not comparable, the
executive summary stated that "the major finding is that poverty is on a declining trend in Kenya, and the risk of falling into poverty is lower today than
in the 1990s" (Kenya National Bureau of Statistics 2007, p. 11). In the case of
Cambodia, there was a further break in continuity in 2009 when the definition of the poverty line was revised. The revision caused the poverty head count
to rise from 14.6 per cent to 23.9 per cent, which is a major difference—due to
a substantial increase in the nonfood allowance (World Bank 2014a, p. 97).

The calculation of comparable nonmonetary poverty rates over time is com-
promised if the available data do not measure the chosen indicators in the same
way at each round of the survey or cease to cover one or more of them at all. In
the case of the estimates of multidimensional poverty made by OPHI, the problem is addressed by producing separate figures, in addition to those for the
Global MPI, based only on indicators that are measured consistently over time.
The short time series based on these standardized figures are shown in the
graphs in the national reports at the end of the book. The two figures available
for any given year on occasion differ appreciably. For example, while the Global
MPI head count for Madagascar published by OPHI for 2008–2009 is 66.9 per
cent, the figure for this year in the standardized time series is 73.3 per cent.

The lesson for the checklist is clear: be careful before "joining the dots."

Comparability across countries

Even more demanding is comparability across countries. The report on poverty in Kenya, for example, compared the 2005–2006 findings with those for its neighbours (Ethiopia, Tanzania, and Uganda) and Burundi, Cameroon, and Nigeria (Kenya National Bureau of Statistics 2007, box 4.2). But are they comparable? Chapter 3 dealt with the thorny issue of purchasing power parities, but there are other important issues that affect our ability to compare figures for different countries.

By their nature, the surveys listed in table 4.1 score relatively well in terms of international comparability. But again, comparability is a matter of degree. Surveys and other data sources vary across countries for good reasons. The objective should be a greater degree of harmonisation, not uniformity. This point is made clearly on the website of the Eurosystem's Household Finance and Consumption Survey: "In view of the considerable cultural and institutional differences between euro area countries, there needs to be some flexibility in the formulation of the questions for the individual countries in order to obtain comparable data" (Household Finance and Consumption Network website, August 2018).[5] As has been argued by Deaton and Dupriez, "we realize that surveys are used for different purposes in different countries, and that a survey that works in one country may be useless in another. Nevertheless, greater standardization is certainly possible in some cases, not only in data collection, but in the reporting and documentation of survey design" (2011, p. 161). In their study of the reliability of food data, for example, Smith, Dupriez, and Troubat found "great variety across surveys in data collection methods and thus in both reliability and relevance" (2014, p. 48).

In considering the goal which could be aimed for, it is useful to distinguish between ex ante and ex post harmonisation. Ex ante harmonisation involves action before the survey goes into the field and hence an early commitment on the part of the relevant statistical agencies. It could involve the selection of sampling methods, the design of the questionnaire (such as the period over which expenditure data are collected), and the methods of data collection. An example of ex ante harmonisation is provided by the regional standardized methodology proposed by the Secretariat of the Pacific Community (2015). Another example, in high-income countries, is the European Community Household Panel (ECHP), which was carried out from 1994 to 2001 in EU member states under Eurostat leadership. The ECHP was succeeded by EU Statistics on Income and Living Conditions (EU-SILC), which involves a lesser degree of harmonisation. EU-SILC is based on

---

[5] *Editors*: The Household Finance and Consumption Survey collects household-level data on households' finances and consumption. The Eurosystem comprises the European Central Bank and the national central banks of the EU member states whose currency is the euro.

> the idea of a "common framework" in contrast with the concept of a "common survey." The common framework is defined by harmonized lists of target . . . variables, by a recommended design for implementing EU-SILC, by common requirements (for imputation, weighting, sampling errors calculation), common concepts (household and income) and classifications . . . aiming at maximising comparability of the information produced. (Eurostat website, "Statistics Explained," August 2018)

Ex post harmonisation can be applied after the data are collected and, although it benefits from the active cooperation of the collecting agency, can be carried out by another body. It typically involves recoding variables to a common template, ensuring the comparability of underlying definitions and the application of common treatments to missing and zero values. A well-known example is the LIS Cross-National Data Center (formerly the Luxembourg Income Study), a cooperative international project which has assembled data-covering income (and more recently wealth, in addition to expenditure, if available) in high- and middle-income countries in Europe, North America, Latin America, Africa, Asia, and Australasia. Data are organised into "waves" corresponding to regular intervals, with the first wave of data from around 1980. The data files (which can be accessed remotely by users) for each country contain variables defined in the same way, so that the user knows that variable "HMI" is in each case the total household income, defined in the same way for each country, in national currency units per year. In the same vein, minimal adjustments are applied to harmonise the household surveys contained in SEDLAC, a database of socioeconomic statistics developed for Latin American and Caribbean countries by the Centro de Estudios Distributivos, Laborales, y Sociales (CEDLAS) in collaboration with the World Bank.

The agency harmonising national sources ex post can, however, go further and make adjustments to the recorded data to bring the different countries into line. This is the case of CEPALSTAT, the Statistical Department of the UN Economic Commission for Latin America and the Caribbean (CEPAL) in the construction of its household surveys database.[6] As described by Bourguignon (2015), the corrections proceed by first considering differential nonresponse by households and, among survey participants, nonresponse by item. Imputing missing items and weighting for nonresponse can narrow some of the gap. CEPALSTAT then compares reported incomes by category and applies an upward correction where the household survey total falls short of that in the national accounts. In broad terms, self-employment income is increased by a factor of two and property income by a factor of three. By itself, such differential adjustment changes not only the total but also the distribution, since people vary in the amount of income they receive from various sources. The effect

---

[6]*Editors*: CEPALSTAT recently abandoned this adjustment procedure (ECLAC 2018, pp. 106–107).

is further amplified by assuming that the uplift in property income applies only to the top 20 per cent (which would not necessarily be valid in countries where older households have substantial savings for retirement).[7]

None of the routes to greater cross-country comparability are easy, and none is beyond question, and it is not surprising that the existing estimates will continue to be less than fully satisfactory. These limitations should be taken into account when considering the results. An obvious example is the fact that a sizeable fraction of the world's countries measure poverty in terms of income rather than consumption (the implications of which are discussed in chapter 8). To be clear: I am not saying that measurement in terms of income is second-best. Rather, the situation means that practice across the world is inconsistent in the measure of household living standards that is used, limiting the comparability of the data. Another example is provided by the fact that the components of household income or consumption may differ across countries, a notable case being the inclusion of the imputed rent of owner-occupiers. (Any substantial extension of the concept of income or consumption may need to be accompanied by an adjustment to the poverty line, as discussed in the previous chapter.)

A third example illustrates the problems that may lie beneath the surface of the data, problems that may arise whenever we want to compare population subgroups.

Suppose we wish to compare the differences in rural and urban poverty across countries. (But the same is likely to happen with other comparisons, for example, by educational level.) This might seem straightforward. Once again, however, we have to stand back and ask how "rural" and "urban" are defined. The basis is evidently geographic, but how are the boundaries drawn? There is in fact no internationally agreed basis for drawing the distinction. The UN, in its advice on the definition, states that "because of national differences in the characteristics that distinguish urban from rural areas, the distinction between the urban and the rural population is not yet amenable to a single definition that would be applicable to all countries or, for the most part, even to the countries within a region" (UN 2017b, para. 4.92). The advice continues: "Where there are no regional recommendations on the matter, countries must establish their own definitions in accordance with their own needs."

Not surprisingly, countries do differ significantly in their approach. The definition of "urban" may be explicit. In India, an "urban" area means any place which meets the following criteria: (1) population of at least 5,000, (2) density of population of 400 per square kilometre or more, and (3) at least 75 per cent

---

[7] The approach adopted by CEPALSTAT was advocated by Altimir "to somehow improve the comparability of income distributions available from household surveys in Latin America" (Altimir 1987, p. 151) and was used in a study by the International Labour Office titled, significantly, *Generating Internationally Comparable Income Distribution Estimates* (van Ginneken and Park 1984).

of the male workforce employed in the non-agricultural sector, although the census office, in consultation with state governments, has the power to declare any settlement to be urban (Bhagat 2005, p. 63; see also Tandel, Hiranandani, and Kapoor 2016). "Rural" is then defined as the complement of "urban"—areas that are not classified as "urban" are classified as "rural." Two alternative definitions of "rural" and "urban" are used in China, and chapter 6 will note that they result in big differences in the shares of the total population in each type of area. In Colombia, the rural population consists of people living outside the boundaries of the municipal capital; in Chile, urban areas are defined as those with housing of more than 2,000 inhabitants, or between 1,001 and 2,000, with 50 per cent or more of the economically active population dedicated to secondary and/or tertiary activities (Tresoldi 2013). These differences matter: "In many situations, areas defined as urban have rural characteristics in terms of occupations (e.g. reliance on agriculture), and also in terms of level of infrastructure and services. Such characteristics may even extend into bigger cities. In some regions—particularly Latin America, this can lead to significant undercounting of the rural population and of the rural poor" (International Fund for Agricultural Development 2011, p. 294, n. 21). National definitions of rural and urban are also subject to change over time. There can be political pressures, such as those related to the funding of local governments, which lead districts to seek reclassification as "urban," and this may lead to major shifts unrelated to any change in the economy or in the level of services. Differences are also important in higher-income countries and, as such, led Brandolini and Cipollone to conclude that "the lack of a standard definition of urban/ rural area precludes a rigorous comparative study. . . . Available microdata, such as those collected at the LIS, do not allow us to achieve a satisfactory harmonisation" (2003, p. 339).

Is this particular problem of comparability absent from the surveys listed earlier in table 4.1, which are explicitly designed to provide comparable data across countries? No. For example, the DHS organisers make clear that the surveys use each country's own rural and urban definitions (DHS Program User Forum, statement on the definition of rural versus urban, 20 February 2013).

As I have said, comparability is a matter of degree. Cross-country comparability has improved considerably, but there are still important limitations that should be carefully considered in order to reach sound conclusions. The lesson for the checklist is clear also in this case: watch out for definitions and read the footnotes.

DATA ON PRICES

Data on prices are crucial for the measurement of poverty. We have already met the PPPs in chapter 3, employed for comparisons of poverty across countries.

Within countries, prices are central to the construction of the poverty line in the basic needs approach. The basket of goods has to be priced.

Questions quickly arise. Is allowance made for any differences in prices in different parts of the country? As put by Angus Deaton:

> In countries like the United States, where transport and distribution systems are highly developed, and where transport costs are relatively low, there is little price variation between localities at any given time. In developing countries, transport is often more difficult, markets are not always well integrated, and even the presence of potential arbitrage cannot equalize prices between different geographic locations. (Deaton 1997, p. 283)

However, even in the United States there are geographical price differences, largely related to housing costs. This is one of the important elements behind the "supplemental poverty measure" developed by the Census Bureau, described in the national report for the United States and mentioned in chapter 2. Such differences contribute to the decision to produce national poverty lines that vary by region or that differ for urban and rural areas. Examples from the national reports of allowing for geographical variation in prices include Cambodia, China, India, Malaysia, the Solomon Islands, Kenya, Mozambique, Niger, Bolivia, Brazil, Jamaica, and Italy, besides the United States.

Then there is the measurement of change in prices, which is critical for the updating of a poverty threshold over time. When you read that the poverty line has been indexed for changing consumer prices, what issues surround the index that is used? And are prices rising more for the poor?

Price indices

The issues regarding the construction of the consumer price index (CPI) are highly relevant to estimates of national and global poverty and a real source of concern. As the World Bank has observed, "Although most countries have well-established statistical systems in place for collecting relatively high-frequency price data, the quality of CPI data varies significantly across countries . . . and suffers from many potential sources of error" (World Bank 2015, p. 243). There can be considerable differences between different indices, and the best choice is not always evident, as is illustrated by the fact that the World Bank poverty estimates based on the $1.90 line make use of the World Development Indicators series on the CPI for 104 countries, but replace them by other national CPIs for twenty countries and by other indices for eight other countries, as well as using subnational CPIs for China and India (Ferreira et al. 2016, table 3).

The behaviour of the CPI is of major significance, given that many developing countries have experienced high rates of inflation, with rises in food and energy prices attracting particular attention. The countries of Eastern Europe and the former Soviet republics experienced some dramatic price changes in the early 1990s as they emerged from the planned system. "By mid-1994, the price of cottage cheese in Kazakhstan was reported to have risen by 29,000 times from its pre-transition December 1990 level, the price of milk by 14,600 times, potatoes by 5,700 times, vodka by 2,600 times and bread made of first category flour by 900 times" (Koen 1997, p. 21). As the author goes on to ask, "how reliable are the aggregate price measures . . . in such circumstances?" But inflation at much lower levels provokes the same question. In Ghana, for instance, recorded inflation in terms of the overall CPI did not drop below 10 per cent a year between 1999 and 2011, with food price increases spiking at over 40 per cent in the early part of the period (McKay, Prttilä, and Tarp 2015, figure 3). The cumulative impact of ten years of prices changing at, say, just 7 per cent a year is a doubling of the price level.

What is a consumer price index? It is a measure of the change over time in the price level faced by households in their role as consumers. There are two key ingredients: (1) price quotations for individual commodities for two different dates, which are aggregated using (2) commodity weights, typically derived from household surveys. The total value of the expenditure is then compared at the two different dates, the weights being held constant. If the prices at the initial date are set at unity (1.0), then the total value at the later date provides a measure of the change in the overall level of prices faced by consumers. As has long been recognised, the conclusions drawn can depend crucially on the choice of weights, which present a variety of possibilities. For this reason, there has been a succession of international conventions. The first international standards for CPIs were established in 1925 by the Second International Conference of Labour Statisticians (ICLS). These standards referred to "cost-of-living" indices rather than CPIs, but later meetings distinguished between a consumer price index defined simply as measuring the change in the cost of purchasing a given "basket" of consumption goods and services, as described above, and a cost-of-living index defined as measuring the change in the cost of maintaining a given standard of living, or level of utility. For this reason, the Tenth ICLS, in 1962, decided to adopt the more general term "consumer price index" to embrace both concepts.

The textbook account of the CPI typically opens by contrasting two different ways of making the calculation. The first uses commodity weights from the initial year and is referred to as a Laspeyres index, named after the economist Étienne Laspeyres, who developed the index in 1871. Price indices had been constructed earlier, notably in 1707 by William Fleetwood, Bishop of Ely, who had been consulted by a student at Oxford threatened with the loss of his fellowship since a fifteenth-century stipulation ruled out students with annual incomes over £5. Fleetwood was able to demonstrate the contemporary value of £5.[8]

---

[8] *Editors*: The details of the story and the place of Fleetwood in the history of price indices are given in Chance (1966).

The second way of making the calculation makes use of commodity weights from the final year and is named after the economist Hermann Paasche.

The choice of weights matters, since the use of Laspeyres weights "tends to overstate the rise in the cost of living by not allowing any substitution between goods to occur" (Diewert 1998, p. 48). This "substitution bias" gives too much weight to goods or services whose relative prices have increased, goods which households can be expected to adjust away from. This in turn matters, since Laspeyres weights are widely used in official price indices. Indeed, the situation is aggravated by the fact that the weights commonly relate, not to the initial year, but to an earlier reference year (referred to in the ILO manual on price indices as a Lowe index [ILO et al. 2004]). As is noted by Kathleen Beegle and her coauthors, "CPI weights are often many years old. As of July 2012, for example, 13 per cent of the African population was living in countries in which the CPI basket was based on data from the 1990s (or earlier)" (2016, p. 37). The Liberian statistical office has commented drily on the country's CPI that it "suffers from outdated goods and services in the consumption basket based on a 1964 survey which was conducted only in Monrovia [the capital]. A new basket of goods and services needs to be reconstructed" (LISGIS 2016, p. i).

Substitution bias is just one of the potentially serious issues confronting the construction of the CPI. There is substitution not only between products but also between sources. A product or service may be supplied from within the household, and failure to allow for such home production may influence recorded inflation. The 2012 ILO survey of 169 countries shows that 37 per cent failed to cover home production (ILO 2013, p. 5). There may have been a shift towards purchasing food outside the home; indeed, this may have been a switch towards a relatively more expensive source where other factors—such as location of employment—determine the choice. (This is an example of a situation where an approach to household behaviour based on capabilities may be illuminating.) In terms of purchased consumption, there may have been shifts in the outlets: "With the advent of discount retail stores in some countries in Africa, failure to adjust where the price data are collected is expected to lead to an overestimate of inflation" (Beegle et al. 2016, p. 36). Substitution also involves new products and the related issue of quality change, issues that received considerable attention in the United States in the Boskin Report and commentaries (Boskin et al. 1996, 1998; Diewert 1998; Deaton 1998).

The weights are only part of the story. When attention is turned to the price quotations, it may be seen that two crucial dimensions are the degree of commodity detail and the extent of coverage of different outlets. Here there is a great deal of variation. In the case of Africa, Beegle and her colleagues note that Statistics South Africa "regularly collects 65,000 price quotations from 27,000 outlets [whereas in] other African countries, the number of CPI quotations ranges from 1,150 (São Tomé and Príncipe) to 51,170 (Ethiopia)" (2016, p. 36).

The difficulties in obtaining reliable data on consumer prices has been graphically described in the case of the Côte d'Ivoire:

> It has been revealed to be impossible to derive reliable/comparable unit prices from surveys. Quantities are declared in units that can be very heterogeneous across space, like bags or basins; furthermore, many times, units are not specified. . . . the 1988–96 price data proved to be very inconsistent with the World Bank figures . . . as well as with the IMF figures . . . in particular with respect to the high inflation following the CFA franc devaluation of 1994. The communicated price data showed very modest inflation in 1994 and 1995, in contrast with the World Bank or IMF figures, which record a 26 per cent inflation rate for 1994 and 14 per cent for 1995. . . . We could not elucidate the origin of such discrepancies. (Cogneau, Houngbedji, and Mesplé-Somps 2016, pp. 324–255)

To sum up this discussion of the domestic CPI, it is evident that there are many potential shortcomings that should lead us to be cautious in using these statistics. In particular, for a variety of reasons, there are arguments that the domestic CPI may overstate the rate of inflation. In this case the poverty line will be adjusted by too much when updated for changes in prices, leading poverty to be overestimated. Conversely, when having developed a new poverty line and using the CPI to calculate the figure to be applied in earlier years, that figure will be set too low, causing an underestimation of poverty at those times. If that is the case, then a fall in the poverty rate will be understated by uncritical use of the CPI.

How large is this problem in practice? One commonly used method to try to answer the question is based on the use of Engel's Law, introduced in chapter 2, which states that the proportion of total spending going to food declines as total spending rises. The idea behind the method is that changes over time in this proportion that cannot be explained by changes in other factors must imply that real incomes (and total spending) have changed. "As a result, any systematic difference over time in the food budget shares of demographically similar households at the same level of real income (CPI deflated) and facing the same relative prices is assumed to reflect mismeasurement in the CPI" (Dabalen et al. 2016, p. 6). The method is not without critics. It relies on the stability of the relationship described by Engel's Law, attributing unexplained change in consumption patterns to one assumed cause.[9] However, it has been applied to investigate possible biases in CPIs in a number of industrialised and developing countries, including the United States, Canada, Australia, New Zealand, Norway, China, Korea, Indonesia, Brazil, and Mexico. Andrew Dabalen and his colleagues apply the method to data from sixteen Sub-Saharan African countries:

> Correcting for CPI bias, poverty falls significantly faster than suggested by current international poverty numbers in 11 countries [Côte d'Ivoire, Demo-

---

[9] *Editors:* Logan (2009) investigates an alternative explanation, while Almås, Beatty, and Crossley (2018) argue that the method is internally inconsistent in its assumptions.

cratic Republic of Congo, Ethiopia, Madagascar, Mozambique, Nigeria, Rwanda, Senegal, South Africa, Tanzania, and Togo]. Based on our estimates, the difference in poverty reduction resulting from CPI-bias adjustment could be as large as −5.7 percentage points per year in Tanzania between 2008 and 2012. Only two countries, Uganda and Ghana, experience significantly slower poverty reduction rates with the correction of CPI bias [around five percentage points per year in Ghana]. The change in poverty trend due to CPI bias correction is statistically insignificant in Mauritius, Cameroon, and Burkina Faso. (2016, p. 3)

The authors conclude that their estimates give "cautious evidence" (p. 20) that African countries may have been more successful in reducing poverty than previously thought.

Do the poor pay more?

When aggregating expenditure across households to arrive at the weight to be applied to each commodity, the CPI typically weights households according to their total consumption, thus giving, in what has come to be labelled "plutocratic bias" (Prais 1959; Muellbauer 1977), more importance to the expenditure of the rich than that of the poor. As Beegle and her coauthors observe, "Plutocratic weights are the natural choice in the deflation of economic aggregates, such as national accounts, but not generally the first choice for measuring poverty and welfare" (2016, p. 37). This introduces the question of "price indices for the poor," which was already mentioned in chapter 3.

There are two respects in which a price index for the poor would depart from the national CPI: the weight attached to different goods and services, and the price quotations applied when measuring inflation. Both differences—in the weights and in the price quotations for goods of comparable quality—are potentially significant.[10] The poor spend a higher share of their income on necessities, notably food. And the prices they face may differ. Due to lack of transport, they use more expensive corner shops rather than cheaper out-of-town supermarkets. They may be constrained to pay for energy with prepayment meters that charge higher prices. If the poor buy smaller quantities, they will fail to benefit from discounts for buying in bulk.

The potential difference that could arise from the application of specific price indices for the poor may be seen from countries that construct price indices based on a budget for basic needs. In the case of Bangladesh, such a Basic Needs Price Index (BNPI) has already been incorporated into World Bank estimates, and the BNPI shows a higher rate of price increase: 85.8 per cent over the period 2005 to 2010, compared with 44 per cent according to the official CPI

---

[10] This may involve bringing together information from different sources. For example, in their study of the Côte d'Ivoire, Grootaert and Kanbur (1994) combine price data from the ICP with expenditure share data from the LSMS.

series reported in the WDI (Ferreira et al. 2015, p. 63). Updating from 2005 to 2010 on this basis would make a considerable difference to the estimated poverty rate: using the CPI, the poverty rate is estimated to fall from 50.5 per cent in 2005 to 24.6 per cent in 2010, whereas with the BNPI the fall is much more modest—to 43.3 per cent (Giménez and Jolliffe 2014, figure 1; World Bank 2013, p. 142).

Evidence from elsewhere is mixed, and care is needed in its interpretation. For example, little difference was found between the changes in the CPI and inflation for the rural poor in Indonesia over 2003 to 2011, but large differences were found for the urban poor, who suffered higher inflation (USAID 2013). The impact of increases in the rice price on the rural poor, who are both consumers and producers of rice, was ambiguous. The same pattern—little difference in rural areas but higher inflation for the urban poor—applied in Ireland over 1996 to 2001, while over 1989 to 1996 the changes in both rural and urban areas in the price index for the poor were similar to those in the index for the population as a whole (Murphy and Garvey 2004). However, these analyses, assuming as they do that poor and nonpoor households faced the same prices, take into account only a difference in weights. The same applies to the experimental study of a CPI for the poor in the United States, which concluded that the urban poor and the general population faced similar price trends for 1984 to 1994; the authors note explicitly that, "within the framework of the CPI program, the only way to construct price indices for demographic subgroups of the population is to adjust the expenditure weights to represent those groups. There is no data for prices paid for items by specific groups of consumers, [or] the outlets in which different consumers are most likely to shop" (Garner, Johnson, and Kokoski 1996, p. 37). Likewise, as seen in chapter 3, Deaton and Dupriez (2011) studied the sensitivity of estimates of global poverty to the use of "poverty weights" when constructing PPPs while using prices that were common for poor and nonpoor.

The prices faced by the poor have in fact been the subject of an extensive literature in developed countries (see, for example, Caplovitz 1968). The presumption that I advanced earlier for the reasons given, that the poor face higher prices, has not always been borne out by the data. A good example of a detailed investigation is the study by Blow and Leicester (2012) of grocery purchases in the United Kingdom in 2006. Goods were defined at the barcode level, which ensured that comparisons were made of prices paid for identical products, overcoming problems of variation in the quality of good purchased. The authors found that, on average, it was richer households that paid more than poorer households, but the differences in prices across income groups were small: "typically only 1–2 per cent between the highest and lowest" (Blow and Leicester 2012, p. 3). However, the study was not able to consider whether rich and poor face a different change over time in prices. The poverty-specific surveys carried out by the Asian Development Bank (ADB), covering sixteen countries in Asia and the Pacific, also tended to show the reverse of the pattern typically presumed: "In general, poverty-specific price data were lower than the 2005 ICP Asia Pacific survey prices" (ADB 2008, p. 44). The price data were obtained by specifying types of goods that tended to be bought by the poor and collecting the data in shops and markets thought to be frequented by the poor. The percentage of prices that were lower for the poor ranged from 75 per cent in Nepal to over 90 per cent in India, Indonesia, Thailand, and Vietnam. These results relate to a particular part of the world and may depend on certain features of the analysis, such as the treatment of different quantities used in the price surveys, but suggest that the second ingredient in PPPs for the poor—the prices faced—is potentially important. Taking both a change in the weights and the prices faced by the poor into account, the ADB concluded that "the application of the new PPPs based on poverty-specific price survey data is likely to alter the estimates of poverty incidence" (p. 65).

As far as the checklist is concerned, the user of poverty statistics for any country should be cautious about accepting at face value statements of the kind that "the poverty line is indexed by changes in consumer prices" and may need to hunt for any evidence of differences in prices paid by the poor.

THE HARD GRAFT

It is easy for me, sitting comfortably in Oxford, to criticise the data that are collected. The hard work is done in statistical offices in the field, negotiating with many parties and training the staff who carry out the surveys or who collect administrative data and information on prices. It is the interviewers who have to translate the ideal survey design into actual returns, working in conditions that are often difficult and sometimes dangerous. The practical problems of carrying out a survey should not be underestimated. Sterling Chadee, director of the Trinidad and Tobago Central Statistical Office, when describing carrying out fieldwork, identified dogs and crime as two of the many problems faced (*Trinidad and Tobago Guardian*, 26 April 2014).

Sampling and interviewing problems

The validity of the sampling approach depends first on the sample design and secondly on how the sampling is carried out. At both stages, things may go wrong—in addition to the inherent random sampling error that is associated with any sample. We are aiming at an estimate of the proportion, H for head count, of the population with consumption below an externally specified amount, say the International Poverty Line. If the sample is a simple random one, drawn from units that are, as far as we know, the same on average in other respects, so that each household has an equal chance of selection, then the estimated "standard error" associated with an observed sample proportion H^* below the poverty line is the square root of $H^*(1-H^*)/N$ where N is the sample size.[11] If we take a 95 per cent confidence interval (often referred to as the "margin of error" in media reports of survey results) of plus or minus twice the standard error (strictly it should be 1.96 times, but twice is easier to remember), then with an observed head count of 0.3 (bearing in mind that these are proportions varying between 0 and 1, not percentages) and a sample of 4,800 (as in the Pakistan example below), the confidence interval is ±0.0132, or ±1.32 percentage points around a poverty rate of 30 per cent. This does not seem particularly concerning, although it would mean that we would be unable to distinguish statistically between poverty rates that vary between years by just a percentage point or two.

In reality, samples are more complex. First, where we are sampling units that we know to be different, such as households in rural and urban areas, the sample may be stratified on that basis. Such stratification in effect means that there are separate samples for each of the different populations. Secondly, the typical survey, for reasons of cost and convenience, chooses to cluster its sampling geographically. There are then two stages, with clusters first being sampled and then households selected randomly from within the chosen clusters. With more complex design, the calculation of the sampling error is affected. The ratio of the new variance of the statistic in question, here the poverty rate, to that from a simple random sample is known as the "design effect," or "deff." Stratification may improve the accuracy, with deff being less than 1, but clustering tends to raise it above 1. The illustrative calculations made by Deaton (1997, table 1.5) of the impact on the mean household per capita expenditure in Pakistan in 1991 showed that the standard error adjusted for the design effect was some 70 per cent higher than that calculated assuming a simple random sample. Assuming the same deff of 1.7 for the poverty rate, this would take the confidence interval to ±2.2 percentage points, which is more worrying but still not large.[12]

Samples may also be smaller than the 4,800 used in the example just given. The median sample size for LSMS surveys is 3,600, although DHS and MICS surveys are typically larger, and this is also true for many national income and expenditure surveys (see table 4.1). But the range of sample sizes is wide. Small

---

[11] The standard error is a measure of the variability of a statistic across all alternative possible samples of the same size. Conceptually, it is the standard deviation of the distribution of the estimates of the statistic, in this case the poverty head count, calculated from all possible samples.

[12] In their review of LSMS surveys, Scott, Steele, and Temesgen (2005) warn that "the design effect varies not just among variables, but also geographically within a country for the same variable and for a specific variable over time . . . [and] can be hugely different between countries" (p. 541). A wide range of figures is also reported in Pettersson and Silva (2005, table VII.2).

sample size may especially be a problem when poverty rates are considered for particular groups in the population, such as different ethnic groups, or for regions. If, say, the sample in question were only 1,000 and we again allow for a design effect of the same amount, the confidence interval around a poverty rate of 30 per cent would rise to ±4.9 percentage points, which is substantial. Now imagine we have two groups, or two regions, one with a poverty rate of 30 per cent and one with a rate of 40 per cent, each rate estimated with a sample size of 1,000. The confidence interval for the *difference* between the two rates (in this case the formula is not given here), taking into account the same assumed design effect as before, would be as large as ±7 percentage points. It would run from 3 per cent (10 minus 7) to 17 per cent (10 plus 7), leaving us in considerable doubt as to the true size of the difference in poverty rates in the population from which the samples were drawn. The official assessment of poverty in Mozambique using the 2014–2015 household budget survey warns that provincial-level poverty rates "should be interpreted with caution due to relatively small sample sizes" (Mozambique Ministry of Economics and Finance 2016, p. 4). In the case of the Solomon Islands, there are large overlaps in the 95 per cent confidence intervals for the estimated poverty rates of most provinces (Solomon Islands National Statistical Office 2015a, figure 2). The US Census Bureau publishes a margin of error alongside all its estimates of poverty rates, but this practice is by no means universal in other countries. "How big a sample is used?" is a question for the checklist.

There is also scope for the estimates to be biased as a result of design faults. A cautionary example in the case of poverty measurement is provided by the early years of the Living Standards Survey in the Côte d'Ivoire. As described by Demery and Grootaert, the survey

> had a sampling bias, which seriously affected estimates of population statistics such as household size. The bias arose from sampling procedures that overrepresented larger dwellings. . . . Estimates of household expenditure per capita in the early years of the survey [1985] are found to be significantly underestimated, resulting in an overestimation of poverty. The sampling bias also resulted in an underestimation of the upward trend in poverty during 1985–88. (1993, p. 263)

The conduct of the survey may mean that the achieved sample departs from that intended. Natural events, for example, may disrupt the planned sample. The report of the Nepal Central Bureau of Statistics on the Annual Survey of Households 2014–2015 has a section on the "Impact of the Earthquake" which explains that "during the survey period, major earthquakes and its aftershocks stunned the country. As an effect, the survey work had to be ceased at [a] few predetermined areas. The survey work could not be completed in 12 PSUs [primary sampling units—the survey clusters]" (Nepal Central Bureau of Statistics 2016, p. 3). The report on the 2012–2013 household survey in the Solomon

Islands noted the impact of the February 2013 tsunami on response rates in the islands of one province (Solomon Islands National Statistical Office 2015, p. 3). Or there may be an emergency of another kind—data collection for the 2014 household income and expenditure survey in Liberia came to a halt after only six of the twelve planned months due to the outbreak of the Ebola epidemic in West Africa. In this case the six months of data collected were reported as being nationally representative, but "seasonal impacts on consumption and expenditures are not reflected in the data, introducing a potential source of bias" (LISGIS 2016, pp. i–ii, x).[13]

Sampling issues are important but may be of less concern than other forms of error, to which I now turn.

The missing

"One of the most fundamental inequalities is between those who are counted and those who are not" (UN 2014, p. 19). In the present context, those who are not counted are those who are omitted from the sampling frame for the household survey and those who are covered but are not respondents to the survey. In statistical terms, these omissions matter to the extent that those omitted are more likely or less likely to be living in extreme poverty. If the poverty rate is the same among the missing population as among those covered, then the poverty estimate obtained by applying the rate for those covered to the whole population is accurate. If the PovcalNet poverty rate is estimated at 20 per cent, then this can be applied to the whole recorded population of the country, not just to that part represented by the surveyed population. There are, however, good reasons to expect those missing from the survey data to differ in their poverty incidence.

Why are people missing? At the top end of the scale, the well-off may be less willing to take part in surveys and therefore are underrepresented. In that case, it would not be appropriate to apply a rate of 20 per cent to those not responding to the survey; zero might be the better assumption. Poverty would be overstated, both in absolute numbers and as an overall rate. At the other end of the scale, those in refugee camps are not typically covered by household surveys and are much more at risk of poverty. In their case, it would not be appropriate to apply a rate of 20 per cent, and the existing practice would understate poverty. For example, in Colombia more than 10 per cent of the population are internally displaced persons, and a study for 2005 showed that the

---

[13] *Editors:* Besides natural disasters or health emergencies, problems may stem from difficulties in staff management. In 2016, the Italian national statistical institute was forced to estimate expenditure data by statistical techniques, which are used *inter alia* for poverty estimation, for about 1,000 households that could not be interviewed in December owing to "contractual issues with the agency in charge of fieldwork" (Istat 2017, p. 18).

poverty rate among this group was 95 per cent, compared to a national poverty rate of 50 per cent (Ibañez 2008).

It is important to distinguish between underrepresentation (those who are covered by the survey but whose response rates are lower) and noncoverage. In the former case, it is possible to make ex post corrections by reweighting the respondents, and this is a common practice in both household surveys and population censuses. For example, there may be good grounds for supposing that urban slum dwellers are underrepresented (Carr-Hill 2013), in which case this can be addressed by oversampling or by ex post stratification. However, where a whole category—such as the institutionalized elderly or pastoralists— are missing from the survey, then it is not simply a question of multiplying up the observed frequencies.

What levels of response are achieved in practice? In the case of the DHS and MICS, which have been used to measure nonmonetary poverty, response is impressively high. The sixty-six surveys conducted by the DHS programme between 1990 and 2000 achieved an average household response rate of 97.5 per cent (Vassen, Tham, and Lê 2005, p. 503). Response by households in the eighteen surveys of the MICS programme carried out in 2014 averaged 96.9 per cent (information taken from survey reports on the UNICEF MICS website).[14] Response rates in surveys used to measure monetary poverty can also reach these levels. For example, household response was 94.1 per cent in the 2011–2012 household budget survey in Tanzania (Tanzania National Bureau of Statistics 2014, p. 10) and 95.2 per cent in the Uganda National Survey for 2012–2013 (Uganda Bureau of Statistics 2014, p. 4), while response was over 90 per cent in four of the eight LSMS surveys described by Scott, Steele, and Temesgen (2005, p. 537). However, the pattern is not universal. In South Africa, response to the 2014–2015 income and expenditure survey in the populous province that includes Johannesburg was only 65 per cent, despite participation in the survey being compulsory (the rate for the country as a whole was 85 per cent). And substantially lower rates have characterised many surveys in high-income countries, where there has often been a falling level of response in recent decades. Response failed to reach 80 per cent in ten of the EU-15 countries in the European Union's harmonised SILC surveys in 2013 and was below 70 per cent in six of these—in Belgium, Denmark, Ireland, Luxembourg, Sweden, and the United Kingdom (Di Meglio et al. 2017, figure 2.1, overall personal response rates). The collapse of communism in Central and Eastern Europe saw a reduction in the willingness of households to participate in official surveys. In Hungary, response to the budget survey fell from an average of 78 per cent in the three surveys in 1983–1987 to 61 per cent in the surveys in 1993–1995

---

[14]Households where nobody was at home in repeated visits are excluded from the calculations of response in the MICS reports. For example, 4.5 per cent of households in Cameroon and 5.9 per cent in Zimbabwe were classified as "unoccupied,"

(Flemming and Micklewright 2000, p. 889). Average response fell short of 60 per cent in 1996–2000 in the budget surveys of Bulgaria, Estonia, and Poland as well as Hungary (Kordos 2005, p. 583).

The exclusion of certain groups by design may be quite extensive. In the case of the Japanese Family Income and Expenditure Survey, for example, those excepted are (1) institutional households; (2) students living alone; (3) households in which the household business is a restaurant or boarding house which shares the same dwelling; (4) households with boarders who share meals (even if this is not the main source of income); (5) households with four or more live-in employees; (6) households where the head is absent for more than three months in the year; and (7) foreigners (Lise et al. 2014, p. 5). In other countries, those not covered may be

1. People resident in a household but not treated as a member, especially servants
2. Foreign officials or military
3. People living in institutions, including hospitals, care homes, prisons, military barracks, factory barracks, religious orders, schools, and universities
4. The homeless
5. Those living in refugee camps
6. Mobile populations, including nomads/pastoralists, guest workers, and those in the course of migration
7. Those living in war zones or dangerous areas

Not all of those in the categories listed above are unrecorded: for example, a young person may be away at school but recorded as a family member. A household survey may include a migration module that tracks internally displaced persons. However, people in the categories listed are at risk of being underrepresented, and in many cases they are indeed missing.

The groups just listed are all potentially important in developing countries. Even in the case of the institutional population, where one tends to think more naturally of developed countries, there are significant institutionalized populations in countries that feature in the poverty calculations. The percentage of the elderly who are institutionalized in Europe and the United States is around 5 per cent, but it is around 3 per cent in Mexico and 2 per cent in Chile (ODI 2015, p. 4), figures that are higher than in Spain (1.3 per cent). The prison population is 0.71 per cent in the United States, but 0.58 per cent in Kenya, 0.4 per cent in El Salvador, and 0.34 per cent in Chile (ODI 2015, p. 6). For others of the groups, there are good reasons to expect their prevalence to be higher in the case of developing countries, such as where there is rapid urbanisation and greater flows of workers in a changing labour market. The significance of the last category—those in dangerous areas—is illustrated by the report of the Sri Lanka Household Income and Expenditure Survey in 2009–2010 that the survey had failed "to cover the entire Northern province as Mannar, Kilinochchi and Mullaithivu districts were out of reach for survey due to massive mine clearance and [resettlement]" (Sri Lanka Department of Census and Statistics 2011, p. 2). All of the northern and eastern provinces were excluded from the 1990–1991 and 1995–1996 surveys due to the earlier civil war.

In order to assess the scale of the problem, there are two requirements. The first is the estimation of the total missing population, relevant to the population total—see below. Overall global totals are not easy to assess. For the groups of nomads/pastoralists, refugees, and those in the military, hospitals, or prisons, Carr-Hill (2015, table 1) gives a minimum of 185 million and a maximum of 253 million, but the addition of other categories would undoubtedly lead to considerably higher figures. The second is an assessment of the proportion of the missing population living in poverty, in order to correct the total calculation. Here the statistical requirements are even more challenging. While it is likely that the incidence of poverty is high in some of the categories, such as those living in refugee camps or the homeless, other groups may be quite heterogeneous, as was found, for instance, in the study of migrant workers in Vietnam by Pincus and Sender (2008).

There are a number of possible sources of information. These include separate surveys or counts, administrative data, and exploiting new technology and data sources. For example, in the case of Afghanistan, the national household survey stratifies on the nomadic population, with the same instrument that aims to enumerate the Kuchi (largely nomadic) population. It may be necessary to employ statistical methods different from those used to date. As was pointed out in the UN *Handbook on Poverty Statistics*, "administrative files provide a first line of potentially useful information in this connection, especially in those instances where attention is paid by policy-makers to disadvantaged groups and where officials are required to monitor conditions and report on actions taken in this area" (Kamanou, Ward, and Havinga 2005, p. 209). Assessing the quantitative impact of adjustments for the missing population would depend on co-operation at the country level, including from high-income countries (on inflows of migrants and refugees). It would require additional funding.

To sum up, the checklist includes the need to be aware of people who are "missing" from the poverty count, and of any adjustments for survey underrepresentation and noncoverage by surveys. As the total living below the International Poverty Line falls over time, the missing population will become proportionately more significant. Moreover, a number of the groups—such as refugees, the homeless, and those living in war zones—have a particular claim on our compassion.

Measuring the total population

The World Bank's poverty figures are often stated in terms of percentages of the total population, but it is the absolute number of human beings living in poverty that is our ultimate concern. To know this, we have to have good population estimates. The 2013 estimate of 767 million living below the International Poverty Line was reached by multiplying the proportions below the threshold in each country by the population of that country and then adding to arrive at a grand total for the world as a whole. The process is then reversed, dividing 767 million by the total world population to arrive at the percentage living in poverty. Errors in the population figures potentially affect the measurement of the scale of the problem and the geographical composition of the poor. The need for scrutiny of the population data is already apparent from the discussion in the previous section of those who are missing from household surveys, and similar considerations apply to the most common source of population data: censuses of the population.

The potential significance of errors in the population data may be illustrated by the case of a country where the census is carried out to the highest professional standards (and where the requirement to conduct a population census is actually embedded in the Constitution): the United States. The US Census Bureau has long been engaged in measures to improve coverage. The report on the 2010 census of population (US Department of Commerce 2012) based its measure of coverage on a comparison of the census numbers with those derived from a "dual system estimate." The dual system estimate is based on a post-enumeration survey that is in turn used to generate statistical estimates of the population total. The difference between the total so generated and the census count is the "net undercount." For the 2010 census, the net undercount turned out to be extremely small: both figures gave a total US population of 300.7 million, the difference being 36,000 (US Department of Commerce 2012, table 3). However, this is a *net* figure: there are both pluses and minuses. The Census Bureau showed that there were in fact 284.7 million correct census enumerations. In the remaining 16.0 million cases, there were either erroneous enumerations (10 million) or whole-person census imputations (6 million). A substantial number of those erroneously enumerated (8.5 million) were duplicates, typically on account of second homes. The loss of 16.0 million was almost exactly counterbalanced, when it came to the net figure, by the 16 million who were found to be missing. Some of the missing may have been covered by the whole-person imputations, but even if all were subtracted, this would still leave 10.0 million. The importance of there being both additions and subtractions arises from the fact that these affect different groups of people. The US analysis of the 2010 census showed, for example, that there was an estimated net *undercount* for renters of 1.09 per cent, but a net *overcount* for owner-occupiers of 0.57 per cent (US Department of Commerce 2012, p. 2). There was a significant net overcount for non-Hispanic whites (0.84 per cent), but significant undercounts for Hispanics (1.54 per cent), non-Hispanic blacks (2.07 per cent), and American Indians on reservation (4.88 per cent) (US

Department of Commerce 2012, table 7, p. 15). If the incidence of poverty and deprivation differs systematically across the groups affected, then it is the 16 million adjustment that is relevant rather than the (close to zero) net undercount.

The US experience, in a country with best-practice census methods, is a salutary warning. What can be said about the sources of population data around the world? There are good reasons to believe that similar issues arise across all countries. As it was put by Kamanou, Ward, and Havinga:

> Problems can arise, however, where some sections of the population do not belong to a defined housing unit or are periodically confined to institutions, such as hospitals, nursing homes, asylums and prisons. Others not listed may not have any fixed abode and thus regularly sleep [or "doss down"] on the streets and in common public areas like parks and railways stations. Even countries like the USA have encountered these problems in census inquiries, and census officials around the world continue to face difficulties in correctly enumerating subgroups like the homeless and illegal immigrants. This problem invariably results in the significant undercount. (2005, p. 228)

Of particular relevance in many developing countries is the role of migration in leading to undercounting (Bhalla and McCormick 2009). In the case of Pakistan, for example, Gazdar comments on the problems with the enumeration of international immigrants "who might be refugees, or whose residential status in the country might be considered semi-legal or illegal. The affected group might also include some legal migrants who nevertheless feel discriminated against" (2003, p. 5).

Even when there is an accurate census, there is the basic issue of estimating the population total between census dates and, in particular, since the last census. As the World Bank's then–chief economist for Africa commented in 2013 in an article titled "Africa's Statistical Tragedy,"

> Most of these [population totals] are extrapolated from the last census. Since the standard for population census periodicity is 10 years, extrapolation is largely the rule. However, in Africa, only 32 countries representing 65 percent of the total population have had a census during the last 10 years. In Angola, for instance, the most recent census was in 1975. Ethiopia, Africa's third most populous nation, had its first census covering the whole country only in 2007. (Devarajan 2013, p. S11)

In the case of Angola, a population census was in fact held the next year, in 2014. This was the first, not since 1975, which was the year Angola became independent from Portugal, but since 1970. Independence was followed by a civil war that did not end until 2002. The 1970 census had recorded the Angolan population at 5.6 million people, while by 2014 the figure had risen four-and-a-half-fold, to 25.8 million.[15] The World Development Indicators for 2015 gave an estimate of the population for 2013 of only 21.5 million. In the circumstances, the WDI estimate might be seen as not that far out. But if the poverty rate were 30 per cent (the most recent figure for Angola from Povcal-Net for the percentage of the population beneath the International Poverty Line, which refers to 2008), a shortfall in the population estimate of about 4 million would mean that the number of Angolans in poverty is underestimated by around 1 million people.

The discussion above has been framed in terms of population censuses, but this is not the only source of population data, and a number of countries have abandoned decennial or quinquennial censuses in favour of using register or other administrative data. Such data also have an important role in extrapolation from the most recent census. (It should be noted that the concern here is not with predicting the future, but with establishing the present population.) The possible margins of error are examined in World Bank (2015), which cites the example of Bangladesh, where, prior to the 2011 population census, the population for that year was projected by the Bangladesh Bureau of Statistics to be some 150 million, but was 164 million according to the UN World Population Prospects 2008 revision. (The 2011 census gave a result close to the former figure.) Moreover, the projections made for a given year change over time. The National Research Council study of population projections noted that "the estimate of the world population in 1950 changed 17 times—13 times upward and 4 times downward—in UN *Demographic Yearbooks* published from 1951 to 1996" (National Research Council 2000, p. 42). In turn, these revisions to the population estimates cause revisions to the poverty estimates. These may be highly significant. In the case of Bangladesh, for example, the number of people estimated to be living below the International Poverty Line was 71 million in 2011, when population data from the WDI 2011 or earlier were employed, but 65 million on the basis of population data from the WDI 2014 and later (World Bank 2015, p. 232, figure 6.1). The review by the US National Research Council (2000) of population projections found that the average absolute error in country population projections five years ahead was 4.8 per cent. The World Bank suggests (2015, p. 232) that this is a reasonable basis for assessing potential error in the population figures underlying the poverty counts and notes that, at present levels, this would mean that some 50 million people would be misclassified.

---

[15] The figure comes from the definitive results to the 2014 census (Instituto Nacional de Estatística 2016, p. 15). The preliminary results, published only four months after the census week, gave a figure of 24.4 million (Instituto Nacional de Estatística 2014, p. 27), and the same source reports the 1970 population (p. 5).

Asking the questions

The asking of the questions is not in itself necessarily straightforward. The report on the Solomon Islands 2012–2013 household survey listed the following "main non-sampling errors" (Solomon Islands National Statistical Office 2015, pp. 4–5):

- Interviewer and respondent fatigue during interview periods
- Misunderstandings in executing the survey on the part of both interviewers and households
- The fact that the questionnaire was in English, which was a second language for interviewers and respondents, leading to problems in communication
- Lack of coordination among interview teams leading to some interviews being missed or incomplete
- Weather, where long periods of rain (and a tsunami) affected enumeration and led to data collection being stopped

The success of the interviewing process depends, of course, on how well the questionnaire is designed. The problems that arise in the framing of the questions are well illustrated by the measurement of a key variable: consumption.

In estimating consumption from recorded expenditure, the first issue concerns the nature of the report. To begin with, *who* is making the report? Ideally, all members of the household should report spending. In practice, responses may only be available from adults, or even only from a primary respondent, such as the head of household. Next one has to ask about the nature of the response. How far is it based on retrospective recall, and how far on prospective record-keeping? The diary method, requiring respondents to maintain a continuous record of all spending, has evident advantages, but inevitably involves some degree of retrospection. Dutifully itemizing each gin-and-tonic as it is consumed may be good for record-keeping, but may make for a less enjoyable evening. Wambile and his coauthors go so far as to argue that

> the theoretical benefits of diaries often fail to materialize because of measurement errors that arise during survey implementation and poor maintenance of diaries. For example, if household respondents are illiterate, innumerate or unmotivated and require assistance from enumerators to complete the diary, a seven-day diary for example, may become a seven-day recall survey with all of the errors associated with recall design (such as recall error and telescoping). (2016, p. 3)

The third issue concerns the length of the recording period. Both memory and willingness to maintain a diary impose limits on the period that can be selected. Short periods, such as seven days, raise the issue of irregular purchases. While expenditure may be smoother than income, spending is less smooth than consumption. Different periods can be adopted for different categories of goods, with a longer period for goods or services that are expected to be purchased less frequently.

The fourth issue concerns the timing of the reporting period. Where the period is less than a year, timing may be of critical importance, particularly where there is a strong seasonality to income and home production. As expressed by the World Bank, "When livelihoods are closely linked with agriculture, well-being will also follow the seasonal pattern . . . with relatively better off periods around harvest time and lean seasons, typically post planting when stocks have dwindled" (World Bank 2015, p. 195).

These may be considered arcane points of limited practical importance. However, experience has shown that they can be highly significant. A well-known example is that of the National Sample Survey (NSS) in India, which is described by Angus Deaton as follows:

> Between 1989 and 1998, the NSS experimented with different recall periods, replacing the traditional 30 day recall period for all goods with a 7 day recall for food and tobacco, and with a 365 day period for durable goods and some other infrequently purchased items. The sample was randomly divided, and half were given the old questionnaire and half the new, so that it is possible to make a clean evaluation of the effects of the change. The shorter reporting period increased reported expenditure on food by around 30%, and total consumption by about 17%. Because there are so many Indians close to the poverty line, the 17% increase was enough to reduce the measured headcount ratio by a half, removing almost 200 million people from poverty. (2005, p. 16)

The potential consequences of the questionnaire design are well demonstrated by another experiment carried out in Tanzania intended to provide information as to the implications of different approaches. The researchers took as the "gold standard" the case where there are individually kept diaries with daily supervision, noting that it costs almost ten times as much as a recall interview. As they observed, this reflects the resources needed for careful tracking "of all commodity in-flows (harvests, purchases, gifts, stock reductions), out-flows (sales, gifts, stock increases, food fed to animals), daily attendance at meals, and acquisitions and disposals by children and other dependents" (Gibson et al. 2015, p. 467). They randomly assigned eight alternative survey designs to 4,000 households, where these included household diaries with less frequent visits and recall interviews where the recall period varied from seven days to a month, including a "usual month." They find that "the results are consistent with errors in measured consumption that are negatively correlated with true values, especially for food and especially in rural areas. Such correlations are plausible as survey reporting tasks become harder for richer households with more varied consumption. This negative correlation creates mean reversion [that is, the measured values will be closer to the average than the true values]"

(p. 474). The implications for poverty measurement depend on the location relative to the means in the different cases, but these were quite close, and where the poverty threshold is below the mean this implies that the poverty rate is understated.

These issues are important in rich countries as well. In 2014, the Italian statistical office implemented an extensive methodological revision of its household budget survey, including changes in sample design and field organisation, a doubling of the diary recording period from seven to fourteen days, and differences in commodity detail. Following the revision, consumption expenditure turned out to be greater than previously measured, especially as a result of the changes made to commodity detail and recording periods; expenditure was found to be higher than earlier estimates particularly for households in the tails of the distribution, for households living in the south, and for larger households (see Istat 2015, p. 150). The improved estimates at the bottom of the expenditure distribution had a considerable impact on poverty rates: taking the average for 2005–2013, relative poverty rates were revised downward by about a fifth, and absolute poverty rates by almost a quarter.

As this illustrates, the measurement of consumption is likely to exhibit variability with respect to several aspects of the survey design and questionnaires, including changes in diary or recall period, changes in the degree of commodity detail, changes in the commodity basket, and changes in who answers the questions.

Notwithstanding the problems in collecting expenditure data, the World Bank is firmly in favour of measuring poverty using a yardstick of low consumption rather than the alternative of low income, arguing, as noted in chapter 3, that these data are better collected than are income data:

> The poor are likely to consume a rather modest range of goods and services, primarily staple food items and a small set of essential nonfood goods and services. Compiling information on the consumption levels of the poor may thus be reasonably straightforward. By contrast, collecting information on the income levels of the poor can be much more complex. The poor are likely to be employed in the informal sector and may derive income from multiple sources . . . many of the developing world's poor are subsistence farmers with incomes that may be particularly difficult to calculate. (World Bank 2015, p. 33)

Problems with measuring household incomes in India are noted by the country's Planning Commission, which reports that a decision to measure living standards by consumption expenditure

> follows from the significant difficulties of capturing household incomes through recall-based (typically with a 30-day reference period) surveys canvased over a moving sample of households. These difficulties are particularly sizeable in the case of households with self-employment as the principal source of income. In

the case of such households, the flow of incomes may be staccato—at the time of harvests in the case of agriculture, uneven over the year (as in trading) or uncertain (in agriculture). Also, these households may be drawing incomes from more than one enterprise where a major proportion of these enterprises do not maintain full accounts/balance-sheets. Consequently, even in the absence of wilful under-reporting of incomes, there are serious problems in capturing the incomes of self-employed households. As per the NSS 68th Round (2011–12) survey, self-employed households form 49.8% of all households in rural India and 35.3% percent of all urban households. (Rangarajan 2014, p. 33)

Angus Deaton goes further, arguing in a developing country context that "all of the difficulties of measuring consumption—imputations, recall bias, seasonality, long questionnaires—apply with greater force to the measurement of income, and a host of additional issues arise" (1997, p. 29). Measurement of household incomes in surveys in rich industrialised countries is helped by a much greater share of the labour force being in the formal wage economy, but it is far from problem-free. Chapter 8 returns to the choice of consumption or income. But in neither case does it seem likely that the collection of information required for the classification of the poor will ever be "reasonably straightforward."

In some cases, collection of information for the different domains in the measurement of nonmonetary poverty may be simpler. Issues with regard to seasonality cause fewer difficulties for indicators such as childhood mortality or education (although they can affect indicators of employment opportunities). There is no need for purchasing power comparisons across countries, nor for collection of price data for different geographical areas or for different population groups. This is not to imply that all is plain sailing. For example, data on birth weight, age, and dates of birth and death all suffer from "heaping," the phenomenon where reporting by survey respondents favours certain numbers, commonly those ending in 0 or 5 (Channon, Padmadas, and McDonald 2011; Lyons-Amos and Stones 2017). Measurement of the human body for the anthropometric measures described in chapter 3 requires careful use of appropriate instruments by well-trained staff (Kostermans 1994). It is not just a matter of interviewers bringing along some bathroom scales and a tape measure at the same time as they are collecting other information.[16]

---

[16] *Editors*: The technical report on the collection of anthropometric data for the survey of Uzbekistan drawn on in Micklewright and Ismail (2001) listed the problems encountered, including: "instruments of measurement imposed terror on children, especially upon children from remote areas. . . . A child fled to the field and hid himself in the cabin of a tractor. . . . In the village of Burbonlyk there were rumors that the children were supposed to be measured in order to be sent to America. The villagers were scared and hid their children" (Expert Centre 1995, pp. 5 and 10).

TRIANGULATION

I have listed quite a number of reasons to regard with caution the poverty results from survey data on households. But just listing is not enough. We need to investigate their importance. As I have already indicated, there are grounds for believing that there are serious issues, but it is also helpful to cross-check the survey findings with alternative sources and to relate the picture depicted to other economic and social statistics. "Triangulation" with other information can help assess the validity of the conclusions and put them in context.

In considering what can be learned from triangulation, it is important to bear in mind that the alternative sources are themselves subject to error and problems of definition. There is a tendency to regard surveys as the potentially "guilty" party that has to be brought into line with other sources, such as the national accounts. But triangulation is not a one-way process; rather, it is a matter of trying to establish a coherent relationship.

Household surveys and national accounts

A major example of triangulation is provided by the comparison of household survey data with the national accounts. The national accounts cannot tell us anything about the situation of individuals, but we can compare the aggregates: the totals of consumption or income. On the face of it, we should arrive at the same total by adding up the individual household survey observations (suitably weighted to allow for the sampling fractions) as are found in the national accounts—at least after netting out an estimate of the consumption and income of the people who are not covered by surveys ("the missing" discussed earlier). In practice, there are wide discrepancies. For example, Deaton and Kozel report a survey estimate of consumption in India of around two-thirds of the national accounts estimate, with the figure having fallen substantially since the late 1960s, by five to ten percentage points each decade (2005, p. 180). Following earlier authors, over thirty years ago John Micklewright and I compared income totals recorded in the main UK household survey in the 1970s with those in the national accounts, distinguishing between different income sources (Atkinson and Micklewright 1983). We found only a small shortfall in the survey figures for wages, and the totals compared reasonably well for the major social security benefits. But the survey total for investment income was only some 50 to 55 per cent of the national accounts figure and for self-employment income around 70 per cent (allowing for problems of comparability in both cases), with both underreporting and differential nonresponse being key likely explanations. The importance for the measurement of poverty will differ with the type of consumption or the source of income. In the case of consumption in India, Deaton and Kozel cite research by Kulshrestha and Kar (2005) that shows, "for the major subgroups that are important in poverty studies (major cereals, more commonly used pulses, edible oils, liquid milk, and vegetables), the two estimates [survey and national accounts] are relatively close" (Deaton and Kozel 2005, p. 182). In the case of income in high-income countries such as the United Kingdom and in other countries where poverty measurement also relies on income surveys, the underrepresentation of investment income may well be a problem for the analysis of top incomes, but less so for measurement at the bottom of the distribution.[17]

The discrepancies between survey and national accounts totals have been a source of lively controversy. One school of thought believes that the household data should be adjusted so that they *do* add up. For another school of thought, such an adjustment would be an anathema. In fact, the existence of discrepancies is scarcely surprising: "the two types of data to be compared here could hardly be more different in the way they are obtained" (Ravallion 2003, p. 646). Whereas the survey data are derived from household responses, the national accounts figures are the outcome of a process that involves estimation of the aggregate flows in the economy and their reconciliation. The underlying definitions differ. The national accounts are drawn up in the context of international standards set by the UN System of National Accounts, although these definitions are followed to varying degrees and are subject to routine revisions as underlying data are consolidated and to periodic revisions when standards change. Household surveys tend to be operated at a national level and are much subject to national concerns and practices. What is more, as concluded in the case of India by the Rangarajan Expert Group, "there are infirmities in both sets of estimates" (Rangarajan 2014, p. 44).

Two major reasons for differences between household survey consumption (income) and the national accounts aggregates are that (1) the two sources record different amounts for the same variables, and (2) the two sources differ in their definitions. (A third reason, already noted, is that surveys do not account for the nonhousehold population, whereas national accounts do.) To start with the former, there are well-rehearsed reasons why reported consumption expenditure in surveys may fall short, when aggregated, of the national accounts total (for example, differential nonresponse or systematic underrecording). Households may be reluctant to fully record their spending on alcohol, for example, whereas the statisticians constructing the national accounts know how much in total was sold. This has led some researchers to adjust upwards total consumer expenditure as reported in household surveys (for example, Sala-i-Martin and Pinkovskiy 2010) to match a chosen national accounts

---

[17] *Editors*: Tony was very aware of other work comparing survey and national accounts totals (recent contributions include Fesseau, Wolff, and Mattonetti 2013) and was involved in research in this area to the end—see the investigation of EU-SILC data for European countries in Atkinson, Guio, and Marlier (2017a).

aggregate. Before the 1990s, this was also the policy of the Planning Commission in India, which "would multiply the total expenditure of each household by that ratio [of the national accounts estimate to the survey estimate of mean consumption] before calculating the number of people living in households below the poverty line" (Deaton and Kozel 2005, p. 179). It is not clear, however, that such an adjustment is appropriate, for several reasons. First, it assumes that all error arises on the side of the surveys, whereas "there can be no presumption that the NAS [national accounts] is right and the surveys are wrong" (Ravallion 2003, p, 647). Second, the "extreme poverty" target under SDG Goal 1 has been set with household survey data in mind, and a different political objective might have been set if the application of the adjustment had been known in advance. Third, the application of a correction at the level of total consumer expenditure seems too gross when the concern is focussed on those at the bottom of the distribution.

A more nuanced approach seeks to adjust the household survey data by addressing the sources for the possible shortfall. This is well illustrated by the differential adjustment by type of income component implemented by CEPALSTAT, discussed above.[18] The detailed research that has been conducted by CEPALSTAT is of considerable interest; however, adjustments that may be reasonable when applied to overall income inequality are not necessarily appropriate for the measurement of global poverty. For instance, one should take into account that adjusting revenues from self-employment is likely to affect those people at the bottom of the distribution who are engaged in the informal sector. While the more nuanced procedure meets the third of the objections raised in the previous paragraph, the first and second objections remain. There are good reasons for not undertaking this final upward adjustment of income by categories: "the agreement is rather wide that such a procedure should be avoided when measuring poverty" (Bourguignon 2015, p. 569). (To avoid any doubt, this does not rule out the earlier stages of corrections for differential nonresponse and for item nonresponse.) Moreover, the experience with income measures does not immediately carry over to consumption expenditure.

The second source of differences—those that arise from differing definitions—may be seen by comparing the two sources where I focus now on the case of consumption. A number of components of the national accounts are readily recognisable as categories of consumption that should appear in a

---

[18] *Editors:* As we noted earlier in the chapter, CEPALSTAT recently abandoned this approach in measuring poverty. Three reasons were put forward: "(a) any discrepancy with the national accounts is interpreted as an omission of the survey, without considering the possible measurement errors in national accounts; (b) since the ability of surveys to capture the income of the richest recipients is limited, the adjustment overcompensates for underreporting by low-income households; and (c) as the information required for the adjustment of income is not available in most countries and is provided with a delay of several years in others, the quality and timeliness of the information are not reliable" (ECLAC 2018, p. 107).

Table 4.2. Linking household survey and national accounts concepts of consumption

Goods and services purchased for final consumption:

+ Goods and services provided by employer

+ Own-produced consumption, including imputed rent on owner-occupied dwellings

+ Goods and services bartered for consumption

+ Current private transfers in kind

= **Household survey definition of final consumption**

To this is then added:

+ Financial intermediation services indirectly measured (FISIM)

+ Insurance service charges

= **National accounts household final consumption expenditures**

+ Social transfers in kind from government and nonprofit institutions serving households

= **National accounts actual household final consumption**

Source: Havinga, Kamanou, and Viet (2010), table 9.3 (adjusted by the author).
Reading note: The table shows which consumption items must be added to "goods and services purchased for final consumption" as estimated in household surveys to derive the "actual household final consumption" available in national accounts.

household survey (see table 4.2, based on Havinga, Kamanou, and Viet 2010, table 9.3).

In considering the definitions in the table, it is important to note first that "actual final consumption" includes social transfers in kind, such as health care and education, and that these items are not easily valued in the hands of the household and may not actually be received. There is certainly no counterpart in the typical household survey, although a sizeable literature has studied how to impute these items and what difference they make to the income distribution and to poverty, as mentioned in the previous chapter. This means, in table 4.2, going to the national accounts aggregate two rows up ("final consumption expenditure").[19] But this too includes items that have no counterpart, such as "financial intermediation services indirectly measured" (FISIM), so that is therefore more appropriate to subtract these, going further back up the table. FISIM is an estimate of the value of the services provided by banks (and other financial intermediaries) for which explicit charges are not made; it can be seen

[19] There is also a case for extending the table downwards, to allow for the subtraction of indirect taxes paid and the addition of subsidies. These are quantitatively significant in many countries and often highly politically salient, and they warrant fuller attention.

as the difference between the interest received by banks from borrowers and the (lower) interest they pay out to savers, this margin being assumed to measure the value of their intermediation services. Total FISIM is then allocated in the national accounts to user sectors, which include households, proportionately to their stocks of deposits and loans held with financial intermediaries. Not only is there no counterpart of FISIM in surveys, but as Deaton and Kozel comment, "in measuring the living standards of the poor, it can reasonably be doubted whether any of the value of financial intermediation is relevant" (2005, p. 183). The possibility of matching the consumption definitions as closely as possible is important not only to assess the mutual coherence of household surveys and national accounts, but also to improve the updating procedure carried out by the World Bank whenever an up-to-date source is not available (see above). Unfortunately, the value of FISIM included in final consumption is not readily available in published tables.[20]

I have paid particular attention to national accounts because they provide a natural benchmark for validation of results from household surveys. We should not forget, however, a more substantive point. National accounts provide the backbone of any description of a country's economic performance. The statistical reconciliation of macro and micro sources is essential to achieve the necessary integration of the analysis of people's living standards into the framework of macroeconomic evaluation (Atkinson 2013).

But in focussing on the comparison with the national accounts, it is important to note that they are not the only source with which we can compare household surveys. Other surveys, such as labour force surveys, employer surveys of wages, and various types of administrative registers, provide useful information to qualify and validate the evidence drawn from household surveys. For example, a serious misalignment in the demographic structure or the labour force participation would cast doubts on the measured distribution of expenditure or income, although sometimes these aspects are dealt with by data producers through reweighting and ex post stratification. These issues are also important when we move to consider multidimensional indicators. Triangulation with other information is necessary in this case as well.[21]

---

[20] *Editors*: According to the 2008 UN System of National Accounts, part of FISIM is attributed to households because they hold deposits and consumer credit. Being treated as services provided by financial intermediaries to households as consumers, this part is included in their final consumption expenditure. Peter van de Ven and Jorrit Zwijnenburg of the OECD Statistics and Data Directorate confirmed to us that in general FISIM attributed to households is not separately published. According to unpublished statistics gathered by the OECD for a selection of countries, this element of final consumption expenditure is fairly negligible in some countries but can account for as much as 2 to 3 per cent of the total in others.

[21] *Editors*: For an example of triangulation focussing on DHS surveys, see Pullum, Assaf, and Staveteig (2017), who compare the estimates for six fertility and mortality indicators from fifty-one DHS surveys with the corresponding estimates elaborated by the UN Inter-Agency

---

Box B. The combined poverty checklist: Concepts and data

Concept

Monetary poverty
 1. Consumption or income?
 2. Counting people or households?
 3. What allowance is made for differences in needs?
 4. How is the depth of poverty measured?

Nonmonetary poverty
 5. What dimensions are covered and what indicators are used?
 6. Do the data relate to individuals or households?
 7. What account is taken of the overlap of deprivations?

Data
 8. Do real data exist and are they available?
 9. Do the data cover the whole country?
 10. Are the data comparable across time?
 11. Are the data comparable with those for other countries?
 12. How are price changes measured?
 13. How big a sample is used?
 14. Who is missing from the data?
 15. Can the resulting estimates be triangulated with other sources?

CONCLUSIONS: AN ALL-ROUND APPROACH (AA)

To translate the concepts of poverty into concrete measures depends crucially on there being data that are fit for purpose. Great progress has been achieved in recent years, but there remain major challenges.

These challenges concern the availability and quality of data, where considerable improvement is still possible. The availability of survey data has increased considerably in most countries, thanks in part to the investment of international organisations, but there remain issues about them being up-to-date and fit for purpose. Dealing with sampling and interviewing problems, tackling nonresponse, asking the right questions, accounting for those missing from survey samples, having reliable counts of the total population, choosing which is the proper price index for the poor, reconciling different aggregate and household-level sources—all are major tasks for data producers. Improvement is clearly possible, but we must be aware of the unavoidable tension between

---

Group for Child Mortality Estimation, the UN Population Division, and the World Health Organization.

improving the statistical instrument and preserving comparability with the past.

These issues are not nuisances to be left to the specialists. They affect results, their comparability over time and across countries, and the soundness of policy conclusions. Like data producers, analysts and users must pay close attention to them. The checklist in box B provides guidance to the questions reviewed in chapters 3 and 4 that one should ask when addressing statistics on poverty, whether globally or nationally.[22]

---

[22] *Editors*: Tony's notes show that he was also planning to include reference in these conclusions to the "total error" approach to measuring poverty that he recommended in the report of the Commission on Global Poverty, involving the evaluation of the possible sources and magnitude of error, particularly nonsampling error (World Bank 2017, p. 50). He was drawn to the total survey error approach developed by sample survey statisticians (Groves et al. 2004) and wrote in his notes that "economists could learn from other social scientists." See also his reference to this approach in chapter 10, p.213.

CHAPTER 5

Global Poverty and the Sustainable Development Goals

At the heart of the Sustainable Development Goals and the earlier Millennium Development Goals is concern for global poverty. Central, therefore, has been the measurement of poverty on a world scale. In the international political process that led to the agreement on the goals, and in the subsequent monitoring of progress, a key role has been played by the statistics on global poverty assembled by the World Bank. These statistics relate to monetary poverty, with which I begin. As such, they are directly relevant to the target associated with SDG Goal 1 of eradicating extreme poverty as measured by the International Poverty Line (see box C). The nonmonetary dimensions of poverty reflected in the other SDGs are taken up later in the chapter.

GLOBAL POVERTY MEASUREMENT BY THE WORLD BANK

The capacity of the World Bank to make estimates of the extent of global poverty dates back to the research initiated by Harvard professor Hollis Chenery when he was the Bank's chief economist in the 1970s. It was on the basis of the studies of Ahluwalia (1974) and Ahluwalia, Carter, and Chenery (1979) that the then-president of the World Bank, Robert McNamara, was able to write in the foreword to the first *World Development Report* in 1978 (as I noted in chapter 1) that "some 800 million individuals continue to be trapped in what I have termed absolute poverty: a condition of life so characterized by malnutrition, illiteracy, disease, squalid surroundings, high infant mortality, and low life expectancy as to be beneath any reasonable definition of human decency" (World Bank 1978, p. iii).

This definition is clearly broad, covering multiple dimensions of deprivation, but the concrete numbers were based on poverty measured in terms of economic resources. Ahluwalia, Carter, and Chenery (1979) made estimates for thirty-six developing countries of the percentage of people living with incomes below a poverty line set on the basis of Indian experience, and they went on to extrapolate to the developing world as a whole.

Box C. 2015 Sustainable Development Goals

1. No poverty
2. Zero hunger
3. Good health and well-being
4. Quality education
5. Gender equality
6. Clean water and sanitation
7. Affordable and clean energy
8. Decent work and economic growth
9. Industry, innovation, and infrastructure
10. Reduced inequalities
11. Sustainable cities and communities
12. Responsible consumption and production
13. Climate action
14. Life below water
15. Life on land
16. Peace, justice, and strong institutions
17. Partnerships for the goals

Each goal has the short form shown above together with a longer form. The longer form for Goal 1 is "end poverty in all its forms everywhere." Specific targets are associated with each goal. In the case of Goal 1, the first two are (a) "by 2030, eradicate extreme poverty for all people everywhere, currently measured as people living on less than $1.25 a day [at 2005 PPPs; $1.90 a day at 2011 PPPs];" (b) by 2030, "reduce at least by half the proportion of men, women and children of all ages living in poverty in all its dimensions according to national definitions."

Source: UN Sustainable Development Goals website.

A short history of World Bank global poverty measures

The attentive reader will have noted that the 800 million figure quoted by Mc-Namara in 1978 is very close to the figure of 767 million shown for 2013 in our first look at the data in chapter 1. Can these two numbers be compared? The short answer is no. The approach adopted by Chenery was the forerunner of that employed by the World Bank today, but there have been major developments, notably as a result of the research carried out in the past twenty-five years at the World Bank by Martin Ravallion and colleagues, where the output of this research is embodied in the Bank's PovcalNet database, on which today's estimates are based. The importance of this research, and the decisions taken in the past to support it, should be underlined. Without the prior investment by its Research Department, the World Bank would not have been in a position to implement the monitoring of the SDG poverty goal. It cannot be accused of having failed to address the question, even if there are many critics of the particular approach adopted.

What have been the essential ingredients in the World Bank calculation?

Better data and the switch to consumption

First, crucial to the exercise is the much-increased, although still limited, availability of high-quality data from household surveys, discussed in the previous chapter. The World Bank uses the available evidence from household surveys to count the number of people living in households where consumption per person falls below the poverty line. Here it should be noted that there was an early switch from the income measure used by Chenery and his colleagues to a consumption-based measure, whenever possible. The box to be ticked in the checklist proposed in box B in chapter 4 is "consumption"; the implications of ticking instead the box for "income" are discussed in chapter 8.

The key role of national poverty standards

The second key feature of the World Bank approach is that the poverty line is set in a way that reflects the national poverty standards set in the poorest countries for which national poverty lines are available: "The World Bank has elected to monitor global poverty by the standards that apply in the very poorest countries of the world" (World Bank 2015, p. 36). At the outset, drawing on the poverty lines set nationally in thirty-three countries, Ravallion, Datt, van de Walle, and Chan (1991, p. 6) based their estimates of poverty in developing countries on two proposed per capita lines: $0.76 a day and $1.02 a day. The latter, which they found to be "more representative," became widely accepted as the basis for $1 a day per person, the "dollar a day" line that gained much attention. As described below, this poverty line later became first $1.08, then $1.25, and, in 2015, $1.90 a day.

The poverty standards set in poor countries are the basis for setting the World Bank poverty line, but there is a further step: the identification of countries for which national poverty lines are available. Not all countries have officially approved poverty lines. Availability determines the set of countries taken into account. In the World Bank estimates for 2005, the set consisted of the fifteen lowest national poverty lines, where these were compared in terms of international purchasing power parity dollars (based on the 2005 round of the ICP). The countries concerned, in order of increasing poverty lines, were *Tanzania*, *Malawi*, Chad, *Nepal*, *Mozambique*, Rwanda, *Niger*, *Uganda*, *Ethiopia*, Mali, the Gambia, Guinea-Bissau, Sierra Leone, *Ghana*, and Tajikistan. The derivation of the national poverty lines is described for the eight italicized countries in the national country reports at the end of the book.[1] The 2015 exercise by the World Bank took the same fifteen countries and updated the national poverty lines in terms of 2011 purchasing power parities. Taking the unweighted mean of the resulting 2011 poverty lines based on PPP dollars resulted in $1.88. Rounded up to $1.90, this led to the figure that the World Bank determined in 2015 should be what is now called the International Poverty Line.

The national studies of poverty are central to the determination of the International Poverty Line, but the circle is not completed. As is discussed further below, we need to go back to the national studies to see how far the results obtained at a global level are coherent with the national findings. For the present, I note that the World Bank approach is a "political definition" of poverty in the terms described in chapter 2. This is no doubt appropriate for an international organisation with a membership comprising nation-states, but it has naturally led to questioning by those seeking to ground the global poverty estimates in a more fundamental approach to poverty measurement.

Purchasing power parities and controversy

The World Bank estimates of global poverty were developed over time, reflecting changes in the two ingredients identified so far: the great improvement in the availability of household survey data and the evolution of national poverty lines. But they also reflected a third ingredient—the application of purchasing power parities—and this has proved controversial. As we have seen in chapter 3, the poverty line applied, say, in India is not obtained by converting dollars into rupees at the market exchange rate; rather, there is an additional adjustment to allow for the fact that the purchasing power in India is different. In the example used of 2011, the market exchange rate was such that a US dollar would obtain 46.67 Indian rupees, but according to the results of the ICP for 2011, to buy the same basket of goods and services in India as $1 would purchase in the United States required only 14.98 rupees. This means that, when interrogating the survey data for that year to estimate poverty in India based on the $1.90 line, we are asking how many people are living in households with consumption per capita less than 28.46 rupees.

In terms of purchasing power, the per capita poverty line rose from $1.02 a day at 1985 PPPs to $1.08 a day at 1993 PPPs, then to $1.25 a day at 2005 PPPs, and lastly to $1.90 a day at 2011 PPPs (Ferreira et al. 2016).

The rise to $1.25 a day was described as the "first major revision of the original $1 a day line" (Ravallion, Chen, and Sangraula 2009, p. 163), and it generated

---

[1] *Editors*: The reports are largely complete for six countries. The exceptions are Malawi and Ethiopia.

considerable debate. The revised estimates implied an upward revision to the global poverty figures: "our new calculations . . . imply that 25% of the population of the developing world, 1.4 billion people, were poor in 2005, which is 400 million more . . . than implied by our old international poverty line based on national lines for the 1980s and the 1993 ICP" (Chen and Ravallion 2010, p. 1621). At the same time, the revisions raised the baseline figures against which the change in poverty could be judged, and the authors stressed that the rate of progress in poverty reduction was little affected. In their analysis, it is important to distinguish the measurement of the level of poverty from the monitoring of poverty over time: "the trends over time and regional profile are robust to various changes in methodology, though precise counts are more sensitive" (p. 1577).

The disconcerting effect on the level of global poverty of this first major revision led many people to seek understanding, notably Angus Deaton in his 2010 Presidential Address to the American Economic Association. (He was the first president, at least in recent times, to take poverty as the subject of the address.) The important point to emerge from this debate was that, while attention had concentrated on the purchasing power comparisons, the new results were the combined effect of changes in the purchasing power parities *and* in the derivation of the International Poverty Line from the national lines. It was based on an entirely new compilation of national poverty lines, which was updated and considerably extended, and on a different method of calculation, which was based on the mean of the national poverty lines for the poorest fifteen countries for which national poverty lines were available in an extended set of seventy-five developing countries.

In 2015 the World Bank moved to the new $1.90 a day line (Ferreira et al. 2016). In seeking to understand the change in the estimated level of global poverty, attention was focussed on the fact that the new estimates made use of a more recent round of the results of the ICP—the round relating to 2011 prices—in place of the 2005 ICP round. The 2011 ICP exercise concluded that, comparing the findings with those in the 2005 round, on average, prices in the developing world were lower than previously found, relative to those in the United States. Such a change led to a significant revision of the view taken of global economic magnitudes, such as gross domestic product (GDP). As summarised in the report on the 2011 ICP, "The relative shares of the three Asian economies—China, India, and Indonesia—to the United States doubled, while Brazil, Mexico, and Russia increased by one-third or more" (World Bank 2014, p. 81). The report goes on to say that "some of the large differences in the Asian economies and developing economies in general can be attributed to the changes in the methodology used for the two comparisons." The economies were larger because a given value in local currency was, with the lower prices represented by the 2011 PPPs, a larger amount in international purchasing power measured with the United States as the benchmark. For the same reason, "the spread of per capita actual individual consumption as a percentage of that of the United States has been greatly reduced, suggesting that the world has become more equal" (World Bank 2014, p. 89). The apparent impact of a switch to the new PPPs was, some commentators argued, a large reduction in global poverty.[2]

The new ICP is important not only because it changed the relative position of rich and poor countries but also because it changed the relative position of different developing countries: "ICP 2011 reversed some of the increase in inequality between poor and rich regions in ICP 2005, but it did not reverse the 2005 changes on a country-by-country basis," noted Deaton and Aten (2017, p. 249). The authors went on to say that "the reduction in Africa in 2011 undid much less of the 2005 increase than was the case in India, so that, just as the ICP 2005 'Asianized' poverty, the ICP 2011 will 'Africanize' it" (p. 250). There is a distinct regional pattern to the revisions, with larger effects in Asia and smaller effects in Africa and in Latin America and the Caribbean. At a country level, I calculated that the adoption of the 2011 ICP conversion factors changed the poverty line in local currency around the world: out of 167 countries for which the 2005 value may be compared with the 2011 value extrapolated backwards, only sixty-three had a change of less than 10 per cent (or were unaffected).

As in the earlier revision, when the World Bank came to redesign its methods in 2015, it not only embodied the 2011 ICP but also incorporated new information about national poverty lines. The World Bank considered a number of possible approaches but, after experimentation, remained close to that employed in the $1.25 revision: basing the poverty standard on the national lines in operation in the same set of fifteen countries used in 2005 and uprating their national poverty lines according to the increase in the national consumer price index, then applying the new ICP 2011 to calculate the poverty line in international dollars. As noted earlier, the unweighted mean of the resulting PPP dollars poverty lines in all fifteen countries was rounded up to $1.90, which represents an increase over $1.25 of 52 per cent. The overall impact on global poverty of the changes in methodology was modest by design: "The updated poverty line of $1.90 in 2011 PPPs reflects the same real standard of living as the $1.25 line did in 2005 PPPs (on average across poor countries)," while "the new line and PPPs do of course lead to changes to poverty counts in individual countries" (Ferreira et al. 2016, p. 164). For 2011, the World Bank estimate of global poverty fell slightly, from 1,011 million people ($1.25 line and 2005 PPPs) to 983 million ($1.90 line and 2011 PPPs) (table 5).

All this may be illustrated by the case of India, starting in 2005. On the basis of the 2005 ICP, the conversion factor (for individual consumption expenditure

---

[2] *Editors*: This is illustrated by the title of a blog post following the publication of the 2011 ICP results: "Global Absolute Poverty Fell by Almost Half on Tuesday" (Dykstra, Kenny, and Sandefur 2014).

by households) was 15.60 local currency units. This implied that an International Poverty Line of $1.25 in 2005 corresponded to 19.50 rupees. In contrast, the 2011 ICP conversion factor extrapolated back to 2005 (World Bank table PA.NUS.PRVT.PP) is 10.43, implying that $1.25 corresponded to a poverty line in 2005 of 13.04 rupees. On its own, this represents a reduction of a third, and it can be expected to reduce substantially the estimated number in poverty in 2005. Conversely, using the 2011 ICP conversion factor, in 2011 the rupee value of the $1.25 international dollar poverty line is 18.73 rupees. The rise in the poverty cutoff between 2005 and 2011 depends on the upward movement in the conversion factor, which in turn reflects the fact that domestic inflation was faster in India than in the benchmark country (the United States), so that India's price advantage had been eroded. But meanwhile the International Poverty Line has been raised to $1.90, so that the new cutoff has become 28.46 rupees (reached by multiplying 18.73 by 1.90/1.25, that is, the increase in the International Poverty Line).

If this sounds as clear as mud, then—apart from my poor exposition—it reflects the fact that there are several moving parts in operation at once. Moreover, it is quite possible that there has been no change in any domestic price, but that the PPP adjustment leads to a change in the local currency poverty line. This is not easily explained to a nonspecialist audience. For these reasons, in the report of the Commission on Global Poverty, I recommended to the World Bank that global poverty estimates should be updated up to 2030 on the basis of the International Poverty Line for each country set in local currency, updated in line with the change in the national CPI or, where available, national index of prices for the poor; the estimates would not be revised in the light of new rounds of the ICP.[3] In the case of India, this would have led to a poverty line in local currency in 2011 of 32.27 rupees, or some 13 per cent higher than that actually employed by the World Bank.[4] A significant difference, but no seismic shock.[5]

This recommendation does not mean that there should not be further purchasing power adjustments in the future. They should, however, be distinct events, not routine adjustments. The major revision of the International Poverty Line would be a recognition that, over time, we have reached a position where we need to recast our view of the relative living standards in different

[3] *Editors*: The recommendation was accepted (World Bank 2016b).

[4] *Editors*: This value is obtained by adjusting the poverty line of 19.50 rupees in 2005 (the one corresponding to $1.25 with the 2005 ICP conversion factor) by the increase in CPI between 2005 and 2011 (65.5 per cent).

[5] *Editors*: Tony's comment may be interpreted in the context of figures he cites earlier—for example, the impact of the $1.25 "major revision" on global poverty or claims of the effect of the change from 2005 ICP to 2011 ICP. However, the implications of a 13 per cent higher poverty line should not be underestimated. Using PovcalNet, we estimate that a rise in the International Poverty Line of this amount in 2011 would add over 100 million people to the number of India's poor, raising the head count from 21.2 to 29.8 per cent.

countries. National governments, as we have seen in chapter 2, make such distinct changes to their poverty standards, and the same can be applied to the International Poverty Line. But it should be signalled, and agreed, as such. By the same token, future changes in the national poverty lines of the fifteen poorest countries (for which data are available) should not affect the International Poverty Line until there is such a major revision. The national poverty lines have, in this respect, served their function. What has been agreed to is the $1.90 line, and this should not be changed because a new poverty standard has been set in Niger or Mozambique.

ESTIMATES OF GLOBAL POVERTY

In this section, I summarise the evidence from the World Bank estimates of global poverty in 2013, to which reference has already been made in chapter 1. The World Bank report *Poverty and Shared Prosperity* (World Bank 2016, p. 42) concludes that the global poor are predominantly rural (80 per cent of the poor worldwide) and young (44 per cent aged under fifteen), poorly educated (39 per cent have no formal education), and mostly employed in the agricultural sector (64 per cent), and that they live in larger households with more children.

Levels and trends

[*Editors*: Tony's notes show that he planned to draw further on the 2016 edition of *Poverty and Shared Prosperity*, which provides the source for the data in figure 5.1. (A new edition was published in 2018—see the foreword.) How would he have gone beyond his brief analysis of poverty levels and trends in chapter 1? His notes suggest that he intended to discuss changes in the composition of global poverty in terms of regions' and countries' levels of average income—along the lines of pages 20–21 in the report of the Commission on Global Poverty (World Bank 2017)—and that he was going to at least mention the "growth elasticity of poverty reduction," that is, the extent to which poverty falls in response to economic growth. This topic was to be revisited in greater depth as one of the two "general issues" in chapter 6 and is addressed by François Bourguignon in his afterword.]

Are the very poor being left behind?

Many national poverty lines lie above the $1.90 threshold of the International Poverty Line. This bears out the naming by the World Bank of the poverty defined by this threshold as "extreme poverty." There is also concern for those in poverty but not extreme poverty. But we can turn the question round. Are we neglecting the distribution among the extreme poor—notably, the situation of the very poorest?

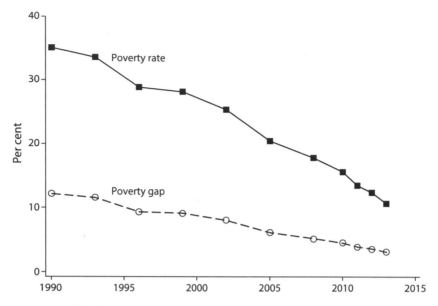

Figure 5.1. Global poverty rate and poverty gap: World Bank estimates based on the $1.90 a day line, 1990 to 2013

Source: World Bank (2016, annex 2A).

Reading note: The World Bank estimated that 35.0 per cent of the world population lived in households beneath the International Poverty Line of $1.90 a day in 1990 and that the poverty gap in this year was 12.2 per cent.

Figure 5.1 shows the global head count for poverty measured by the $1.90 line—the poverty rates that were already shown in chapter 1 (figure 1.2)—together with the World Bank's estimates of a measure of the depth of poverty beneath the same line: the poverty gap, described in chapter 3. Both measures fall considerably between 1990 and 2013—the head count by more than two-thirds (from 35.0 to 10.7 per cent) and the poverty gap by almost three-quarters (from 12.2 to 3.2 per cent). This means that the drop in the share of people living in poverty was accompanied by an even larger reduction in the shortfall in consumption or income from the poverty line. This conclusion is confirmed by looking at the figures for the FGT2 index, which, as explained in chapter 3, takes the square of individual poverty gaps and hence assigns greater weight to larger gaps (and thus to the poorest people). The FGT2 (not shown in the graph) also fell by almost three-quarters, from 5.8 to 1.5 per cent (same source as for figure 5.1). This last piece of information shows that based on the World Bank's published evidence, the last quarter-century saw an improvement in the distribution among the poor.

Women and children in poverty

In 2014, Carly Fiorina, the former CEO of Hewlett-Packard and a Republican presidential hopeful, said that "women remain the most underutilized resource in the world and the most subjugated people in the world. Seventy percent of the people living in abject poverty are women." She was quoted by Jon Greenberg (2014) of the *Tampa Bay Times*, who went on the hunt for the source of this widely quoted, but never footnoted, statistic.[6]

Rural and urban poverty

Poverty as measured is very much a rural phenomenon, as emphasised at the start of this section. The World Bank differentiates for China, India, and Indonesia between the rural and urban populations, and its estimates clearly show a higher poverty rate in rural areas. The head-count poverty ratios in Indonesia in 2010 were higher by a half in rural areas (19.8 per cent rural versus 12.0 per cent urban); in India in 2011–2012, the rural rate was nearly double (24.8 per cent rural versus 13.4 per cent urban). In China in 2012, the rural head-count rate was 13 per cent, whereas urban poverty was close to zero. For the world as a whole, the World Bank's *Economic Premise* profile shows that the rural population accounted for 58.4 per cent of the total population, but 77.8 per cent of those living in households in extreme poverty (Olinto et al. 2013, figure 7).[7]

---

[6] *Editors:* We presume that Tony would have built on his discussion of poverty among women and children in the report of the Commission on Global Poverty (World Bank 2017, pp. 112–116), although, as noted there, the data used for the global poverty estimates are limited in what they can reveal. For example, they tell us how many women live in households whose consumption is below the poverty line rather than how many women have individual consumption below the line. His notes for this subsection also include the abstract of Newhouse, Suarez-Becerra, and Evans (2016), a background paper for the *Poverty and Shared Prosperity* report (World Bank 2016), which compares the poverty rate for children in eighty-nine countries according to the $1.90 line with that among adults: 19.5 per cent and 9.2 per cent, respectively, taking all countries together.

[7] *Editors:* We do not know how Tony would have continued. As part of the discussion, he would probably have reminded the reader of the problems with defining "rural" and "urban" described in chapter 4. (This relates not only to the World Bank estimates that he planned to discuss here but also to the estimates based on national poverty lines in the national reports at the end of the book that Tony was to draw on in chapters 6–9: one of the most frequent breakdowns of national estimates in the reports is between rural and urban poverty.) He might have cited existing research, such as Sahn and Stifel (2003), which was in his files, and Ravallion, Chen, and Sangraula (2007). Besides estimates and definitions, we think he would have addressed differences in the nature of rural and urban poverty—do they mean the same thing when, for example, differences in infrastructure and public services are taken into account?

DO NONMONETARY POVERTY MEASURES TELL THE SAME STORY?

In Nepal, where monetary poverty measured by the $1.90 line fell by two-thirds between 2003 and 2010, OPHI's Global Multidimensional Poverty Index— described more fully below—showed a sharp fall in the head count, from 64.7 per cent in 2006 to 44.2 per cent in 2011, providing strong supporting evidence for the two approaches yielding similar conclusions. In Kenya, where the apparent conflict between the trend shown by the World Bank's PovcalNet estimates and the national figures cannot readily be resolved on account of breaks in comparability (and lack of recent data),[8] the decline in the OPHI Global MPI head count from 60.1 per cent in 2003 to 51.2 per cent in 2009 provides evidence of progress, albeit at a more modest rate. In this section, I consider the role of nonmonetary measures and the extent to which they are confirmatory and how far they show a different picture. If, as might be expected, there are countries where the nonmonetary poverty rate can be predicted quite accurately from the monetary head count, but others where the figure lies far from the predicted value, what can we learn?

The SDGs as a whole[9]

As seen in chapter 3, the Global MPI developed by OPHI uses ten indicators to measure three dimensions of poverty, "education," "health," and "standard of living" (see table 5.1). Two indicators each relate to education and health, and six relate to standard of living. The three dimensions are weighted equally in the calculations of the MPI, implying that the ten indicators are weighted unequally—those for education and health each have a weight of one-sixth while those for standard of living have a weight of one-eighteenth. A methodological note on the OPHI website states that "each person is identified as de-

---

[8] *Editors*: When Tony was writing, the most recent national poverty estimate for Kenya was for 2005–2006. (This remains the case for the World Bank estimates in the April 2018 version of PovcalNet.) However, in editing the national report for Kenya, we have been able to draw on data for 2015–2016 that were published in March 2018 (see figure KEN).

[9] *Editors*: Tony planned to relate the topics covered by the SDGs to the multidimensional measurement of poverty, in particular the measures developed by OPHI in conjunction with UNDP. (He may also have wanted to refer to the Eurostat measures of material deprivation for the EU.) His description of the OPHI measures would have gone beyond that in chapter 4—he seems to have held back there in the same way as the details of the World Bank's measurement of monetary poverty are not made clear until the current chapter. The description of the OPHI measures in the first part of the text has been drafted by us; we have not attempted to relate these measures to the SDGs, as Tony would have done, or to summarise the criticisms of them. (The broad arguments for and against the approach are covered in chapter 3.) Our description predates the revision of the Global MPI in September 2018, announced while this book was in production. This revision made minor changes to several indicators and was intended to align the Global MPI more closely with the SDGs (Alkire and Jahan 2018; Alkire, Kanagaratnam, and Suppa 2018).

Table 5.1. Dimensions, indicators, deprivation cutoffs, and weights in the Global MPI

Dimension	Indicator	Household Deprived if:	Weight
Education	Years of schooling	No household member aged ten years or older has completed five years of schooling	$\frac{1}{6}$
	Child school attendance	Any school child is not attending school up to the age at which he or she would complete class 8	$\frac{1}{6}$
Health	Child mortality	Any child has died in the family in the five-year period preceding the survey	$\frac{1}{6}$
	Nutrition	Any adult under seventy years old or any child for whom there is nutritional information is undernourished in terms of weight for age	$\frac{1}{6}$
Living standard	Electricity	Household has no electricity	$\frac{1}{18}$
	Improved sanitation	Household's sanitation facility is not improved (according to Millennial Development Goal guidelines), or it is improved but shared with other households	$\frac{1}{18}$
	Improved drinking water	Household does not have access to improved drinking water (according to MDG guidelines), or safe drinking water is at least a thirty-minute walk from home (round-trip)	$\frac{1}{18}$
	Flooring	Household has only a dirt, sand, dung, or "other" (unspecified) type of floor	$\frac{1}{18}$
	Cooking fuel	Household cooks with dung, wood, or charcoal	$\frac{1}{18}$
	Assets ownership	Household does not own more than one of the following assets: radio, TV, telephone, bicycle, motorbike, or fridge, and household does not own a car or lorry	$\frac{1}{18}$

Source: Alkire and Robles (2017, table 1). (See editors' note to the main text on the September 2018 revision of the Global MPI indicators.)

Reading note: In the Global MPI, two indicators (years of schooling and child school attendance) are used to measure deprivation in the dimension of education, each with a weight of one-sixth.

prived or non-deprived in each indicator based on a deprivation cutoff" (Alkire and Robles 2017, p. 4); the cutoffs for each indicator are also listed in the table. The four indicators for education and health all refer to the status of the individuals in the household, and all household members are considered in the assessment, rather than taking a reference person. However, it is the household that is identified as deprived or not on any indicator rather than the person, and the same is true of the classification of multidimensional poverty based on the indicators. For example, it is sufficient that at least one person has five years of schooling for classifying the household and all its members as not deprived according to the first education indicator, and this is regardless of the household size.[10] The reference unit is the household—a person is multidimensionally poor if the household they live in is classified as multidimensionally poor.

A household is multidimensionally poor if it is identified as deprived in at least a third of the weighted indicators. For example, it is poor if no household member aged ten or over has five years of schooling (weight = 1/6) *and* the household has no electricity (weight = 1/18) *and* the household has a dirt, sand, or dung floor (weight =1/18) *and* the household cooks with dung, wood, or charcoal (weight = 1/18). The threshold of a third of the weighted indicators means that, in principle, a household could be classified as poor on the basis of the indicators for just one dimension—for example, both the health indicators—"which raises questions as to how their poverty is 'multidimensional'" (Alkire and Santos 2014, p. 265), although this is reported to be rare in practice.[11]

Households and the persons living in them classified as poor in this way are considered by the authors of the Global MPI to be in "acute" poverty according to international norms (such as the Millennium Development Goals, referred to in two of the indicators). However, several other classifications are also proposed and used in OPHI's publications. The "vulnerable to poverty" are defined as persons in households deprived in at least a fifth of the weighted indicators; deprivation in at least half of the weighted indicators is defined as "severe poverty." In another variant, "destitution" is again defined as a household being deprived in a third of the weighted indicators, but with more demanding cutoffs for eight of the ten indicators—for example, a forty-five-minute walk for water rather than thirty minutes (Alkire and Robles 2017, table 2). The depth of poverty is also measured by the average deprivation score of those classified as poor.

For countries for which OPHI makes estimates of nonmonetary poverty, the text of each national report at the end of the book includes the latest estimate of the national rate [*Editors*: available in the spring of 2018] and the separate rates for rural and urban areas. The accompanying graph contains OPHI's

---

[10] *Editors*: This approach is consistent with assuming that proximity to a minimally literate person has positive externalities for all household members. This point is discussed by Basu and Foster (1998).

[11] *Editors*: Sabina Alkire and Maria Emma Santos (2014) note in their paper that this point was put to them by Tony.

short time series of estimates, if available. The latest estimate in the time series may differ from the figure in the text (and sometimes appreciably) on account of OPHI standardizing the calculations to take account of differences over time in survey content. (See the discussion of comparability over time in chapter 4.)

Multidimensional poverty indices

A number of countries now have official national Multidimensional Poverty Indices based on the Alkire-Foster methodology. In most cases the MPI is reported alongside the official statistics for monetary poverty, rather than with consumption or income included as a component. (Mexico is an exception in that it includes income as a dimension in its MPI.) What is covered? The MPI in Colombia, for example, covers five dimensions: family education, the situation of children and young people, employment, health, and access to public facilities and housing condition, using fifteen indicators (Salazar, Díaz, and Pinzón 2013). The MPI for Costa Rica has five dimensions: education, health, housing, work, and social protection, with twenty indicators. (The dimensions covered in MPIs in other Latin American countries were given earlier in chapter 3, table 3.1.) I return to the results from these national MPIs in the chapters that follow, but here I stay with the figures from the Global MPI.

The 2016 *Human Development Report* (UNDP 2016) contains estimates of the Global MPI for 102 countries.[12] The relevant table is titled "Multidimensional Poverty Index: Developing Countries," the label "developing" being used broadly—around a quarter of the 102 countries are classified by the World Bank as upper-middle-income. (Another quarter are low-income, and half are lower-middle-income.) The figures all refer to a year during the period 2005–2015. For the moment I focus on the head count, the proportion of the population that is multidimensionally poor, leaving the measures of the intensity of poverty to one side. That is, the proportion of the population living in households that have a score of at least a third of the total possible score across the ten weighted indicators of deprivation used in the Global MPI.[13]

Not surprisingly in view of the composition of the group of countries, the head counts range widely, from less than 1 per cent (Armenia, Belarus, Mon-

[12] *Editors*: Tony was working with the 2015 report, but we have updated his analysis to the 2016 report, which was published after his death. However, in doing so, we became aware that the "Multidimensional Poverty Index" published by UNDP differed slightly from OPHI's Global MPI during 2014–2016 (although the same three dimensions and ten indicators were used). We are grateful to Sabina Alkire for correspondence on this point. (See the news item on the OPHI website, "HDRO and OPHI Unify Global Multidimensional Poverty Measures to Better Monitor Progress on SDGs," 28 February 2018.)

[13] *Editors*: The 2016 report contains the following warning: "Not all indicators were available for all countries, so caution should be used in cross-country comparisons. Where an indicator is missing, weights of available indicators are adjusted to total 100 percent" (UNDP 2016, note to table 6).

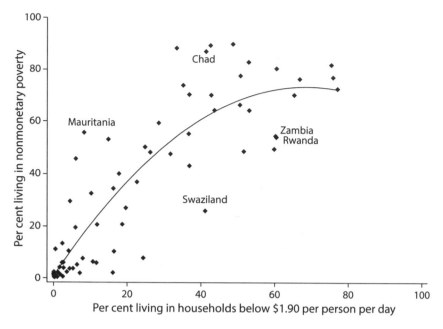

Figure 5.2. Nonmonetary and monetary poverty rates for seventy-two countries (per cent)

Source: UNDP (2016, table 6) and PovcalNet (October 2017 version). The line superimposed on the graph is from the OLS regression of the nonmonetary rate on the monetary rate and its square. *Reading note*: Twenty-six per cent of the population of Swaziland live in households suffering from nonmonetary poverty, and 41 per cent live in households below $1.90 per person per day. (These estimates refer to 2010; the latter figure is an extrapolation from the linear trend for 2000–2009.)

tenegro, St. Lucia, Serbia, and Ukraine) to nearly 90 per cent (Ethiopia, Niger, and South Sudan). The mean value is 32 per cent and the median is 26 per cent.

Confirming or confronting?

How do these rates of nonmonetary poverty compare with those for monetary poverty discussed earlier in the chapter, the figures estimated by the World Bank based on the International Poverty Line? The two are plotted against each other in figure 5.2. A problem in making this comparison is that the PovcalNet database contains no estimates of monetary poverty for some countries, and for others an estimate is available only for a very different year than for the non-monetary figure in the UNDP report, with the difference being too great to try to overcome. As a result, the graph contains only seventy-two countries.[14]

[14]The data are for the same years in thirty-four countries, while for two countries there is a difference of one year. For the remaining countries, in twenty-six cases the monetary poverty

The average nonmonetary poverty rate in this somewhat smaller group of countries is 34 per cent. This is ten percentage points more than the average for the monetary rates based on the $1.90 line. But nothing should be read into this difference. The averages reflect the thresholds used to measure whether a household is poor, thresholds that in a sense are arbitrary. For example, were we to consider instead the head count for "severe" multidimensional poverty in the Global MPI, the relationship between the two averages would be reversed—the nonmonetary rates would have the lower mean. What is of interest, however, is the pattern of the data in the graph. In general, the incidence of nonmonetary poverty is higher where monetary poverty rates are higher—the two sets of figures show quite strong positive correlation. The curved line superimposed on the graph summarises the statistical relationship. (The minor downturn at the right-hand end of the line should be ignored.) Countries close to the line are where the nonmonetary rate can be predicted quite well from the monetary head count. But there are countries that are well away from the line, such as the four named African countries. Swaziland and Chad have the same proportion of the population below the $1.90 line—41 per cent. But while Swaziland has a rate of multidimensional poverty at the median level of 26 per cent, the rate in Chad is 87 per cent, almost at the top of the range. (The three countries close to Chad in the diagram with higher nonmonetary rates of nearly 90 per cent are those mentioned earlier, reading from left to right: Ethiopia, South Sudan, and Niger.) Mauritania, Rwanda, and Zambia all have nonmonetary poverty rates of about 55 per cent. But in Mauritania only 8 per cent of the population are in households with per capita consumption below the $1.90 line, while in Rwanda and Zambia the figure is 60 per cent.[15]

---

rate was obtained by linear interpolation from figures for earlier and later years than for the nonmonetary rate, and in ten cases by linear extrapolation from figures for two earlier years (to a maximum of two years ahead).

[15] *Editors*: We think that Tony would have continued this section in several directions. First, in the case of Swaziland and Chad, we believe that he would have investigated which of the ten indicators of nonmonetary deprivation drive the difference in the head counts and that he would have used this example to make a general point about understanding variation in rates of multidimensional poverty. Second, as flagged earlier in the text, he would have discussed further what we learn from such "outliers," countries well away from the regression line on the graph—including Mauritania, Rwanda, and Zambia. Third, he would have asked if the relationship between monetary and nonmonetary poverty rates varies between different parts of the world—his spreadsheets show him investigating the relationship separately for Asia, Africa, and Latin America and the Caribbean. Fourth, he would have looked at the measures of the intensity of multidimensional poverty, perhaps comparing them with measures of the depth of monetary poverty. Fifth, he would have addressed the question of whether the changes over time in monetary and nonmonetary poverty are congruent. Is the pattern that he reports for Nepal at the start of the section the norm? (On this, see Alkire, Roche, and Vaz 2017.)

DRILLING DOWN: FROM GLOBAL TO LOCAL

One of the principal aims of this book is to build vertical bridges between the global estimates produced by international agencies and national studies of poverty. To this end, I consider in the four chapters that follow the evidence about poverty in Asia (both East Asia and the Pacific and South Asia) in chapter 6, Africa in chapter 7, Latin America and the Caribbean in chapter 8, and high-income countries in chapter 9. The definition of "high-income" follows that employed by the World Bank[16] and is taken to "trump" the regional definitions, so that a country in Latin America classified as high-income is treated in chapter 9, not chapter 8. In each chapter, I seek to draw together the national poverty reports—the material shown at the end of the book for each of the sixty countries. Each national poverty report contains a discussion of the methods employed and a single graph summarising the findings on poverty (and inequality) over time. (There are separate graphs for rural and urban China.)

The reader will find that, when considering the national poverty report for country X, I might make reference to country Y. (For example, I refer to China when discussing poverty in Poland.) I have not become suddenly geographically confused. Rather, I see chapters 6 to 9 as building horizontal bridges between the measurement of poverty at a national level in different countries. Such cross-references underline where there is scope for mutual learning. The EU analyses of income and poverty, for example, have demonstrated the value of peer evaluation.

Key questions

The chapters deal with several key questions. The first key question asks, how do the figures that make up the global poverty count relate to those at the national level? If the inhabitants of a country look up the numbers on the World Bank website, will they be surprised by what they find? In some cases, the answer is yes. The Pacific Community publishes National Minimum Development Indicators for the island nations that are among its members, and the rates of "basic needs poverty" are shown in figure 5.3, plotted against the World Bank numbers. Not all Pacific countries are to be found on the World Bank website, but for the nine countries shown—in each case the two figures are for the same year—the findings are not totally reassuring. There are of course many reasons why national findings may differ from those of the World Bank, including differences in the data sources, in the methods by which the data are analysed,

---

[16] As noted in chapter 1, the classification is revised each year, so countries can move between groups. For the 2017 fiscal year, high-income economies were those with an annual GNI per head of $12,476 or more, calculated employing the World Bank Atlas method.

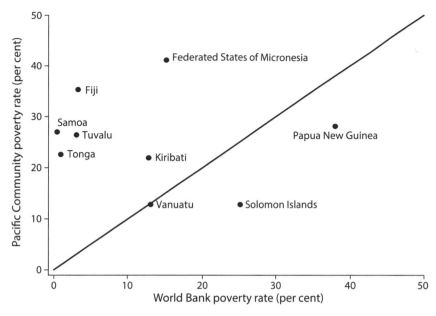

Figure 5.3. Pacific islands: National estimates of poverty rates published by the Pacific Community ("basic needs poverty") and World Bank estimates ($1.90 line)
Source: Secretariat of the Pacific Community website (National Minimum Development Indicators) and PovcalNet (October 2017 version). The data for each country refer to the same year for the two measures (years vary between 2006 and 2013).
Reading note: The estimate of the national poverty rate for "basic needs poverty" published by the Pacific Community is 28 per cent in Papua New Guinea (in 2009) and the World Bank figure based on the $1.90 a day line is 38 per cent (in the same year).

and in the definitions adopted. One of the most evident is that the national poverty lines differ in level from the International Poverty Line. Countries may set their lines above or below $1.90 a day.[17] At the same time, when discussing this question, we may find that the *levels* are different, but the *trends over time* are parallel. In such cases, we may be more concerned with the trend than with the level and conclude that the estimates are congruent even if differently located.

[17] In comparing the estimates, we have therefore to allow for such differences in the level of the poverty threshold. Suppose that the national poverty line is set at $(1 + x)$ times the $1.90 line. Measured poverty is, other things equal, higher (or not lower, strictly speaking). In thinking about how much higher, it is helpful to note that this is equivalent to reducing all consumption amounts by a factor $(1 + x)$. Seen this way, the impact of the difference in levels of consumption may be measured in terms of the growth elasticity of poverty, to which reference has already been made, except that the growth is now negative.

The second key question is, how do the national monetary poverty estimates relate to multiple deprivation indices of nonmonetary poverty? As discussed earlier in this chapter, but now placed in the context of national studies, do the nonmonetary measures give us a very different picture at the national level? If, as earlier, we examine how far we can predict the nonmonetary indices from knowledge of the monetary poverty head count, can we learn from the outliers?

The third key question is, what do the national studies tell us about who is poor?

The fourth key question concerns the relation at a national level between poverty estimates and measures of income inequality. Recent debate about success and failure in reducing poverty has turned the spotlight on the relation with overall inequality: that is, how far macroeconomic growth has benefitted groups at different points in the distribution of consumption (or income) from top to bottom. Put simply, where poverty reduction has been disappointing, is that because the gains from growth have gone to those in the middle or to those at the top? In what follows, I concentrate on the dynamics of inequality—how it has changed over time. It may also be the case that the *level* of inequality affects the poverty performance. Countries where there is a high level of inequality may attach lower priority to tackling poverty, or the high level may reflect institutional and social differences that get in the way of effective antipoverty policies.

The evidence about changes in inequality comes, with three exceptions, from national studies. It is important to note that these studies are not comparable across countries. In reading the national reports, one cannot assume that inequality is measured in the same way in every country. Moreover, I have not made use of the secondary data sets that are available as a result of the work of the World Bank, UNU-WIDER, the OECD, and academic researchers, such as Solt (2009), referred to earlier in chapter 4. I should explain why. We have to work with household surveys that have already been conducted. The only way in which they can be made comparable to a satisfactory degree is by ex post harmonisation using the individual data records, as has been described in the previous chapter. Such an ex post exercise is very demanding in terms of resources and depends on agreement about the common protocol. In chapter 4, I described the LIS project, which, commencing with seven countries in the 1980s, has been able to produce data on this basis covering now fifty high-income and middle-income countries. The LIS data are the first of the "exceptions" referred to at the beginning of this paragraph. The second is the EU-SILC (European Statistics on Income and Living Conditions), which is an ex ante harmonised data collection activity, now covering not just the EU but also Iceland, Norway, Switzerland, and Turkey. The third exception concerns the PovcalNet multi-country database of the World Bank. This database, described in chapter 4, is at the heart of the World Bank global poverty estimates, so that it is clearly necessary to give it careful attention. These apart, I do not have recourse to secondary data sets, since I am not confident that they provide a satisfactory basis for our analysis. They have the attraction of being readily downloadable, and they are widely used by researchers, but they differ in definitions and underlying methodology. Efforts are made to correct for these differences at an aggregate level—for example, by subtracting a fixed amount where the data relate to income rather than consumption—but such adjustments are too gross.

The inequality measures used here are on the whole unadjusted estimates drawn from national studies, from EU-SILC, or from LIS. It is of course the case that differences in definition and methods may affect the comparability of the *changes* as well as the levels. The reader should bear this firmly in mind.

CONCLUSIONS

The statistics assembled by the World Bank have played a key role in raising public concern about global poverty. In this chapter, I sketched the story of the International Poverty Line because it shows how the output of an essentially technical procedure, ingeniously based on using the poverty lines adopted within poor countries to pin down the global standard, has eventually gained global political legitimacy. The $1.90 line has today acquired an independent political status, which is sanctioned by its inclusion in SDG Goal 1.

It has been a remarkable achievement. Its consolidation calls for driving the research efforts in two directions. First, the theoretical elaboration of a multidimensional view of deprivation, sustained by new analytical tools and richer data, has brought to the fore the importance of measuring the nonmonetary dimensions of poverty, which is also reflected in many other SDGs. There is clearly a need to investigate the relationship that links the two sets of indicators—monetary and nonmonetary—to understand whether they confirm or confront each other. Second, we must come full circle and travel back from global to local. Are the global figures in line with national poverty studies? This is essential to assessing the reliability of the global figures and understanding whether they tell us how the world is changing. But it is also important to evaluate the political feasibility of the measures to eradicate poverty, which are mostly carried out at the national level.

This brings me to consider national cases, which is done in the next four chapters. I start with Asia, where we have seen a large role played by the two largest populations—those of China and India.

CHAPTER 6

Poverty in Asia and the Pacific

The aim of the country chapters is twofold:

1. To set out the key questions: describing poverty in individual countries by investigating how far national studies bear out the global statistics, how poverty is evolving over time, who is living in poverty, whether the very poor are being left behind, and the evidence about nonmonetary poverty.
2. In each chapter, to take up one or two crucial issues (in each case different issues) in the fight against poverty, where the discussion is focussed on the region in question but reference is made worldwide.

In the present chapter, there are national poverty reports for a wide range of countries in Asia and the Pacific: Bangladesh, Cambodia, China, Fiji, India, Indonesia, Malaysia, Nepal, the Philippines, Solomon Islands, Sri Lanka, Thailand, and Vietnam. These thirteen countries vary in scale from China (population 1.4 billion) and India (1.3 billion), the first countries considered, to the Solomon Islands (0.6 million), and they range in longitude from 70°east (Rajkot in India) to the International Date Line (Fiji).[1]

Asia is widely regarded, from the global poverty estimates, as a "success story" in terms of poverty reduction, and a key question with which this chapter is concerned is, how far is this assessment borne out by the national studies of poverty in a variety of Asian and Pacific countries? Following a review of the experience at the national level, I concentrate on two issues in this chapter. They are relevant to the Asian countries on which this chapter focusses, but also for a whole range of countries in other parts of the world, where these issues are crucial for policy debate. The reader will therefore find discussion from all parts of the globe. If Ghana appears, then it is not because of my lack of geographical knowledge or an editorial mistake.

The first general issue is the relation between growth, inequality, and poverty reduction. The countries considered include a number where rapid growth

---

[1] *Editors*: Tony wanted to include Georgia in this chapter rather than in chapter 9. (Georgia is not in the high-income group; see box A in chapter 1.) However, we have not modified the structure of his draft, and we have left his discussion of Georgia in that later chapter. Taking Georgia into account, the range in longitude begins at 40°east in the disputed region of Abkhazia on the Black Sea. Georgia straddles Europe and Asia, as reflected in its membership in different international organisations: Georgia is a member of the Council of Europe and is a country supported by the European Bank for Reconstruction and Development, but it is also a "regional member" of the Asian Development Bank.

has moved them from low-income to lower-middle- or upper-middle-income status in recent years. Has growth been a sufficient vehicle for achieving poverty reduction, as living standards have risen relative to the $1.90 line? "Trickle-down" has come under much criticism, but does it actually work? Or can poverty, measured by the International Poverty Line, be reduced only if inequality is reduced? If that is the case, then achievement of Sustainable Development Goal 1 poses a challenge of a different kind. There is a different policy trade-off.

The second issue concerns another major potential policy dilemma: the relation between poverty reduction and action on climate change. Climate is much debated, and it has long been recognised that there is a distributional dimension involving social justice across generations. But there is also the issue of the distribution of consumption today. The issue is one of distribution among countries, and across regions, so that the discussion ranges beyond Asia and the Pacific, but it also concerns within-country distribution. We need to face the question of how far climate change mitigation and poverty alleviation are complementary and to what extent they are potentially in conflict.

NATIONAL REPORTS

First, I examine the evolution of poverty at the level of individual countries. The global poverty figures have been dominated, as we have seen in the previous chapter, by the two very large countries—China and India—and I begin with these. Examining the underlying national sources is crucial, and as we shall see, in neither country is the measurement of poverty straightforward.

China

In China in 2012, according to the World Bank estimates, 6.5 per cent of the population lived in households with consumption below the International Poverty Line, or some 87 million people—more than the total population of Germany. (The reason for looking at 2012 rather than a more recent year is explained below.) Among the urban population, the poverty rate was less than 1 per cent (0.4 per cent), whereas the rural poverty rate was 13 per cent, so that one can see the overall poverty rate as being determined very largely by the latter. It is not therefore surprising that much attention is now focussed on rural poverty, and it is indeed for rural China that an official poverty line has been established. Results are presented for urban China in figure CHN2 (see the national report), but it is difficult to interpret these since there is no official poverty line, and different investigators have used different lines (see Riskin and Gao 2009). It is also important that the period since 1981 has seen a major shift in population from rural to urban China, as illustrated in figure 6.1. Until 2013, there were separate household surveys of the rural and urban populations, and in the national report the findings are presented separately (so that China, unlike other countries, has two graphs). I return later to the question of the extent to which comparability is ensured from 2013 with the introduction of the nationwide integrated survey in that year.

As we have seen in chapters 4 and 5, there is no agreed definition of rural and urban, and the Chinese data have a number of specific features. Two types of definition are used. Under the first, "the official designation 'urban' in China does not denote usual place of residence, . . . but the label 'non-agricultural' on the personal register (hukou)" (Hussain 2003, p. 3). It is therefore a personal characteristic, not a spatial location, and has as a consequence that some members may be recorded as "urban," whereas others in the same household are recorded as "rural." At the same time, location has a role in the conduct of the household surveys from which the poverty estimates are obtained. The survey is conducted in rural or urban districts according to their administrative classification. Where, in the latter case, a household consists entirely of people with a personal classification as "rural," they are transferred to the rural sample. The result is that "the rural definition for the on-going China's rural household survey could be regarded as this first definition based on Hukou" (Zhang and Wang 2011, p. 8). The second definition reflects the process of urbanisation with the classification of areas by the National Bureau of Statistics (NBS) depending on the state of construction of housing and public facilities. In 2009, the rural population on the first definition represented about two-thirds of the total but only half on the second, which appears to form the basis for the data in figure 6.1. In 2008, annual net household income per capita for rural residents was 5 per cent lower on the latter basis than on the former (Zhang and Wang 2011, p. 9).[2]

The rise in the urban population is in part due to extensive migration, but it also reflects administrative reclassification. As noted in chapter 4, political pressures may lead districts to seek reclassification, and this may lead to major shifts. In the case of China, Goldstein has described how, in the 1980s, "many localities have been added to the city and town rosters, through annexation to existing urban places or through reclassification, greatly expanding the number of such localities, the number of persons living in urban places, and the number of urban residents who are engaged in agricultural activities" (1990, p. 675).

The decline in poverty in China as recorded in the World Bank estimates is truly dramatic. In thirty years, from 1981 to 2012, the poverty rate in rural China fell, in round numbers, from 95 per cent to not much more than 10 per

[2]*Editors*: Figure 6.1 draws on World Bank data. Similar data are given on the National Bureau of Statistics *China Statistical Yearbook 2017* website (table 2–1); the urban totals there are a little higher than the World Bank figures and the rural totals a little lower (by a few million in each case).

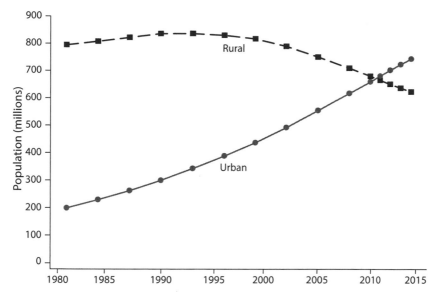

Figure 6.1. Rural and urban population of China, 1981 to 2014 (millions)
Source: PovcalNet (October 2016).
Reading note: The population was 635.7 million in rural China in 2013 and 721.7 million in urban China.

cent. The figures are given in figure CHN1.[3] The total number, shown in figure 6.2, has fallen from around 750 million to 85 million. The decline since 1990 has been particularly rapid, with the fall of 575 million accounting for more than half the reduction in global poverty over that period. The fall in urban poverty is equally impressive: from 60 per cent in 1981 to close to zero according to the International Poverty Line. In a speech in 2011, the then president, Hu Jintao, referred to "the extraordinary achievements that China has made in poverty alleviation . . . and to [the contribution] to the global anti-poverty drive,"[4] and these claims are fully borne out by the numbers.

A second important conclusion concerns the relation with national estimates. The government has for many years set an official poverty line for rural China (as noted, there is no official poverty line for urban China). The official line from 1980 to 2007 is referred to as the "extreme poverty line"; the line was

[3] *Editors*: The World Bank series shows estimates for 1993 and 1996, whereas no national data are available for that year. Elsewhere, there is an apparent difference of a year between the observations for the two series, reflecting an issue with some graphs that is explained in our note that precedes the national reports.

[4] *Editors*: The statement is reported in a news item, "Xinhua: China Raises Poverty Line by 80 Pct to Benefit over 100 Mln," on the website of the Embassy of the People's Republic of China in the United States of America

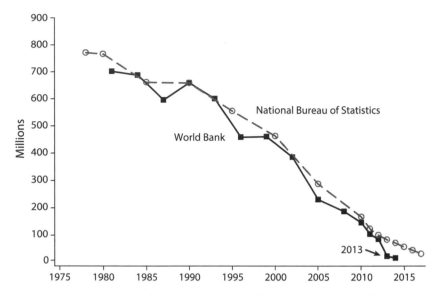

Figure 6.2. Number of people in poverty in rural China, 1978 to 2017 (millions)
Source: PovcalNet (October 2016 and April 2018 versions) and National Bureau of Statistics (see national report). The World Bank figures are obtained by applying the rural poverty rates from PovcalNet to the rural population totals in the same source.
Reading note: The World Bank estimates that 21.5 million people in rural China were in poverty in 2013 and 14.9 million in 2014, while the National Bureau of Statistics figures are 82.5 million and 70.2 million, respectively.

replaced by the "low income line," put into effect from 2008 to 2010; this in turn was replaced by the "new poverty line" effective since 2011, but with poverty rates calculated on the same basis back to 1978 (shown in figure CHN1). The new poverty line in 2010 was 2,300 yuan per person per year at 2010 prices, whereas the low income poverty line had been set at 1,247 yuan for the same year. The striking feature of the poverty rates in figure CHN1, as well as the total rural poverty numbers in figure 6.2, is how closely the new poverty estimates of the National Bureau of Statistics and those of the World Bank follow each other, at least to 2012.[5] It is reassuring that the country that contributed the most to the decline in total global poverty should be based on numbers where the national and World Bank figures are in line. At the same time, we should note that the new poverty line is some 20 per cent higher than the

[5] The World Bank notes that its poverty estimates for China "are based on grouped distributions, which are often not as precise as direct estimates based on the full distribution of household income and consumption aggregates" (World Bank 2016b, p. 49). See also the discussion of PovcalNet in chapter 4.

International Poverty Line (see national report), and we might expect the NBS estimate to be higher; it is therefore the similarity in the trend on which we should focus.

At this point, however, we should look at the poverty rate in 2013, when the World Bank figures show a sharp reduction since the previous year (2012), a reduction that contributes substantially to the fall in global poverty in that year. The data point is singled out in figure 6.2. The fall in rural China was 62.9 million, which was over half of the global fall between 2012 and 2013 of 114 million. In contrast, the figures supplied by the NBS show a fall of 16.5 million.[6] In seeking to understand the reasons for this reduction, we learn from information supplied by the NBS (for example, Xu 2015) that there are several factors in operation:

1. The move in 2013 to an integrated nationwide household survey, which was not fully comparable with the previous household surveys, in which rural and urban areas were sampled separately. In particular, the definition of "urban residents" was extended to include rural migrants who had lived in urban areas for more than six months. It also treated university students as permanent residents in the household.

2. Modification of the list of items to include imputed rents on owner-occupied housing, the reimbursement of medical expenses, and expenditure on university students. At the same time, irregular expenditures, such as those for building a house or for a wedding or funeral, were excluded. It should be noted that imputed rents are taken into account when calculating total consumption per head, but not in the case of rural residents when calculating total income per head.

3. The official poverty line had previously been increased in 2011, and was higher than the International Poverty Line, to an extent that depends on the appropriate purchasing power parity, about which there is disagreement.

Of these changes, the first—the inclusion of new items, with no adjustment to the poverty threshold—may be expected to reduce the poverty count in both rural and urban areas. There are elements operating in the opposite direction: the omission of irregular items, and the fact that the inclusion of students brings both extra spending and an additional person (thus reducing the per capita consumption). But these are unlikely to outweigh the additions. The second— the transfer of rural migrants to the urban sector—is likely to raise the poverty rate in both rural and urban counts. This would be the case if those mi-

[6]*Editors*: The rural poverty rates, shown in figure CHN1, fell between 2012 and 2013 by 9.6 percentage points (World Bank) and 1.7 percentage points (NBS). Tony's version of figure 6.2 finished in 2013 for the World Bank series and in 2014 for the NBS figures (and his comment on the global fall in poverty drew on the October 2016 version of PovcalNet). We have updated the graph, adding data for one more year and three more years, respectively, but we have not added to Tony's commentary.

grants who were previously transferred to the rural sample would in general be better off than the average rural resident (see the earlier comment about rural income per capita under the different definitions of "rural"), but less well off than the average urban resident. The third factor means that the changes in consumption per head are operating at different points in the distribution, so that their relative impacts cannot be readily assessed. In view of this, it seems safest to regard the post-2013 World Bank estimates as a separate series.

The estimates of poverty according to the extreme and low poverty lines are also shown in figure CHN1 in the national report. How do these national estimates correspond to the World Bank figures? These poverty lines for rural China, which had each in turn been the official rural threshold, are distinctly low. The extreme poverty line applied until 2007, when it was 785 yuan per person per year, while the low poverty line, which replaced it, was 1,196 yuan in 2008. Applying the 2005 ICP purchasing power parity indicates that both lines were well below $1.00 per person per day (international dollars).[7] This is consistent with the findings in figure CHN1 that the results for the extreme and low poverty lines lie well below the World Bank estimates. It is noticeable, however, that the rate of decline is rather slower, particularly in the early 2000s. Inspection of the graph for rural China suggests that the rate of decline in the poverty rate is noticeably slower than indicated by the Chinese figures contained in the World Bank global estimates.

In the absence of a poverty line for urban areas, urban poverty has been measured in a variety of ways. Hussain (2003) constructed a basic needs line, based on a daily calorie intake of 2,100. The food bundle was derived from the consumption pattern of the lowest quintile group, scaled to meet the calorie requirement, and the nonfood component estimated on the basis of the statistical relationship between nonfood and food spending. A similar approach was followed by Khan (1998, 2004), whose results for 1988, 1995, and 2002 are shown in figure CHN2. While the general trend is similar to that in the World Bank series, the rate of decline is slower and appears to miss the stagnation in China's performance in poverty reduction in the period between 1988 and 1995, "when urban poverty showed little decline and, indeed, some increase according to certain indicators" (Khan 2004, p. 24). The graph also shows the estimates of Gustafsson and Ding (2016, 2017), which extend to the more recent period, and the same comments apply.

What about inequality in China? There is much recent discussion of "rising inequality in China," and this is indeed the title of the valuable 2015 book edited by Shi Li, Hiroshi Sato, and Terry Sicular, to which they add the subtitle "Challenges to a Harmonious Society." The reference looks back to the 1970s,

---

[7] *Editors*: The World Bank's 2009 poverty assessment for China commented that the extreme poverty line in 2007 of 785 yuan represented only PPP$0.57 per person per day using the 2005 ICP and was the lowest amongst a sample of seventy-five countries (World Bank 2009, p. v).

when the Gini coefficient for income per head, if fully comparable with today's figures, was indeed low: 21 per cent in rural China in 1978 and only 16 per cent in urban China (figures CHN1 and CHN2). Nor does it appear to have risen greatly in the subsequent decade, despite the celebrated restatement of the Kuznets curve[8] by Deng Xiaopeng: "We must permit some regions, some enterprises, and some workers and peasants to have a greater income first. . . . the entire national economy will constantly move forward like a series of waves and the peoples of every nationality then quickly become rich" (I owe this quotation to Howes 1993, pp. 3, 4). In fact, the degree of inequality did not seem to rise markedly, since there were countervailing forces such as egalitarian wage reform. As summarised by Dwight Perkins: "Despite the poor quality of the data, there is no support for the view that inequality in China fell significantly during periods such as that of the Cultural Revolution [1966 to 1976] or rose as a result of market-oriented reforms. . . . There is no doubt that the economic benefits of the reforms in the 1979–87 period were widely shared" (Perkins 1988, p. 639).

What happened after this in China under its Communist government? In the case of the Soviet republics and Eastern Europe, the record of Communist governments regarding income inequality was mixed. Some countries, such as Russia, had levels of measured income inequality not dissimilar to those in relatively egalitarian OECD countries, while others, such as Czechoslovakia, achieved levels well below (Atkinson and Micklewright 1992, chapter 5).[9]

India

In the case of India, the World Bank observes that,

> for this report, as with many other countries, the total poor population in India is based on estimates rather than actual numbers provided through a household survey collected in the year of reference, in this case, 2013. Such estimates are subject to a great deal of uncertainty, which typically arises because of revisions

---

[8] The Kuznets curve refers to the possibility that, as a result of structural change, income inequality first rises and then falls as the economy modernises. This generates an inverted-U-shaped curve for the degree of income inequality (Kuznets 1955).

[9] *Editors*: Tony's drafting of his discussion of China finished at this point. He would surely have gone on to comment on the large increases in inequality in China from the mid-1980s, which make the reduction in poverty all the more striking: the Gini coefficient for income per capita rose to 39 per cent in 2009 in rural areas and to 34 per cent in urban areas (see figures CHN1 and CHN2). He might have pointed to the flattening out (and small falls) in both cases towards the end of the period, while warning against reading too much into recent trends. He could have referred again to President Hu Jintao's November 2011 speech in which the president stated: "By 2020 . . . the current trend of a widening rich-poor gap will be reversed." The current president, Xi Jinping, has declared a goal of eradicating rural poverty by the same year (report to the Nineteenth National Congress of the Communist Party of China, 18 October 2017, website of *China Daily*).

of national accounts in each country. This is also the case in India, on which the estimates for 2013 and the adjusted historical series reflect the government's periodic revisions of the growth in private consumption expenditure and the population. Notwithstanding the revisions, no methodological change underpins the 2013 poverty estimates for India with respect to 2012. In addition, the poverty estimates for India at the global poverty line are historically based on the Uniform Reference Period consumption aggregate, which involves a 30-day recall among respondents in the recording of all items of consumption. For 2011/2012, this implies a poverty rate of 21.2 percent at the US$1.90 poverty line. Since 2009, however, the Multiple Mixed Reference Period has also been used in the collection of consumption data. The methodology is closer to best international practice. It relies on recall periods among respondents of 7, 30, and 365 days, depending on the items of consumption. If the consumption estimate derived from the latter methodology had been used to estimate India's poverty rate, the result at the US$1.90 poverty line would have been a substantially lower 12.4 percent in 2011/2012. The application of the methodology is still being tested. Its adoption would eventually lead to a substantial downward revision of the poverty numbers in India (World Bank 2016, p. 49).[10]

South Asia (Bangladesh, Nepal, Sri Lanka)

Nepal has changed a great deal in recent decades. As has been described by Uematsu, Shidiq, and Tiwari, "Nepal's first comprehensive poverty assessment was published in 1991. The report—based on the Multi-Purpose Household

---

[10] *Editors*: This quotation from the World Bank's *Poverty and Shared Prosperity* report for 2016 is all that we have from Tony's draft for this subsection. (He had also assembled the data for the national report on India, although most of the text was written by us.) We guess that he would have used the quotation to reiterate issues in measuring households' consumption expenditure, perhaps referring back to the comments made by Angus Deaton that he quoted in chapter 4 on the same matter of a change in recall period in India. He might have also noted that the successive revisions to the official poverty line in India by the Planning Commission, which included other changes besides the recall period, had the net overall effect of increasing the poverty rate (compare series 1 and 2 and then 2 and 3 in figure IND). He would certainly have commented on the large fall in poverty in both the World Bank figures and the national estimates (for example, from 54.9 per cent in 1973 to 27.5 per cent in 2004, measured by series 1) and the close similarity of the two sets of estimates over 1993–1994 to 2011–2012, while drawing attention to the debate there has been over some of the numbers (see, for example, Deaton and Kozel 2005). He might also have contrasted the relatively small changes in measured inequality in India with those in China. The differences in the picture of rural versus urban poverty, depending on the set of estimates used (see the national report), could well have drawn his attention. He would surely have commented on the perspective given by the data on nonmonetary poverty (on this, see, for example, Alkire and Seth 2015; Alkire, Oldiges, and Kanagaratnam 2018).

Budget Survey conducted in 1984/85—depicted dire living conditions in Nepal more than 30 years ago. Using what was considered then a very conservative poverty line, at least 40 percent of the population was deemed absolutely poor" (2016, p. 2).[11]

Since then, there has been a dramatic reduction in the extent of measured poverty, even if less than that shown in the World Bank's PovcalNet figures, which are the basis for the global poverty estimates. These show the overall poverty rate as falling from 61.9 per cent in 1995 to 14.99 per cent in 2010, which means that poverty, measured on the basis of $1.90 a day, fell to a quarter of its previous level in fifteen years. In contrast, the calculations undertaken by the national statistical office in conjunction with the World Bank show a fall, with the 2010 poverty threshold, from 63.8 per cent in 1995 to 30.8 per cent in 2010, which means that poverty was halved. The reduction is still very impressive, but a half is very different from a quarter. This calculation takes no account, however, of the revision of the series[12]

South East Asia (Cambodia, Malaysia, Thailand, Vietnam)

[*Editors*: The national reports for Cambodia and Malaysia are reasonably complete, but there is only minimal information for Thailand and Vietnam.]

Indonesia and the Pacific (Indonesia, Fiji, the Philippines, the Solomon Islands)

[*Editors*: We have deleted text discussing changes in the distribution of income in the Philippines following the 1983–1985 recession that Tony had parked in the draft, taken from the *World Development Report 1990* (World Bank 1990, p. 111), which we presume he intended to draw on when discussing trends in poverty in this country. There are national reports for Indonesia, Fiji, and the Solomon Islands, but only a skeleton report for the Philippines.]

---

[11] Estimates of poverty in Nepal had been made for years prior to 1991—see Acharya (2004, p. 199). The National Planning Commission carried out a national survey in 1976–1977 and the Nepalese central bank conducted a budget survey in 1984–1985.

[12] *Editors*: Tantalisingly, this sentence was incomplete, and we have left it unchanged. The national report for Nepal describes three series of national estimates, of which the one Tony referred to is series 2. The much lower figures shown in series 1 are based on a different poverty line. The single observation for series 3 in 2011–2012 is obtained with both a different poverty line and a shorter recall period for food expenditure. (It is to this data point that Tony's sentence probably refers.) There are also national reports for the other two countries covered by this subsection.

GROWTH, INEQUALITY, AND POVERTY REDUCTION

Trickle-down and the distribution of consumption

[*Editors*: This section and the one that follows were to cover the two "crucial issues . . . in the fight against poverty" (see the opening of the chapter) that Tony wished to address in chapter 6. They are taken up by François Bourguignon and Nicholas Stern in their afterwords to the book.]

TACKLING POVERTY AND CLIMATE CHANGE

Complementary or competitive?

CONCLUSIONS

CHAPTER 7

Africa: Diversity of Experience

In 1957, Ghana, previously known as the Gold Coast, became independent from Britain. In the subsequent sixty years, the political landscape in Africa changed out of recognition. All seventeen British colonies and protectorates became independent, the last being Zimbabwe in 1980, after a Unilateral Declaration of Independence by a white minority government in 1965. In French colonial Africa, the countries becoming independent in 1960 included the Côte d'Ivoire, the Republic of the Congo, Gabon, Mali, Senegal, and Togo. The Belgian Congo became independent in the same year. The Portuguese colonies of Angola and Mozambique became independent in 1975, following the Carnation Revolution in Portugal, which replaced the earlier dictatorship. Today there are some fifty independent countries in Sub-Saharan Africa.

The economic landscape too has changed dramatically, but poverty remains a serious issue in Africa, and the continent is the focus of much attention on account of famine and deprivation. Africa is often seen—in contrast to Asia—as the "problem case" in the fight against global poverty. "Over the last 30 years, world-wide absolute poverty has fallen sharply. . . . But in African countries the percentage has barely fallen" (Our-Africa website, 2016). As observed by the World Bank, "A significant change in the geography of poverty has meant that Sub-Saharan Africa was hosting more than half the world's poor in 2013" (World Bank 2016, p. 35). The slower rate of poverty reduction in Sub-Saharan Africa has been illustrated in chapter 1 in figure 1.3. Where has this left individual African countries today? Figure 7.1 shows the proportion of the population now living beneath the International Poverty Line of $1.90 per day in each of fifty African countries. The year to which the figure refers varies, depending on the availability of data, but in most cases is after 2010. The poverty rate is over 35 per cent in half the countries and below 10 per cent in only nine.

At the same time, the key feature of African experience is diversity. In this chapter, I seek to learn from these differences, building on national case studies that span North Africa as well as Sub-Saharan Africa. The national reports for eighteen countries, nearly a third of those covered in the book, are for Botswana, Côte d'Ivoire, Egypt, Ethiopia, Ghana, Kenya, Liberia, Madagascar, Malawi, Mauritius, Mozambique, Niger, Sierra Leone, South Africa, Tanzania, Tunisia, Uganda, and Zambia.

The national reports include descriptions of how ministries and statistical offices have calculated their own national poverty lines, and the key questions

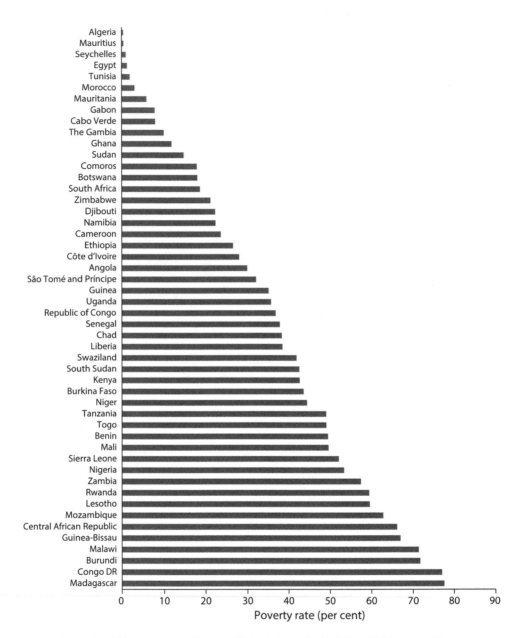

Figure 7.1. African countries: Persons living in households below $1.90 poverty line (per cent)

Source: PovcalNet (April 2018). Data are for years between 2005 and 2016 and refer to household consumption (except in the Seychelles, where the figure is based on household income).

Reading note: The World Bank estimates that 77.6 per cent of the population of Madagascar were living in households below the $1.90 per person per day poverty line in 2012.

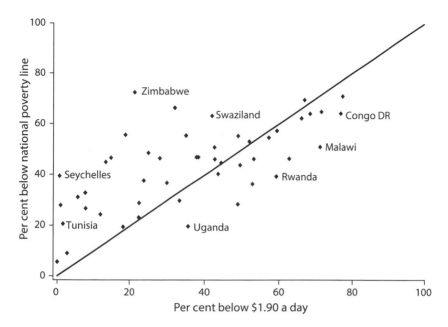

Figure 7.2. African countries: Persons in households below national poverty line and persons in households below $1.90 poverty line (per cent)

Source: World Development Indicators and PovcalNet (April 2018). Data are for years between 2004 and 2015 but are for the same year in each country.

Reading note: Zimbabwe has a poverty rate of 72.3 per cent when poverty is measured using the national line and a rate of 21.4 per cent when poverty is measured using the $1.90 per person per day line. (These estimates refer to 2011.)

addressed below include how trends in poverty measured by these lines compare with those shown in the World Bank estimates based on the International Poverty Line. As a prelude, figure 7.2 shows how the levels of poverty on the two definitions, national and international, compare for a single year. (The years vary, but in each country the data are for the same year.) The graph is not restricted to the countries covered by the national reports and includes all but two of the countries in figure 7.1. The national poverty rates are shown on the vertical axis, and the rates based on the $1.90 line are on the horizontal axis. Somewhat over half of the data points lie above the 45-degree line— these are the countries where the poverty rate based on the national definition is higher than that based on the international definition. These countries, which are mostly on the left-hand side of the graph, are those that are richer on average, where the national calculations of the poverty line tend to be more generous.[1]

---

[1]Median GNI per capita in the year in question (Atlas method) for countries above the 45-degree line is more than double that for countries below the line.

NATIONAL REPORTS

[*Editors*: There are complete or largely finished reports for ten countries—the Côte d'Ivoire, Ghana, Kenya, Mauritius, Mozambique, Niger, South Africa, Tanzania, Uganda, and Zambia—with only limited data for the other eight. As in chapter 6, Tony would have included a detailed discussion of the four groups shown below.]

North Africa (Egypt, Tunisia)

Western Africa (Ghana, Liberia, Niger, Côte d'Ivoire, Sierra Leone)

Eastern Africa (Uganda, Ethiopia, Kenya, Mauritius, Tanzania)

Southern Africa (South Africa, Botswana, Madagascar, Malawi, Mozambique, Zambia)

A COLONIAL LEGACY?

The countries considered above differ in many respects, and there have been many attempts to arrive at a classification of African states. In such typologies, one leading factor has been the colonial history, where there are representatives among the eighteen countries covered by the national reports of the former colonial empires of France, Germany, Italy, Portugal, and the United Kingdom. The first general issue discussed in this chapter is the impact, if any, of the colonial history. This does of course also involve many of the countries considered in the previous chapter on Asia, where we have to add the Netherlands and Spain to the list of colonial powers, and, in rather different ways, the countries of Latin America and the Caribbean, which are the subject of the next chapter, and from chapter 9 those countries formerly ruled by Great Britain: Australia, Canada, Ireland, New Zealand, and the United States.[2]

CORRELATES OF SUCCESS?

Whatever view one takes of the colonial past, the diversity of experience in Africa today raises the more general question as to what could explain the differences in success in tackling poverty. What can be learned from comparing countries that have successfully reduced poverty, measured according to the International Poverty Line, and that have set ambitious poverty goals at the national level?

In their study of *Growth and Poverty in Sub-Saharan Africa*, Channing Arndt, Andy McKay, and Finn Tarp (2016) divide countries into three categories: "rapid growth and rapid poverty reduction," "rapid growth but limited poverty reduction," and "un-inspiring negative growth and poverty reduction." With a small change in names, the same groupings are used here.[3]

Growth and lower poverty

Growth but little progress on poverty

In Zambia, the government initiated in 1991 a series of poverty assessments that evolved into the Living Conditions Monitoring Surveys (LCMS), which

---

[2] *Editors*: We do not know how Tony was going to tackle this section. His spreadsheets have calculations of the average per cent poor across African countries grouped according to the former colonial power. (The countries go beyond those covered by the eighteen national reports and include, for example, the former Belgian colonies of Rwanda, Burundi, and Congo DRC.) The poverty measures he considered were the per cent below the International Poverty Line and the nonmonetary figures published in the *Human Development Report* for 2015, discussed in earlier chapters. These calculations could only have been a starting point, and there is a large literature on which Tony could have drawn. We think it likely that he would have referred to the work of Rumman Khan, Oliver Morrissey, and Paul Mosley on the "Colonial Legacy and Poverty Reduction in Sub-Saharan Africa" (2016), although we cannot tell whether he would have agreed with their conclusions. (His files also included Bowden, Chiripanhura, and Mosley 2008.) Other research on Africa that he might have cited includes Acemoglu and Robinson (2010), Austin (2010, 2015), and Bossuroy and Cogneau (2013). See also our comments in the foreword on Tony's interest in top incomes in colonial Africa. In the case of India, his notes refer to the work of Dadabhai Naoroji (for example, Naoroji 1901).

[3] *Editors*: All that we have for the rest of this section are the bits on Zambia and the Côte d'Ivoire that Tony had placed in the manuscript ready to work into the text for the two subsections concerned.

continue to be conducted, most recently in 2015 (Zambia Central Statistical Office 2016). The Central Statistical Office summarised the findings of the 2010 survey:

> During the 1990s, levels of national poverty were sometimes more than 70 per cent. During the same period rural poverty was persistently in excess of 80 per cent. By 2004, levels of poverty were still high at about 67 per cent. Furthermore, since 2005 the Zambian economy has continued to register positive real GDP growth of not less than 5 per cent. Much of this economic growth was observed during the implementation of the Fifth National Development Plan (FNDP), which covered the period 2006–2010. However, there has been no notable corresponding improvement in the wellbeing of the people, especially in rural areas. (Zambia Central Statistical Office 2012, p. 172)

Poor in both growth and poverty reduction

The chapter on the Côte d'Ivoire in Arndt, McKay, and Tarp (2016) is entitled "The Fall of the Elephant." (Its national football team is nicknamed "Les Eléphants.") Rising poverty has been a major concern in the Côte d'Ivoire. Over the past thirty years, from 1985 to 2015, the national poverty rate has risen from 10 per cent to not far short of 50 per cent (see figure CIV in the national report). The World Bank PovcalNet estimates are lower, as we would expect since the national poverty threshold has been higher than the $1.90 standard, but the upward trend is similar in the two sets of figures, with the gap widening as the national poverty line rose to be 40 per cent higher than the $1.90 line. This rise, it may be noted, took place despite the fall in the inequality of income, where the Gini coefficient fell by ten percentage points between 2002 and 2015. Concern about the levels of monetary poverty is reinforced by the fact that the score on nonmonetary multiple deprivation in the Côte d'Ivoire exceeds by some ten percentage points that which would be expected at the level of recorded PovcalNet monetary poverty. (This expectation is based on the relationship between the two measures shown in figure 5.2 in chapter 5.) Moreover, while secondary school attendance increased between 1988 and 2008, there was little improvement in primary school attendance, which remained below 60 per cent (Cogneau, Houngbedji, and Mesplé-Somps 2016, table 14.A1).

The evolution of poverty since 1985 illustrates why a historical account is often best seen in terms of a series of episodes rather than as an unfolding trend.[4] The country's experience has been summarised by the Côte d'Ivoire

---

[4] *Editors*: This is a point Tony made prominently with reference to inequality in his presidential address to the Royal Economic Society (Atkinson 1997). Much of the rest of this paragraph is Tony's translation from the French text in the report by the Institut National.

Institut National de la Statistique (2008, section 1.1) as follows. The first ten years were marked by an unfavourable economic conjuncture, with deteriorating terms of trade, a sharp fall in cocoa prices after 1988, and a structural adjustment programme imposed by the International Monetary Fund (IMF) that involved major budget cuts and prevented growth from keeping up with rapid population growth. Consumption per capita in constant PPP dollars (2005 ICP) fell by 30 per cent between 1988 and 1993 (Cogneau, Houngbedji, and Mesplé-Somps 2016, table 14.1). Devaluation in 1994 and international aid were associated with a subsequent period up to 1998 when growth was more rapid and exceeded population growth. Consumption per capita recovered some of the lost ground, but this was lost by the end of the third period, from 1998 to 2008, which was marked by military-political crises (a military coup in 1999 and an army rebellion in 2002) and a de facto partition of the country. These were accompanied by a decline in living standards and a considerable loss of life, accompanied by massive displacement of the population. Not surprisingly, this unhappy sequence of events saw the poverty rate rise sharply from 2002 to 2008. Writing about the two decades from 1988 to 2008, Cogneau, Houngbedji, and Mesplé-Somps concluded that the country "could never recover from the initial shock created by the halving of cocoa producer prices and huge budget cuts" (p. 337).

CONCLUSIONS

CHAPTER 8

Poverty in Latin America and the Caribbean

On crossing the Atlantic, we come to countries that are in general richer and where rates of poverty measured by the international yardstick have been lower. At a national level, poverty lines are typically set at higher levels than the International Poverty Line of $1.90 a day. Yet these are countries where levels of overall inequality are high and rates of poverty reduction over the recent period as a whole have been slow. There was a period of hope in the first decade of this century, but doubts about the future are now being expressed. In order to examine experience at the national level, the chapter studies the recent history of poverty and inequality in eleven countries in Latin America and the Caribbean: Bolivia, Brazil, Colombia, the Dominican Republic, Guatemala, Jamaica, Mexico, Panama, Peru, Trinidad and Tobago, and Uruguay.

The national studies raise one key issue, identified in chapter 3, which is the choice between measuring poverty in terms of consumption or of income. In the countries examined in chapters 6 and 7, poverty is usually measured in terms of low *consumption*, whereas most Latin American countries have typically posed the problem in terms of low *income*. This choice is made in part on practical grounds, reflecting the kind of information that is available, but there is a more fundamental difference between different conceptions of poverty, as we have seen in the theoretical discussion of chapter 3—a difference that is illuminated by the capability approach to ethical judgements developed by Amartya Sen and Martha Nussbaum. This chapter therefore follows analysis of the national reports by investigating the practical significance of the difference.

The second issue—equally fundamental—is the contrast between the poverty of individuals and the poverty of groups. Economics is dominated today by the view, modifying John Donne, that "each household is an island, entire in itself." We count up the number of people living in households judged to be in poverty, treating each in isolation. As argued in chapter 2 and developed in this chapter, such an approach is not consistent with a capability view of poverty, but we need to go further and consider poverty as defined for salient groups. These can take different forms, but the present chapter illustrates the point by reference to the poverty of minority indigenous peoples. This is an issue with particular salience in Latin America and the Caribbean, but it arises in the countries discussed in earlier chapters, such as India, and in rich countries such as Canada.

Before all this, we should return to the pervasive issue of data quality, which all of the continent has had to confront. It is well illustrated by the following account by the official bodies concerned with poverty measurement in the Dominican Republic:

> In the last three decades, there have been in the Dominican Republic a multiplicity of figures for the extent of monetary poverty which differ significantly even in the order of magnitude for the same period. This phenomenon is due, in part, to the use of different methodologies to measure poverty that refer mainly to the construction of the basic shopping basket, the definition of the indicator of well-being, and the underlying sources of data. This has meant as a consequence that the set of estimates for those decades do not allow comparability and, accordingly, do not permit an adequate assessment of the situation and trends of monetary poverty.
>
> This was brought to a head by the discrepancy of more than 1.7 million for the year 2002, and of more than 1.1 million in the year 2004, between the figures published on the one hand jointly by the World Bank and the IDB [Inter-American Development Bank], and on the other hand the figures published by CEPAL [the UN Economic Commission for Latin America and the Caribbean]. The discrepancy had important implications for the allocation of public expenditure earmarked for the fight against poverty, as well as for its characterization and hence the design of such policies. (Dominican Republic 2012, p. 15 [my loose translation])

The account goes on to note that "the presence of differences in estimates of monetary poverty has not been a problem exclusive to the Dominican Republic. Several countries of Latin America have had to face this problem: Peru, Mexico, Colombia and Paraguay [three of which are discussed in this chapter]. In the cases of Peru and Mexico, with very notable divergences in their estimates, the problem was addressed by the formation of a Committee of poverty" (p. 15).

In the case of the Dominican Republic, a range of committees was established with a high-level inter-institutional committee and a technical committee, which included representatives from the central statistics office, the ministry for economic planning and development, the ministry of social policy, the ministry of labour, the ministry of public health, the central bank, the UNDP, the World Bank, and the UN Economic Commission for Latin America and the Caribbean (CEPAL). One concrete result was a clearly defined official poverty line based on new calculations and summarised in the national report for the Dominican Republic at the end of the book.

Other issues of data quality are familiar from elsewhere and include the problem of constructing series of poverty estimates that are comparable over time and across countries. A joint initiative of the Universidad Nacional de La Plata in Argentina and the World Bank has tried to provide such series of data in the Socio-Economic Database for Latin America and the Caribbean (SED-LAC). The methodological guide to the database comments that "governments have been improving their household surveys over the past decade, changing coverage and questionnaires. The issue of comparability is, hence, of a great concern. In particular, how comparable (across countries and over time) are the statistics shown in SEDLAC?" (CEDLAS and World Bank 2014, p. 2). Understandably, the authors of the guide do not give a definitive answer to their question, and they warn that "the final decision whether making a comparison or not depends on the preferences and specific needs of each user" (p. 3). As seen in chapter 4, the issue of comparability for Latin American countries has been tackled in a different way by CEPALSTAT, which has favoured a more interventionist approach than SEDLAC, based on an extensive adjustment to the survey data in the light of the national accounts.

To start the chapter's analysis of the available data, figure 8.1 shows the percentage of the population in households with incomes below the $1.90 International Poverty Line in each of the twenty-five Latin American and Caribbean countries for which the World Bank provides estimates in PovcalNet [*Editors*: updated to April 2018]. Some of the figures are distinctly elderly—the data from Belize, Guyana, St. Lucia, Suriname, and Trinidad and Tobago are from the 1990s—but most refer to 2014 to 2016. As was the case in the previous chapter, the numbers vary substantially, ranging from 0.1 per cent in Uruguay (a high-income country in the World Bank classification) to 52.8 per cent in Haiti (a low-income country). But levels of poverty are in general far lower than in Africa. In nineteen countries, the poverty rate is below 10 per cent, a level that characterises only nine of the fifty African countries in figure 7.1 (the analogous graph in chapter 7).

The number of poor people across these Latin American and Caribbean countries sums to 28 million.[1] Where do they live? Some 6 million are in Haiti, where, as we have seen, over half the country's population are below the International Poverty Line as judged by their household income. (I turn to the picture given by consumption data below.) But 7 million—a quarter—live in Brazil, easily the most populous country in the region with some 210 million people. The inhabitants of Brazil and of Mexico (over 125 million) account for more than half the region's total population. What happens

---

[1] *Editors*: This number is derived from Tony's application of poverty rates in figure 8.1 (updated by us) to population totals for 2015. It is very close to the estimate given in the latest regional summary (for 2013) on the PovcalNet website in April 2018.

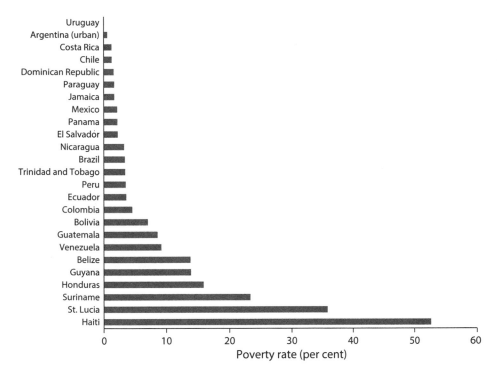

Figure 8.1. Latin American and Caribbean countries: Persons in households below $1.90 poverty line (per cent)

Source: PovcalNet (April 2018). Data are for years between 1992 and 2016 and refer to household income (except in Jamaica, where the figure is based on household consumption).

Reading note: The World Bank estimates that 52.8 per cent of the population of Haiti were living in households with incomes below the $1.90 per person per day poverty line in 2012.

to poverty in these two big countries—with only modest poverty rates in the top half of figure 8.1—has a large impact on the number of poor in the region as a whole.

These poverty rates and numbers of poor people refer to poverty according to a standard of $1.90 per person per day. But as noted, national poverty lines are typically set at higher levels than this in the countries that are the subject of this chapter. This is reflected in the pattern shown in figure 8.2, which plots the poverty rates for twenty countries with measurement by each national line on the vertical axis against the rates when poverty is measured using the international line on the horizontal axis. All countries come above the 45-degree line: the poverty rates are everywhere higher with the national threshold, many of them by a long way. The national rates average 30 per cent, while the $1.90 a

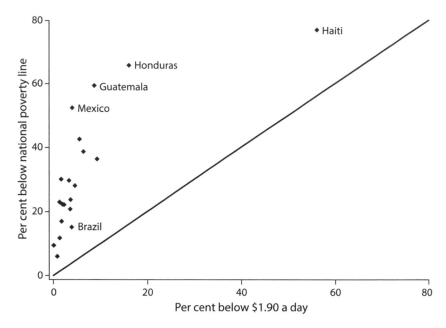

Figure 8.2. Latin American and Caribbean countries: Persons in households below national "moderate" poverty line and persons in households below $1.90 line (per cent)

Source: PovcalNet (April 2018) and SEDLAC. Data refer to various years but, for each country, to the same year for both poverty rates.

Reading note: Honduras has a poverty rate of 65.7 per cent when poverty is measured using the national "moderate" line and a rate of 16.0 per cent when poverty is measured using the $1.90 per person per day line. (These estimates refer to 2016.)

day rates average only 7 per cent. The reader may like to compare the graph with figure 7.2 for Africa, where a large number of countries have a lower rate when measured by a national yardstick.

The national poverty estimates in figure 8.2 are from the collection made by SEDLAC and relate to measurement based on "moderate" poverty lines. That is, a poverty line that includes allowance for both food and nonfood items. For all but one country in the graph (Jamaica), the SEDLAC data also include figures for poverty rates based on a lower "extreme" poverty line. These lower lines are mostly based on the cost of a basic food basket alone, with no allowance for any nonfood items. (Several examples are described in the national reports.) If we switch from the moderate to the extreme national poverty figures, the differences between the national estimates and those based on the International Poverty Line fall considerably. But the national figures still average 14 per cent, twice the average of the international ones. In passing, it is worth noting that the International Poverty Line is also defined by the World Bank as a threshold for extreme poverty (see chapter 1). We therefore have two definitions of "extreme," one based on national standards and one on an international standard.

NATIONAL REPORTS

[*Editors*: There are complete or largely finished reports for five countries: the Dominican Republic and Jamaica from the Caribbean and Bolivia, Brazil, and Colombia from South America. The reports for the other six countries are skeletons. The only text for this part of the chapter that Tony had drafted was the paragraph on Bolivia. In the case of nonmonetary poverty, besides the multidimensional measures for the region that Tony drew attention to in chapter 3 (see table 3.1), we note the work of Santos and Villatoro (2018), which covers seventeen Latin American countries at two points in time, one around 2005 and one around 2012.]

Caribbean (the Dominican Republic, Jamaica, Trinidad and Tobago)

Central America (Guatemala, Mexico, Panama)

South America (Bolivia, Brazil, Colombia, Peru, Uruguay)

The development of poverty in Bolivia, measured in terms of income, is summarised in figure BOL in the national report. The experience of this country provides answers to the four questions about poverty at the national level posed at the end of chapter 5. First, the movements in the World Bank estimates of the proportion of the population living below $1.90 a day are closely in line with the changes over time in the national poverty estimates—at least as far as the period since 2000 is concerned. As is to be expected of a relatively richer country, the national poverty line is set at a higher level, and the country's own "extreme" poverty count is more than double the World Bank count, but both show a major reduction. This reduction took place in the twenty-first century. Between 2000 and 2012, the World Bank poverty rate was reduced to a third of its previous value, taking some 2 million people out of extreme poverty. The proportion suffering extreme poverty on the national definition was halved, and the proportion below the moderate poverty line declined by a third. The answer to the second question—do the estimates of nonmonetary poverty tally with the national figures for monetary poverty—cannot be answered in full, as we have estimates only for two years, 2003 and 2008. However, we see that between these two dates the nonmonetary poverty rate also fell sharply, by nearly sixteen percentage points. The reality of the dramatic success in reducing monetary poverty is therefore underlined by the fall in nonmonetary poverty.[2] Third, the burden of poverty measured by the national estimates varies sharply. The extreme poverty rate in 2012 was 12 per cent in urban areas but 41 per cent in rural areas, and poverty was much higher among indigenous people—37 per cent compared to 12 per cent for the rest of the population. Fourth, what is the relation of poverty with economic growth and with the changes in income inequality? The period since 2000 has seen GNI per head in Bolivia double in terms of PPP, with the growth coming largely after the mid-2000s. This might suggest a strong poverty responsiveness, a conclusion reinforced by the fact that the period from the late 1990s to the mid-2000s, when growth was relatively stagnant, saw little poverty reduction. On the other hand, the earlier World Bank figures suggest that poverty rose in the 1990s, when growth was comparatively strong, although in this case the national poverty estimates are not in agreement. We must also look at the behaviour of income inequality, where the Gini coefficient fell between 2006 and 2012 by twelve percentage points. Inequality remains high, but there has been a major reduction in a short period.

INCOME OR CONSUMPTION

The World Bank estimates of poverty for Latin American and Caribbean countries shown in figure 8.1 are based on data for households' incomes. And in the great majority of cases, the series of figures given in PovcalNet for each of these countries showing how poverty has evolved over time are also based exclusively on income—there are typically no estimates that use data on households' consumption. By contrast, all the figures for African countries considered in chapter 7 are based on consumption (with the exception of the latest estimate for Seychelles, now classified as a high-income country).

The exceptions in Latin America and the Caribbean are Jamaica, Haiti, Mexico, and Nicaragua. For Jamaica, there are only estimates based on con-

---

[2] *Editors*: Tony drew here on the OPHI estimates of multidimensional poverty for Bolivia. Alternative estimates based on five non-income dimensions for a rather longer period, 1999 to 2011, are given by Villarroel and Hernani-Limarino (2013). They conclude that the head count fell substantially over these years, with the downward trend accelerating from 2005.

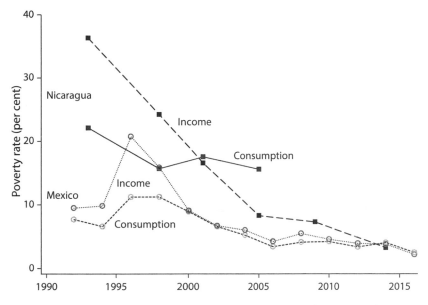

Figure 8.3. Mexico and Nicaragua poverty rates with the $1.90 line (per cent): Income versus consumption

Source: PovcalNet (April 2018).

Reading note: In 1993, the World Bank estimates that 36.3 per cent of the population of Nicaragua were living in households below $1.90 per person per day when measured using household income and 22.1 per cent when measured using household consumption.

sumption. For Haiti, there are two figures for 2012 using the International Poverty Line of $1.90, one based on income and one on consumption, and there is a very large difference between them: a poverty rate of 23.5 per cent with consumption but 52.8 per cent with income. (The latter is used in figure 8.1 for consistency with other countries.) (PovcalNet contains an estimate of the poverty rate in Haiti for just one other year, 2001, based on income—56.1 per cent.)

In the case of Mexico and Nicaragua, there are figures both for income poverty and for consumption poverty stretching back into the 1990s (see figure 8.3). For Mexico, there is a close correspondence between the two rates from 2000 onwards, for both the level and the trend. But the picture for the 1990s is very different.[3] For Nicaragua, there are four years for which estimates are given on both bases. In the last of these, 2005, the consumption-based rate was

---

[3] *Editors*: The graph is based on the April 2018 version of PovcalNet. The October 2016 version used by Tony showed an income poverty rate from 2004 onwards that was several percentage points higher than the estimate in figure 8.3 (see his comment on data for 2012 in chapter 3 [p. 62]), but with smaller differences between income and consumption poverty in the 1990s,

notably higher than the income poverty rate. In 2001 they were essentially the same, while in 1998 and 1993 the rates using consumption data were substantially lower. The two series therefore give a quite different picture of the trend in poverty reduction over the period concerned, one showing a fall of less than ten percentage points and the other a fall of almost thirty percentage points.[4]

THE POVERTY OF GROUPS

[*Editors*: Although the introduction to the chapter mentions only indigenous peoples, Tony's section and subsection titles imply that he also planned to discuss the broader issue of poverty among ethnic minorities. In both cases, his notes show that he intended to refer to other parts of the world beyond Latin America and the Caribbean, applying his strategy for addressing his chosen "general issues" in chapters 6 to 9. For example, he had taken notes on poverty among different minorities in Nepal from World Bank (2006); his national reports at the end of the book include estimates of poverty rates for different ethnic groups in other countries, such as those for India and South Africa; and he had collected data on poverty among indigenous children in Canada from Macdonald and Wilson (2013), who observe: "Poverty is not solely a question of income levels. Status First Nations children, in addition to a higher poverty rate, often live in communities that are without comparison in Canada when it comes to the impoverishment of services and infrastructure" (p. 19).]

Ethnic minorities

Poverty among indigenous peoples

According to the United Nations Permanent Forum on Indigenous Issues (2016), there are some 370 million indigenous peoples living in seventy countries across the world. There is evidence that they face much higher rates of poverty. The World Bank (2016a) study in Latin America, where there are estimated to be some 42 million indigenous people, found that they face poverty rates that are on average twice as high as for other Latin Americans. Measured in terms of the percentage of people living on less than the International Poverty Line (taken in this case as $1.25 in PPP dollars in the late 2000s), 9 per cent were below this threshold compared with only 3 per cent for non-

---

[4] *Editors*: We do not know how Tony was planning to develop this section further. He returns to the definitions of consumption and income in chapter 9 when discussing the meaning of poverty in rich countries.

indigenous people, based on a weighted average for Bolivia, Brazil, Ecuador, Guatemala, Mexico, and Peru (World Bank 2016a, figure 10). Nor can the difference be fully explained by demographic and economic differences between indigenous peoples and the rest of the population. In Bolivia, Ecuador, Guatemala, Mexico, and Peru, only about half the gap in poverty rates between indigenous and non-indigenous peoples can be accounted for in this way (Calvo-Gonzãlez 2016).

CONCLUSIONS

CHAPTER 9

Poverty in Rich Countries and a Global Measure of Poverty

An important feature of the SDGs is that they are now global, encompassing rich as well as poor countries. And poverty remains a concern in many OECD countries, and indeed to the OECD itself, which has pioneered much research. This chapter includes national case studies for seventeen countries: Australia, Canada, Finland, France, Germany, Greece, Ireland, Italy, Japan, New Zealand, Norway, Poland, Portugal, South Korea, Sweden, the United Kingdom, and the United States.

To allocate more than a quarter of the national reports to rich countries may seem excessive. But to begin with, these countries have a long history, extending back to the nineteenth century, of measuring poverty from which we can learn. More importantly, we have to ask why, after a long period of rising living standards, poverty is still on the agenda, and this is a key issue discussed in the chapter. From this, I go on to reconsider what is meant by poverty in rich countries. This takes us to the final issue, which in a sense brings the book full circle. A great deal of attention has been paid to global inequality and the possible impact of factors such as globalization. Researchers have asked whether the reduced gaps between Asian countries and the OECD have reduced world income inequality by more than it has been increased by greater within-country inequality. We need to ask the same question about global poverty, but this requires a global poverty standard that goes beyond the International Poverty Line. In this chapter, the capability approach is employed to provide a foundation for such a "societal" poverty line applicable to the world as a whole.

NATIONAL REPORTS

National poverty studies have a long history. In the United Kingdom, the starting point for the scientific study of household poverty is often taken, as in earlier chapters of this book, to have been the work in York by Seebohm Rowntree in 1899 (Rowntree 1901), although there had been earlier studies. In the Soviet Union, there had been a long history: "By the time the Bolsheviks came to power, Russia had already acquired quite a respectable history of investigations into people's living standards" (Matthews 1986, pp. 13–14). In Poland, "poverty measurement was first attempted . . . in the early twenties just after the country regained its independence" (Kordos 1991, p. 3).

Eastern Europe and the former Soviet Union (Poland, Georgia)

When John Micklewright, then at the European University in Florence, and I began in the early 1990s to study poverty and the distribution of income in Eastern Europe and the former Soviet Union, there was a widely held belief that the period before the fall of communism was a statistical desert. Little was known, and the limited data collected were not published. Poverty was regarded as a distinguishing feature of capitalism and the introduction of the idea that it might also occur under communism was discouraged or forbidden: Matthews wrote of the Soviet Union that "public discussion of poverty as such is virtually banned in the USSR itself, and even specialist Soviet writers cannot easily broach it" (1986, p. xi).

This was a convenient myth, because it meant that the study of poverty post-communism could start from a clean slate and did not have to face the tricky issues of comparison with what happened before. It was convenient because it avoided the awkward questions that arise when we seek to compare poverty under different economic and political systems. However, we did not believe that it was true—it was largely a myth. We knew that in countries such as Poland, researchers led by Jan Kordos of the Central Statistical Office (which celebrated its centenary in 2018) were investigating how many people were living below the social minimum. Even cursory perusal of the annual statistical yearbooks for other Eastern European countries revealed tables summarising the findings from the regular household income surveys, and there were other official publications, such as those of the Hungarian statistical office (Hungarian Central Statistical Office 1975). We knew that in the London School of Economics library there were rows of reports for the different countries gathering dust. The *World Development Report* of 1990 contained an analysis of poverty in Poland and other countries which drew on a background paper by Branko Milanovic on poverty in Hungary, Poland, and the former Yugoslavia (Milanovic 1990). And Alastair McAuley (1979), a colleague during my time at the University of Essex, had done important work on poverty and the distribution of income in the Soviet Union.

Recovering data on income inequality and poverty in pre-1990 communist countries became something of an obsession, and we wrote a full book on Eastern Europe and the former Soviet Union (Atkinson and Micklewright 1992). Here space is limited, and I restrict attention to two representatives of today's countries: Poland and Georgia.[1]

In Poland, the Institute of Labour and Social Affairs first calculated a social minimum level of income in 1980, and an annual series was carried out

---

[1] *Editors*: We have retained Tony's discussion of Georgia in this chapter, a country not mentioned in the list in the opening paragraph (Georgia is not a high income country.) Tony had thought of covering Georgia in chapter 6 instead, as we note there.

every year from 1983 (see figure POL). The social minimum was not a social assistance level; it was quite independent of social security benefits and was based on a basket of goods. It was therefore a basic needs approach, not a political line. The basket covered all goods, not just food. The latter was based on nutritional requirements, and the prices based on actual prices recorded in the Household Budget Survey. The minimum was adjusted for shortages, notably in 1984–1988, when there were widespread shortages of meat and the food standard was reduced in recognition of the fact that households might not have been able to obtain the food. As Algernon Moncrieff claims to his visiting aunt in Oscar Wilde's play *The Importance of Being Earnest*, "there were no cucumbers in the market this morning . . . not even for ready money." In this case, there was no shortage (he had eaten the entire plate), but the Polish adjustment underlines a potentially important reason why consumption may differ from income and the need to take account of the supply side of the market.

What do the data tell us about poverty under communism in Poland? The first striking conclusion from figure POL is that the recorded national estimates of the poverty head count in the 1980s are high—in excess of 20 per cent in several years. Poverty rose from 11 per cent in 1980 to more than double that level in 1983 (23.7 per cent) during what Milanovic (1990) calls "the crisis years." Szulc attributes the rise to the "great price increase in 1982, which was not compensated by incomes augmentation" (1990, p. 7). These periods of increase must have been of concern to the regime and may have been a source of growing opposition, leading to the formation of Solidarity in 1980, led by Lech Wałęsa, and its suppression at the end of 1981. Poverty in Poland, measured by the yardstick of the social minimum, rose by some ten percentage points during the period of martial law in the early 1980s.

Judged by the standards of other European countries, how do the figures for poverty under communism in its last decade compare? The LIS-based estimates for the mid or late 1980s show the proportion living with equivalised household income below 60 per cent of the median was 8 per cent in the Netherlands, 11 per cent in Finland, 12 per cent in Sweden, rising to 17 per cent in France and in Spain, 18 per cent in the United Kingdom, and 19 per cent in Italy. The LIS-based figure for 1986 in Poland for the same relative poverty measure was 17 per cent (also shown in figure POL), identical to the national figure for that year based on the social minimum. The conclusion that I draw is that poverty in communist Poland was not lower than in Western countries, but neither was it demonstrably much higher.

What happened after 1990? The initial years saw a large rise in poverty as measured by the social minimum approach from pre-1990, although this rise has been questioned (see the national report). As put by the OECD, the estimates "tend to point to a similar diagnosis: poverty increased in the early 1990s but may recently have peaked" (OECD 1996, p. 89). Interestingly, the OECD in its regular Economic Surveys of Poland never returned to the subject in the twenty years (and eleven reports) that followed. Poverty had dropped off the agenda. The evidence post-1995 is in fact not easy to interpret. The LIS-based estimates suggest that in 2013 the proportion living in households with equivalised disposable income below 60 per cent of the median was little different from that in 1995. On the other hand, the Eurostat estimates on the same basis indicate a three-percentage-point reduction between 2004 and 2014, and support is provided by the decline in income inequality. Here we see the value of being able to appeal to measures of nonmonetary poverty, which show a very marked decline from 2005 to 2015. Taken together, this suggests that progress has been made in Poland in recent years towards tackling poverty in the round. Finally, figure POL has one more piece of evidence: the poverty rate for 1996 to 2016 based on the subsistence minimum that is calculated by the Institute of Labour and Social Affairs along with the (higher) social minimum. This rate is estimated by the Central Statistical Office and is based on consumption rather than income. The figures show a substantial rise of eight percentage points to a level of 12.3 per cent in 2005. But this is followed by a fall—albeit not continuous—to 4.9 per cent by the end of the period, confirming the direction of travel in the other measures in the graph.

As we move east to the former Soviet Union, including Georgia, we begin to appreciate why it has been claimed that we know little about poverty under communism. This is not entirely fair. As already noted, there had been work on living standards in Tsarist Russia, and this did not come to an end with the Revolution: family budget studies continued, in 1922 there was an All-Russian Statistical Conference devoted to the topic, and there were calculations of subsistence minima in the Soviet Union in the 1950s (Matthews 1986, pp. 16, 19). But there were increasing restrictions on the publication of such information. The subject was still discussed, and new work was undertaken in the 1980s on minimum budgets. The last prime minister of the Soviet Union, Nikolai Ryzhkov, told the Congress of People's Deputies that in 1989 nearly 40 million people lived below the poverty line (Atkinson and Micklewright 1992, p. 178).

The 40 million figure referred to the number of persons with per capita household income beneath a subsistence minimum calculated by the Soviet statistical office, Goskomstat, and equal in 1989 to 81 roubles per person per month (or 88 roubles, depending on the prices used in the calculation). Published data from Goskomstat on the distribution of income at this time identified the numbers below a line equal to 75 roubles per capita, noting that it had become customary to refer to these people as poor. The incidence of poverty, measured in this way, varied enormously across the fifteen constituent republics of the Soviet Union, from 2 per cent in Estonia to 51 per cent in Tajikistan (Atkinson and Micklewright 1992, table 8.4). The figure for Georgia, 13 per cent, was the median. But we know little about how these estimates were reached. The methods are not described in the same careful way as in Poland and, as far as one can judge, the quality of the underlying data fell short. The figures were based on the USSR Family Budget Survey, which had a very poor reputation.

Following the breakup of the Soviet Union, each republic inherited part of the Family Budget Survey. In 1996, Georgia introduced a new survey with assistance from Statistics Canada and the World Bank and, the year after, an official poverty line. Figure GEO shows poverty rates for 1996–2000 based on this line and for 2004–2015 based on the subsistence minimum now used by the National Statistical Office of Georgia.[2]

Anglo-Saxon countries and Ireland (the United States, the United Kingdom, Australia, Canada, New Zealand, Ireland)

The 2008 OECD report "Growing Unequal?" summarised the changes in poverty head counts between the mid-1990s and the mid-2000s, taking an income poverty line set at 50 per cent of the median. The majority (sixteen out of the twenty-six countries selected) showed a rise. These included all of the Anglo-Saxon countries listed above, apart from Great Britain, which had experienced a large increase in the previous decade. (To avoid confusion, Great Britain is the United Kingdom excluding Northern Ireland.) This certainly suggests that there has been no progress in reducing poverty in the Anglo-Saxon countries, and indeed that performance with regard to poverty in high-income countries is travelling in the wrong direction. However, how far is this a true summary? Have all Anglo-Saxon countries been equally unsuccessful in reducing poverty?

As we have seen, poverty measurement in the United Kingdom and the United States began with poverty lines that originated in a basic needs approach. The US official poverty series continues in that tradition, although there is debate as to how far the price index used for updating overstates the rate of inflation, not allowing sufficiently for quality change, so that the effective purchasing power has risen. There are also estimates for the United States, using a relative poverty line based on a percentage of median income, which are more directly comparable in terms of measuring trends over time with the relative poverty lines now employed in the United Kingdom and in the other Anglo-Saxon countries and Ireland. In each case, the poverty estimates are obtained from household surveys, with, in the case of the United Kingdom, an admixture of income tax data to correct for undercoverage at the top.

Table 9.1 draws together the results from the national reports to show how poverty and income inequality have changed over the past thirty years. Since the economic crisis of 2007–2008 may have had a significant impact (see below), the changes in poverty are also shown for the period ending in 2008. As may be seen, the picture is more nuanced than the simple summary suggested. Of

---

[2] *Editors*: Tony left this subsection unfinished, with no notes on his plans for its completion.

Table 9.1. How have poverty and income inequality changed in Anglo-Saxon countries and Ireland?

	Change in Poverty Rate, 1984 to 2014 (Percentage Points)	Change in Poverty Rate, 1984 to 2008 (Percentage Points)	Change in Gini Coefficient, 1984 to 2014 (Percentage Points)
Australia	+1.4	+2.3	+5.3
Canada	0	+0.4	+1.8
Ireland	+0.7	−1.2	−1.2
New Zealand	+6.0	+5.0	+7.2
United Kingdom	+3.1	+5.1	+6.9
United States	−0.4	−0.9	+6.4

Source: National reports. Poverty is defined as living in a household with income below 60 per cent of the median (50 per cent in Canada and the United States). Australia poverty rates are from 1985 to 2010, and Gini coefficients are from 1981 to 2013. Ireland poverty rates are from 1994 for poverty and from 1995 for the Gini coefficient. There is no 2008 poverty rate for New Zealand, and the 2007 rate (which is identical to the 2009 rate) has been used.
Reading note: In the United States, the poverty rate fell by 0.4 percentage points between 1984 and 2014.

the six countries, half saw a change of less than one percentage point over the past thirty years. There were large increases in New Zealand and the United Kingdom, but they stand out. The charge that can be levelled against the Anglo-Saxon countries is not that poverty has generally risen, but that they have failed to bring about a significant reduction.

Where there is greater similarity is in the increase in income inequality. In four of the six countries, the Gini coefficient was higher at the end of the period by at least five percentage points. This should be carefully stated. Many politicians and leaders of international bodies, having discovered inequality, assert that we have a problem of "rising inequality." Careful inspection of the national reports will reveal that inequality is not rising in as many countries today; rather, the problem is that inequality has risen in the past, and that we are facing the problem of a high level of inequality.

Two countries stand out in the poverty figures in table 9.1: New Zealand and the United Kingdom.[3]

[3] *Editors*: How would Tony have developed this subsection, which includes the UK experience that he knew so well? It is clear that he intended to focus on child poverty in his discussion of New Zealand and the United Kingdom. He planned a box on the UK Child Poverty Act of 2010, which underlined the then-Labour government's commitment to "eradicate child poverty." This legislation set targets for various monetary and nonmonetary measures of child poverty and imposed a duty on governments to move towards them by 2020–2021 (see the national report). In the case of New Zealand, his notes include the following text from Perry (2016, p. 91):

Northern and Southern Europe compared (Finland, Norway, Sweden, Portugal, Spain, Italy, Greece)

Mainland Western Europe (France, Germany)

Japan and Korea

It is not easy to reconstruct the history of income inequality in Japan. The LIS key figures contain only one year of data (2008) and the World Development Indicators provide only (slightly different) data for the same year. There are a variety of national sources, which have strengths and weaknesses. For example, the National Survey of Family Income and Expenditure has a large sample (55,000 households) but excludes single-person households. Kohara and Ohtake provide long-run series for the Gini coefficient, but they relate to before-tax income (2014, figure 17.1).[4]

THE PERSISTENCE OF POVERTY

[*Editors*: Tony's files included figure 9.1, which shows long time series of both relative and absolute poverty measures for the United States and a much shorter series for relative poverty in the Eurozone. (The relative poverty rates are both based on thresholds of 60 per cent of median equivalised household income,

---

"In 2002, in the context of the Agenda for Children, the Labour-led government made a commitment to eliminate child poverty and, in the Speech from the Throne in November 2005, the Governor-General described the Working for Families package as 'the biggest offensive on child poverty New Zealand has seen for decades.' [But] in response to the Children's Commissioner's Expert Advisory Group's 2012 Report on Solutions to Child Poverty, the current National-led government declined to take up the recommendations for a suite of official measures and a set of official targets for reducing child poverty." (The Labour-led government that took power in October 2017 has made reducing child poverty a priority.) We think Tony would also have included discussion of Ireland's national antipoverty strategy, which dates to 1997, and of changes that have taken place in Ireland in "consistent" poverty, the country's official definition of poverty (low income combined with material deprivation, defined further in the national report), possibly commenting on the relatively better performance of Ireland vis-à-vis other countries in table 9.1.

[4]*Editors*: There is a national report for Japan with information on measurement of poverty as well as inequality, but there is no report for Korea.

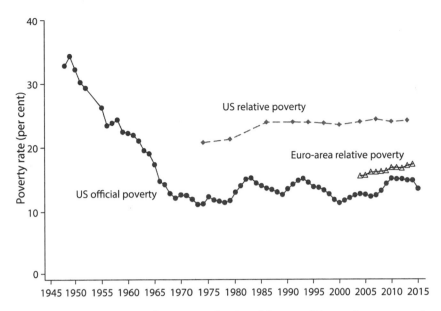

Figure 9.1. The persistence of poverty in the United States and Europe (per cent poor)
Source: US Census Bureau; LIS Key Figures (downloaded September 2016); and Eurostat website, tessi010, Euro (19) (downloaded October 2016). Relative poverty is defined as equivalised household income below 60 per cent of the median; the US official measure is also based on income. *Reading note*: In 2013, 24.1 per cent of the US population were living in households with incomes below 60 per cent of the median.

while the absolute rate refers to the US official poverty line.) We think he planned to use the graph to help introduce this section. His notes show that somewhere in the chapter he planned to cover "poverty measurement in the European Union. Delors and the back of an envelope. Investment in household surveys. The Laeken indicators and their development. Europe 2020."]

The long wait to tackle relative poverty

The Great Recession[5]

In France, the study by Pan Ké Shon has asked why "the level of the 'poverty in living conditions' indicator remained broadly stable during the period of ex-

---

[5] *Editors*: We have just the two paragraphs on France and Greece from Tony. Changes in poverty and income inequality in rich countries in the early years after the financial crisis of 2007–2008 are discussed in Jenkins et al. (2013).

ceptional economic crisis which began in 2008. It even declined in 2011 and 2012. What are the reasons for these unexpected movements and for the divergence between the material deprivation indicators and the monetary poverty rate (which has been increasing since 2008)?" (2015, abstract).

In the case of Greece, the impact has been summarised by Mitrakos as follows:

> The available data indicate that income inequality and relative poverty increased, yet not dramatically, during the current crisis, although the composition of the poor population changed considerably. However, the sharp decline in disposable income and the dramatic increase in unemployment led to a significant deterioration in economic prosperity and absolute poverty, i.e., when the poverty line in real terms remains stable in the pro-crisis levels. (2013, abstract)

The meaning of poverty in rich countries

What does poverty really mean in rich countries? We may need to rethink what the terms "consumption" and "income" mean. Should soup kitchens and food banks be regarded as providing consumption of equal value to purchases made freely in a supermarket? Should income from begging be regarded as equal in value to a welfare cheque? Is money received from selling plasma, as described by Edin and Shaefer (2015, p. 93), equivalent to a pay cheque? The qualitative nature of the transaction, and the degree of agency, need to be taken into account. This may lead to consumption financed by certain kinds of income being discounted by a factor less than 1 that takes account of the conditions on which it is obtained, or even discounted altogether. In other words, $1 of income is not treated the same regardless of the conditions under which it was obtained.[6]

A GLOBAL POVERTY MEASURE

Poverty in rich countries has conventionally been treated as separate from poverty in the developing world. Within academia there have tended to be two

---

[6] *Editors:* Had Tony finished this section, we think he would have developed other issues flagged in his discussion of poverty in rich countries in chapter 1 (pp. 20–22): the coverage by household surveys of groups particularly prone to poverty, including those at the margins of society, and what nonmonetary indicators add to our knowledge of the poor in high-income countries. And chapter 4 signals his intention for more discussion here of the EU's measurement of material deprivation. He might also have returned to the issue of a rights-based approach to measuring poverty and referred, for example, to the reports of the visits to the United States in 2017 and to the United Kingdom in 2018 of the UN special rapporteur on extreme poverty and human rights (Alston 2017, 2018, 2018a).

disjoint literatures, and the methods applied have been different. The SDGs, however, seek to change this. The goals are formulated as concerned with poverty in all nations. What is more, poverty is to be assessed both by the International Poverty Line and according to national criteria, recognising that, as societies evolve, so too do the standards by which they judge poverty.

In order to develop a common framework, we have to come to terms with the different national approaches, and this is a challenge. In chapter 2, I have argued that the capability approach offers one route forward. It is not necessarily the only vehicle for reconciliation, but the proposed calculations have the virtue of simplicity. Put succinctly, the poverty line is set at the International Poverty Line for countries with mean consumption per head below a certain level, but then rises with mean consumption: for example, using the main version considered here, it rises by 30 per cent (the "gradient") of any increase in mean consumption per head. That is, if mean consumption per head rises by $10, the poverty line rises by $3 (where the dollars here and in the remainder of this chapter are again all international purchasing power dollars). What is the "certain level" where the poverty line begins to rise? This is governed by the parameters already specified: there is a switch where 30 per cent of mean consumption reaches the International Poverty Line. Or put another way, the poverty line starts to move upwards when a country's mean consumption is three and a third times the International Poverty Line. The reader may like to look again at the discussion of figure 2.1 in chapter 2.[7]

Implementing a global poverty count

To put the global poverty approach into effect, I have used the PovcalNet data of the World Bank.[8] These data have their limitations (discussed in chapter 4) in country coverage and in the lags with which data can be incorporated. For instance, in my calculation I have dropped eight countries whose data come from before 2000. This leaves me with a total of 147 countries. I should also note that the methods applied here differ in certain respects from those applied by the World Bank, so that the numbers reached are not fully compara-

---

[7] Ravallion and Chen (2013) have proposed such a new class of "truly global poverty measures," although their approach is a little different. With an absolute poverty line at $1.25 a day at 2005 prices, they set the relative poverty line at $1.25 for countries whose mean consumption is at or below this level. (This applies to only a small number of countries.) Where the country mean consumption exceeds $1.25 a day, the poverty line is set equal to $1.25 plus 50 per cent of the excess of mean consumption over $1.25. On this basis, they make estimates of poverty measures for the world as a whole covering the period 1990 to 2008.

[8] *Editors*: Tony used data from the October 2016 version of PovcalNet, and in this chapter we have not attempted to update his calculations. His comments on PovcalNet do not necessarily hold for later releases. For example, estimates of poverty in Iraq and Malta are present in the April 2018 version. At the regional level his estimates are very close but not perfectly coincident with the World Bank's figures available in the PovcalNet archive

ble with those in chapters 1 and 5. My aim is to suggest what can be learned from this approach, not to provide definitive estimates. My father used to say, "If all else fails, read the instructions," and I repeat here the warning on the World Bank website:

> PovcalNet was developed for the sole purpose of public replication of the World Bank's poverty measures for its widely used international poverty lines, including $1.90 a day and $3.20 a day in 2011 PPP. The methods built into PovcalNet are considered reliable for that purpose. However, we cannot be confident that the methods work well for other purposes, including tracing out the entire distribution of income. We would especially warn that estimates of the densities near the bottom and top tails of the distribution could be quite unreliable, and no attempt has been made by the Bank's staff to validate the tool for such purposes.

In addition to the $1.90 and $3.20 lines, the PovcalNet website also reports estimates for the $5.50 line. In the present case, PovcalNet is being used to extrapolate upwards from $1.90 a day for those countries where the relative poverty line exceeds $1.90. No use is made of data below $1.90 a day, nor is there any attempt to trace the entire distribution. The poverty lines for high-income countries stretch some way up the distribution, reaching a maximum value at $21.25 a day for Luxembourg in the case of the first of the two calculations I make in what follows (the 30 per cent gradient). This is eleven times the International Poverty Line, and we clearly need to take the estimates for rich countries with some caution. However, with the 30 per cent gradient, the new poverty line lies between $1.90 and $5.50 for forty-nine countries out of ninety-one. In other words, they lie within the range for which the World Bank employs the data. For another twenty-one countries, the line falls between $5.50 and $9.50, which is five times the International Poverty Line. The remaining twenty-one countries are all rich nations from the OECD area and have a mean societal poverty line of $15.20; for the United States, the line equals $18.91.

With the qualification made above, the PovcalNet data are a most useful resource, and the World Bank has greatly aided scientific research by making the data available. They cover 90 per cent of the world population. The countries that are missing are in some cases understandable, such as Somalia or Iraq; in other cases, such as Malta and New Zealand, the omissions are puzzling. It is hard to judge how far they as a group would have a higher or lower poverty rate than the 90 per cent covered, but *faute de mieux* the numbers reported here are increased by the percentage necessary to bring the total population into line with the estimated world population in 2013, which is the reference year for all my calculations.

As discussed earlier, there are two key parameters. The first is the International Poverty Line, which I maintain as $1.90. The second is the gradient, or the percentage rate at which the relative poverty line is adjusted as mean consumption rises. A variety of values have been used in national poverty studies. The statistics published by Eurostat for the EU member states and a number of other countries show a range including 40 per cent, 50 per cent, 60 per cent, and 70 per cent.[9] The LIS Key Statistics takes 40 per cent, 50 per cent, and 60 per cent of the median. In chapter 2, I argued that the national poverty lines suggested a rate that was lower than 40 per cent, and a rate of a third is used by Ravallion and Chen (2011) on the basis of their new analysis of national poverty lines. In subsequent papers (Ravallion and Chen 2013; Chen and Ravallion 2013), the authors, however, base their global poverty measure on a gradient of 50 per cent, noting the important point that the earlier value of a third was based on mean consumption as measured in the national accounts, whereas the poverty line is being calculated from mean consumption as recorded in the household surveys. As we have seen in an earlier chapter, there can be a significant difference, with the national accounts figure typically more extensive. Taking a higher percentage therefore makes a great deal of sense. For future reference, we may note that their estimate of the number of people in poverty across the world in 2008 was 2,912.1 million, or nearly three billion, with an overall poverty rate of 43.6 per cent (Ravallion and Chen 2013, table 2).

The finding of Ravallion and Chen that four people in ten in the world are poor is a conclusion that many people will find shocking, but others will find it hard to credit. The latter group will ask about the robustness of the conclusion to the choice of the key parameters. They will note that, as described above, many official studies consider a range of possible values for the gradient. They may argue that there are other considerations apart from the current national poverty lines. Indeed, we must recognise that the determination of the key percentage is a decision that will involve inputs from a range of sources. In order therefore to provide a guide to the sensitivity of the results, I begin with 30 per cent and then consider 50 per cent.

Figure 9.2 illustrates these two cases, plotting the poverty line that applies against mean consumption per head. As noted earlier, with a gradient of 30 per cent (the top diagram), the poverty line starts to rise at a value of average consumption that is three and a third times the International Poverty Line of $1.90—that is, at $6.33 per person per day. With a gradient of 50 per cent, however, the line starts to rise when consumption per head is only twice the International Poverty Line, at $3.80, and then of course it rises more steeply, at a rate of $5 for every $10 increase in consumption per head. This second case is shown in the lower diagram. (The reader can now see the answer to the question posed in chapter 2 as to how the diagram in figure 2.1 would look were

[9] In using the statistics published by Eurostat, the relevant series here is that for people "at risk of poverty." There is also a measure for people "at risk of poverty and social exclusion," which is a measure combining both monetary and nonmonetary measures. It is also important to note that for most countries the income data relate to income in the year preceding the survey, so that data labelled 2016 relate to income in 2015.

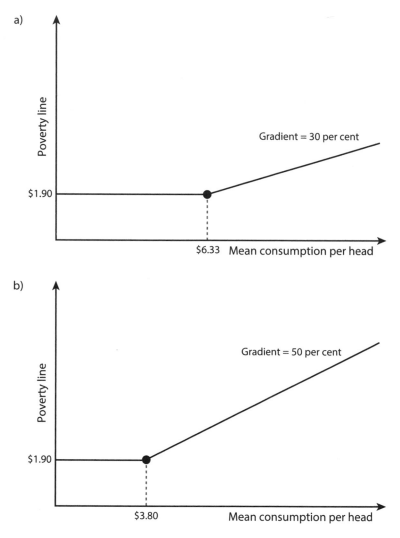

Figure 9.2. Poverty lines for estimating global poverty with (a) gradient after a switching point of 30 per cent and (b) gradient after a switching point of 50 per cent
Reading note: With a gradient of 30 per cent, the poverty line is $1.90 until a country's mean consumption per head reaches $6.33, at which point it increases by 30 cents for each rise of $1 in mean consumption per head.

the gradient of the line to be 50 per cent.) Both these differences—a switching point at a lower level of mean consumption per head and a steeper rise in the poverty line beyond the switching point—will mean a higher estimate of global poverty. Table 9.2 summarises the resulting calculations.

With the combination of the International Poverty Line set at $1.90 and a gradient of 30 per cent, fifty-six of the countries covered by PovcalNet were to the left of the switching point of $6.33 in 2013. For them, the calculation is the same as that discussed in the earlier parts of the book. The poverty rate for the group as a whole was 26.1 per cent, and, adjusted to the total world population to allow for undercoverage of PovcalNet, there were 830 million people in poverty. Nearly double the number of countries (ninety-one) were to the right of the $6.33 switching point. For this group as a whole, the poverty rate was 9.8 per cent. Adjusted again to the total world population, the number of poor people in this group was 390 million, giving an estimate of world poverty (the total number of the poor in the two groups) of 1,220 million people, or about one and a quarter billion. Of these, 296 million are people living in households with per capita consumption or income higher than $1.90 a day: they do not live in what the World Bank defines as "extreme" poverty but are poor according to the societal standard. In terms of figure 2.1 in chapter 2, these are the individuals in area III, while the remaining 94 million people, who are living below the $1.90 line, are in area II.

With the gradient at 50 per cent, the estimate of the total number poor rises sharply, to 2,029 million, or just over two billion. This total is composed of a smaller number of poor people (718 million persons, after adjusting to the world population) in countries to the left of the now lower switching point ($3.80), and a substantially higher number of poor people in countries to the right of the switching point (1,311 million persons, again after adjustment). In this second calculation, there are 113 countries covered by PovcalNet to the right of the switching point and only thirty-four countries to its left: the choice of the 50 per cent gradient reduces the value of the switching point, causing twenty-two countries to move to a higher poverty threshold than the $1.90 line that applied with the 30 per cent gradient.

As when the gradient is at 30 per cent, the poverty standard has been raised compared to the situation with the uniform $1.90 line, recognising that society evolves and becomes richer. In this case, with a gradient of 50 per cent, 1,105 million people are considered poor according to a relative threshold (area III in figure 2.1) on top of those living in extreme poverty, who total 924 million (areas I and II). The global head-count poverty rate more than doubles, from 12.9 per cent with the International Poverty Line applied everywhere to 28.3 per cent with the "societal" line. This estimate based on the societal line seems to suggest an improvement relative to that for 2008 by Ravallion and Chen (2013), but this conclusion is unwarranted, as the estimates are not directly comparable. Whatever the differences, the societal approach is a promising way

Table 9.2. Global poverty in 2013

	30 Per Cent Gradient and Switching Point at $6.33 a Day		
	Countries to Left of Switching Point	Countries to Right of Switching Point	All Countries
Countries in PovcalNet (number)	56	91	147
Population (millions)	3,177	4,002	7,179
People in "extreme" poverty (millions)	830	94	924
People in relative poverty (millions)	–	296	296
People in poverty, total (millions)	830	390	1,220
People in "extreme" poverty (per cent)	26.1	2.4	12.9
People in relative poverty (per cent)	–	7.4	4.1
People in poverty, total (per cent)	26.1	9.8	17.0

	50 Per Cent Gradient and Switching Point at $3.80 a Day		
	Countries to Left of Switching Point	Countries to Right of Switching Point	All Countries
Countries in PovcalNet (number)	34	113	147
Population (millions)	2,308	4,871	7,179
People in "extreme" poverty (millions)	718	206	924
People in relative poverty (millions)	–	1,105	1,105
People in poverty, total (millions)	718	1,311	2,029
People in "extreme" poverty (per cent)	31.1	4.2	12.9
People in relative poverty (per cent)	–	22.7	15.4
People in poverty, total (per cent)	31.1	26.9	28.3

Source: Author's calculations using PovcalNet, October 2016 version. Only countries in PovcalNet with data for 2000 or a later year are considered in the calculation. Population totals and numbers of people in poverty are adjusted for a factor equal to the ratio of the midyear estimate of the world population in 2013 to the total population of the PovcalNet countries considered in the calculation. "Extreme" poverty means living in a household with consumption (or income) per capita below $1.90 per person per day. "Relative" poverty means living in a household with consumption (or income) per capita above $1.90 per person per day but below the societal poverty line.

Reading note: With a 30 per cent gradient, there are fifty-six countries in PovcalNet to the left of the switching point—that is, which have mean per capita consumption or income below $6.33 ($1.90/0.3) per day.

to bridge the gap between poor and rich countries in the measurement of poverty.[10]

CONCLUSIONS

[10] *Editors*: Tony had not yet drafted further comment on his figures or on the Ravallion and Chen (2013) estimates (which were based on the 2005 ICP). He would surely also have referred to the global poverty estimates in Jolliffe and Prydz (2017), work stimulated by his recommendation in the report of the Commission on Global Poverty for a societal poverty measure of the type implemented in this chapter (World Bank 2017, p. 14). (The 2018 edition of the World Bank report *Poverty and Shared Prosperity* contains further discussion of this approach.) He may also have had in mind to estimate global totals for earlier years so as to establish trends over time, as in both Ravallion and Chen (2013) and Joliffe and Prydz (2017), complementing his presentation of trends in different regions in chapter 1 based on applying everywhere the International Poverty Line of $1.90. We note that Jolliffe and Prydz (2017) estimate a reduction in the global poverty head count from 33.4 per cent in 2008 to 29.3 per cent in 2013 (table 5), although they apply a different methodology: they drop the flat portion of the poverty line corresponding to $1.90 and take the line to be simply "a dollar a day plus 50 percent of median daily consumption" (p. 17), hence one that is always increasing. We think Tony would have discussed too the work of Ugo Gentilini and Andy Sumner, who suggest a different approach to estimating a figure for world poverty, taking this simply as the sum of national head counts based on national poverty lines: "Using data from 160 countries covering nearly 92 per cent of world population, we estimate that globally 1.5 billion people live in poverty as defined within their own countries" (Gentilini and Sumner 2012, p. 3). The same authors, together with Joshua Greenstein, argue for "the importance of national ownership and the incorporation of context-specific measures of poverty, and that any new poverty goals should be designed with political mobilization as a consideration" (Greenstein, Gentilini, and Sumner 2014, p. 132). While Tony would have agreed with this sentiment—reflected in his emphasis on the importance of national measures in much of this book—we think he would have argued for the merit of an approach establishing a *common framework* for measurement, such as the one that he developed with François Bourguignon and implemented in this chapter. Finally, he would also have returned to the ethical considerations that he discussed in chapter 1. As implemented, the approach to a societal measure of poverty here in chapter 9 reflects the "global cosmopolitan" position that he explained at the start of the book, where an equal weight is given in the count to people across the world. But he flagged in chapter 1 that he would also be considering in the current chapter the use of a "limited sympathy" measure where the weights vary, producing "a *nationally specific* count of world poverty. The magnitude of world poverty as seen from India will be different from that seen from the United States" (pp. 13–14).

CHAPTER 10

Conclusions: Beyond $1.90 a Day

The role of social science is to provide answers to the questions posed by society and to convey the limits to the answers that can be given in the present state of knowledge. The measurement of poverty is in this respect challenging. It is a concept that is contested, and its centrality to much political debate means that opinions are not only divided but also hotly expressed. Some deny categorically that we can say anything about the extent of global poverty and whether or not it is being successfully tackled. Others quote estimates from the World Bank or other researchers as though they are gospel truth. In this book, I have tried to steer a middle course.

In charting a middle way, I have tried to introduce readers to some new ideas. New thinking is, I believe, necessary to resolve old issues, but it is also necessary because the measurement of poverty is not a static subject. The world is changing, notably on account of the rise of countries that were classified as "low-income" a generation ago, but also because all societies evolve and their ambitions with regard to tackling poverty change over time. To meet the changing world, the analysis of poverty has to become richer and more subtle. Economists, statisticians, sociologists, and political scientists, among others, have to open their minds to new ways of thinking.

SUMMING UP

Global welfare economics

The first challenge to the existing mode of thought is to extend our evaluation of societies, and specifically the measurement of poverty, beyond the national boundaries that are the basis for current welfare economics. And it is not just economics. The Berkeley philosopher Debra Satz writes that "the dominant paradigms in political philosophy and social policy have been either statist or nationalist. [Both believe] either that the very idea of international justice does not make any sense or that our primary loyalties are to those at home" (Satz 2003, p. 625).

Such an extension beyond national concepts of welfare appears to some to be a fruitless endeavour. In his *In Defense of Globalization*, the economist Jagdish Bhagwati writes:

What sense does it make to put a household in Mongolia alongside a household in Chile, one in Bangladesh, another in the United States, and still another in Congo? These households do not belong to a "society" in which they compare themselves with the others, and so a measure that includes all of them is practically a meaningless construct. (2004, p. 67; I owe this quotation to Brandolini and Carta 2016)

As is argued in chapter 2, the question of "belonging" to a society is a very relevant one. In this, I agree with Bhagwati, but I do not believe that it leads us to adopt an isolationist position. It totally ignores any sense of world solidarity, where the citizens of a country have a degree of empathy with their fellows elsewhere in the world. As was argued presciently by Herbert Frankel some seventy-five years ago in his presidential address to the Economic Society of South Africa, "there exists a world economic solidarity which makes it imperative for national governments to abandon the idolatry of national sovereignty and universality if they are to promote the economic well-being of their peoples" (1942, p. 180). At the other extreme from Bhagwati is the position of global cosmopolitanism, where everyone counts for one. Frankel went on to say that "the new economic ideal which we require must take the form of a world popular economic front against poverty" (p. 181).

For many people, neither extreme appeals, and I have described in chapter 1 an intermediate path where there is a commitment to help others but to a limited degree. Such an "extended but limited" approach recognises that people may read this book because they are worried about poverty and deprivation around the world, but that they may give this less weight than poverty at home, and that concern for poverty at home in turn has its limits. This statement is less stark than those of the extremes but is, I believe, more relevant, and one of the aims of the book is to illuminate the path from a more subtle moral judgment such as this to practical measurement.

Poverty as a multifaceted concept

A major theme running through the book is that "poverty" may carry many different meanings, as has been discussed in chapter 2. There is not a single monolithic concept. The meaning and interpretation of poverty is contested, and we need to consider different approaches to its measurement. The variety of meanings is evident from the formulation of the SDGs themselves. The first, and the best known, is the first target under Goal 1, which may be paraphrased as eradicating by 2030 extreme poverty for all people everywhere, measured as people living on less than the International Poverty Line. The target is set explicitly in terms of achieving a minimum level of economic resources. But the second target under the same Goal refers to "poverty in all its dimensions," where the concept is broadened to include nonmonetary indicators. Such non-monetary dimensions of deprivation are highlighted in many of the other SDGs. In this book, I have been particularly interested in the relation between monetary and nonmonetary measures of poverty. Are countries that are doing well at reducing the number living on less than the International Poverty Line also doing well at reducing deprivation measured in terms of nutrition, ill health, poor housing, and other nonmonetary indicators? Poverty cannot simply be summarised by a single number.

In order to understand what lies behind these differing indicators, we have to ask the fundamental question as to the source of our concern about poverty and to recognise that people may legitimately hold different views. The measurement of poverty is not a purely technical subject. This book is not like a guide to plumbing, because the right answers depend on views that are politically influenced and, at heart, matters of moral judgement. They are influenced by culture and by history. My hope is that the book will widen the ways in which poverty is viewed, allowing for a greater diversity of approaches.

Importance of a checklist

The fact that there is a complex path from moral judgement to concrete measures of poverty means that it is essential that we understand just what, at the end of the day, is being measured. It can make a great deal of difference how the underlying concept of poverty is translated into concrete measures. It is not surprising if outsiders feel bewildered by the variety of statistics on offer. Optimists may point to one set of statistics that shows rapid progress. Pessimists may point to another set of statistics that indicates that we are falling behind. It is for this reason that I have suggested a simple checklist.

The checklist is drawn up in chapters 3 and 4. The first part deals with the theoretical concepts. What exactly is being measured? How are we comparing poverty in China with that in the European Union? Who is being measured? How far do the reported measures take account of inequality within the household? If they do not, then we cannot say anything about how many women are in poverty. Do nonmonetary measures of poverty tell the same story as monetary measures, or do they, as we saw in chapter 2 to be the case in Pakistan, suggest that poverty is more serious? But what dimensions are covered by multidimensional measures? How are they weighted? How do they measure the extent to which different deprivations overlap?

The implementation of the poverty definitions is the subject of chapter 4, which describes the data that are needed and asks how far the existing sources are fit for purpose. Do we in fact have any appropriate data, and are they available? Any social scientist who has relied on secondary data (that is, data collected by someone else, not by the researcher) knows that gaining access may be the greatest of the problems faced. Are the data sufficiently comparable over time for them to be used to monitor progress? Are they sufficiently comparable with the data for other countries to be combined in reaching a global total? Then there are the issues of practical implementation. How was the sample of households drawn and interviewed? How big is the sample? Who is missing? What account is taken of geographical differences? What is done if the household survey shows a different picture (usually less rosy) than that recorded in the national macroeconomic accounts?

Drawing together the different elements of the checklists in chapters 3 and 4, I conclude that what we need is an All-round Approach (AA) to poverty measurement that not only serves to clarify the way in which a particular estimate has been reached—which boxes have been ticked—but also alerts us to the fact that there are alternative choices that could lead to different conclusions about the extent and direction of change in measured poverty. This may be viewed as a variation on the "total survey error" approach, which has been advocated in the statistical literature (see, for example, the review by Groves and Lyberg 2010). This approach, less widely known in economics than in other social sciences, dates back to the article by Deming (1944), in which he set out a thirteenfold classification of factors affecting the ultimate value of a survey and needing to be taken into account when drawing conclusions. In the present case, the checklist is intended to perform a similar function.

Our knowledge is imperfect but useful

What are we to make of the estimates of global poverty that were previewed in chapter 1 and examined in greater detail in chapter 5? There are those who believe that seeking to measure global poverty is a futile exercise. The obstacles to making such a calculation are too great to even attempt an estimate of the number of people living in poverty. At the other extreme are those who have complete confidence in the estimates made by the World Bank, by other international agencies, and by national governments, and who even quote their findings down to the decimal point. As we have seen in the country case studies, there are countries where the data to be found in international data sets can be taken with confidence but others where the World Bank or other data are potentially misleading.

My position regarding the measurement of global poverty is intermediate. Any estimate of worldwide poverty is surrounded by a margin of variation due to differences in concepts and implementation—hence the checklist. In examining the evidence for individual countries, as in the national case studies, it will become evident that the numbers for some countries are more reliable than those for other countries. It also becomes clear that countries, for quite legitimate reasons, calculate poverty on different bases. This is often lost from sight in public pronouncements, and it is important to convey to policymakers and other users that they are operating with statistical information about which there is considerable scope for variation. The key take-away message for the reader is that estimates of poverty, at all levels, and on all different approaches, are imperfect, but they are fit for purpose.

Monetary and nonmonetary poverty

Many years ago, there was an advertising campaign for a well-known beer that claimed to refresh the parts that other beers could not reach. To a significant extent, this is the role of nonmonetary indicators of poverty. Income measures, rooted in the household, cannot inform us about intra-household inequality, in contrast to measures of health or nutritional status. Income measures cannot capture the degradation of the environment. But nonmonetary measures are also an important source of triangulating evidence.[1]

Growth, inequality, and poverty

[*Editors*: This heading and those that follow show that Tony intended to summarise his findings on each of the eight "general issues" he had planned to deal with in chapters 6 to 9.]

The twin challenges of poverty and climate change

A colonial legacy?

Correlates of success

Consumption or income?

---

[1] *Editors*: We presume that Tony would have continued this discussion given the importance he attached to using both monetary and nonmonetary indicators.

The poverty of groups

Persistence of poverty in rich countries

Measures of global poverty

WE KNOW ENOUGH TO ACT

The evidence assembled in this book shows that many countries are making definite progress in tackling monetary and nonmonetary poverty. In some countries, progress has been dramatic, as in China, and dramatic progress has been achieved in some countries after a period of stagnation or backsliding. But there remains much to be done, as reflected in the title of the 2012 World Bank report on Vietnam: "Well Begun, Not Yet Done." Moreover, progress is mixed. Within continents, such as Africa, there are both success stories and cases of no progress. The failure of rich countries in recent years to give priority to reducing poverty is seen as a disgrace by those for whom it is a major source of concern.

Facing up to failure

The failure to take effective action cannot be attributed to lack of information. As I have argued, the data are greatly improved and—when responsibly interpreted—fit for purpose. "Responsibly" means taking account of the full range of possibilities as to why the numbers may be misleading. We need to check, for example, that the changes in the proportion below the International Poverty Line are consistent with what is observed in terms of nonmonetary poverty, and that the numbers entering global databases are congruent, once conceptual and methodological differences are taken into account, with the findings of national poverty studies.

Rather, I have formed the view, when reading hundreds of poverty reports, that the key is the engagement of top politicians and policy-makers. Their sustained support and the close monitoring of the extent of their engagement are essential. We have seen how in the United States it was the priority given to poverty by President Lyndon Johnson, immediately on taking office, that led to the War on Poverty, which has had lasting impact. It was the lack of interest of his successors, or outright hostility in the case of President Ronald Reagan, that meant that the impact was not developed further. In many countries, reducing poverty has formed part of national plans or been the subject of special programmes, such as the National Strategy for Growth and Reduction of Poverty in Tanzania.

Finale: A third challenge

This book has been concerned with one of the two major challenges faced by the world today: tackling global poverty and ensuring sustainability in the face of climate change and shortage of resources. The two challenges are larger than can be met by any national government or by short-term measures. Resolution does not depend on a single president or political party. Given the presence of presidents and governments that close their eyes to the issues or are indifferent about global progress, this is reassuring. However, it does raise questions about the role of democracy. We have failed to consider the different levels at which democratic principles apply. There can be little doubt that some of the successes have been achieved, not at the level of national governments, but at the levels of villages, cities, and provinces (states in the United States). Local politics has, however, all too often been allowed to wither on the vine. The aim of many politicians has been to build careers at this level and then move on. At the other extreme, and much more recent, has been the creation of political entities at the supranational level, such as the European Union, a model that has been influential in the creation of bodies such as the Union of South American Nations. Development of supranational bodies has been much criticised as undemocratic and remote. Remoteness may be one reason why even where there are direct elections, people fail to vote. Where there is an indirect representative democracy, then it depends on the willingness and capacity of national representatives to close the gap and ensure that the views of their voters are given due weight. At both levels, local and supranational, conventional thinking about democracy needs to be reconsidered.

With the fall of the Berlin Wall and the dissolution of the Soviet Union, the attitude of Western democracies has been that their view of the world's political organisation has triumphed. They have paid little attention to the fact that there are alternatives. One cannot help noting that one of the most successful countries in tackling poverty is China, a country ruled by an elite who attach greater importance to achieving a harmonious society than to the principle of "one person one vote." The Western democracies have not recognised that the United States and Europe have signally failed to tackle poverty in their own countries. Rethinking the role of democracy is a third major challenge facing us today.

The dangers come when the poverty objective is relegated to a lower level of ministry. In the United Kingdom, under the Labour governments of Tony Blair and Gordon Brown, we had senior politicians who attached considerable weight to solving poverty and established a national target for the elimination of child poverty. Both the prime minister and the chancellor of the exchequer, the head of the Treasury, were active on the global stage, notably at the G8 summit on Africa in 2008, which achieved agreement on aid and debt relief. Since 2010, with the change of government, the national poverty policy has been relegated to the Department of Work and Pensions. Not only does poverty not enter its title, but the Treasury has looked to the department for cost savings, not for progress in achieving the goals that the government has accepted as part of the Europe 2020 objective, an objective that will probably, in the UK case, be a casualty of Brexit. There is a nice contrast with Bangladesh, where the report on progress in 2014–2015 was produced by the Macroeconomic Wing of the Ministry of Finance. At the EU level too, poverty reduction, although one of the five key targets, receives little priority, and this may reflect that it is not a key responsibility of the highly influential Directorate-General for Economic and Financial Affairs.

The conclusion that I draw is that our leaders have accepted ambitious goals for tackling poverty, globally and nationally, and we need to hold them to account.

Growth, Inequality, and Poverty Reduction

François Bourguignon

Writing this afterword that is meant to complement an unfinished book by the world's authority in the field of poverty and inequality was a real challenge. My ambition was to write a piece that was a straight continuation of the existing chapters and Tony's outline and to try to be a truthful transcriber of what he had in mind and did not have enough time to write. At every moment, however, the doubts kept coming: "Would Tony have agreed with that statement?"; "What would he have said about that issue?"; "He certainly would have explained this much better than me"; "How come he was so clear and I am so obscure?" Yet, remembering how attentive, open, and indulgent he was to what others thought and said, hope returned: "Maybe, he would have liked this idea, or this way of presenting this argument" . . . before doubt surged back again. As usual, the questions he had in mind were truly fundamental, and the issue of the relationship between poverty, inequality, and growth is no exception. He planned to deal with it in chapter 6 in connection with the evolution of poverty in Asian countries. How sad it is that we'll never know what he was about to say.

In Tony's mind, poverty and inequality were indeed tightly linked. They are even partly equivalent where the poverty line is defined as a proportion of the median standard of living, as is the case in the EU. Thus, poverty can be thought of as an inequality measure focussed on the bottom of the distribution. As discussed in chapter 2, this definition of poverty according to the overall affluence of the society where people live was clearly favoured by Tony. I remember very clearly his comment fifteen years ago that the lack of a cell phone would soon be seen as a sign of poverty, the equivalent of the "linen shirt" that, 250 years ago, Adam Smith said a labourer would be ashamed not to wear in public. He was clearly right.

Things are different for developing countries, which this afterword will mostly refer to, as Tony intended to do. There an absolute poverty line is indeed crucial, as it is a determinant of whether people survive or not. That the poverty line should be defined in absolute terms in low-income countries and should take precedence over a relative poverty line is made clear from figure 2.1 in chapter 2, borrowed from one of our joint papers (Atkinson and Bourguignon 2001).[1] Under these conditions, the level of poverty in a developing

---

[1] In the report of the Commission on Global Poverty, Tony allowed for a positive intercept of the upward-sloping, income-dependent poverty line as if even a relative definition of the pov-

country results both from the volume of resources available in the whole economy and the way they are allocated in the population. Dynamically, changes in the level of poverty depend on both economic growth *and* changes in the distribution of living standards. It is in that sense that Tony thought that the relationship between poverty, inequality, and growth was a fundamental issue. As he stated in chapter 1 (p. 2): "Greater knowledge about uneven development has played an essential role in demonstrating the need for development policy to consider a wider set of objectives than economic growth." Indeed, this question has been central to the debate on poverty reduction for a very long time, with some people believing that growth is the only cure to absolute poverty, as its benefits necessarily trickle down to poor people, while others have emphasised the role of distribution and redistribution, whether through transfers of purchasing power or human capital investment among the poor.

That Tony wanted to handle the issue of the trickle-down of growth and its relationship with inequality and poverty in connection with Asian countries is easily understandable, as growth has been particularly strong in that region over the last two or three decades, whereas poverty has drastically declined in some cases, despite increasing income inequality. Yet the relationship is equally important in other regions of the world in order to understand the pace, and possibly even the direction, of poverty change.

I summarise here how we understand today the complex relationship between poverty, inequality, and growth, emphasising the logic of that relationship and some of its implications for policy.

I first focus on the nature of the growth-poverty-inequality relationship, the main point being that, if poverty is defined in purely economic terms, i.e., excluding welfare dimensions like education or health, then there is a kind of arithmetic link between the extent of poverty, the income share of the bottom part of the distribution of living standards, and the mean standard. This implies that understanding how economic development and growth affect poverty requires us to understand the interaction between growth and inequality—or more generally, the overall distribution of income or living standards. After a short section on the concept of the growth-elasticity of poverty, I concentrate on the relationship between growth and inequality. First, I deal with the causality links that go from growth to inequality, and then to poverty. Second, I reverse the causality and analyse the way in which inequality may affect the rate of growth of the economy and therefore poverty. The conclusion stresses several lessons to be drawn from this short review of issues for policy—emphasising in particular the concept of pro-poor growth policies—and research.

---

erty threshold would comprise an absolute component (World Bank 2017, figure 2.2). What matters, however, is not so much that intercept but the level of income at which the two lines—one flat and one upward-sloping—cross and the slope of the relative poverty line beyond that point. In what follows, it is thus assumed that the flat line is the relevant poverty threshold for developing countries.

THE ARITHMETIC OF POVERTY, INEQUALITY, AND GROWTH

The argument that follows refers to where poverty is defined and measured in absolute terms, that is, with respect to a fixed threshold for the standard of living rather than a threshold that varies with the mean or the median standard of living in society.

To see why growth is a key factor of poverty reduction when poverty is measured in absolute terms—or in "anchored absolute" terms, to use Tony's distinction in chapter 2—consider the hypothetical case where growth is such that the standard of living of all people in a given country increases by the same proportion during a given period, say 10 per cent over three years. This clearly implies that all the poor people initially with a living standard between 10 per cent below the poverty line and the poverty line itself will leave poverty, whereas those remaining below the poverty line will be closer to it, the distance to the poverty line falling by 10 per cent of the initial income.[2] Thus, both the poverty head count and the poverty gap will fall.[3] By how much will depend on what share of the poor population finds itself initially less than 10 per cent below the poverty threshold and how far the others are from it. It thus depends on the distribution of living standards among the poor.

In reality, things are not that simple. Growth is not uniform within the population, so that inequality may change over time.

Consider the case of China between 1990 and 2012, which is partly dealt with in chapter 6. Using the International Poverty Line of $1.90, two-thirds of the Chinese were in poverty in 1990.[4] Over the period under scrutiny, average consumption expenditure per capita increased by a factor of 4.5, i.e., an annual growth rate equal to 7 per cent. If all people had enjoyed that same rate of growth in their living standard—which will be called "distribution-neutral growth"—all the people whose living standard was between $1.90/4.5 and $1.90 in 1990 should have been out of poverty by 2012. This is almost the entire poor population. The poverty head count should thus have fallen from 66.6 per cent to practically zero. Instead, as noted in chapter 6, it was 6.5 per cent. What does that mean? Simply that not all people enjoyed the same growth. The standard of living of poor people grew at less than 7 per cent, whereas that of the non-poor grew faster. Inequality must have increased. Indeed, this can be checked looking at the Gini coefficient, a frequently used measure of overall inequal-

---

[2] By a living standard that is initially "10 per cent below the poverty line" I mean an income that if increased by 10 per cent of itself would just reach the poverty line.

[3] Despite Tony's insistence on describing the extent of poverty by both the poverty head count and the poverty gap, in this afterword I will generally focus on the former, the excuse being that, except if otherwise specified, the latter generally behaves in the same way.

[4] Here and in what follows I use the World Bank's PovcalNet database.

ity. According to the data of the National Bureau of Statistics, it surged during that period, from 35 per cent to 47 per cent (Li 2016).[5]

Very much the same story holds for the other Asian giant, India. The poverty head count with the $1.90 International Poverty Line was 46 per cent in 1993 and 21 per cent in 2011. If growth had been distribution-neutral, however, poverty should have dropped to 15 per cent. In India too, inequality had increased, and this reduced the impact of growth on poverty.

The opposite outcome is also possible. In Moldova, a lower-middle-income country and the poorest country in the European continent not included in Tony's sixty-country database for his national reports, the proportion of Moldovans below the national poverty line—slightly below $5 per person per day (in international purchasing power dollars)—was 21.9 per cent in 2010.[6] Average real consumption expenditure per capita grew by a total of 8 per cent by 2015. Distribution-neutral growth would have implied a fall of 4.9 percentage points in the poverty head count. Instead, the head count fell by 12 percentage points because growth favoured the poor more than the nonpoor. Inequality had gone down—the Gini coefficient had dropped from 32 to 27 per cent. Unlike the preceding cases, Moldova is thus an example of a country where distributional change rather than growth has been the major driver of poverty reduction.

As suggested by the preceding examples, observed changes in poverty measures can thus arithmetically be decomposed into two parts: (1) a "growth" effect, or the change due to growth if growth were distribution-neutral; (2) the "redistribution" effect, or the change due to the modification of the distribution of living standards that took place at the same time as growth.[7] The change in poverty thus results from a uniform proportional increase in standards of living and a redistribution of the total income thus generated. In the case of Moldova considered earlier, the growth effect reduced the poverty head count from 21.9 to 17 per cent, whereas the distribution effect reduced the head count further to 9.9 per cent.

Viewed in this way, poverty changes over time are essentially the joint arithmetic result of the growth and distribution effects. Understanding the way poverty changes and at what speed in a country thus requires understanding the determinants of growth and distributional changes, and most importantly the interaction between them.

It is of course tempting to give more importance to one of these two factors. Indeed, the development literature and its logical emphasis on the con-

[5] PovcalNet reports inequality figures separately for urban and rural areas; Tony also focusses on these subnational figures in chapter 6 and in his national report for China at the end of the book.

[6] Data on Moldova come from https://data.worldbank.org/country/moldova.

[7] The decomposition of the change in poverty into a growth and distribution effect was first proposed by Datt and Ravallion (1992)

cept of absolute poverty tended to focus on growth as the primary factor for poverty reduction. Over the very long run, it is true that it is difficult to imagine that the distribution of standards of living can change continuously in the same direction, thus converging towards full equality or full inequality, however it might be defined. It would then follow that growth should be the main determinant of poverty reduction in developing countries. This point is well illustrated by the title of the influential paper by Dollar and Kraay (2002), "Growth Is Good for the Poor,"[8] and its restatement almost fifteen years later, "Growth Is Still Good for the Poor" (Dollar, Kleineberg, and Kraay 2016). These papers clearly plead in favour of the emphasis on policy in developing countries being on growth rather than on distributional issues, a view largely shared for a long time by the international development community.

Such a view misses several important points, however. The first, of course, is that growth may not be distribution-neutral in the medium run. If the objective is to eradicate absolute poverty as soon as possible, distributional changes and the potential impact of growth on distribution must be taken into account. For instance, the absolute poverty head count has remained practically constant in the United States for the last thirty years despite substantial growth, and with no change in the real poverty threshold, because growth benefitted mostly the top of the income distribution and inequality surged. The second point is that the distributional features of an economy at a given point of time are likely to have some impact on its dynamics, a point well put by Ravallion (2007) in a paper teasingly entitled "Inequality *Is* Bad for the Poor." Finally, it turns out that, even when distribution-neutral, the impact of growth on poverty depends on the shape of the distribution of standards of living in a country and, in some specific way, on its degree of inequality.

I explore this last point further in what follows before focussing on the relationship between growth and inequality.

THE GROWTH-ELASTICITY OF POVERTY

The growth-elasticity of poverty is the pace at which the poverty head count, or another measure, falls for each one percentage point of growth. The observed elasticity thus is the ratio of the observed percentage reduction of poverty to the percentage change in the mean living standard of the population. It ranges

[8] These authors showed that the elasticity of the mean income or consumption expenditure of the poorest 20 per cent of the population with respect to GDP growth is not significantly different from unity, meaning that poor people benefit equally from growth as the rest of the population. This definition of "poverty" is substantially different from conventional measures of absolute poverty. It compares more to the concept of "shared prosperity" recently introduced by the World Bank, although this refers to the bottom 40 per cent of the population rather than Dollar and Kraay's 20 per cent.

from negative values, when poverty is increasing despite the increase in mean income, to positive values, which may be extremely high, as when growth is negligible but poverty declines because of pure distributional changes. In the example of Moldova, the growth-elasticity of poverty between 2010 and 2015 was particularly high at 6.7. In India, it was slightly above unity over the period 1993–2011. That elasticity is often defined with reference to GDP per capita rather than the mean standard of living as given by household surveys so as to reflect the speed at which aggregate growth reduces poverty. The difference may sometimes be substantial, as when the share of national income accruing to households declines.[9]

A difficulty with the preceding concept of growth-elasticity of poverty is that it merges the growth and distribution effects. The true growth-elasticity should be defined in terms of distribution-neutral growth, to isolate it from the distribution effect. In the case of Moldova, for instance, this distribution-neutral growth elasticity is 2.4 rather than 6.7 because of the substantial equalizing of the distribution of consumption expenditures per capita that took place between 2010 and 2015. In India, the correction goes in the opposite direction raising the elasticity to 1.4 from 1.1 over 1993–2011—because the distribution of consumption became more unequal.

The pace at which distribution-neutral growth reduces poverty logically depends on the shape of the distribution of standards of living below the poverty line and thus on the extent of inequality in that distribution. Ravallion (2001) showed that the corresponding elasticity actually decreases with the degree of inequality of the whole distribution of standards of living. Later I provided a general specification of that elasticity that also included the ratio of the poverty line to the mean income and, implicitly, the initial level of poverty (Bourguignon 2003). Overall, the distribution-neutral growth-elasticity of poverty was shown to increase as both poverty and inequality were falling.

That poverty reduction is necessarily slower with the same rate of growth in an economy with more inequality is an interesting phenomenon. It suggests that there is a kind of double dividend in lasting reductions in inequality in a country. On the one hand, redistribution today reduces poverty (provided it does not benefit only the middle classes). On the other hand, a lower level of inequality accelerates the speed at which distribution-neutral economic growth will reduce poverty tomorrow.

Yet there is some ambiguity in this result. Increasing the top incomes in a given country would clearly raise the level of inequality but does not presumably modify the distribution of income below the poverty line and therefore

---

[9] A controversy built up in India several years ago precisely on this point. The rate of growth of average expenditure per capita as measured by the national household survey turns out to be five times smaller than the rate of growth of GDP. As discussed in Deaton and Kozel (2005), part of the problem was purely statistical, however.

the speed at which distribution-neutral growth would reduce poverty. That the growth-elasticity of poverty is found to fall with standard measures of inequality like the Gini coefficient defined on the whole distribution is due to these measures capturing inequality not only at the top but also at the bottom of the distribution.

HOW GROWTH AFFECTS INEQUALITY

Distribution neutrality is an unlikely outcome of economic growth, which is rarely balanced in the sense that all sectors of activity grow exactly at the same rate. The labour force and other factors of production like equipment, buildings, and infrastructure do not expand at the same rate either. On top of this, some factors, like land, are generally in fixed supply. It follows that the structure of the price system changes with growth, the same being true of the rewards to the various factors of production owned by people. Some people may thus benefit more from growth than others, whereas some may even lose if they operate in declining sectors or supply a factor of production for which demand is falling.

Is there any regularity in this process, and can it be said that the distribution of standards of living evolves in a specific manner with economic growth? In a famous presidential address to the American Economic Association, Simon Kuznets (1955) elaborated on the main mechanisms that could link economic growth and changes in the structure of incomes. He emphasised two such mechanisms. The first one is the concentration of savings among the well-off, which should lead to further concentration of wealth and income with growth. The second one is the shift away from agriculture that almost universally accompanies growth. This mechanism could be responsible for more inequality in a first stage of development, as urbanisation and industrialisation make the income gap between urban and rural areas more salient, and less in a second stage as these processes continue but most people have already left low-productivity activities in rural areas. Kuznets then hypothesised, based on very scant historical evidence, that "long secular swings" in inequality have taken place in England, the United States, and Germany, with an increase in the first half of the nineteenth century in England and the second half in the United States and Germany, and a decline in the first half of the twentieth century.

This inverted-U shape of the relationship between the degree of inequality and the level of affluence of a country, also known as the "Kuznets curve" (referred to briefly by Tony in chapter 6), became very popular in the mid and late 1970s, when rough estimates of income inequality in developing countries were put together to show that Kuznets's relationship held across countries at different levels of development—a literature triggered by Paukert (1973). However, this conclusion was based on sketchy data, a single observation per country, and very few countries. When better data became available, with observations at several points of time for several countries, more precise tests of the Kuznets curve hypothesis were conducted that essentially led to its rejection. Today a consensus seems to have formed that there is no systematic relationship for developing countries between the level of development, as measured by GDP per capita, and the degree of inequality, as shown by available inequality measures.[10]

Such a negative result is not surprising when one considers the variety of growth experiences around the world and their context. It does not mean that there are no common mechanisms linking growth and inequality across countries and development experiences, including of course those stressed by Kuznets. It means that other, essentially heterogeneous factors that accompany or affect growth are at play. In the first place, the growth strategies pursued by the various countries may themselves be different. For instance, development agencies increasingly discuss growth strategies in terms of whether they are "pro-poor." Clearly, a growth strategy focussing on the accumulation of human capital among the poor is likely to have a distributional impact different from a strategy based on the development of infrastructure. Another obvious factor of heterogeneity across countries is their redistribution policies.

Two additional points on the distributional impact of growth need to be made. The first one is in line with Tony's emphasis on the issue of data quality in chapter 4. Cross-country work in the field of inequality is most often plagued with comparability issues, this being sometimes also the case across time within a given country. Much of the work conducted to estimate the effect of growth on inequality is affected by this problem. This was the case with earlier work on the Kuznets hypothesis, as noted in Atkinson and Brandolini (2001). As shown in a recent comprehensive survey of cross-national income inequality databases headed by Ferreira and Lustig (2015), data constraints are still important today and may explain the inconclusiveness of this research area.

The second point is on the direction of the relationship between growth and inequality. Growth may affect inequality, but in the opposite direction, inequality itself may affect growth. Recognising that policies aimed at changing the distributional features of an economy may affect economic growth makes the econometrics of the Kuznets curve tricky. Not taking explicitly into account such policies, as well as other exogenous distributional shocks, means that any measure of the impact of growth on inequality is biased. Do observed distributional changes reflect the impact of growth per se, or rather the impact of distribution policies that also affect growth and are not accounted for? If

---

[10] For a recent contribution with an extensive survey of the literature and new tests on supposedly good-quality data, see Gallup (2013). Of course, this conclusion would not hold if developed countries were included in the analysis, due to inequality being substantially lower there.

policies that affect both distribution and growth are sufficiently different across countries or over time, estimating the pure effect of growth on distribution is problematic.

HOW INEQUALITY MAY AFFECT GROWTH

The story of the empirics of the relationship whose causality runs from inequality to growth is very similar to that with the cross-national Kuznets curve. Initial estimates by Alesina and Rodrik (1993) and Persson and Tabellini (1994) pointed to a significant negative impact of inequality on the rate of economic growth in a sample of countries where inequality data were available. Better data, longer observation periods, and panel data rather than pure cross-sectional econometrics showed later that this relationship was extremely fragile. The estimated effect of inequality on growth appeared significantly negative in some cases, nonsignificant in others, and even significantly positive in still others.[11]

Besides the problems linked to the quality of the inequality data used in those analyses, considerable developments over the last twenty years or so on the theory side help us understand the inconclusiveness of the empirical analysis. This is essentially due to the multiplicity and diversity of the channels through which the distributional features of an economy may affect its dynamics, and to the fact that the relative importance of these channels may vary considerably across countries. Four of them, particularly emphasised in the recent literature, are discussed below.

The first channel is the concentration of savings in the richest part of the population, as emphasised by Kuznets. In view of this concentration, it might be expected that a lower share of income going to the top of the distribution—for instance, through progressive taxation—would reduce the overall saving rate in the economy and therefore capital accumulation and the pace of growth.[12] Another, related version of the argument is that the taxation of capital income, which tends to be concentrated among the rich, is a disincentive to investment and potentially slows down growth. Reciprocally, this line of reasoning is also a trickle-down argument, according to which lowering the tax on high incomes would accelerate growth and *in fine* benefit the whole population, including the poorest. This is the argument recently used by Donald Trump to justify a regressive tax reform in the United States. When abolishing the tax on financial wealth a few months after assuming power, the French

---

[11] Ehrhart (2009) gives a rather comprehensive survey of that literature, including its theoretical aspects.

[12] This reasoning is often associated with the name of Kaldor, even though Kaldor (1955) had it in the opposite direction, from an exogenous rate of growth to the distribution of income between capitalists—the high savers—and workers.

president, Emmanuel Macron, preferred to use the mountaineering image of incentivizing the lead man on the rope (*premier de cordée*) so that the whole rope team make it sooner to the summit.

This argument suggests that inequality has a positive impact on growth, and conversely, that redistribution has a negative effect. There is in fact no evidence of the former or the latter.[13] An important drawback of the savings argument concerns the equality between savings and investment. Not all savings contribute to domestic growth if, for instance, they are invested abroad—as is the case with capital flight in many developing countries. On the other hand, the limited evidence available in developed countries is mostly inconclusive on the disincentive effect of top-income taxation on investment and growth. Some researchers found a positive effect of top marginal income tax rates on growth, whereas others found a negative effect, although both effects were rarely significant.[14]

The second channel is the mirror image of the preceding one. It is concerned with the demand side of the economy. Given that the share of additional income spent on consumption tends to decrease as income rises, a more unequal distribution of resources in an economy reduces the demand for goods and services. This may thus slow down investment and growth so that any excess savings available would be invested abroad. This line of reasoning seems to have lost ground in the literature, presumably because the expansion of international trade is often thought to weaken demand constraints. This is only partly true, however, as many goods and services are not fully tradable.

The third channel also works in the opposite direction to the first one and suggests that inequality may be detrimental to growth. It focusses on the imperfection of the credit market, in particular the constraint that potential investors without enough wealth or collateral face on the credit market, which prevents them from investing, however profitable, privately and socially, their would-be investments might be. Under these conditions, having less wealth in the hands of rich people and more in those of poor would-be investors should increase the rate of capital accumulation and its average rate of return. A less unequal distribution of wealth—or, as in this case, easier access to the credit market—should be associated with faster growth. An obvious illustration of this mechanism is the case of children who may be more talented than others but who are not sent to high school or college by their poor parents. Microeconomic evidence on credit market imperfections and their negative impact on the development of small and medium enterprises (SMEs) is also plentiful.

[13] See Lindert (2004) for developed countries. Ostry, Berg, and Tsangarides (2014) found no significant effect of redistribution either, but did find a negative small effect of inequality on growth. However, the "synthetic" data set they used is problematic.

[14] Milasi and Waldmann (2018) find a significant nonlinear effect on a panel of developed countries and briefly survey previous evidence. An early paper by Easterly and Rebelo (1993) on developing countries found no significant relationship either.

More generally, one could refer to all situations of unequal access to income-generating or income-enhancing facilities as responsible for more inequality and slower growth. This concerns not only education and credit but also access to decent jobs—i.e., the issue of labour market discrimination—training, health care, or security. To some extent, it is the inequality of opportunity rather than of income or expenditure that is relevant here.

Stressing that some market imperfections are responsible for more inequality and poverty, on the one hand, and less economic efficiency and dynamism, on the other, is essential. This is because there is a complementarity between poverty and inequality reduction and growth along some policy dimensions, and also because it highlights the importance of identifying these imperfections and developing policies to correct them. The implicit policy framework is not standard redistribution of today's income, where taxes are levied on the rich and the revenue is redistributed to the poor. Redistribution with this model goes through different channels that *ultimately* increase the capacity of poor people to generate more income today and tomorrow. Many of the numerous field experiments carried out today in developing countries aim at designing such policies and there is micro-evidence that they may indeed reduce poverty by increasing economic efficiency. How important the aggregate effect of these policies may be, however, on the long-run rate of growth and the overall pace of poverty reduction is difficult to determine.

The last inequality-growth channel I want to emphasise refers to the political economy of redistribution and politics. In a nutshell, the argument is that too high a level of inequality in a society will trigger a strong social demand for redistribution, which, in some instances, may be detrimental to economic growth. A simple, widely cited model is the one where people decide upon the extent of redistribution through a vote on the level of a uniform tax rate. Assuming an egalitarian redistribution of the tax revenue, for instance through lump-sum cash grants, people below the mean income are in favour of a high tax rate, as they will pay less than what they receive, and the opposite is true of people above the mean. If the median voter is the decisive voter, it follows that the tax rate increases with the gap between mean and median gross income (income before taxes and benefits), a gap which is an indicator of income inequality. Then, if a higher tax rate really discourages savings and investment, the rate of growth would be negatively affected by the original level—pretax and benefit—of inequality. Of course, this line of reasoning completely ignores the positive impact that redistribution may have otherwise on the economy and its rate of growth, a view that was at the very centre of Tony's work (for example, Atkinson 1999, 2014a). But it has the merit of moving the spotlight onto the political and social consequences of excessive inequality.

Evidence is difficult to gather on the relationship between redistribution and inequality, on the one hand, and taxation and growth, on the other, not least because of the difficulty of measuring redistribution in a comparable way across countries. However, the view that redistribution is triggered by too high a level of inequality does not fit the observation of developed countries where data on pre- and post-redistribution inequality are available. This is true when comparing Nordic countries to others, or the United States and the United Kingdom to France or Germany. Nor is it the case that among those countries, the ones that redistribute more grow less rapidly, as can be seen from the high-growth performances of the Nordics over the last three decades and more. The determinants and consequences of redistribution are more complex than in the simple model above.

The social demand for redistribution may also express itself through purely political channels, without necessarily being satisfied. Hence the view that excessive inequality may lead to social tensions, political instability, or political changes, which, in turn, are detrimental to the investment climate and growth. For instance, numerous observers have related the Trump election in the United States to the continuous rise of inequality, the slow growth of purchasing power in the bottom half of the income distribution, and the stagnation of poverty over more than thirty years. If true, inequality will have thus led to a populist government whose decisions it is difficult to imagine will be without negative and possibly disastrous economic consequences in the long run.

The case of Brexit in the United Kingdom or the rise of populist and nationalist parties in several European countries, including the Front National in France,[15] could lend themselves to the same kind of analysis. However, because disposable income or consumption inequality has varied relatively little over the last two or three decades in most cases, it is probably not the inequality of standards of living that matters there but other types of inequality: unemployment or job precariousness, unequal opportunities both in the near future and for future generations, and a sense of social exclusion felt by part of the population despite their living standards being above a basic minimum.

In sum, there are multiple and diverse channels through which the distributional features of a society may affect the pace of economic growth and, through it, the pace of absolute poverty reduction. The extent to which more inequality will be associated with slower or faster growth ultimately depends on the relative importance of these various channels when comparing different countries. More important, however, is that, within a given country, the fact that the various channels are not pointing in the same direction gives scope for redistribution and antipoverty policies that will not affect growth, at least over the medium and long run. Redistribution may indeed affect savings and investments negatively in some cases. But this negative effect on growth will be compensated for—and possibly more than compensated for—if the increased tax revenues are spent on human capital accumulation by poor people or more generally on providing the means for poor people to generate income

---

[15] Recently renamed the "Rassemblement National."

to which they do not currently have access. As a matter of fact, in poor countries, even straight redistribution through cash transfers may have that effect by improving human capital and easing liquidity constraints. Of course, the argument is even stronger when there are reasons to expect the negative savings/investment effect to be moderate.

The same line of argument in favour of redistribution, or preventing excessive inequality, applies to the case where it is thought that inequality may lead to economically costly social and political tensions.

Another important conclusion to draw from the preceding discussion is the importance of the actual concept of inequality used in identifying these various channels: gross or net incomes, wealth, access to income-generating facilities, or opportunities in a more general sense. A fundamental problem is that data that would permit measurement of these various aspects of inequality are often missing and the nature of the measures to be used in gauging these inequalities is unclear.

CONCLUSION

Several lessons can be drawn from these brief remarks on the complex relationship between poverty reduction, inequality, and growth. They are important for reflecting on the design of antipoverty policies and directions for future research.

The first lesson is that there is no spontaneous, general and unidirectional relationship between growth, inequality, and poverty, and therefore no uniform policy prescription. The relationship between them is too complex to yield uniform features across countries. Within countries, however, there are policies that can reduce poverty and inequality and contribute to overall economic growth. These "pro-poor" growth policies may be of different types—human capital accumulation, training, SME development, agricultural extension, rural electrification, affirmative action to fight ethnic and gender discrimination, etc. Designing them to comply with their threefold objective—faster growth, less inequality, and faster poverty reduction—while fully taking into account their financing and potential adverse effects on growth, as well as their inherent country-specificity, should be the objective of antipoverty policy analysis.

Although most of the argument in this afterword has referred to absolute poverty and therefore developing countries, the preceding conclusion clearly applies equally to relative poverty. This complementarity between poverty and inequality reduction and economic efficiency was central to Tony's work.

A second important lesson is about the diversity of the concepts of inequality needed to analyse the role of inequality in the development process, at all levels of development. It is striking that some key channels through which inequality may affect growth refer not to the standard concept of disposable income, or consumption expenditure inequality, but to inequalities of a different nature: gross or market incomes, wealth, jobs, opportunities. These essentially positive ways of approaching inequality echo the normative analysis of chapter 2. Capabilities, for instance, may be considered a normative concept to define poverty. The inequality of their distribution in the population, by not allowing some people to express their talent, may also be a positive constraint on efficiency and growth.

It follows that the measurement of these extended concepts of both poverty and inequality become increasingly important for a good understanding of the economics of inequality, growth, and poverty and for the design of the appropriate policies. Tony's absence will be badly felt in this endeavour.

Poverty and Climate Change

Nicholas Stern

Tony Atkinson was a foundational figure in the study of poverty, shaping fundamentally the way in which we understand its meaning, its measurement, and its causes. He was a world leader in the formulation and analysis of policies to reduce poverty. He thought deeply about what might drive poverty in the future. And Tony was a true internationalist with profound interest in global issues and global responses and the meaning of mutual responsibility.

He recognised the immense dangers, particularly for poorer people, of unmanaged climate change. He asked about the implications for living standards—across nations and within societies, both now and in the future—of attempts to grapple with the issues and to make and implement policy. Thus, for Tony, the relationship between poverty and climate change was of crucial importance. That is why he wanted to include a discussion in this book. We talked through the issues and questions many times in the dozen or so years before he died. This short afterword is an attempt to reflect on those discussions and to respond to Tony's questions.

This afterword begins with an examination of the drivers and consequences of climate change and the urgency and scale of necessary action. In the next section, we then show why climate change matters so much for poverty: it is the poorest who are, and will be, hit earliest and hardest. The arguments for acting to manage climate change are not just concerned with protecting future generations from the immense risks, vitally important though this is. The transition to low- or zero-carbon development is the growth story of the twenty-first century. Strong, sustainable, and inclusive, it is the only lasting growth story on offer and is the subject matter of the following section.

The understanding both of the huge threats of unmanaged climate change and of the attractiveness of the alternative paths of low-carbon growth underpinned the extraordinary success of COP21 of the United Nations Framework Convention on Climate Change (UNFCCC) in reaching the climate agreement in Paris in December 2015.[1] More than 190 countries have signed and ratified

---

[1] The UNFCCC is an international environmental treaty, adopted on 9 May 1992. The Conference of the Parties (COP) is the supreme decision-making body of the convention. All states that are parties to the convention are represented at the COP and have been meeting since 1995 (COP1) to assess and negotiate the global response to the threat of climate change.

the agreement. Over 190 countries have also adopted the 2030 Sustainable Development Agenda, including the seventeen Sustainable Development Goals (SDGs), agreed upon at the United Nations in 2015. Together these two global agreements constitute a remarkable global agenda,[2] unique in human history. Multilateralism is not dead, notwithstanding the presence of real threats. The fourth section, the first of three that focus on the politics of climate change, describes key aspects of this agenda, including the central role of sustainable infrastructure and how the Paris agreement came into being.

The fifth section discusses political economy, including the vested interests that might oppose effective action. The following section examines the challenges of a "just transition": radical change in production and consumption methods, particularly concerning energy, will inevitably involve dislocation. That should be managed in a way that offers new opportunities and support to those who might experience or suffer from such dislocation.

Prospects for the future are the subject of the concluding section. Momentum is building, but too slowly, and action is urgent. We need acceleration now.

WHAT DRIVES CLIMATE CHANGE? HOW CAN IT BE MANAGED?

The greenhouse effect, which leads to global warming and climate change, arises because the molecules of some gases oscillate at a frequency similar to that of infra-red light and the resulting interference inhibits the escape of energy from the atmosphere. Much of the energy from the sun's rays is reflected back from the earth's surface as infra-red. It is the oscillation frequencies that determine which are the greenhouse gases (GHGs). The principal amongst these in terms of "radiative forcing" is carbon dioxide, although there are others,[3] such as methane, which vary in potency and duration.[4] With higher concentrations of GHGs in the atmosphere, the warming effect is stronger. We generally measure warming in terms of increase in average global surface temperature relative to the end of the nineteenth century, i.e., before fossil fuel–led growth got under way on a global scale.

We are currently seeing a temperature increase of 1°C, which takes us to the upper border of the benign Holocene period, which has been with us since the warming after the end of the last ice age around 10,000 years ago. The Holocene is now ending, and the changes that human activity has brought have

---

[2] There are 193 countries that have adopted both.

[3] Apart from carbon dioxide and methane, other greenhouse gases generally considered are nitrous oxide, hydrofluorocarbons, perfluorocarbons, sulphur hexafluoride, and nitrogen trifluoride.

[4] Methane, for example, is much more potent than carbon dioxide in terms of radiative forcing, but does not last nearly as long in the atmosphere.

moved us into the Anthropocene. During the Holocene, temperatures have been in a narrow range, roughly plus or minus 1°C. This is the period when settled farming emerged, with the cultivation of cereals, and our civilisation developed beyond hunting and gathering. Scientists have argued, for very sound reasons, that a rise in global surface temperature above 2°C is "dangerous" (IPCC 2013). We are already seeing intense effects at 1°C. We have not seen, as a world, a rise of 3°C for around three million years (way before *Homo sapiens* emerged around 250,000 years ago), and global temperature increases of 4°C or 5°C have not occurred for tens of millions of years.

The damage from climate change arises primarily via water in some shape or form: storms, floods and inundation, droughts and desertification, sea level rise. Temperature matters too: some places are likely to become so hot as to be impossible for humans to survive in them. With a rise of 3°C or 4°C, probably hundreds of millions, perhaps billions, of people would have to move. We are on a path of emissions which corresponds, over a period of a century or so, to warming of around 3°C, if the Paris COP21 country targets for emissions reductions are achieved (on Paris COP21, see the section on the new global agenda below) and of perhaps 4°C or 5°C if we follow something like pre-Paris business as usual (BAU). All temperature forecasts following from an assumed path of emissions are uncertain, as we cannot model with full confidence and there are inherent uncertainties in the system.

Brief illustrations of the damage we might experience include the following. At 3°C or 4°C, most of the snows from the Himalayas would be gone. That would cause severe disruption to the main rivers of Asia—including the Yellow, Yangtze, Mekong, Ganges, and Indus—on which countries with populations of billions depend. It is interesting that Tony's plan for a discussion of climate change was strongly linked to Asia (chapter 6). Similarly, the snows from the Andes and the Rockies, which serve so much of the Americas, would also melt. Much of Bangladesh would be submerged. Many of the world's big cities are coastal, from the major cities of Australia to Shanghai, Cairo, Amsterdam, Copenhagen, New York, and Rio de Janeiro, and many would probably be devastated by sea level rise. Hurricanes, cyclones, and typhoons would increase dramatically in intensity. These are just illustrations. The lives and livelihoods of hundreds of millions would likely be destroyed.

Not only are the direct consequences of climate-related disasters likely to be immense, but the indirect effects of climate-related shocks could cause profound long-term damage to prosperity and well-being. Indirect effects could wipe out decades of development, cause regions to fall back into poverty, and damage people's health irreversibly (Hallegatte et al. 2016). Climate change worsens the effect of natural disasters on people's lives, and these disasters, such as hurricanes or floods, destroy or damage assets for poor people and rich people alike, and for whole communities. Waterborne diseases and pests spread faster during heat waves, floods or droughts result in death, health expenditure, and lost labour income, and droughts or crop diseases cause crop losses and food price shocks.

Until sources and sinks[5] for GHGs start to come into balance, temperatures are likely to go on rising as concentrations increase.[6] Responding effectively to the challenge of stabilising temperature below a rise of 2°C will involve reducing emissions dramatically from current BAU paths—by at least 20 per cent in the next two decades—and peaking emissions within a few years. Further, for a target of 2°C, we must bring sources and sinks into balance (in this sense "net zero" emissions) in the second half of the century, around 50 years from now. The later they come into balance, the higher the temperature at which we will see temperature stabilisation.

The magnitude of that challenge is illustrated by the following. The world's infrastructure will roughly double in the next fifteen years, the world economy will double in twenty years (at a growth rate of a little over 3 per cent a year), and the world's population will double in forty years (with the shape of towns and cities determined in the next ten or twenty years). All this will take place in two decades during which emissions must drop by 20 per cent or more. We can see that large-scale action is urgent. The next two decades will be decisive. If the new infrastructure, economy, and cities that we add in that time look anything like the old, then we will have probably locked in temperature increases of well over 3°C during the next century or so.[7]

The urgency and scale of the necessary action has not yet been sufficiently widely understood or accepted. But this is the tough logic of the science and of basic economic projections, which look very robust. Tony understood all this very well. He rightly attached very high importance to clear communication of the basic facts and analyses which must inform policy-making. There is no more important message to communicate than the criticality of radical change in our infrastructure and in our patterns of growth in the next two decades.

THE POOREST ARE HIT EARLIEST AND HARDEST FROM A FAILURE TO MANAGE CLIMATE CHANGE

In 2005, Hurricane Katrina caused more than 1,800 deaths and is estimated to have been the costliest Atlantic hurricane, with damages around $125

---

[5]"Sinks" absorb GHGs from the atmosphere. The most important examples are forests and oceans, particularly in relation to carbon dioxide.

[6]Actually, given lags in the system, temperatures are likely to go on rising for a period even after concentrations peak.

[7]As Pfeiffer and his colleagues (2016) show, for 2°C, nearly all power infrastructure must be low- or zero-carbon from now on. Baldwin and her colleagues (2018) show that investment in the construction of coal-fired power plants must stop in 2020 in order for the Paris goals to be met.

billion. Hundreds of thousands were displaced, and most of the deaths and displacements were amongst the poorest (Krause and Reeves 2017; Platt Boustan et al. 2017). In July of the same year, a cyclone struck Mumbai and Maharashtra, and more than 1,000 died. Again, it was the poorest who suffered most (Ranger et al. 2011; Hallegatte et al. 2010). The 2010 floods in Pakistan affected more than one-fifth of its land area and 20 million people, with a death toll of around 1,800 (Kirsch et al. 2012). It is the poorest who suffer most when an extreme weather event strikes, whether in the southern United States or in South Asia. Poorer people are more likely to live on vulnerable land such as floodplains, to have homes that are less robust, to be less able to get away quickly, and to be less likely to have insurance.

Hurricanes, cyclones, and floods are associated with sudden, devastating disasters that have highly destructive effects, but poor people are also the most vulnerable and exposed to the more gradual, slower, and more pervasive environmental disasters. Many of the latter are associated with lack of water over time, whether through extended periods of low rainfall or gradual degradation of land resources through desertification. Others are associated with a shift to more intense and more variable weather patterns. Although slower to manifest, the impacts can be as destructive as those of more sudden disasters, if not more so in many circumstances. Poorer people engaged in agriculture are more likely to be working on marginal land and less likely to have access to irrigation or the drainage required to manage intense rainfall. (For a recent study on the vulnerability of poor people, see Winsemius et al. 2018).

Historical evidence shows that there was an increase in the severity, duration, and frequency of droughts between 1950 and 2010 in many of the world's most vulnerable regions, including the Sahel and Congo regions of Africa and the areas surrounding the Mediterranean (Spinoni et al. 2013). The severity and frequency of slow-onset climate disruptions, such as drought, are also set to increase. The World Bank predicts that by 2080, with unmitigated climate change, the number of drought days could rise by more than 20 per cent across the world. This would in turn increase the number of people exposed to droughts by 50 to 90 per cent, most of them poor (Hallegatte et al. 2016).

Many of the consequences of climate-induced droughts are already being felt. In the Horn of Africa, prolonged drought conditions following the erratic 2015–2016 El Niño event (the strongest on record) have persisted in Ethiopia, Kenya, Sudan, South Sudan, Djibouti, and Somalia. This drought, when coupled with other complex drivers such as conflict and poverty, has resulted in around 12 million people facing severe hunger, extensive loss of livestock and assets, and ultimately widespread internal displacement (Akumu and Frouws 2017). This has resulted in the movement of millions of people across the region searching for stability and security.

The impacts of drought are also not confined to Africa; there is increasing evidence that the worst drought on instrumental record in the Fertile Crescent of the Middle East contributed to the resultant migration of millions of people to urban areas in Syria between 2007 and 2010 (Kelley et al. 2015). This in turn exacerbated already strained services and infrastructure and became a contributing factor to the devastating Syrian conflict.

The above evidence comes from climate-related disruptions that we have seen as the temperature increases have risen to 1°C, but we have seen that we risk rises of 3°C or more. From the transformation of lives and livelihoods arising from such increases, hundreds of millions, perhaps billions, would likely have to move. There would be grave risks of widespread, severe, and extended conflict.

In all cases, it is the poorest who are most vulnerable and who suffer the greatest impacts. Tony recognised very clearly the double inequity here. The poorest of the world, wherever they are, have contributed least to the causes of climate change, but they suffer the most.

THE NEW STORY OF GROWTH

The rise of 3°C to 5° C in global surface temperature that we could see without strong action would induce radical change in the human geography of our planet, with widespread and severe devastation. The magnitude of these grave risks alone constitutes a powerful argument for strong action to reduce climate risk, even if this were to involve some significant reduction in income or substantial costs. That was the argument in the original UNFCCC treaty of 1992, which adopted the simplistic view that we should pay the marginal cost to be cleaner and less polluting, if that cost was less than the damage avoided—a simple, essentially static cost-benefit approach. The argument then turned to who should pay the marginal costs, with some commentators *inter alia* invoking the historic responsibility of rich countries. That simplistic view would not be wrong if the static model fully captured the essence of the issues and associated choices.

However, the narrow static argument is profoundly misleading, because we can now see that there is powerful dynamic learning, as well as substantial economies of scale, when we turn our focus to developing and using less wasteful low-carbon technologies. The arguments for strong and early action intensify still further when we recognise that burning fossil fuels causes dangerous particulate pollution, which presently kills or harms several million people a year around the world. And in the future, if such burning persisted, it would kill and harm via climate change. Further, we can see how to design our cities in ways which make them much less congested and polluted, as well as more productive and attractive places to live and work. And we understand much better how to look after our grasslands, forests, and oceans—our "natural infrastructure"—in ways which turn them into effective sinks for carbon dioxide rather than sources of carbon dioxide released from their damage or destruction, for example, through deforestation. Taking care of our natural infrastructure will make it part of a healthy and robust ecosystem which offers vital and productive services, including key elements of our water supply.

In his introduction to chapter 6, Tony challenged us directly to "face the question of how far climate change mitigation and poverty alleviation are complementary and how far they are potentially in conflict." We can now see that, for the most part, actions to reduce emissions are complementary with actions to reduce poverty. This follows in part from the features of the dynamics of low-carbon growth just described. There are many other direct examples. Decentralised solar power combined with micro credit can bring electricity to poor people for whom it might not otherwise be available. The system of root intensification for rice raises productivity and saves on water and energy by not flooding paddy fields; that in turn reduces methane emissions. Public transport saves energy and benefits poor people.

In other words, the transition to the low-carbon economy offers us an alternative and dynamic growth agenda. Developing relevant new growth models in theory and practice is a key and urgent task for economic theorists, applied economists, and economic decision-makers, in both the public and private sectors.

Tony took the understanding of growth very seriously, and some of his early theoretical papers were on endogenous technical progress and discovery (see, for example, Atkinson and Stiglitz 1969). (He was also the first to stress the importance of the time scale of growth models.) He was very focussed on processes of change. We discussed the challenges of developing a dynamic "public economics as if time matters," which was the subject of my paper in the issue of *Journal of Public Economics* in Tony's honour (Stern 2018). Tony founded the journal in the 1970s and edited it for more than twenty-five years. This was the type of approach to analytical public economics which he did so much to develop and foster.

That we can both grow and cut emissions has already become clear. Since 1990, the UK economy has grown by nearly 70 per cent and emissions have been cut by more than 40 per cent. In the last three or four years, emissions in China have plateaued and annual growth is still above 6 per cent and output is much cleaner and less polluting, i.e., growth is moving toward the "higher quality" that China is now seeking. Many countries—primarily in Europe but also including the United States and Uzbekistan—have managed to decouple GHG emissions and GDP growth (Aden 2016).

What we are now beginning to see—and must understand, promote, and deliver—is something still stronger than the possible coexistence of growth and emissions reductions. Examples of growth which is actually stronger and better as we make our transition to the low-carbon economy are beginning to emerge. One reason is that we have seen very powerful technological advances in the last dozen or so years during which the world has begun to make low-carbon and clean development a priority. The costs of generating power from onshore and offshore wind and of solar-generated power have fallen dramatically since 2010 (IRENA 2018). Technological improvements, including higher solar PV module efficiencies and larger wind turbines, drive such cost reductions. Many of these advances are the result of learning-by-doing and economies of scale. In many parts of the world, renewable power now offers the cheapest form of new energy capacity. The share of renewables and energy efficiency in public research and development spending also each increased from just 7 per cent of the total in 1985 to 20 per cent in 2015 (IEA 2017). The prices of batteries for electric vehicles are now a fifth of what they were in 2010 (Chediak 2017). Many more breakthroughs and discoveries are on the way. It is very likely that the great waves of discovery we have already seen are just the beginning of an intense and fruitful process. As well as the remarkable technical progress in renewables and energy efficiency, many of our future advances will flow from the better design of cities and the sound management of our natural infrastructure.

The new model of growth can also be enhanced by, and create, stronger communities. Reusing and recycling happen in communities. Networks such as public transport and broadband connect communities. "Combined heat and power" occurs in communities. Protecting and enhancing forests depends on societies acting in a cohesive way. Indeed, the commitment to build environmentally friendly and attractive towns and cities can arise more naturally in stronger communities and, in turn, draw people together as they work towards a shared goal of improving their town or city and experience together the benefits that work produces. The importance of the connectedness and mutual dependence of human beings was fundamental to Tony's understanding of a good society. (See, for example, his reference to John Donne in chapter 8.)

Many alternative technologies, such as decentralised solar power, allow people with no electricity to gain access to it, enabling their children to study in the evenings and providing greater security for women and girls, who would otherwise be out fetching firewood, often over long distances. Better public transport enables poorer people in particular to travel more efficiently to jobs and enhances their opportunities. And the impact of pollution in cities is generally worse for poorer people, who live in places and travel in ways that make them more vulnerable.

This new sustainable and inclusive growth story is based on fostering and investing in the development of human, social, natural, and physical capital. Human capital is the health, education, and capabilities of individuals to build their lives and livelihoods. Social capital refers to good governance and cohesive and supportive communities. Natural capital is embodied in environmental and natural resources. And physical capital includes the productive assets, particularly infrastructure, which we create from savings out of income. Building these forms of capital together and in ways which involve creativity, complementarity, and technical progress will bring sustainability. By sustainability we mean ensuring that future generations have opportunities for well-being at least as good as our own, assuming they behave similarly towards those that follow. Sustainability turns on the capital of various types we pass on to future generations.

This new growth agenda and these new growth models really can bring us strong, sustainable, and inclusive growth. The transition to the low-carbon economy is the growth story of the twenty-first century. It has sustainable infrastructure at its core. Investing in this new sustainable infrastructure sharpens supply and boosts demand, both in the short term and the medium term. It launches Schumpeterian innovation and investment in the medium term. And there is no longer-term high-carbon growth story: any such attempt would self-destruct in the hostile environment it would create.

The study and fostering of this new growth agenda is a task for us all. Tony would have pressed us to take part and would likely have been in the vanguard.

THE NEW GLOBAL AGENDA

As described in the introduction, 2015 brought a new global agenda: the Sustainable Development Goals in September, and the Paris UNFCCC agreement in December, with more than 190 countries involved in each case. The creation of such an agenda was remarkable and an outstanding manifestation of multilateralism. This agenda expresses a joint commitment, with explicit goals for 2030 in the SDGs, to sustainable development in which all are to be involved: developing, emerging, and developed countries. In Paris COP21, it recognises mutual interdependence, expresses an obligation for mutual support, anticipates the severe risks to future generations, and enhances our obligations to offer them chances in life as good as those we inherited (in other words, a commitment to sustainability). The 2015 agreements were truly remarkable and showed that the narrow self-interest in the behaviour of "Homo economicus" at the centre of so much economic modelling misses much that is crucially important in how we can behave. In other words, goodness, responsibility, and foresight can be widespread and form the foundation of agreement and commitment.

We cannot take such collaboration based on shared values for granted, and it is worth describing briefly how these agreements were reached. The SDGs followed on from the Millennium Development Goals (MDGs), agreed to in 2000 to cover advances for the next fifteen years—i.e., to 2015—with improvements calibrated relative to 1990. These were targets for developing countries, with developed countries obliged to support. It transpired that, as intended, the MDGs provided a powerful impetus to and coherence for development and development assistance in the period to 2015. These eight goals covered dimensions around the reduction of income poverty, education, health, the environment, and collaboration for action. They showed the energising effects of shared targets and commitments. And aid budgets in many countries, including the United Kingdom, were increased and focussed on the goals. When I led the writing of the report of the Commission for Africa in 2004–2005 (from the UK Treasury) ahead of the UK-led G8 summit in Gleneagles, Scotland, in July 2005, it was clear that the MDGs provided powerful impetus and a valuable framework. These goals were a key factor in the simultaneous mass movement "Make Poverty History," which pressed, successfully, for commitment to action at Gleneagles.

The SDGs built on the MDGs and set targets for 2015–2030 across seventeen dimensions that fall largely under the same headings but are now broader and deeper. They include inequality as well as poverty, are more explicit on gender issues, and focus throughout on sustainability, the environment, and climate, explicitly in around two-thirds of the goals and implicitly in the others. Goal 13 is directly on climate change: "Take urgent action to combat climate change and its impacts." Crucially, the goals apply to all countries. The difference between the SDGs and the MDGs is a recognition of the great changes in the world economy and the sharply increasing pressures on the global commons. The SDGs were very important for Tony in discussing social objectives, and he set them out explicitly in box C in chapter 5.

Crucially, the SDGs advanced beyond the MDGs in applying to all countries and in bringing sustainability to centre stage. They were concerned now with the rights of future generations and equity in relation to those who would follow, as well as current poverty. They emerged from the largely positive experience of the MDGs in shaping and galvanising action and the growing recognition of what dirty and damaging growth could do to our environment and our future opportunities.

The Paris agreement of December 2015, COP21, built on two understandings, as I have already argued: first, that the risks of unmanaged climate change are grave, and second, that the new growth agenda presents very attractive development opportunities. It also built on the achievements of earlier COPs.

COP15 in December 2009 in Copenhagen had attempted to reach international agreement for climate action. The conference, for which preparation had been insufficient, was cold, chaotic, and quarrelsome. Some of the behaviour of negotiators made it appear as though rich countries were scheming together to push the poorer countries into particular positions. Nevertheless, COP15 produced the outline of an agreement (an "accord") which was the foundation of an agreement in Cancún, Mexico, COP16, a year later, a meeting which was much less quarrelsome and for which much better preparations had been made. There was a strong and shared desire for an agreement and concern that the divisiveness of Copenhagen not be repeated.

Key aspects of the Cancún agreement were targets for emissions for 2020 for developed countries and some targets for developing countries.[8] The former were supposed to be "binding" and the latter "indicative." The developed countries made a commitment to generate flows of climate finance, $100 billion per annum from developed countries to poorer countries.[9] It looks, broadly speaking, as though the emissions targets for 2020 set out in Copenhagen/Cancún, at least for major countries or groups (G20), are likely to be achieved (UNEP 2017).

Part of the hesitation in coming to a formal agreement in Copenhagen was the concern from developing countries that attempts to reduce emissions might slow growth and poverty reduction. This "tension" was a question that Tony planned to tackle in his discussion of climate change. In discussing the new growth story in the previous section, I argued that we can now see that the alleged hard trade-off between climate responsibility and poverty reduction or growth is fundamentally misleading. And I gave examples from power supply, agriculture, and transport of how emissions reductions and poverty reduction come together.

It was the increasing realisation that the transition to the low-carbon economy was this century's growth story that made a profound contribution to the success of Paris COP21. That argument continues to grow in strength and acceptance, but it is not yet won. And there are many, including vested interests (see next section), who resist vigorously.

The key elements of the Paris COP21 agreement were: (1) a global temperature target of well below 2°C, with efforts to hold to 1.5°C; (2) Naturally Determined Contributions (NDCs) describing each country's emissions intentions for 2030; (3) intended financing flows of $100 billion each year from richer to poorer countries; (4) conventions on measurement of emissions; (5) plans to ratchet up action to be developed by 2020, recognising that the set of NDC intentions is not consistent with the temperature targets (they look more like a 3°C path); (6) long-term planning (including at the country level) to achieve a balance of sources and sinks in the second half of the century; and (7) the establishment of a technology transfer mechanism to support innovation and deployment.

The success of Paris depended also on the activities of many who were not national decision-makers or negotiators, including businesspeople, mayors of cities, and NGOs. There were many shared understandings and coalitions built

[8] The emissions intentions embodied in Cancún in large measure arose from the agreement in the Copenhagen accord to come forward with such intentions in the months following the Copenhagen COP.

[9] I was directly involved in negotiating the annual $100 billion, working with Prime Minister Meles Zenawi of Ethiopia, who was representing a group of African countries in these discussions. I did not have a formal role but was able, on behalf of Meles Zenwai, to liaise with Mike Froman of the United States, who was working with Secretary of State Hillary Clinton.

around Paris which contributed strongly. Behaviour during the process itself and the very strong commitment to get an agreement was testimony to the sense of responsibility to future generations, which was deep and widely shared, together with a recognition of the internationalism that was necessary to take on that responsibility and tackle climate change. In our discussions over the years, Tony had long argued that economic analysis and the modelling of behaviour should look beyond the portrayal of the natural state of humans as being narrowly self-interested and calculating only for themselves.

Two examples of the generation of collaborative behaviour around specific issues can illustrate. First, developing countries had earlier insisted, up to COP15 in Copenhagen and beyond, on a narrow interpretation of "common but differentiated responsibility" (a key UNFCCC principle) to mean that rich countries should have binding obligations on emissions and poor countries need only indicate broad intentions. Recognising that, in the future of emissions, developing and emerging countries would play a bigger role than developed countries (due to the sheer weight of numbers and the embodiment of their growth), Paris COP21 took NDCs from all countries on a similar basis. And the fact that they were not binding in a formal way involving sanctions also brought countries together. In any case, it became clear that the enforcement of sanctions around the idea of "binding" simply lacked any credibility. Dropping the notion of "binding" avoided divisiveness over its meaning and to whom it applied. It also may have made the countries more ambitious. And as we have seen, countries are indeed influenced by the goals which they voluntarily set for themselves.

Second, during Paris many rich countries joined together with small-island states and African governments to press for efforts to keep temperature increases below 1.5°C, recognising the severe threats faced by these states and our joint responsibilities as a world.[10]

The global agenda constructed in 2015 has stood the test of time. For example, Paris COP21 came into force, with the necessary ratifications, extraordinarily rapidly—within eleven months. In contrast, the Kyoto Protocol agreed to at the COP of 1997 took eight years to ratify. And the Paris agreement has so far withstood President Trump's intention, announced in June 2017, to withdraw (although we note that technically that could not take place until just after the 2020 presidential election in the United States).[11] Country after country in COP22 in Marrakesh in November 2016, just after the 2016 presidential

[10] The group of countries pressing for an explicit statement in relation to 1.5°C became known as the "high-ambition coalition."

[11] As per the terms of the Paris agreement, the submission of an intent to withdraw can only be made three years after the agreement entered into force (4 November 2016), which means that the earliest date the United States can submit one is 4 November 2019. This would then take a year to finalise, with withdrawal happening at the earliest on 4 November 2020. The next US presidential election is scheduled for 3 November 2020.

election, stated clearly that their commitment would carry on. And at the Hamburg G20 summit in June 2017, the G20, minus the United States, said that "Paris is irreversible"—very strong language for such communiqués. Internationalism must be promoted, nurtured, and decided, but it lives.

POLITICAL ECONOMY AND VESTED INTERESTS

As time went by, Tony became more and more convinced of the importance of understanding the workings of political economy. Reform should of course be well designed, and Tony was preeminent here, but its success also depends on understanding how it might be opposed and how counterarguments and vested interests can be tackled. He was a great believer in rigorous analysis and transparency of results. He noted that the evaluation of policy reform requires the identification of who gains and who loses, and by how much; so too does an analysis of who might be opposed, and how strongly. Also, he championed our duty as academics to communicate—witness his important European Economic Association presidential address in 1989 entitled "Public Economics and the Economic Public" (Atkinson 1990).

There has been powerful opposition to action on climate change, much of it driven by vested interests, particularly those with large fossil fuel interests in the United States. Naomi Oreskes and Erik Conway (2010), for example, have shown in their excellent book *Merchants of Doubt* how such interests have tried to sow doubt about scientific studies that show the dangers involved in the activities of these interests. These authors use tobacco/health and fossil fuels/climate as central examples and demonstrate that fossil fuel interests have funded "climate deniers."

Others, particularly on seeing the diminishing credibility of the denial of climate science, have tried their hand at "lukewarming." They say that they accept the science but think that the potential impacts of climate change and its damages are only modest and that alternative techniques are very costly (see, for example, Ridley 2015). Climate science and the very rapid pace of technological advance of low-carbon technologies are proving the lukewarmers wrong. Such arguments must be confronted head on: they are not only wrong, but dangerous in the inaction they promote. Delay is potentially deeply damaging.

This is not the place to go into these issues in any further detail. But as we analyse and propose reform and study public policy, they do illustrate Tony's insistence on the importance of examining political economy. Tony believed strongly in the power of analysis to come to an understanding of the workings of the world, warts and all, and in our duty to communicate clearly and strongly.

A JUST TRANSITION

We have seen that action on climate change and the embrace of the new strong growth story will involve radical change and large-scale innovation and investment. It will involve moving away quickly from fossil fuels in energy, finding new approaches to transport, adopting very different city design, protecting forests and grasslands, and so on. This will inevitably mean that many activities must change quickly and that some, such as coal mining and coal use, must be radically reduced. Economic history teaches us that industrial revolutions, or waves of technological change, involve dislocation. We need a "just transition," both morally (coal miners are not personally responsible for climate change) and politically, if the reform is to be carried through at the pace necessary.

It is not enough to point to the many new jobs created by the new industries. That is an important and highly relevant argument, but it is not the whole story. Some of those working in the old industries can find jobs in the new. But not all of those working with horses in the early twentieth century became chauffeurs or workers in car factories. There should be active retraining and fostering of new skills; so too financing for new ventures. And those for whom new activities would not be possible should be provided with social protection.

Much of the loss of employment would be highly localised—in coal regions or states, for example. Regional investment and innovation should be an important part of the response. Sometimes major public activities can be relocated. For example, in the United Kingdom, social security administration, record-keeping, and management was moved to the Newcastle area, which had suffered from the slowdown of the coal and shipbuilding industries. Unfortunately, history has given us many examples of how not to manage such transitions. This includes the United Kingdom, which, as a country early to the industrial revolution and waves of technological changes, has had to manage such dislocations but has not always done so very well.

Much technological change which is under way, such as robotics and AI, will transform employment and the way we work. The transition to the low-carbon economy will be interwoven with these other manifestations and drivers of technical change. In our discussions, Tony saw very clearly the importance of managing these transitions much better than we have done in the past. He emphasised the importance of looking back to the lessons of economic history, looking forward to what is coming, understanding the dynamics of change, and working to embrace change. In so doing, we have a responsibility to create a world where our children can prosper, where everyone, but particularly poorer people, has opportunities, and where poorer people are not casualties or collateral damage of change.

PROSPECTS

Tony was an intellectual activist who believed in understanding the causes and drivers of change. He studied policies which could advance living standards or well-being on all dimensions, particularly for poor people. He saw unmanaged climate change as a grave danger, particularly for the poorest people of the world. And he saw the great potential of the transition to the low-carbon economy in driving sustainable and inclusive growth for the twenty-first century.

Tony had not been heavily involved in research on these issues. But he saw the dangers, the opportunities, and the importance of strong research, in particular research focussed on explaining how to deliver the new story of growth, manage change, and radically reduce the grave risks of climate change. He was immensely encouraging to those who were working on these issues, myself included.

His intention to discuss these issues in this book marked Tony's strong interest in them and recognition of their importance. Had he been able to write that part of chapter 6 himself, I am sure he would have helped us advance in our understanding of climate change and poverty.

I think that Tony was beginning to share my optimism about what we can do to deliver a much more attractive form of growth—growth which is sustainable and inclusive and which can contribute to the rapid reduction of poverty as well as the immense risks to poor people, and the whole world, from climate change. I am sure that he shared my deep concern as to whether we could create the political will to act quickly enough.

Tony did not believe that an absence of political will was something that just happens. He thought that political will can be strengthened by clear and rational analysis and argument. Whilst that task is often difficult, it is the duty of academics to take on the policy issues with great openness and rigour and engage in strong public debate. No one delivered on that duty better than Tony. He was an example and inspiration to us all. He combined powerful argument and analysis with public engagement in *Inequality: What Can Be Done?* (2016), heroically written whilst his terminal disease was with him. We hope that this, his last book on poverty, will not only play a similar role in increasing our understanding of world poverty and of what can be done, but also be a shining example to future researchers of the duty to bring their work to the most important issues of their time, while showing them how it can be done.

EDITORS' NOTE

Each national report consists of text, structured according to the headings below, followed by a graph (two in the case of China). For nineteen of the sixty countries, where Tony had neither assembled national estimates of poverty into a spreadsheet nor started to draft text for a national report, we have drawn graphs containing just the PovcalNet estimates based on the $1.90 a day line and, where available, the estimates of nonmonetary poverty rates made by the Oxford Poverty and Human Development Initiative (OPHI) (or, in the case of Sweden, the percentage of the population below 60 per cent of median income and the material deprivation rate, both estimated by Eurostat). For a number of other countries, Tony had assembled the necessary data and had drawn graphs based on them, but the text of the report has been written by us.

We have updated World Bank figures from PovcalNet to the April 2018 release of the data, OPHI figures to the Winter 2017–2018 release (these therefore predate the revision to the Global MPI in September 2018 that is mentioned in a footnote in chapter 5), and figures based on EU-SILC and from LIS Key Figures to information available in July 2018 (from the Eurostat and LIS websites, respectively). We have also updated a substantial number of national estimates by drawing on national sources, although by no means all of them.

Readers interested in particular countries will naturally wish to pursue the latest information available. The great majority of the sources used in the national reports are available free of charge on the websites of national statistical offices, government ministries, research centres, and international organisations. (For some older data, Tony could also draw on material that he had been collecting for decades, which is now stored in the Economists' Papers Archive in the library of Duke University.) In addition, we refer readers to the short country "poverty briefs" on the World Bank's website, produced in response to a recommendation by Tony in the report of the Commission on Global Poverty (World Bank 2017, pp. 28–29).

Poverty lines: This describes the national poverty line or lines that lie behind the series of national estimates of poverty rates plotted in the graph for each country. Where there are more than one series, these are labelled "series 1," "series 2," etc. In a number of cases, Tony gives values of national poverty lines in international purchasing power dollars (using data on local currency to PPP dollars from the World Development Indicators: WDI PPP API_PA.NUS.PPP_DS2, downloaded 4 October 2016). We suspect that he intended to do this for all countries and to analyse the results in the main text of the book in chapters 3 or 4 and/or in the regional chapters, chapters 6 to 9.

Poverty today: The latest figure is given for the percentage of the population living in households beneath the International Poverty Line of $1.90 per person per day (2011 PPP dollars) taken from PovcalNet, contrasting this with one or more national estimates of the poverty rate based on the line or lines described under the previous heading.

In the draft that Tony left, he also reported the latest PovcalNet estimate of the poverty gap based on the $1.90 line. However, in reporting national estimates, he included only the latest poverty rate but no national measure of the depth of poverty. We have followed this practice in our editing, although many of the national sources cited do also provide estimates of the poverty gap and the FGT2 index, and it may be that in time Tony would have added these to the reports.

Who is poor?: This section gives a snapshot of how the incidence of poverty varies across the population based on the national poverty line currently in use. The information is often underdeveloped, but rural-urban and regional differences feature frequently. The descriptions are based exclusively on estimates of monetary poverty, but Tony may have planned to augment them with figures for nonmonetary poverty—the OPHI Country Briefings typically include regional breakdowns and rural-urban differences, and in editing the reports we have included the latter under the "nonmonetary poverty" heading.

Change over time: This section is often underdeveloped or missing altogether. It is restricted to a monetary definition of poverty (see below on nonmonetary poverty).

Nonmonetary poverty: For countries for which OPHI makes estimates, this section includes the latest estimate of the head count that forms part of the Global Multidimensional Poverty Index (Global MPI). The accompanying graph contains OPHI's short time series of harmonised estimates, if available, based on calculations that are standardized to take account of any differences over time in survey content (see chapter 4). Not infrequently, these estimates do not extend to the year for which the latest head count is given as part of the Global MPI. The OHPI Country Briefings on which Tony drew provide information on the intensity of multidimensional poverty as well as its incidence, but only estimates of the latter are given in the national reports. In the case of EU countries, the text of each report refers to "the Eurostat indicator" of material deprivation. These are the measures described in chapter 3: the percentage of the population that cannot afford at least three (material deprivation) or four (severe material deprivation) items from a list of nine items. (The figures come from the Eurostat website.) A number of countries have national estimates of multidimensional poverty, produced by a government department, the statistical office, a research institute, or university researchers; these estimates are often, but not always, based on the Alkire-Foster method underlying the OPHI estimates. Tony's drafts of the national reports did not always refer to these national estimates, and the same applies to the versions that the reader will find here; series based on these figures are only rarely included in the graphs.

Overall inequality: This section reports figures for the Gini coefficient for income and/or consumption inequality, sometimes commenting on how they have changed over time.

The poverty rates plotted in the graphs refer typically to the percentage of individuals living in households with income or consumption (per capita or equivalised by a different scale) beneath the line in question. That is, each individual is weighted 1, although occasionally other weights are applied and this is made clear in the text of the report. (For example, the poverty rate series is for equivalent adults in the case of Kenya.) (See the discussion of this issue in chapter 3.) For brevity's sake, the labels for each series in the graphs omit most of this detail. The Gini coefficients also usually refer to the distribution of individuals by their household income or consumption (again, per capita or equivalised by a different scale). In each graph, the World Bank series from PovcalNet based on the $1.90 line is plotted without breaks, although there may well be cases where this is not appropriate due to changes in the methods used to conduct the surveys on which the estimates are based, as sometimes confirmed by the discussion in the reports of national estimates based on the same data. The one exception is for China, where we have indicated a break when both the rural and urban series switch from using household income to household consumption. Occasionally, the World Bank estimates and the national estimates are reported with a one-year difference despite clearly being based on the same survey, which may arise when surveying spans calendar years; we have not always been able to rationalize this situation and select the appropriate year. The vertical (and horizontal) scales in the graphs vary, and hence care should be taken when comparing graphs for different countries, although we have harmonised the scales to a considerable degree. The sources for the national poverty estimates and Gini coefficients are usually cited within each report. The national estimates of poverty for Latin American and Caribbean countries are taken in a number of cases from the SEDLAC database maintained by the Centro de Estudios Distributivos, Laborales, y Sociales (CEDLAS), part of the Universidad Nacional de La Plata, Argentina, and available on the CEDLAS website. (The database also contains separate statistics calculated on ex post–harmonised data sets, which are not used in the national reports.) Estimates for high-income countries are sometimes taken from Eurostat and from LIS Key Figures (see the note on reference years for Eurostat data based on EU-SILC in Atkinson et al. 2017, pp. 6–7). The graphs do not have the reading note beneath them that is present for the graphs in the main text. (See Tony's comment on this feature in his preface.) The graph names use the standard three-letter ISO country codes. All the data plotted in the graphs are available for download at www.tony-atkinson.com.

The brief country descriptions below the graphs draw on the World Bank classification of countries by level of GNI per capita in 2015 given in chapter 1 in box A and on estimates of GNI per capita in that year using the Atlas [series NY.GNP.PCAP.CD] and PPP [NY.GNP.PCAP.PP.CD] methods and population totals [series SP.POP.TOTL] taken from the World Development Indicators (downloaded February 2018).

The list of references for each report, which have been compiled in the section following the national reports, sometimes includes sources that have not been cited. We have retained these apparent redundancies from Tony's draft in case they contain material that he planned to draw on in a later revision or that he simply wanted to provide as useful references for anyone wishing to delve into the analysis of poverty in the country concerned.

The length of each national report is constrained not to exceed two pages (except for China).

National Poverty Reports for chapter 6

BANGLADESH

Poverty lines: The Bangladesh Bureau of Statistics has used a cost of basic needs method to measure poverty since 1995–1996. First, the cost is computed of a fixed food bundle of eleven food items (rice, wheat, pulses, milk, oil, meat, freshwater fish, potato, other vegetables, sugar, and fruits) providing the minimal nutritional requirements for a diet corresponding to 2,122 Cal per day per person (the food-poverty line). Second, two different allowances for nonfood consumption are computed: a "lower" allowance reflecting the median amount spent on nonfood items by households whose total consumption is approximately equal to their food-poverty line, and an "upper" allowance corresponding to the amount spent on nonfood items by households whose food consumption (rather than total consumption) is approximately equal to their food-poverty line. The sum of food and upper nonfood allowances constitutes the upper poverty line, which forms the basis for series 2 in the graph (Ministry of Finance 2015, p. 3). The updating of the poverty line over time is described in World Bank (2013, box 1-1 and appendix 1). (It is unclear whether the poverty rate for 1991 in series 2 shown in the graph is calculated on a basis consistent with those for later years.) Series 1 is from Khan and Sen (2006, p. 320), based on income, and series 2 is from Ministry of Finance (2015, table 1). Poverty is measured with the Household Income and Expenditure Survey (HIES), where a household is classified as poor if its total consumption expenditure per capita is beneath the relevant line (series 2).

Poverty today: The World Bank estimates show that the proportion of the population living in households with consumption per head below $1.90 a day in 2016 was 14.8 per cent and that the poverty gap was 2.7 per cent. Series 2 of the national estimates shows that the proportion of the population living in households with consumption below the upper poverty line in 2010 was 31.5 per cent, when the World Bank figure was 19.6 per cent.

Who is poor?

- The national estimate of the poverty rate in 2010 (series 2) was 35.2 per cent in rural areas and 21.3 per cent in urban areas.

- Regional poverty rates varied from 26.2 per cent in Chittagong to 39.4 per cent in Barisal.

(Ministry of Finance 2015, table 4)

Change over time: According to the official estimates based on the upper poverty line (series 2), Bangladesh experienced a steady decline in consumption-based poverty rates between 2000 and 2010: the poverty rate declined 1.78 percentage points per year between 2000 and 2005, and 1.70 percentage points in the period 2005 to 2010. "This suggests that the series of shocks that affected Bangladesh in 2007/2008 did not significantly slow down the speed of poverty reduction" (World Bank 2013, p. xii).

Nonmonetary poverty: The OPHI Global MPI head count, based on deprivation according to a third or more of the weighted indicators, shows that 41.3 per cent of the population were in poor households in 2014 (estimate based on Demographic and Health Survey [DHS] data). Split by rural and urban subpopulations, the rates were 48.2 and 22.5 per cent, respectively. The harmonised time series of the head count (see editors' note) shows a decline in the national rate, from 67.1 per cent in 2004 to 49.6 per cent in 2011.

Overall inequality: The Gini coefficient for household per capita consumption in 2010 was 29.9 per cent; it had remained little changed from 2000 (30.7 per cent) (World Bank 2013, p. 13). Gini coefficients for per capita income rose substantially between 1991 (30.3 per cent) and 2000 (40.5 per cent), the rise being somewhat larger in rural areas and smaller in urban areas, and they rose again to 2005 (43.8 per cent) (Khan and Sen 2006, p. 315, table 14.3 [rural] and 14.5 [urban]; Khan 2005, table VII). Khan (2005) questions the comparability of the HIES data over time. Estimates of the Gini coefficient for both per capita income and per capita consumption over 1984 to 2010 (not shown in the graph) are given in Ministry of Finance (2015, figure 10), with the source given as the World Bank.

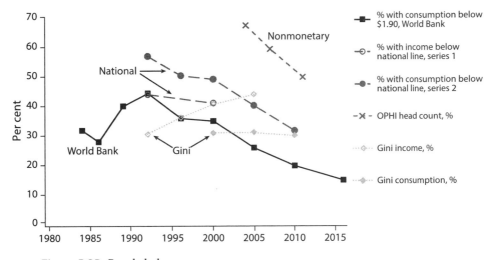

Figure BGD. Bangladesh

Bangladesh is a lower-middle-income country, according to the World Bank classification, with GNI per capita in 2015 of $1,190 (Atlas) and $3,550 (PPP) and a population in that year of 161.0 million people.

CAMBODIA

Poverty lines: A national poverty line was developed with assistance from the World Bank in 1997, based on data from the Cambodia Socio-Economic Survey (CSES) 1993–1994. The line included a food component based on 2,100 Cal per person per day and a nonfood component estimated from the nonfood expenditures of households with total per capita expenditure around the level of the food poverty line in the 1993–1994 survey. However,

> in the 1990s, the CSES databases were not comparable to each other: in coverage, definitions of variables, or data collection methods. Only the CSES of 2004 and the surveys conducted thereafter covered the whole country and have been reasonably comparable to each other. . . . Effectively, the poverty rates based on the poverty line of 1997 were considered comparable and officially accepted for 1993/1994, 2004 and 2007 only. (Ministry of Planning 2013, box 1; see also the comments of Gibson 2005, chapter 4)

A new line and poverty estimates (using household expenditure per capita) were developed by an Inter-ministerial Working Group using the 2009 CSES, the changes from the earlier line, and estimates that included (1) a food component based on 2,200 Cal per person per day (priced separately in Phnom Penh, other urban areas, and rural areas), (2) a nonfood component equal to the average expenditure on certain items by households between the second and third deciles of total household expenditure (separate figures for Phnom Penh, other urban areas, and rural areas), (3) the exclusion of imputed income from rent for homeowners (previously included), and (4) a switch from calculating total expenditure that includes the estimated depreciation values of consumer durables to taking expenditure on durables bought in the last twelve months. In 2009, the poverty line was 6,347 riels per day in Phnom Penh, 4,352 riels in other urban areas, and 3,503 riels in rural areas (Ministry of Planning 2013, table 3). Series 1 shows estimates based on this line, allowing for changes in prices before and after 2009. Series 2 shows estimates by a World Bank team working in parallel with the Inter-ministerial Working Group, using similar methods to arrive at a poverty line and to estimate poverty rates. In 2009, the poverty line for series 2 was 5,326 riels per day in Phnom Penh, 4,273 riels in other urban areas, and 3,914 riels in rural areas (World Bank 2014, table 32) (series 1 and 2 from World Bank 2014, figure 49; series 1 for 2012 from Asian Development Bank 2014, figure 3; series 2 for 2012–2013 from World Bank 2016).

Poverty today: The World Bank estimates that in 2012 the proportion of the population living in households with consumption per head below $1.90 a day was 2.17 per cent and that the poverty gap was 0.28 per cent. National estimates show 19.8 per cent (series 1) and 20.5 per cent (series 2) of the population in poverty in 2011; these estimates are close, but the subnational figures for this year differ much more: 10.9 per cent in Phnom Penh, 22.5 per cent in other urban areas, and 20.7 per cent in rural areas in series 1 and 1.5 per cent, 16.1 per cent, and 23.7 per cent, respectively, in series 2 (Asian Development Bank 2014, figure 3; World Bank 2014, table 38).

Who is poor?

Change over time:

Nonmonetary poverty: The OPHI Global MPI head count, based on deprivation according to a third or more of the weighted indicators, shows that 33.0 per cent of the population were in poor households in 2014 (estimate based on DHS data). Split by rural and urban subpopulations, the rates were 38.1 and 7.1, per cent respectively. The harmonised time series of the head count (see editors' note) shows a decline in the national rate, from 59.2 per cent in 2005 to 45.9 per cent in 2011.

Overall inequality: The Gini coefficient for household expenditure in 2004–2011 is from World Bank (2014, table 5) and for 2012 from World Bank 2016.

[*Editors*: Data that Tony compiled for Cambodia include the series in the graph for the percentage of people in households below $1.90 per person per day taken from the October 2016 release of PovcalNet. The October 2017 and April 2018 releases contained no data for Cambodia, and the notes for the October 2017 release in the "What Is New" section of the website state:

> We have removed poverty estimates for Cambodia until further analytical work is carried out. Close examination of the household survey and price data suggested problems with the household survey–based welfare aggregate, producing implausibly low poverty rates. According to these estimates, Cambodia's poverty rate was much lower than what is expected from its GDP per capita. Furthermore some non-income welfare indicators are much lower in Cambodia than in countries with comparable extreme poverty rates. We have removed the Cambodia data pending further analytical work to improve the reliability of the household survey-based consumption aggregate.

We do not know whether estimates in other series in the graph have also been called into question.]

Cambodia is a lower-middle-income country according to the World Bank classification, with GNI per capita in 2015 of $1,070 (Atlas method) and $3,290 (PPP) and a population in that year of 15.6 million people.

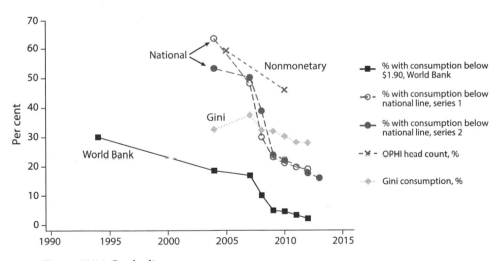

Figure KHM. Cambodia

CHINA

Poverty lines: The government has for many years set an official poverty line for rural China. (There is no official poverty line for urban China.) The official line from 1978 to 2007, applied in series 1, is referred to as the "extreme poverty line"; the line was replaced by the "low-income poverty line," effective from 2008 to 2010 and applied in series 2; this in turn was replaced by the "new poverty line," effective from 2011 and applied in series 3. The new poverty line is based on expenditure needs for adequate food and clothing (housing costs are low in rural China); estimates for the poverty thresholds for this series back to 1978 adjust the 2011 line using the Rural Poor CPI, which is heavily weighted to food consumption. (The sources for all three series are: National Bureau of Statistics [NBS] 2017, table 1-1, p. 356; the source for 2017 for series 3 is NBS 2018. These sources give both poverty rates and numbers in poverty—the series 3 figures for the latter are shown in figure 6.2 in chapter 6.)

The series 3 poverty line in 2010 was 2,300 yuan per person per year at 2010 prices, whereas the series 2 line had been set at 1,247 yuan. NBS (2015, p. 108) states that the new poverty line for rural China in 2011 was PPP$2.30 a day, or 21 per cent higher than the International Poverty Line of $1.90. It similarly states that, if account is taken of the additions for housing, including imputed rents, then the rural poverty line would be 20 per cent higher. The urban poverty estimates are from Khan (1998, 2004) and Gustafsson and Ding (2016, 2017). The former applied a basic needs line to data from CASS (Chinese Academy of Social Science) surveys (Khan 1998, table 13; 2004, table 14). The latter took the lowest *dibao* line (for Yunnan) in the twelve provinces covered by CHIP (China Household Income Project) surveys of urban households in the years in question (Gustafsson and Ding 2017, table 7.3). (*Dibao* is a minimum income programme—see, for example, Gao 2017; the CHIP data, among other sources, are discussed in Gustafsson, Li, and Sato 2014.)

In 2013 there was a major change in the data source, with the introduction of the integrated nationwide household survey in place of the previously separate surveys for rural and urban China conducted by NBS (see the discussion in chapter 6). (Information on the earlier separate surveys and the new integrated survey is given in Gustafsson, Li, and Sato 2014.) Both sets of urban poverty figures take income per capita as the welfare measure and include an estimate of imputed rent for owner-occupiers. The World Bank estimates are based on income for 1981–1987 and consumption expenditure thereafter; the series jumps upwards after 1987 in both rural and urban areas. From 2013, the NBS estimates of rural poverty using the new integrated national household survey are based on consumption; however, households with consumption per capita below the poverty line but with much higher income are not classified as poor. Previously, rural poverty was defined by NBS as either income per capita below the poverty line and consumption per capita below 1.2 times the line or consumption per capita below the poverty line and income per capita below 1.2 times the line (NBS 2004, p. 8; World Bank 2009, box 1.2).

Poverty today: The World Bank estimates show that in 2014 the proportion of the population living in households with consumption per head below $1.90 a day was 1.4 per cent and that the poverty gap was 0.3 per cent. For rural China, the proportion living in households below $1.90 a day was 2.4 per cent; for urban China, the percentage was 0.5 per cent. The national estimate for rural poverty in 2014 (series 3) was 7.2

per cent (and 3.1 per cent in 2017). The national estimate for urban poverty (*dibao* line) in 2013 was 1.0 per cent when the World Bank estimate was 0.5 per cent, as in 2014.

Who is poor?

- In 2013, the rural population accounted for 85 per cent of those in poverty according to the World Bank estimates of households with consumption per head below $1.90 a day.

- In 2014, the official rural poverty rate estimated by NBS (series 3) was 7.2 per cent, but varied from 2.7 per cent in the East Region, 7.5 per cent in the Middle Region, to 12.4 per cent in the West Region. Half the rural poor (51.3 per cent) were living in the West Region. Five provinces (Guizhou, Yunnan, Xizang, Gansu, and Xinjiang) had poverty rates in excess of 15 per cent.

- In 2014, people in rural China living in provinces designated as "minority areas" had a poverty rate that was double the national rate; they accounted for 31.4 per cent of the total rural population below the poverty line.

- In 2014, the rural poverty rate for children aged under sixteen was 9.5 per cent; the rate for those aged sixty and over was 9.5 per cent, compared with the national average for rural China, which was 7.2 per cent.

- In 2014, the poverty rate in rural areas for those living in households where the head had completed high school was 4.7 per cent; 5.7 per cent where the head had completed middle school; 10.7 per cent where the head had only completed primary school; and 14.5 per cent where the head was illiterate.

(NBS 2015)

Change over time:

Nonmonetary poverty: The OPHI Global MPI head count, based on deprivation according to a third or more of the weighted indicators, shows that 4.0 per cent of the population were in poor households in 2014 (estimate based on the China Family Panel Studies survey [CFPS] data). Split by rural and urban subpopulations, the rates were 6.7 and 1.9 per cent, respectively. Alkire and Shen (2017) provide alternative estimates and also review earlier literature for China.

Overall inequality: The Gini coefficient for household income per capita in 2010 was 38 per cent in rural China and 33.0 per cent in urban China (Li 2013, appendix table). (The same figures are shown in Li 2016, figures 1 [rural] and 2 [urban].) The effect of excluding migrant workers is shown by Li, Sato, and Sicular (2013, table 2.7) to raise the urban Gini coefficient in 2007 from 31.7 per cent to 34.0 per cent.

The People's Republic of China is an upper-middle-income country according to the World Bank classification, with GNI per capita in 2015 of $7,950 (Atlas method) and $14,160 (PPP) and a population in that year of 1,371.2 million people.

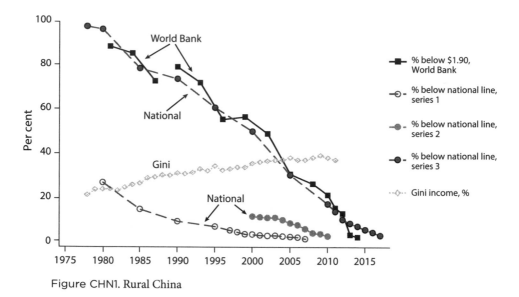

Figure CHN1. Rural China

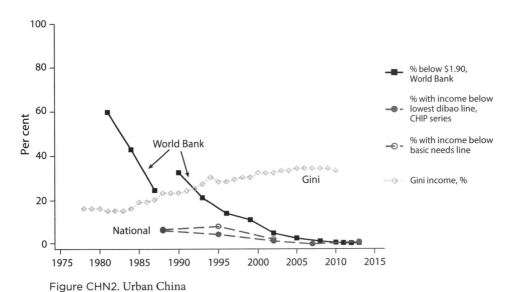

Figure CHN2. Urban China

FIJI

Poverty lines: The basic needs poverty line, which underlines the series 2 estimates of the poverty rate, has two components: a food poverty line (FPL) and a non-food poverty line (NFPL). "The FPL consists of [a] basket of foods, which for the 2002–03 analysis was derived from expenditure patterns of the middle quintile (20%) of the Rural and Urban groups of iTaukei and Indo-Fijians. The actual quantities of basic food items were according to food plans that the Fiji Food and Nutrition Centre estimated to give minimal levels of the energy and essential nutrients" (Narsey 2011, p. 84). More details are given by Narsey (2008), who also describes the NFPL. Poverty estimates are based on data from the Household Income and Expenditure Survey and are shown in the graph from 2002–2003; results from the survey of 1990–1991 are considered unreliable (Narsey 2006, p. 1).

Poverty today: The World Bank estimates show that in 2013–2014 the proportion of the population living in households with consumption per head below \$1.90 a day was 1.4 per cent and that the poverty gap was 0.2 per cent. The national estimate of the poverty rate (series 2) for the same year was 28.1 per cent. The figures for national series 1 are other estimates made by the World Bank taken from 2017 World Development Indicators for 2002 and 2013 and Narsey (2012, table B.4) for 2008; the series 2 figures are from Narsey (2011, table G.1) for 2002 and 2008 and Fiji Bureau of Statistics (2015, table 1) for 2013. Narsey (2012, appendix B) discusses the differences in methodology between his estimates (series 2), made on behalf of the Fiji Bureau of Statistics, and the World Bank's estimates (series 1). Narsey's series 2 estimates use equivalised household income as the measure of welfare, while the World Bank figures are based on equivalised consumption expenditure, excluding expenditure on durables and health. (In both cases the equivalence scale is 1.0 for a person aged fifteen and over and 0.5 for a person aged under fifteen.) In addition, the World Bank estimates are based on a somewhat different procedure for calculating the poverty line (while still maintaining the FPL and NFPL elements).

Who is poor?

- The incidence of rural poverty according to national estimates was 36.7 per cent in 2013–2014, down from 43 per cent in 2008–2009. The urban poverty rate in 2013–2014 was notably lower, 19.8 per cent, but was a little higher than in 2008–2009, when the figure was 18 per cent (Fiji Bureau of Statistics 2015, p. 1, series 2 definition of poverty). Narsey (2012, p. 106) notes that the incidence of rural poverty rose between 2002 and 2008 on the series 2 definition but was unchanged on the series 1 definition.

Change over time:

Nonmonetary poverty: Fiji is not included in the countries covered by OPHI.

Overall inequality: The Gini coefficient for household income per equivalent adult (equivalence scale as for national poverty rate series 1 and 2) is from Narsey, Raikoti, and Waqavonovono (2010, table 32).

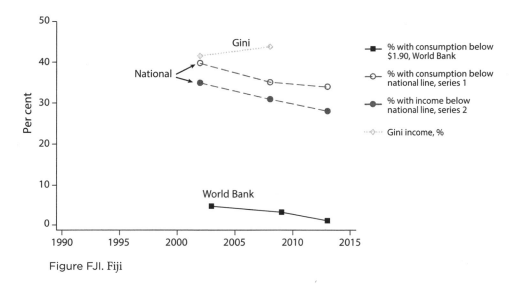

Figure FJI. Fiji

Fiji is an upper-middle-income country according to the World Bank classification, with GNI per capita in 2015 of $4,780 (Atlas method) and $8,700 (PPP) and a population in that year of 0.9 million people.

GEORGIA

Poverty lines: The National Statistical Office of Georgia (Geostat) publishes figures for both relative poverty and absolute poverty, both based on household consumption. The relative poverty lines used are 40 per cent and 60 per cent of median consumption expenditure. The methodology for the series for absolute poverty (series 2, downloaded 7 August 2017 from www.geostat.ge) is not fully transparent, but Geostat publishes on its website a description of the calculation of a subsistence minimum which appears to underlie this series. The guide notes that

> subsistence minimum is defined on the basis of a food basket. The minimum food basket represents a basket of defined quantities of food products and contains the amount of food that is physiologically required (proteins, fats and carbohydrates) for a working age male to lead a normal life and have the ability to work.... Monthly intermediate cost of the food basket is multiplied by the price bargaining coefficient, calculated on the basis of comparison of prices collected by the Price Statistics Division and obtained from the Integrated Household Surveys (IHSs). The coefficient currently stands at 0.865. After these adjustments, the final cost of the minimum food basket for a working age male is obtained in a given month. The cost of the minimum food basket is divided by 0.7 to calculate the subsistence minimum (the share of food products in the subsistence minimum cost equals 70%, thus, the cost of non-food products accounts for 30% of the subsistence minimum cost). (Geostat 2017)

Estimates of poverty are based on the Integrated Household Survey, which began in 1996 with financial and technical assistance from Statistics Canada and the World Bank. (Before the breakup of the Soviet Union, Georgia contributed to the Soviet Union's Family Budget Survey, providing 2,055 households to the survey in 1988; see Atkinson and Micklewright 1992, table S6). Earlier estimates of poverty include those in World Bank (1999, 2002, 2009). The 1999 report states: "An official poverty line, set by the Law on the minimum subsistence basket, exists in Georgia since April, 1997. It follows a normative approach and it is anchored to unrealistically high nutrition norms of the pre-independence period" (World Bank 1999, p. 2). The 2002 report (World Bank 2002, table 1) provides estimates of poverty based on this subsistence minimum for 1997–2000 (series 1, consumption per equivalent adult). The relationship between the two subsistence minima behind the two series of national poverty estimates is unclear.

Poverty today: The World Bank estimates show that in 2016 the proportion of the population living in households with consumption per head below $1.90 a day was 4.2 per cent and that the poverty gap was 1.0 per cent. The Geostat estimates (series 2) show 22.4 per cent of the population living in absolute poverty in 2014 and 20.8 per cent in 2015, when the World Bank figure was 4.0 per cent.

Who is poor?

- The absolute poverty rate (series 2) in 2015 for the population in urban areas was 16.7 per cent, and it was 24.7 per cent for the population in rural areas.

Change over time:

Nonmonetary poverty: The OPHI Global MPI head count, based on deprivation according to a third or more of the weighted indicators, shows that 0.8 per cent of the population were in poor households in 2014 (estimate based on Multiple Indicator Cluster Surveys [MICS] data) (OPHI Country Briefing, June 2016).

Overall inequality: Geostat reports a Gini coefficient for total cash incomes (defined as total cash inflows including cash incomes and transfers and other cash inflows) for 2015 of 47 per cent and for consumer expenditures (defined as cash consumption expenditures and noncash expenditures) of 40 per cent (downloaded October 2016; these are the series shown in the graph, but the Geostat website in August 2017 gave somewhat lower figures for 2015: 43 per cent and 38 per cent, respectively). It is unclear whether or not an equivalence scale has been used.

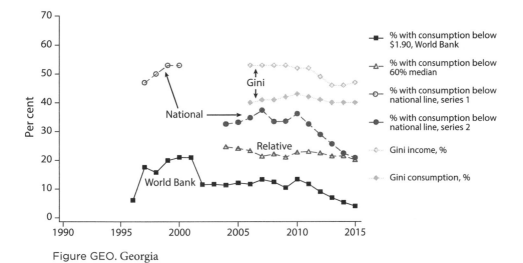

Figure GEO. Georgia

Georgia is an upper-middle-income country according to the World Bank classification, with GNI per capita in 2015 of $4,120 (Atlas method) and $9,410 (PPP) and a population in that year of 3.7 million people.

INDIA

Poverty lines: The national series are based on lines recommended by expert groups and established by the Planning Commission of the Government of India (now the National Institution for Transforming India): series 1 (Lakdawala), series 2 (Tendulkar), and series 3 (Rangarajan). (The data are from Rangarajan 2014: series 1 from table 2.1, series 2 from table 2.2, series 3 from tables 4.4 and 4.6.) All three use per capita consumption expenditure. Their origin lies with a calculation of the monthly expenditure (on food and other items) per capita recorded in 1973–1974 household survey data associated with an intake of 2,400 Cal per capita per day in rural areas and 2,100 Cal in urban areas, values taken as the rural and urban poverty lines and applied in series 1 after allowing for interstate differences in prices. The report of the third group, Rangarajan (2014), describes the evolution of the lines and implementation in the measurement of poverty using the National Sample Survey (NSS), including, for example, allowing for differences in state-level price changes and a change in recall period for expenditures in the NSS (see also More and Singh 2015). State-level lines for series 2 for 2011–2012 varied from Rs 695 per month per capita in rural areas and Rs 861 in urban areas (both in Odisha) to Rs 1,270 and Rs 1,302, respectively (both in Nagaland); all-India figures were Rs 816 in rural areas and Rs 1,000 in urban areas (Planning Commission 2014, p. 100).

The series 3 line (Rangarajan) is a significant departure but is still based on estimates of food expenditure to meet nutritional requirements (newly set as 2,155 Cal, 48 gms of protein, and 28 gms of fat per capita per day in rural areas and 2,090 Cal, 50 gms, and 26 gms, respectively, in urban areas) and allowance for other items, with separate calculations for rural and urban areas and state-level variation for differences in prices. The net effect of the Rangarajan group's changes was a 19 per cent increase in the rural line and a 41 per cent increase in the urban line, reflected in notably higher poverty rates (compare series 3 with series 2), although about two-thirds (rural) and one-quarter (urban) of the increases were due to a switch in recall period used in the NSS. (For criticism of the Rangarajan line, see Deaton and Drèze 2014; for discussion of the sensitivity of poverty estimates to the choice of recall period and discussion of inconsistencies in the series over time, see Deaton and Kozel 2005.)

Poverty today: The World Bank estimates that in 2011–2012 the proportion of the population living in households with consumption per head below $1.90 a day was 21.2 per cent and that the poverty gap was 4.3 per cent. National estimates show rates for the same year of 21.9 per cent (series 2) and 29.5 per cent (series 3).

Who is poor?

• The World Bank estimates for 2011–2012 show that the poverty rate, based on the $1.90 line, in urban and rural India was 13.4 per cent and 24.8 per cent, respectively. National estimates for series 2 for the same year show rates of 13.7 per cent in urban areas and 25.7 per cent in rural areas, a similar difference to that in the World Bank figures. But series 3 figures show a much smaller difference between urban and rural areas, with rates of 26.4 per cent and 30.9 per cent, respectively (sources as above), reflecting the larger rise in the urban line (see above). In 2004–2005, both series 1 and 2 give an estimate for the urban rate of 25.7 per cent, while the figure for rural poverty is 28.3 per cent in series 1 and 41.8 per cent in series 2 (Rangarajan 2014, tables 2.1 and 4.4; Planning Commission 2014, p. 99).

- National estimates (series 2) at the state level range for 2011–2012 from under 9 per cent in Goa, Kerala, Himachal Pradesh, Punjab, and Sikkim to between 35 and 40 per cent in Arunchal Pradesh, Manipur, Jharkhand, and Chattisgarh. (This does not include the seven "union territories," several of which have small populations.) The rate in Delhi (a union territory with some 17 million people) was 9.9 per cent (Planning Commission 2014, p. 101). Deaton and Drèze (2014) note that "for half of India's major States, urban poverty is higher than rural poverty" in the series 3 estimates and argue that this is counterintuitive.

- National estimates (series 1) for 2004–2005 show poverty rates of 37.1 per cent for "scheduled castes," 44.7 per cent for "scheduled tribes," 28.0 per cent for "all Hindus," 33.0 per cent for "Muslims," and 17.9 per cent for "other minorities" (Planning Commission 2014, p. 103).

Change over time:

Nonmonetary poverty: The OPHI Global MPI head count, based on deprivation according to a third or more of the weighted indicators, shows that 41.3 per cent of the population were in poor households in 2011–2012 (estimate based on the India Human Development Survey [IHDS] data). Split by rural and urban subpopulations, the rates were 53.5 and 14.8 per cent, respectively. The harmonised time series of the head count (see editors' note) shows a decline in the national rate, from 57.3 per cent in 1998–1999 to 49 per cent in 2005–2006 (see also Alkire and Seth 2015 and Alkire, Oldiges, and Kanagaratnam 2018).

Overall inequality: Series 1: The Gini coefficient for per capita expenditure is from the World Bank Database from World Income Inequality Database, version 3, September 2015, downloaded June 2016. Series 2: The Gini coefficient for equivalent disposable income is from LIS Key Figures (downloaded 12 June 2016; see Vanneman and Dubey 2013).

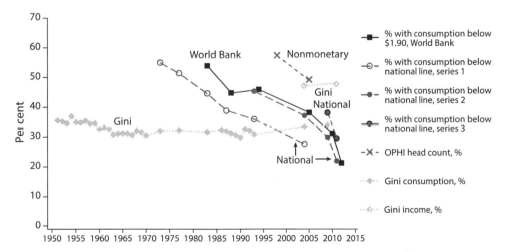

Figure IND. India

India is a lower-middle-income country according to the World Bank classification, with GNI per capita in 2015 of $1,600 (Atlas method) and $6,020 (PPP) and a population in that year of 1,311.1 million people.

INDONESIA

Poverty lines: Badan Pusat Statistik (Statistics Indonesia) provides national estimates of absolute poverty rates on its website that go back to 1970; there is a break in the data in 1996, with two figures provided for that year. These data are shown in the graph as series 1 up to 1996 and series 2 from 1996 onwards (downloaded October 2016). Priebe (2014) describes the evolution of Statistics Indonesia's measurement of poverty and concludes that neither of the two series is consistent over time due to adjustments to the method of calculating the poverty line and to changes in the household survey (Susenas) used to estimate the number of people in households that are poor. He argues that "only the time series since 2007 can be safely assumed to be comparable" (Priebe 2014, p. 202). However, Priebe also notes continuity in the basic method: the poverty lines have always comprised food and nonfood components, with the former reflecting an intake of 2,100 Cal per person per day; the same household survey has been used throughout the period; and consumption expenditure per capita has always been taken as the welfare measure. See also the discussion by Booth (2016), who describes the break in the data in 1996 as stemming from an upwards revision in both the food and nonfood components of the poverty line and thus reflecting a more generous view of "basic needs" (Booth 2016, p. 178). The calculation of a poverty estimate for 1970 is not mentioned by Priebe (2014), who describes estimates by Statistics Indonesia first being made for 1976; the same is true of the account in Booth (1993).

Poverty today: The World Bank estimates show that in 2016 the proportion of the population living in households with consumption per head below $1.90 a day was 6.5 per cent and that the poverty gap was 1.2 per cent. National estimates (series 2) for 2014 show a poverty rate of 11.1 per cent, when the World Bank figure was 7.9 per cent.

Who is poor?

• The World Bank estimates for 2014 show that 7.5 per cent of the urban population was poor measured by the $1.90 line and 8.4 per cent of the rural population. National estimates (series 2 poverty line) for the same year show poverty rates of 8.3 per cent in urban areas and 14.0 per cent in rural areas, a notably larger difference.

Change over time:

Nonmonetary poverty: The OPHI Global MPI head count, based on deprivation according to a third or more of the weighted indicators, shows that 15.5 per cent of the population were in poor households in 2012 (estimate based on DHS data). Split by rural and urban subpopulations, the rates were 20.7 and 10.2 per cent, respectively. The harmonised time series of the head count (see editors' note) shows a decline in the national rate, from 20.8 per cent in 2007 to 15.5 per cent in 2012. (In this case the harmonised rate in 2012 gives the same level of poverty as the rate used in the Global MPI.)

Overall inequality: The series for the Gini coefficient for household per capita expenditure since 2002 is from the website of Statistics Indonesia, "Consumption and Expenditure/Selected Consumption Indicators" (downloaded October 2016); earlier observations are from Booth (2000, table 1); and Krongkaew and Ragayah (2006, table 2).

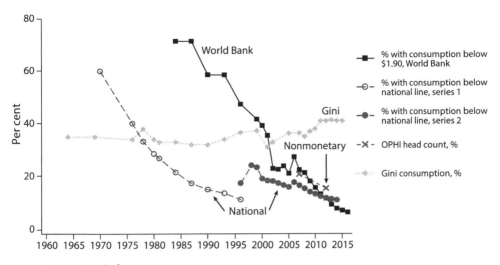

Figure IDN. Indonesia

Indonesia is a lower-middle-income country according to the World Bank classification, with GNI per capita in 2015 of $3,440 (Atlas method) and $10,680 (PPP) and a population in that year of 275.6 million people.

MALAYSIA

Poverty lines: The official poverty line income (PLI) was first formulated in 1977 and was used until 2005, updated annually by the CPI, to monitor the country's progress in eradicating poverty. As the name suggests, the poverty line is applied to income, not expenditure. The food element was based on the dietary needs of a five-person household consisting of one adult male aged twenty to thirty-nine, one female adult aged twenty to thirty-nine, and three children of either sex aged one to three years, four to six years, and seven to nine years, aimed at delivering 9,910 Cal (with an additional 10 per cent added to the estimated cost). Estimates for clothing and footwear costs for the family of five were obtained from the Ministry of Welfare Services, and an allowance for other nonfood expenditures was based on the actual expenditures of households with low monthly incomes. Households with incomes below the PLI were considered to be poor irrespective of their size or composition. "For example, a one-person household was classified as 'poor' if its income was insufficient to meet the food and nonfood needs of the reference five-member household" (UNDP 2007, p. 22), whereas very large households could be misclassified as nonpoor. The only spatial price variation in the 1977 PLI was to use different lines for Sabah and Sarawak; no distinction was made between rural and urban areas.

In 2005 the PLI was substantially revised to make it more comprehensive and more generous than its 1977 predecessor. The PLI now varies with the size, composition, and location of the household. The food component is calculated from dietary requirements, and the nonfood PLI component is based on the expenditures of those households in the Household Expenditure Survey (HES) whose total expenditure was roughly 20 per cent higher than the food PLI. The poverty estimates, however, are based on the Household Income Survey (HIS), which is larger than the HES. The income measure taken is gross income, not net income (UNDP 2007, p. 70). In addition, a lower poverty line is used "to capture 'hard-core' or extreme poverty. Formerly, a household was considered to be in extreme poverty if its income fell below half the standard PLI. In the revised 2005 methodology, a household is considered extremely poor if its income is less than the food component of the PLI" (UNDP 2007, p. 73).

Poverty today: The World Bank estimates show that in 2009, 0.3 per cent of the population were living in households with incomes per head below $1.90 a day and that the poverty gap was less than 0.1 per cent. This rate had been below 1 per cent since 1997. The estimates based on the national poverty line (series 2) show that 3.8 per cent of households had incomes below the PLI level in 2009. The estimates refer to poor households and not to the number of individuals living in poor households (see UNDP 2007, p. 18; the same source [p. 68] also gives estimates on the latter basis which are a few percentage points higher). The percentage of households below the official absolute poverty line is from Department of Statistics Malaysia 2014, table 7 (downloaded from the department's website, November 2016); see also Snodgrass (2002, table 2-1). The estimates are shown in two series because the poverty line was revised upwards when the 2004 methodology was introduced in place of the earlier 1977 methodology, with estimates on the new basis made back to 1999 (see UNDP 2007). The series for relative poverty (percentage below 50 per cent of median equivalised household income) are taken from UNDP (2007, table 4.8).

Who is poor?

- The national estimate of the poverty rate is higher among larger households, so that the poverty rate for individuals exceeds that for households: in 2004, the household poverty rate was 6.0 per cent, but that for individuals was 8.7 per cent.

- The poverty rate among children was higher, at 12.6 per cent in 2004.

- The poverty rate among rural households in 2004 was 12.3 per cent, and it was 2.7 per cent among urban households.

- The household poverty rate in 2004 varied substantially across regions, from 1.6 per cent in Kuala Lumpur to 25.5 per cent in Sabah (one of the two regions of East Malaysia or Malaysian Borneo).

(UNDP 2007, tables 4.7 and 4.4)

Change over time:

Nonmonetary poverty: Malaysia is not included in the countries covered by OPHI.
Overall inequality: Income inequality as measured by the Gini coefficient has fallen by some ten percentage points over the past thirty years (Department of Statistics Malaysia (2009, 2012; 2014, table 6); Ragayah (2008, table 1); the 1967 observation from Krongkaew and Ragayah (2006, table 2).

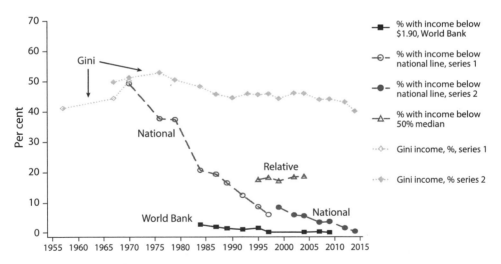

Figure MYS. Malaysia

Malaysia encompasses Peninsular Malaya and the states of Sabah and Sarawak on the island of Borneo. It is an upper-middle-income country according to the World Bank classification, with GNI per capita in 2015 of $10,450 (Atlas) and $26,140 (PPP) and a population in that year of 30.3 million people.

NEPAL

Poverty lines: The threshold is defined as the cost of satisfying minimum caloric requirements (set at 2,220 Cal) and basic needs for nonfood goods and services, where the latter is based on the share of nonfood spending by households whose food spending is around that required for the minimum food basket. In 2010, the poverty line (introduced in 1995–1996) was replaced by one that was 35 per cent higher in real terms to reflect rises in general living standards. The new line was Rs 19,262 per person per year, which corresponded to PPP$2.33 per person per day. Poverty is measured using households' consumption expenditure per capita.

Poverty today: According to the World Bank estimates, in 2010–2011, 15.0 per cent of the population were living in households with consumption per head below $1.90 a day and the poverty gap was 3.1 per cent. Using the 2010–2011 Nepal Living Standards Survey (NLSS) and the new 2010 poverty line, the official estimate of the Central Bureau of Statistics (CBS) is that 25.2 per cent of the population were poor ("CBS View on Poverty in Nepal," table 3, downloaded October 2017). This estimate (series 3) is not comparable with those for earlier years on account of both the change in the poverty line and a switch to measuring food consumption with a seven-day recall period rather than the thirty-day period used for the previous estimates (Uematsu, Shidiq, and Tiwari 2016, annex I). Series 1 is based on the pre-2010 poverty line and series 2 on the line adopted in 2010, with both series based on food consumption measured with a thirty-day recall period (Uematsu, Shidiq, and Tiwari 2016, table 2, based on the NLSS conducted in 1995–1996, 2003–2004, and 2010–2011). Applying the national 2010 poverty line, series 2 shows 30.8 per cent of the population living in households in poverty in 2010–2011.

Who is poor?

- In 2003, applying the 1995 threshold, the poverty rate in rural areas was some three times that of urban areas (World Bank 2006, table 1.3). In 2010–2011, the CBS estimates based on the new poverty line and the seven-day recall period for food (series 3) show the poverty rate to be 27.4 per cent in rural areas and 15.5 per cent in urban areas ("CBS View on Poverty in Nepal," table 3).

- In 2003–2004, poverty rates (series 1 poverty line) were highest among Hill-Terai Dalits (46 per cent) and the Hill Janjatis (44 per cent). Both groups experienced falls in poverty (by a fifth and a tenth, respectively) between 1995–1996 and 2003–2004, but these decreases were more modest than those among the Upper Castes and the Newars (which fell by a half and a quarter, respectively) (World Bank 2006, p. iv).

- In 2003–2004, 30 per cent of households reported that their food expenditure was "less than adequate for their family's needs" (World Bank 2006, table 1.7).

- In 2010–2011, the CBS estimates (series 3) show the poverty rate to have been under 10 per cent where there were three or fewer persons in the household, but as high as 37.6 per cent where there were seven or more persons. People in poor households of this latter size made up 49 per cent of the poor. The poverty rate was 12.3 per cent where no child aged under six was present in the household and 46.5 per cent with three or more children of this age present ("CBS View on Poverty in Nepal," table 5).

Change over time: Applying the 2010 poverty line to all years shows that the poverty rate was halved between 1995 (63.8 per cent) and 2010 (30.8 per cent) (Uematsu, Shidiq, and Tiwari 2016, table 2). On comparability over time, see Prennushi (1999), drawn on in the discussion in chapter 4.

Nonmonetary poverty: The OPHI Global MPI head count, based on deprivation according to a third or more of the weighted indicators, shows that 38.8 per cent of the population were in poor households in 2016 (estimate based on DHS data). Split by rural and urban subpopulations, the rates were 52.0 and 30.6 per cent, respectively. The harmonised time series of the head count (see editors' note) shows a decline in the national rate, from 64.7 per cent in 2006 to 44.2 per cent in 2011. Different figures for 2006–2014, also produced on a harmonised basis, are given in National Planning Commission and OPHI (2018, table 4-1).

Overall inequality: The Gini coefficient for household per capita expenditure showed a marked increase from 1984 to 2003, but from 2003 to 2010 much of this increase was reversed (although, it should be noted, changes were made in the 2010 NLSS in the reporting of food consumption, which may have affected the comparability with the earlier surveys) (World Development Indicators).

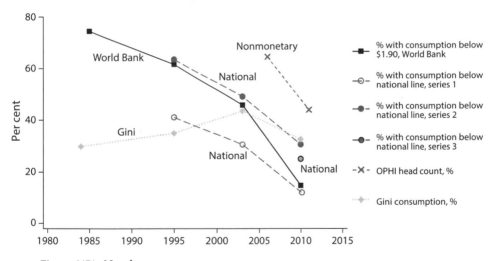

Figure NPL. Nepal

Nepal has been a republic since 2008, when the previous monarchy was replaced. (Following a period when the monarch ruled without parliament, a multi-party democracy was established in 1991. In 1996 there began a long insurgency and civil war. There were serious earthquakes in 2015.) It is a low-income country according to the World Bank classification, with GNI per capita in 2015 of $740 (Atlas method) and $2,500 (PPP) and a population in that year of 28.5 million people.

PHILIPPINES

Poverty lines:

Poverty today: The World Bank estimates show that in 2015 the proportion of the population living in households with consumption per head below $1.90 a day was 8.3 per cent and that the poverty gap was 1.6 per cent.

Who is poor?

Change over time:

Nonmonetary poverty: The OPHI Global MPI head count, based on deprivation according to a third or more of the weighted indicators, shows that 11.0 per cent of the population were in poor households in 2013 (estimate based on DHS data). Split by rural and urban subpopulations, the rates were 13.7 and 8.1 per cent, respectively.

Overall inequality:

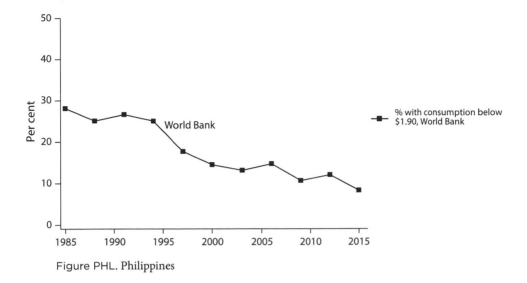

Figure PHL. Philippines

The Republic of the Philippines is a lower-middle-income country according to the World Bank classification, with GNI per capita in 2015 of $3,520 (Atlas method) and $8,900 (PPP) and a population in that year of 100.7 million people.

SOLOMON ISLANDS

Poverty lines: "A Solomon Island–specific 'poverty line' is specified as the minimum expenditures needed to obtain basic food and non-food goods taking into account prevailing consumption patterns in the country" (Solomon Islands National Statistical Office [SINSO] 2015, p. vi). Food needs are calculated on the basis of a daily intake of 2,200 Cal, and the food poverty line varies by location according to food prices. In the headline poverty indicator, nonfood basic needs are based on the food budget share of those households whose spending on food is equal to the food poverty line, and again this varies by location. The poverty line is expressed per adult equivalent (children aged zero to six count as 0.5 and people of all other ages count as 1.0). In 2012–2013, the poverty lines for temporal comparisons (excluding imputed rent) ranged from SBD$3,162 to SBD$8,784 per year. The former figure corresponded to PPP$1.33 per adult per day and the latter to PPP$3.69.

Poverty today: The World Bank estimates show that in 2012–2013 the proportion of the population living in households with consumption per head below $1.90 a day was 25.1 per cent and that the poverty gap was 6.8 per cent. The proportion of the population with consumption per equivalent adult below the national poverty line in 2012–2013 was substantially lower at 12.7 per cent and the poverty gap was 3.2 per cent (SINSO 2015, p. 12). A calculation for 2012–2013 employing a temporally consistent poverty line (excluding in this case imputed rent) gave a figure of 14 per cent, and the figure on the same basis for 2005–2006 was 22.4 per cent; these are the two data points shown in the graph as series 2 and series 1, respectively (SINSO 2015, p. 23 and appendix III). Poverty is assessed with the Household Income and Expenditure Survey (HIES). The report on the 2012–2013 survey notes that "the 2012/13 HIES is fundamentally different in design and implementation from the previous HIES 2005/6, and thus caution must be taken in any direct comparison of results" (SINSO 2015a, p. x). Thus, the report on poverty warns that "there are important variations in procedures between the two surveys that cannot be adjusted for, unlike the variations in consumption aggregates. These variations reduce the weight that can be placed on the inference of a fall in poverty" (SINSO 2015, p. 43). This is why the national estimates for 2005–2006 and 2012–2013 are shown as separate series in the graph. (There was an earlier nationwide survey in 1992, but it is described as "limited in scope" [SINSO 2015a, p. iii].)

Who is poor?

- Poverty in the Solomon Islands is largely a rural phenomenon; the population is heavily rural, and the poverty rate is higher in rural areas (13.6 per cent) than in urban areas (9.1 per cent).

- There is considerable variation in the poverty rate by province, from 5.6 per cent in the Central Province to 22.2 per cent in Guadalcanal and 31.5 per cent in Makira; both of the latter provinces were significantly affected by cyclone and storm damage just before and during the survey period.

- The poverty rate for persons in households headed by a woman was 12.0 per cent, slightly lower than that for persons in households headed by men (12.8 per cent).

- The poverty rate for persons in households where the head did not complete primary education was 15.8 per cent, compared with 6.5 per cent where the head had tertiary education.

- The majority of the population are Melanesian; the poverty rate was lower for those in households whose head was non-Melanesian (5.7 per cent).

- The poverty rate was higher (15.1 per cent) for persons in households where the head was working on his or her own account rather than for another party compensating the head with wage income (10.4 per cent for those working in the private sector and 4.0 per cent for those in the public sector).

(SINSO 2015; rates for 2012–2013 estimated on a basis consistent with the national figure of 12.7 per cent)

Change over time:

Nonmonetary poverty: The Solomon Islands are not included in the countries covered by OPHI.

Overall inequality: The 2012–2013 report contained estimates of the Gini coefficients for both expenditure (excluding imputed rent) and total income of 40.8 per cent and 53.9 per cent, respectively. These indicate "a high degree of inequality" (SINSO 2015a, p. 67). The earlier study for 2005–2006 found that the Gini coefficient for per capita equivalised expenditure was 39.0 per cent, but this is not comparable.

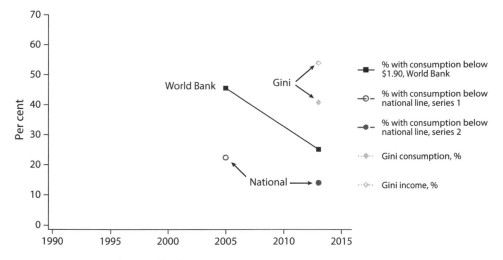

Figure SLB. Solomon Islands

The Solomon Islands consist of six major islands and over 900 smaller islands in an archipelago to the east of Papua New Guinea. The capital, Honiara, is on the island of Guadalcanal. The Solomon Islands are a lower-middle-income country according to the World Bank classification, with GNI per capita in 2015 of $1,910 (Atlas method) and $2,180 (PPP) and a population in that year of 0.6 million people.

SRI LANKA

Poverty lines: Sri Lanka used a variety of poverty lines prior to the establishment in 2004 of the official poverty line (OPL) (Sri Lanka Department of Census and Statistics 2004). The base year for the OPL is 2002, and the line is defined as the level of per capita expenditure for a person to be able to reach a nutritional level of 2,030 Cal in 2002. For other years, back to 1990–1991 and from 2002 onwards, the poverty line is updated by the Colombo consumer price index (CCPI). The OPL for 2002 is Rs 1,432. Updating using the CCPI to 2005 and applying the 2005 PPP figure of 40.04 yields a figure of PPP$1.49 a day, so that the OPL at that time was some 20 per cent above the then World Bank poverty line (PPP$1.25). It has remained close to that level. At the same time, the OPL fell as a proportion of mean per capita expenditure and was below 30 per cent in 2012–2013. The poverty line does not vary geographically. However, household per capita expenditure (the welfare indicator compared with the poverty line) is adjusted for differences in prices between districts (subdivisions of provinces).

Poverty today: The World Bank estimates show that in 2016 the proportion of the population living in households with consumption per head below $1.90 a day was 0.7 per cent and that the poverty gap was 0.1 per cent. The national poverty figures are based on the Household Income and Expenditure Survey (HIES). The HIES began as the Labour Force and Socio-Economic Survey in 1980–1981, which was carried out for a second time in 1985–1986. The HIES was first conducted as a separate survey in 1990–1991 and repeated in 1995–1996, 2002, 2006–2007, 2009–2010, 2012–2013, and 2016. The coverage of northern and eastern parts of the country was affected by the civil war that ended in 2009. For example, the 2006–2007 survey excluded all of Northern province and the Trincomalee district of Eastern province, and all of Northern and Eastern provinces were excluded from the 1990–1991 and 1995–1996 surveys; these two provinces were first fully included in the HIES only in the 2012–2013 survey. National poverty figures are published covering the period from 1990–1991 (Sri Lanka Department of Census and Statistics 2017, figure 2). The proportion of the population estimated to be poor in 2016 was 4.1 per cent.

Who is poor?

- The poverty rate in 2016 measured according to the official poverty line ranged from 1.7 per cent in Western province to 7.3 per cent in Eastern province and 7.7 per cent in Northern province. Northern and Eastern provinces, excluded wholly or partly from the HIES before 2012–2013, made up 23.9 per cent of the poor (and 21.1 per cent in 2012–2013).

(Sri Lanka Department of Census and Statistics 2017, table 1)

Change over time:

Nonmonetary poverty: Sri Lanka is not included in the countries covered by OPHI. (Some nonmonetary aspects are integrated with measurement of monetary poverty in Weerahewa and Wickramasinghe 2005.)

Overall inequality: The Gini coefficient for household income and household expenditure (not per capita) is from HIES 2012–2013 final report, table HI, and HIES 2016 final report, table 5.

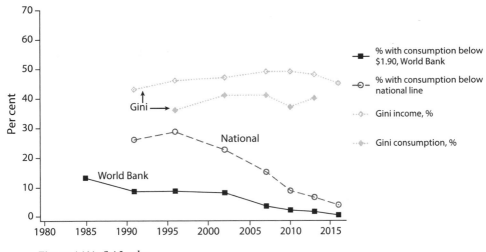

Figure LKA. Sri Lanka

Sri Lanka is a lower-middle-income country according to the World Bank classification, with GNI per capita in 2015 of $3,800 (Atlas method) and $11,480 (PPP) and a population in that year of 21.0 million people.

THAILAND

Poverty lines:

Poverty today: The World Bank estimates show that in 2013 the proportion of the population living in households with consumption per head below $1.90 a day was less than 0.1 per cent and that the poverty gap was 0.0 per cent (to one decimal place).

Who is poor?

Change over time:

Nonmonetary poverty: The OPHI Global MPI head count, based on deprivation according to a third or more of the weighted indicators, shows that 0.9 per cent of the population were in poor households in 2012 (estimate based on MICS data). Split by rural and urban subpopulations, the rates were 1.1 and 0.6 per cent, respectively.

Overall inequality:

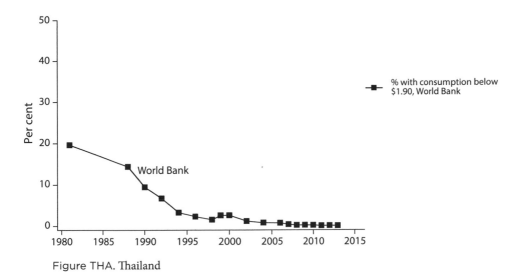

Figure THA. Thailand

Thailand is an upper-middle-income country according to the World Bank classification, with GNI per capita in 2015 of $5,690 (Atlas method) and $15,210 (PPP) and a population in that year of 68.0 million people.

VIETNAM

Poverty lines:

Poverty today: The World Bank estimates show that in 2014 the proportion of the population living in households with consumption per head below $1.90 a day was 2.6 per cent and that the poverty gap was 0.5 per cent.

Who is poor?

Change over time:

Nonmonetary poverty: The OPHI Global MPI head count, based on deprivation according to a third or more of the weighted indicators, shows that 7.1 per cent of the population were in poor households in 2013–2014 (estimate based on MICS data). Split by rural and urban subpopulations, the rates were 8.8 and 3.6 per cent, respectively (see also Baulch and Masset 2003; Tran, Alkire, and Klasen 2015).

Overall inequality: The Gini coefficients for per capita consumption and income are from Benjamin, Brandt, and McCaig (2016, table 1).

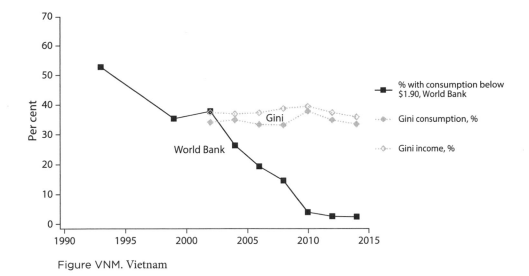

Figure VNM. Vietnam

Vietnam is a lower-middle-income country according to the World Bank classification, with GNI per capita in 2015 of $1,950 (Atlas method) and $5,690 (PPP) and a population in that year of 91.7 million people.

National poverty reports for chapter 7

BOTSWANA

Poverty lines:

Poverty today: The World Bank estimates show that in 2009 the proportion of the population living in households with consumption per head below $1.90 a day was 18.2 per cent and that the poverty gap was 5.8 per cent.

Who is poor?

Change over time:

Nonmonetary poverty: Botswana is not included in the countries covered by OPHI.

Overall inequality:

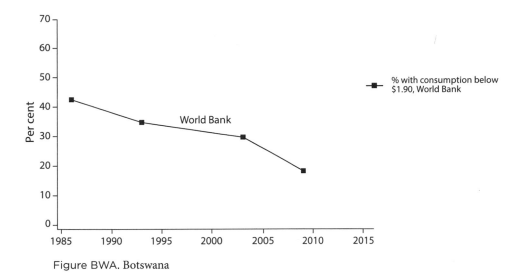

Figure BWA. Botswana

Botswana is an upper-middle-income country according to the World Bank clas-sification, with GNI per capita in 2015 of $6,680 (Atlas method) and $15,600 (PPP) and a population in that year of 2.3 million people.

CÔTE D'IVOIRE

Poverty lines: The national poverty line in 2015 was 269,075 Francs CFA per person per year, or 737 Francs CFA per day, the latter corresponding to PPP$3.11. In 2008 the corresponding figure was PPP$3.05. The poverty line varies by administrative district, reflecting differences in purchasing power, with the economic capital of Abidjan, Côte d'Ivoire's largest city, as the reference point; the lowest figure in 2015 was 85.7 per cent of the Abidjan figure in urban areas of the Montagnes district and 73.9 per cent in rural areas of the same district. Historically, the poverty line is a relative one, taken as the bottom decile of consumer expenditure per capita recorded in the EPAM survey (see below) of 1985 (75,000 Francs CFA per capita per year at that time), adjusted in subsequent years for changes in prices. An "extreme" poverty line is taken as the bottom decile in each survey year, providing, by definition, an extreme poverty rate of 10 per cent (Institut National de la Statistique 2015, p. 27).

Poverty today: The World Bank estimates show that in 2015 the proportion of the population living in households with consumption per head below $1.90 a day was 28.2 per cent and that the poverty gap was 9.1 per cent. In terms of the national poverty line, the proportion of the population with consumption expenditure below the line in the same year was substantially higher, at 46.3 per cent. The source of data used in the estimates is the Enquête sur le Niveau de Vie des Ménages (ENV), earlier the Enquête Permanente Auprès Ménages (EPAM), providing information for 1985, 1993, 1995, 1998, 2002, 2008, and 2015. The national series shown in the graph is taken from Institut National de la Statistique (2015, figure 3.1). Dabalen and Paul (2013) question the extent of the rise in poverty shown in this series given changes to the methodology of the ENV and EPAM; see also the appendix of Cogneau, Houngbedji, and Mesplé-Somps (2014).

Who is poor?

- In 2015, according to the national poverty line, rural areas (49.9 per cent of the total population) had a poverty rate of 56.8 per cent, compared with 35.9 per cent in urban areas. Across administrative regions, the rate in 2015 varied between 22.7 per cent in the city of Abidjan to 71.7 per cent in Kabadougou in the northwest of the country.

- The poverty rate in 2015 was similar whether the head of the household was male (46.4 per cent) or female (45.9 per cent).

- The poverty rate in 2015 varied with the labour market status of the household head: 22.1 per cent in public-sector employment, 32.5 per cent in private employment, 36.5 per cent when self-employed, 50.0 per cent when unemployed, and 59.5 per cent when employed in agriculture.

- The literacy rate for those (aged over fifteen) below the national poverty line in 2015 was 33.3 per cent, compared with 52.3 per cent for those above the poverty line.

(Institut National de la Statistique 2015)

Change over time:

Nonmonetary poverty: The OPHI Global MPI head count, based on deprivation according to a third or more of the weighted indicators, shows that 58.8 per cent of the population were in poor households in 2011–2012 (estimate based on DHS data). Split by rural and urban subpopulations, the rates were 78.0 and 35.0 per cent, respectively. The harmonised time series of the head count (see editors' note) shows a decline in the national rate, from 61.5 per cent in 2005 to 55.2 per cent in 2011–2012.

Overall inequality: In 2015, the Gini coefficient for consumption expenditure per capita was 40.2 per cent, reflecting a decline from 50.0 per cent in 2002 (Institut National de la Statistique 2015, p. 11).

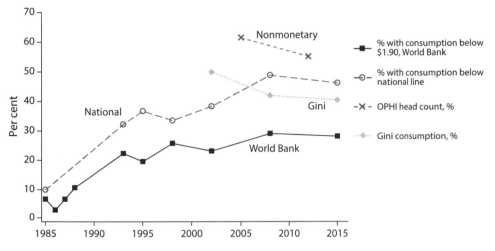

Figure CIV. Côte d'Ivoire

Côte d'Ivoire is a West African country. A military coup in 1999 was followed by a civil war that led in turn to a division of the country. The presidential election in 2010 that followed a peace agreement led to further fighting and the involvement of UN peacekeepers. The Côte d'Ivoire is a lower-middle-income country according to the World Bank classification, with GNI per capita in 2015 of $1,490 (Atlas method) and $3,240 (PPP) and a population in that year of 22.7 million people.

EGYPT

Poverty lines:

Poverty today: The World Bank estimates show that in 2015 the proportion of the population living in households with consumption per head below $1.90 a day was 1.4 per cent and that the poverty gap was 0.2 per cent.

Who is poor?

Change over time:

Nonmonetary poverty: The OPHI Global MPI head count, based on deprivation according to a third or more of the weighted indicators, shows that 3.6 per cent of the population were in poor households in 2014 (estimate based on DHS data). Split by rural and urban subpopulations, the rates were 4.4 and 2.1 per cent, respectively. The harmonised time series of the head count (see editors' note) shows a decline in the national rate, from 8.2 per cent in 2005 to 6.0 per cent in 2008.

Overall inequality:

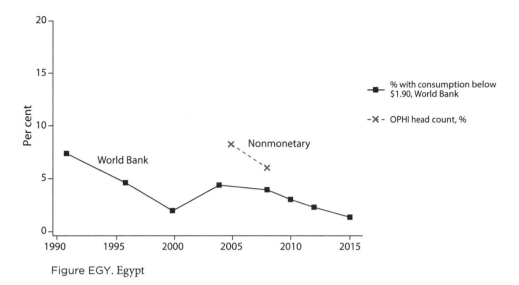

Figure EGY. Egypt

The Arab Republic of Egypt is a lower-middle-income country according to the World Bank classification, with GNI per capita in 2015 of $3,310 (Atlas method) and $10,690 (PPP) and a population in that year of 91.5 million people.

ETHIOPIA

Poverty lines:

Poverty today: World Bank estimates for 2015–2016 show that 26.7 per cent were living in households with consumption per head below $1.90 a day and that the poverty gap was 7.7 per cent.

Who is poor?

Change over time:

Nonmonetary poverty: The OPHI Global MPI head count, based on deprivation according to a third or more of the weighted indicators, shows that 83.1 per cent of the population were in poor households in 2016 (estimate based on DHS data). Split by rural and urban subpopulations, the rates were 92.4 and 31.9 per cent, respectively. The harmonised time series of the head count (see editors' note) shows a decline in the national rate, from 93.6 per cent in 2000 to 85.2 per cent in 2011.

Overall inequality:

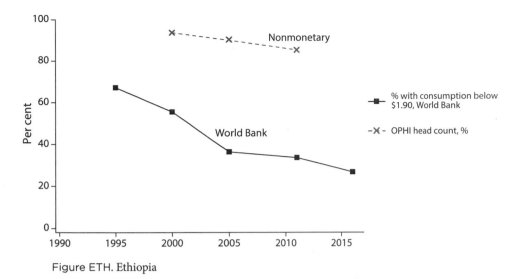

Figure ETH. Ethiopia

Ethiopia is a low-income country according to the World Bank classification, with GNI per capita in 2015 of $600 (Atlas method) and $1,620 (PPP) and a population in that year of 99.4 million people.

GHANA

Poverty lines: National estimates are based on lines initially selected as ratios of mean consumption expenditure per capita in 1988: an upper line of two-thirds and a lower line of one-half. They were later replaced by nutrition-based lines (2,900 Cal per equivalent adult), with an allowance for nonfood needs. In 1998–1999 the new lower line was 700,000 cedis per adult per year and the upper line was 900,000 cedis—50 per cent and 64 per cent, respectively, of the mean consumption level. In 2005–2006, on uprating by the 1999 to 2006 change in the CPI, the upper line was 3,708,900 cedis per adult equivalent per year. Applying the 2005 PPP conversion rate (4,475.82) yields a figure of PPP$2.27 a day, so that the line in 2005 was 82 per cent above the World Bank poverty line at that time (PPP$1.25). In 2012–2013 the upper line was 1,314 cedis per equivalent adult per year. (The currency was rebased in 2007 with 10,000 old units equal to 1 new unit.) Deflating this figure by the CPI reported by Ghana Statistical Service (GSS), and applying the 2005 PPP figure of 0.454, yields a figure of PPP$3.175 a day, which is approximately two and a half times higher than the World Bank line. In addition to this "upper poverty line," there is an "extreme poverty line," based only on nutritional needs, set at 792.05 cedis in 2013–2014. This extreme line was some 60 per cent of the upper line, and hence close to the World Bank line of $1.90. The two lines were revised in 2012–2013 to take account of changing consumption patterns, resulting in the estimates based on the upper line shown in the graph, series 2 for 1992–2006 (from GSS 2007, tables 2 and A1.5) and series 3 for 2006–2013 (from GSS 2014, tables 3.1 and 3.2), but the discontinuity is not large. Series 1 is based on the original upper line introduced in 1988 (from Coulombe and McKay 1995, table 2). The equivalence scale is complex, with assumed needs differing between men, women, children of different ages, and the elderly (GSS 2014, table A8.2).

Poverty today: The World Bank estimates that 12.1 per cent of the population in 2012–2013 were living in households with consumption per head below $1.90 a day and that the poverty gap was 3.5 per cent. In the same year, the poverty rate using the upper line was 24.2 per cent (series 3), and the rate with the extreme line was 8.4 per cent.

Who is poor?

- The rural poverty rate was 37.9 per cent and the urban rate was 10.6 per cent.

- The rate ranged from 3.5 per cent in the capital, Accra, to 9.9 per cent in urban coastal localities, to 26.4 per cent in urban Savannah, to 30.3 per cent in rural coastal localities and 55.0 per cent in rural Savannah.

- The rate for households with a female head at 19.1 per cent was lower than for households with a male head (25.9 per cent).

- The rate for households where the head was a public employee was 7.1 per cent, for private employees 10.8 per cent, for the unemployed 28.1 per cent, and for the self-employed in agriculture 39.2 per cent.

- The rate for households where the head had secondary education was 8.0 per cent, where the head had a middle school leaving certificate 16.2 per cent, and where the head had no qualifications 37.6 per cent.

(GSS 2014, table 3.1, figures 4.1–4.3, estimates based on the upper poverty line)

Change over time: The national figures are based on the Ghana Living Standards Survey (GLSS) rounds for 1987–1988, 1988–1989, 1991–1992, 1998–1999, 2005–2006, and 2012–2013. Each round covers a nationally representative sample of households spread over a period of twelve months. The GLSS questionnaires were significantly different after the second round: "The questionnaire used for the third round . . . included a much more detailed expenditure section, in which households were visited repeatedly at two–three day intervals over a month, and in which there was a significant increase in the number of items" (Coulombe and MacKay 1995, p. 2). Thus, there is good reason to expect the third round to yield higher estimates of expenditure and hence lower poverty rates (see also McKay, Pirttilä, and Tarp 2015).

Nonmonetary poverty: The OPHI Global MPI head count, based on deprivation according to a third or more of the weighted indicators, shows that 33.7 per cent of the population were in poor households in 2014 (estimate based on DHS data). Split by rural and urban subpopulations, the rates were 49.4 and 17.6 per cent, respectively. The harmonised time series of the head count (see editors' note) shows a decline in the national rate, from 58.7 per cent in 2003 to 41.9 per cent in 2008. The national study (GSS 2013) estimated a poverty rate of 42.7 per cent for the Multidimensional Poverty Index (MPI) in 2010.

Overall inequality: The Gini coefficient for consumption per head rose from 37.3 per cent in 1990 to 40.9 per cent in 2012–2013 (McKay, Pirttilä, and Tarp 2015, table 6).

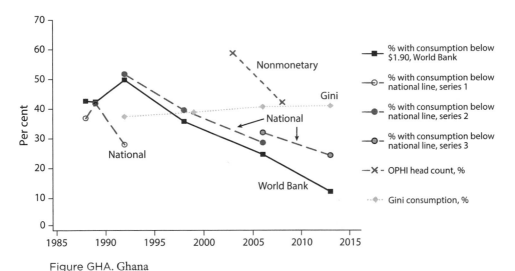

Figure GHA. Ghana

Ghana is in West Africa. In 1957, it was the first British colony in Africa to declare independence. Ghana is a lower-middle-income country according to the World Bank classification, with GNI per capita in 2015 of $1,470 (Atlas method) and $4,070 (PPP) and a population in that year of 27.4 million people.

KENYA

Poverty lines: The national line is based on a food poverty line, from which an overall line is constructed. The food line is calculated separately for rural and urban areas and starts from a daily calorie requirement (2,250 Cal per person) and is related to a spending requirement via an iterative process based on the distribution of food consumption. The overall poverty line is derived by an iterative process on the total nonfood expenditure of households with a defined position in the distribution of food expenditures relative to the food poverty line. The poverty line is adjusted for price variation during the year and by province. The overall poverty line in 2005–2006 in monthly adult equivalents was Kshs 1,562 for rural areas and Kshs 2,913 for urban areas. (The equivalence scale allots 0.24 for children aged zero to four, 0.65 for children aged five to fourteen, and 1.0 for all people aged fifteen and over.) Converting to individuals from adult equivalents (1.26 individuals per adult equivalent) and taking a weighted average of rural and urban lines according to population shares (80 per cent rural) yields a national average per person of PPP\$2.26 per person per day. Besides figures for overall poverty, the Kenya National Bureau of Statistics also publishes figures for food poverty (food consumption expenditure beneath the food poverty line) and "hardcore" poverty defined as total consumption expenditure beneath the food poverty line (Kenya National Bureau of Statistics 2007.) National estimates of overall poverty are based on the Kenya Integrated Household Budget Survey (KIHBS) for 2005–2006 and 2015–2016 (series 2) and the Welfare Monitoring Survey (WMS) for 1992–1997 (series 1); the series shown in the graphs refer to percentages of adult equivalents and not to individuals.

Poverty today: The World Bank estimates that 42.8 per cent of the population in 2005–2006 were living in households with consumption per head below \$1.90 a day and that the poverty gap was 16.0 per cent. In terms of the national poverty line, the proportion of the population with consumption per equivalent adult below the relevant overall poverty line (urban or rural) in the same year was 46.6 per cent; the food poverty rate was 45.8 per cent, and the hardcore rate 19.5 per cent. In 2015–2016 the rates were 36.1 per cent, 32.0 per cent, and 8.6 per cent, respectively (Kenya National Bureau of Statistics 2007; 2018, table 4.1 in both cases). (These estimates, unlike the series in the graph, refer to percentages of individuals and not adult equivalents.)

Who is poor?

- The overall poverty rate among individuals in rural areas in 2015–2016 was 40.1 per cent according to the national poverty line, compared with 27.5 per cent in peri-urban areas and 29.4 per cent in core urban areas.

- The rate across the forty-seven counties of Kenya varied from 16.7 per cent in the capital, Nairobi, to 79.4 per cent in Turkana. The counties with the highest rates were in the northeast of the country.

(Kenya National Bureau of Statistics 2018, table 4.3 [figures for individuals])

Change over time: National poverty rates for 2005–2006 and 2015–2016 based on the KIHBS cannot be compared with rates estimated for 1997 and earlier years based on the WMS (see the explanation in chapter 4). Nonetheless, the Kenya National Bureau of Statistics concluded that "the results show that national absolute poverty declined from 52.3 per cent in 1997 to 45.9 per cent in 2005/6" (Kenya National Bureau of Statistics 2007, p. 43 [figures refer to rates for equivalent adults and not individuals]). In the graph shown here, the series based on KIHBS and WMS are distinguished separately (Kenya National Bureau of Statistics 2007, table 4.8; 2018, table 4.1). The differences in the WMS and the KIHBS are listed in the 2007 report (p. 54), while differences in the three WMS surveys are discussed in Kabubo-Mariara and Ndeng'e (2004).

Nonmonetary poverty: The OPHI Global MPI head count, based on deprivation according to a third or more of the weighted indicators, shows that 39.9 per cent of the population were in poor households in 2014 (estimate based on DHS data). Split by rural and urban subpopulations, the rates were 51.4 and 17.3 per cent, respectively. The harmonised time series of the head count (see editors' note) shows a decline in the national rate, from 60.1 per cent in 2003 to 51.2 per cent in 2008–2009.

Overall inequality: In 2005–2006, the Gini coefficient for household expenditure (excluding rent) per equivalent adult was 38.0 per cent, reflecting a decline from 41.7 per cent in 1997 (Kenya National Bureau of Statistics 2007, p. 83).

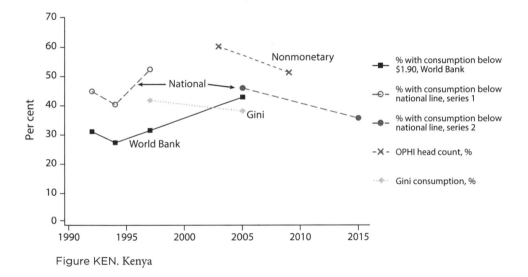

Figure KEN. Kenya

Kenya is in East Africa. It is a lower-middle-income country according to the World Bank classification, with GNI per capita in 2015 of $1,310 (Atlas method) and $3,060 (PPP) and a population in that year of 46.1 million people.

LIBERIA

Poverty lines:

Poverty today: The World Bank estimates show that in 2014 the proportion of the population living in households with consumption per head below $1.90 a day was 38.6 per cent and that the poverty gap was 11.7 per cent.

Who is poor?

Change over time:

Nonmonetary poverty: The OPHI Global MPI head count, based on deprivation according to a third or more of the weighted indicators, shows that 71.2 per cent of the population were in poor households in 2013 (estimate based on DHS data). Split by rural and urban subpopulations, the rates were 84.9 and 60.5 per cent, respectively. The harmonised time series of the head count (see editors' note) shows a decline in the national rate, from 83.9 per cent in 2007 to 69.4 per cent in 2013.

Overall inequality:

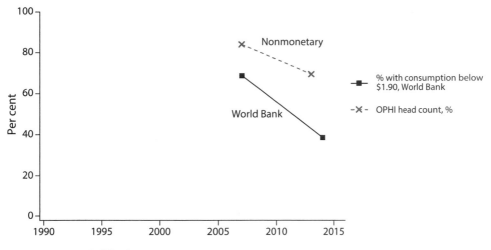

Figure LBR. Liberia

Liberia is a low-income country according to the World Bank classification, with GNI per capita in 2015 of $380 (Atlas method) and $720 (PPP) and a population in that year of 4.5 million people.

MADAGASCAR

Poverty lines:

Poverty today: The World Bank estimates show that in 2012 the proportion of the population living in households with consumption per head below $1.90 a day was 77.6 per cent and that the poverty gap was 39.0 per cent.

Who is poor?

Change over time:

Nonmonetary poverty: The OPHI Global MPI head count, based on deprivation according to a third or more of the weighted indicators, shows that 66.9 per cent of the population were in poor households in 2008–2009 (estimate based on DHS data). Split by rural and urban subpopulations, the rates were 73.7 and 24.9 per cent, respectively. The harmonised time series of the head count (see editors' note) shows an increase in the national rate, from 67.0 per cent in 2000 to 73.3 per cent in 2008–2009.

Overall inequality:

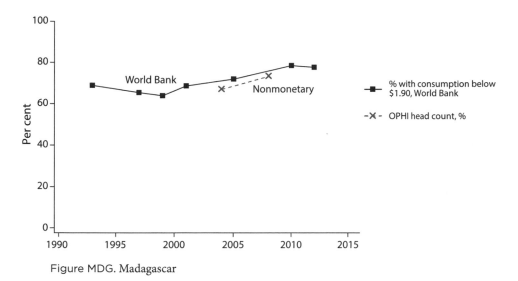

Figure MDG. Madagascar

Madagascar is in the Indian Ocean, off the coast of East Africa. It is a low-income country according to the World Bank classification, with GNI per capita in 2015 of $420 (Atlas method) and $1,400 (PPP) and a population in that year of 24.2 million people.

MALAWI

Poverty lines:

Poverty today: The World Bank estimates show that in 2010–2011 the proportion of the population living in households with consumption per head below $1.90 a day was 71.4 per cent and that the poverty gap was 33.6 per cent.

Who is poor?

Change over time:

Nonmonetary poverty: The OPHI Global MPI head count, based on deprivation according to a third or more of the weighted indicators, shows that 53.7 per cent of the population were in poor households in 2015–2016 (estimate based on DHS data). Split by rural and urban subpopulations, the rates were 58.9 and 23.2 per cent, respectively. The harmonised time series of the head count (see editors' note) shows a decline in the national rate, from 72.1 per cent in 2004 to 66.7 per cent in 2010.

Overall inequality:

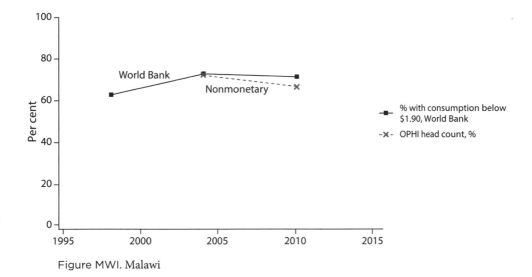

Figure MWI. Malawi

Malawi is a low-income country according to the World Bank classification, with GNI per capita in 2015 of $340 (Atlas method) and $1,140 (PPP) and a population in that year of 17.2 million people.

MAURITIUS

Poverty lines: Mauritius has no official poverty line. To measure poverty Statistics Mauritius uses a relative poverty line set at half of the median monthly household income per adult equivalent (series 1). Household income—used to measure poverty—comprises disposable income and an estimate of imputed rent for homeowners. The number of adult equivalents in a household is taken as N to the power 0.7, where N is equal to the number of adults plus 0.7 times the number of children (persons aged less than sixteen). A family with two adults and two children is therefore 2.36 adult equivalents. To measure changes in poverty over time, Statistics Mauritius also uses an anchored poverty line set at half of the median monthly household income per equivalent adult in a given year, indexed by the change in consumer prices (series 2); the base year is 1996–1997 in the data shown in the graph. (The 2017 data point given in Statistics Mauritius [2018] uses 2012 as the base year and has been scaled in the graph to be comparable.) Series 1 and 2 are taken from Statistics Mauritius (2015, tables 1 and 23; 2018, tables 7 and 8), and both are based on data from the Household Budget Survey (HBS).

Poverty today: The World Bank estimates for 2012 show that 0.5 per cent of the population were living in households with consumption per head below $1.90 a day per person and that the poverty gap was 0.1 per cent. The national estimates for the same year of the proportion of individuals in households with equivalised income below 50 per cent of the median (series 1) and below 50 per cent of the median in 1996–1997 (series 2) was 9.8 per cent and 5.3 per cent, respectively. The figures for 2017 were 10.3 per cent (series 1) and 3.4 per cent (series 2).

Who is poor?

- For males, the poverty rate in 2012 according to the relative poverty line was 9.0 per cent; for females, it was 10.5 per cent.

- The poverty rate for those aged under sixteen was 14.8 per cent, and for those aged sixty and over it was 7.0 per cent.

- The poverty rate for those aged twenty and over with below-secondary-level education was 12.9 per cent; the rate for those who had at least a Cambridge school certificate qualification from secondary education was 2.2 per cent.

- Among the population aged sixteen and over, the poverty rate was 5.9 per cent for persons with a job, 20.9 per cent for persons unemployed, and 10.2 per cent for those who were economically inactive (students, retired, homemakers, etc).

(Statistics Mauritius 2015, pp. 10–12)

Change over time: The relative poverty series shows a modest rise over 2000–2012, which, as Statistics Mauritius (2015, p. 4) notes, is in line with a rise in the Gini coefficient. However, the anchored series shows a slight net fall over the same period.

Nonmonetary poverty: Mauritius is not included in the countries covered by OPHI.

Overall inequality: The Gini coefficient for the household (not individual) distribution of monthly household disposable income (not equivalised) is estimated with the HBS and is taken from Central Statistics Office (2005, table 4.2) and Statistics Mauritius (2015, table 2; 2018, table 3). Subramanian (2001, page 2) gives a figure of 0.5 for 1962 but it is unclear if it is comparable with the series included here.

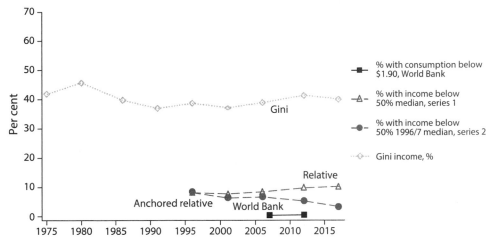

Figure MUS. Mauritius

Mauritius is an island nation in the Indian Ocean. It is an upper-middle-income country according to the World Bank classification, with GNI per capita in 2015 of $9,780 (Atlas method) and $19,290 (PPP) and a population in that year of 1.3 million people.

MOZAMBIQUE

Poverty lines: There have been four national assessments of poverty, each based on the Inquérito ao Orçamento Familiar (IOF, Family Budget Survey), conducted in 1996–1997, 2002–2003, 2008–2009, and 2014–2015. The first used thirteen different poverty lines, based on local prices and local consumption patterns in the 1996–1997 survey. For the second assessment, each of these lines was adjusted in accordance with the changes in local prices and local consumption patterns observed in the 2002–2003 survey, while the third assessment used another set of thirteen lines estimated using the 2008–2009 survey (van den Boom 2011, p. 18). These lines were reestimated again in the fourth assessment (Ministério de Economia e Finanças 2016, appendix 7), the last of these implementing the PLEASe methodology described in Arndt and Mahrt (2017). (A slightly different account of measurement in the first three assessments is given in Arndt et al. 2017.) Series 1 is from the third assessment (Ministry of Planning and Development 2010, table 3-5) and is represented as one series, although the change in calculation of lines for 2008–2009 threatens comparability over time. Series 2 is from the fourth assessment (Ministry of Economics and Finance 2016, table RE-1) and includes reestimation for earlier years, although it is unclear whether this produces figures that are fully consistent. Poverty measurement uses consumption expenditure per capita.

Poverty today: The World Bank estimates show 62.9 per cent of the population living in households with consumption per head below \$1.90 a day per person in 2014–2015 and a poverty gap of 28.0 per cent. For the same year, the national estimate of the poverty rate was 46.1 per cent (series 2). The fourth poverty assessment recognised a problem of underrecording of consumption in the 2014–2015 survey, suggesting that this had worsened from the situation already noted in the 2002–2003 and 2008–2009 surveys. The three adjustments to the data implemented to try to allow for this problem reduced the estimated poverty rate for 2014–2015 to 44.9 per cent, 41.9 per cent, or 40.9 per cent (Ministry of Economics and Finance 2016, table RE-2).

Who is poor?

- In rural areas the poverty rate in 2014–2015, according to the national poverty line, was 50.1 per cent, compared with 37.4 per cent in urban areas.

- Across provinces, the poverty rate varied between 11.6 per cent in the capital city of Maputo and 18.9 per cent in Maputo province to 57.1 per cent in Nampula and 60.6 per cent in Niassa. A surprisingly high estimate for Maputo in 2002–2003 was one of the puzzles that led to van den Boom's (2011) investigation; Niassa had the second-lowest estimated poverty rate in 2008–2009.

(Ministry of Economics and Finance 2016)

Change over time: The World Bank figures show a different pattern of change between 1995–1996 and 2008–2009 to the national estimates produced by the Ministry of Economy and Finances (series 1 and 2). The former shows a fall that accelerates between 2002–2003 and 2008–2009, while the ministry's estimates show a more L-shaped pattern of change. The pattern in series 1 was one of the stimuli for the reevaluations of national estimates in Mozambique by van den Boom (2011) and Alfani et al. (2012), both of whom produce alternative estimates for 1995–1996 to 2008–2009 that show a pattern with less of a L-shaped decline. They comment also on the differences in the pattern of change over time in poverty rates at the provincial level.

Nonmonetary poverty: The OPHI Global MPI head count, based on deprivation according to a third or more of the weighted indicators, shows that 69.6 per cent of the population were in poor households in 2011 (estimate based on DHS data). Split by rural and urban subpopulations, the rates were 83.9 and 38.2 per cent, respectively. The harmonised time series of the head count (see editors' note) shows a decline in the national rate, from 82.3 per cent in 2003 to 70.3 per cent in 2011. The fourth national poverty assessment also contains estimates of nonmonetary poverty, based on the Alkire-Foster method, for each of the four IOF surveys, using six items (no household member having completed first-level primary school, no access to safe water, inadequate sanitation, grass roofing, no electricity, and very limited possession of durable goods). The proportion of the population deprived on three or more items (not shown in the graph) fell by twenty-five percentage points between 1996–1997 and 2014–2015, from 92.7 per cent to 67.4 per cent (Ministry of Economics and Finance 2016, table RE-4).

Overall inequality: In 2014–2015, the estimate of the Gini coefficient for consumption per capita was 47 per cent, reflecting an increase from 40 per cent in 1996; the figures are shown as one series, although the extent to which changes and problems in the IOF surveys affect the comparability of the estimates is unclear (Ministry of Economics and Finance 2016, table RE-3).

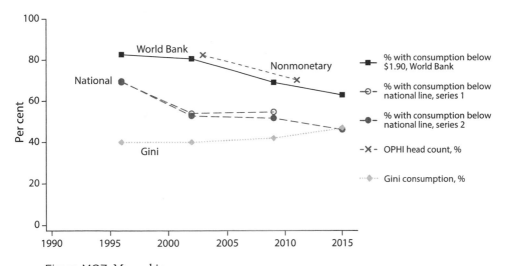

Figure MOZ. Mozambique

Mozambique is a low-income country according to the World Bank classification, with GNI per capita in 2015 of $580 (Atlas method) and $1,170 (PPP) and a population in that year of 28.0 million people.

NIGER

Poverty lines: Estimates of poverty have been made by the Institut National de la Statistique for 2005, 2007–2008, and 2011, using household surveys conducted in those years (Enquête Nationale sur les Conditions de Vie des Ménages et l'Agriculture, ECVMA). The poverty rate is based on measuring consumption expenditure per capita. In 2005, a food poverty line was calculated using a standard of 2,100 Cal per person per day with a nonfood element added based on the recorded expenditure of households whose consumption per capita of food was close to the food line. The selected basket of food was valued separately in rural and urban areas, and the overall poverty line was 144,750 Francs CFA per year in urban areas and 105,827 Francs CFA in rural areas. For 2007–2008, the poverty line was adjusted upwards by the national inflation rate since 2005 (Institut National de la Statistique 2008, pp. 16–17). For 2011, an exercise analogous to that in 2005 was undertaken to reestimate the poverty line, although there is some ambiguity as to whether the same standard of kilocalories was used (Institut National de la Statistique 2013, pp. 11–14). The series shown in the graph is from Institut National de la Statistique (2008, table 2.2; 2013, table 3). (The UN Economic Commission for Africa [2016, p. 13] reports a figure of 45.1 per cent for 2014 based on the ECVMA carried out in 2014, but this has not been included in the series shown in figure NER.) There were a number of important differences in the methodology between the three household surveys; for example, the 2007–2008 survey collected data over seven consecutive days, whereas the 2005 and 2011 surveys relied on retrospective interviews, asking respondents to recall their past food consumption. These differences led the World Bank to reestimate poverty rates for the three surveys using a 2011 poverty line fixed in real terms and attempting to allow for differences in survey methods; the procedure involved using a statistical model based on data from the 2011 survey to assign a value for consumption expenditure per capita to households in the 2005 and 2007–2008 surveys. Results are given in World Bank (2015, table 3), with estimated poverty rates of 53.7 per cent in 2005 and 52.6 per cent in 2007–2008. These figures are lower than those published by the Institut National de la Statistique for the same years: 62.1 per cent and 59.5 per cent, respectively (shown in the series in figure NER).

Poverty today: The World Bank estimates for 2014 show that 44.5 per cent of the population were living in households with consumption per head below $1.90 a day per person and that the poverty gap was 13.5 per cent. The Institut National de la Statistique estimates the poverty rate in 2011 to have been 48.2 per cent, when the World Bank figure was 50.3 per cent.

Who is poor?

- The poverty rate in urban areas in 2011, according to the official poverty line, was 17.9 per cent and 54.6 per cent in rural areas.

- Regional poverty rate estimates varied from 10.2 per cent in the capital city of Niamey to 57.8 per cent in Maradi.

- Poverty rates were highest in large households: 59.6 per cent in households with ten to fourteen people and 66.8 per cent in households with fifteen people or more. (These two types of household made up 23.9 per cent and 8.2 per cent, respectively, of the population.)

(Institut National de la Statistique 2013)

Change over time: The change over time in the monetary poverty rate between 2005 and 2011 differs sharply between the two series, although they both show a marked reduction.

Nonmonetary poverty: The OPHI Global MPI head count, based on deprivation according to a third or more of the weighted indicators, shows that 89.3 per cent of the population were in poor households in 2012 (estimate based on DHS data). Split by rural and urban subpopulations, the rates were 96.2 and 53.9 per cent, respectively. The harmonised time series of the head count (see editors' note) shows a small reduction in the national rate, from 93.5 per cent in 2006 to 90.0 per cent in 2012.

Overall inequality: The Gini coefficients refer to annual consumption expenditure per capita and are based on the same surveys as the poverty rates, using the unadjusted data (World Bank 2014, table 5). The data show the Gini coefficient rising from 28.6 per cent in 2005 to 31.4 per cent in 2011.

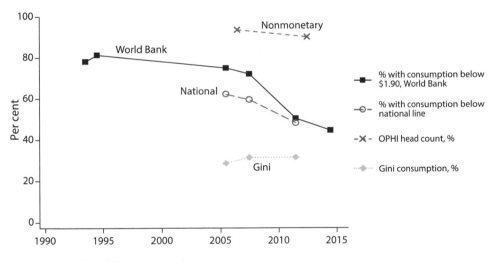

Figure NER. Niger

Niger is a lower-middle-income country according to the World Bank classification, with GNI per capita (PPP) in 2015 of $950 (a figure using the Atlas method is not published by the World Bank) and a population in that year of 19.9 million people.

SIERRA LEONE

Poverty line:

Poverty today: The World Bank estimates for 2011 show that 52.2 per cent were living in households with consumption per head below $1.90 a day per person and that the poverty gap was 16.7 per cent.

Who is poor?

Change over time:

Nonmonetary poverty: The OPHI Global MPI head count, based on deprivation according to a third or more of the weighted indicators, shows that 81.0 per cent of the population were in poor households in 2013 (estimate based on DHS data). Split by rural and urban subpopulations, the rates were 92.0 and 56.3 per cent, respectively. The harmonised time series of the head count (see editors' note) shows a marginal increase in the national rate, from 79.1 per cent in 2008 to 80.7 per cent in 2013.

Overall inequality:

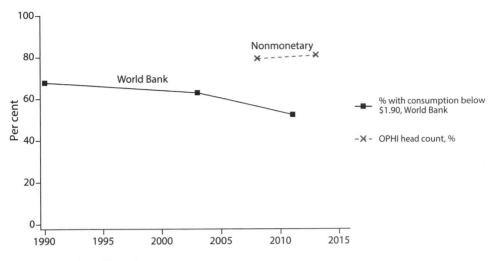

Figure SLE. Sierra Leone

Sierra Leone is a low-income country according to the World Bank classification, with GNI per capita in 2015 of $550 (Atlas method) and $1,560 (PPP) and a population in that year of 6.5 million people.

SOUTH AFRICA

Poverty lines: Various poverty standards have been used since the 1940s (Budlender, Leibbrandt, and Woolard 2015). (Chapter 4 notes comments by Beegle et al. [2016] on problems of comparability over time.) The series in the graph are based on the Income and Expenditure Survey (IES) for 2005–2006 and 2010–2011 and the Living Conditions Survey (LCS) for 2008–2009 and 2014–2015. The figures relate to individuals in households with per capita expenditure below the lower-bound poverty line (LBPL) (series 1) and food poverty line (FPL) (series 2). The surveys for 2005–2006 and 2008–2009 used four-week expenditure diaries, and those for 2010–2011 and 2014–2015 used two-week diaries (both combined with recall for some items). (Response to the 2014–2015 survey was 84.9 per cent, ranging from 95.6 per cent in Limpopo province to 65.3 per cent in Gauteng, which includes Johannesburg.) Alternative series (not shown) exist for the percentage of people living in households with per capita income below R 3,000 (at 2000 prices) in van der Berg and Louw (2004, table 5) from 1970 to 2000, and in Leibbrandt et al. (2010, table 1.3). The series in the graph stem from the first calculations of an official poverty line in 2012, subsequently revised to "take account of changing needs, preferences and social conditions" (Statistics South Africa 2017, p. 114). The food poverty line is the estimated cost per capita to meet a nutritional standard of 2,100 Cal per day, with consumption patterns of households in decile groups 2 to 4 of per capita expenditure taken as a reference group for determining a food basket. The lower-bound poverty line takes account of nonfood needs by calculating the nonfood expenditure of households, with total expenditure similar to the FPL. A higher "upper-bound" line calculates the nonfood expenditure of households with food expenditure similar to the FPL, but it is the LBPL that "has emerged as the preferred threshold that is commonly used for the country's poverty reduction targets" (Statistics South Africa 2017, p. 15). In 2015, the FPL was R 441 per month per person and the LBPL was R 647; in 2011, the lines were R 335 and R 501, respectively. In the earlier versions used for estimates in Statistics South Africa (2014), these two lines for 2011 were R 321 and R 443, resulting, for example, in an estimate of persons below the FPL that was 1.2 percentage points lower than the figure shown in the graph for series 2. Series 1 and 2 are from Statistics South Africa (2017, Table 2.1).

Poverty today: The World Bank estimates for 2014–2015 show that 18.9 per cent of the population were living in households with consumption per head below $1.90 a day per person and that the poverty gap was 6.2 per cent. The national estimates of the head count the same year were 40.0 per cent (series 1) and 25.2 per cent (series 2) and 36.4 per cent and 21.4 per cent, respectively, in 2011.

Who is poor?

- The poverty rate in rural areas in 2014–2015 according to the LBPL was 65.4 per cent and 25.4 per cent in urban areas.

- The poverty rate by province ranged from 19.0 per cent in Gauteng and 21.3 per cent in the Western Cape to 57.0 per cent in Limpopo and 59.1 per cent in Eastern Cape.

- For males, the poverty rate was 38.2 per cent; for females, it was 41.7 per cent.

• The proportion of each of the main racial groups living in poverty was 47.1 per cent for Black Africans, 23.3 per cent for Coloureds, 1.2 per cent for Indians/Asians, and 0.4 per cent for Whites.

(Statistics South Africa 2017, tables 3.14, 3.13, 3.9, and 3.10)

Change over time: The World Bank figures shows a fall of 8.6 percentage points between 2006 and 2009, while national figures show a smaller fall of 3.4 points (series 1) or a rise of 5.1 points (series 2). All three series show an increase in poverty between 2010–2011 and 2014–2015, by 2.4 points (World Bank), 3.6 points (series 1), and 3.8 points (series 2).

Nonmonetary poverty: The OPHI Global MPI head count, based on deprivation according to a third or more of the weighted indicators, shows that 9.2 per cent of the population were in poor households in 2014–2015 (estimate based on National Income Dynamics [NIDS] survey data). Split by rural and urban subpopulations, the rates were 17.2 and 3.6 per cent, respectively. The harmonised time series of the head count (see editors' note) shows a decline in the national rate, from 17.8 per cent in 2008 to 10.5 per cent in 2012. National estimates (not shown) using the Alkire-Foster method with the Census and Community Survey data show the percentage of people deprived in at least a third of weighted indicators as 17.9 per cent in 2001, 8.0 per cent in 2011, and 7.0 per cent in 2016 (Statistics South Africa 2017, table 2.5).

Overall inequality: The Gini coefficient of per capita income (and consumption) for 2006–2015 is from Statistics South Africa (2017, figure 2.7) and for 1993 and 2000 from Leibbrandt et al. (2010a, table 5.17). (The two sources give the same value for 2005–2006.)

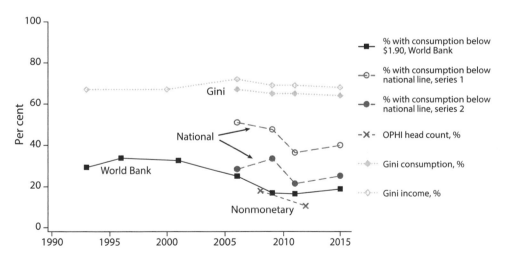

Figure ZAF. South Africa

South Africa is an upper-middle-income country according to the World Bank classification, with GNI per capita in 2015 of $6,070 (Atlas method) and $12,830 (PPP) and a population in that year of 55.0 million people.

TANZANIA

Poverty lines: Poverty estimates for mainland Tanzania are made using the mainland Household Budget Survey (HBS), which has been conducted in 1991–1992, 2000–2001, 2007, and 2011–2012, using expenditure per adult equivalent as the welfare measure. Two lines are employed: the food poverty line based on the cost of purchasing a food basket providing 2,200 Cal per person per day, using information on a reference group of households in the bottom half of the expenditure distribution (less the first decile group), and the basic needs poverty line, calculated as the food poverty line divided by the food share of households, with consumption per adult equivalent close to the food poverty line (measured as 0.715). In 2012, the monthly basic needs poverty line per adult equivalent for mainland Tanzania was 36,482 TZS, and the food poverty line was 26,085 TZS. Series 1 and 2 measure poverty by the basic needs line; series 2 is taken from the report of the 2011–2012 survey (National Bureau of Statistics 2014, table 7.4) and series 1 from the report of the 2007 survey (National Bureau of Statistics 2009, table 7.2).

A number of changes in methodology took place between the 2007 and 2011–2012 surveys, which is one explanation for the existence of the two series. These are detailed in National Bureau of Statistics (2014, pp. 9–10) and World Bank (2015, appendix 1.A) and include adjustment to the recall period for nonfood items, a more detailed probe of them (food expenditures continued to be collected in a twenty-eight-day diary), and, it is argued, better survey implementation and supervision. The equivalence scale used takes into account both age and sex with values ranging from 0.4 for those zero to two years old of either sex to 0.8 and 0.72 at age sixty or more for men and women, respectively, to 1.2 for male fifteen- to eighteen-year-olds (National Bureau of Statistics 2009, table A.6). Separate estimates of poverty are made for Zanzibar, a semiautonomous group of islands with its own Household Budget Survey and poverty lines. Figures for 2004–2005 and 2009–2010 are given in the Zanzibar Household Budget Survey report for 2009–2010 (Office of Chief Government Statistician–Zanzibar 2012, table 7.3; see also World Bank 2017).

Poverty today: The World Bank estimates show that in 2011–2012 the proportion of the population living in households with consumption per head below $1.90 a day was 49.1 per cent and that the poverty gap was 15.4 per cent. According to national estimates (mainland Tanzania, series 2) for the same year, 9.7 per cent of the population was below the food poverty line and 28.2 per cent were below the basic needs line (National Bureau of Statistics 2014, table 7.4.)

Who is poor?

- The poverty rate in 2011–2012, according to the basic needs line, was 33.3 per cent in rural areas, compared with 4.1 per cent in Dar es Salaam and 21.7 per cent in other urban areas.

- The poverty rate was 16.4 per cent for households with four members, but 41.9 per cent for households with ten members or more.

- The poverty rates were virtually identical for households with male heads (28.4 per cent) and with female heads (27.1 per cent).

- In 2011–2012, 40.8 per cent of households were in poverty where the head had no education, compared with 5.4 per cent for those where the head had secondary education.

(National Bureau of Statistics 2014, tables 7.4, 8.1, 8.3, and 8.5)

Change over time: The national poverty estimates, using the basic needs poverty line, show a fall from 38.6 per cent in 1991–1992 to 28.2 per cent in 2011–2012. The fall is continuous, contrasting with that in the World Bank series, which shows a rise between 1991–1992 and 2000.

Nonmonetary poverty: The OPHI Global MPI head count, based on deprivation according to a third or more of the weighted indicators, shows that 56.6 per cent of the population were in poor households in 2015–2016 (estimate based on DHS data). Split by rural and urban subpopulations, the rates were 68.6 and 27.7 per cent, respectively. The harmonised time series of the head count (see editors' note) shows a decline in the national rate, from 65.6 per cent in 2008 to 61.1 per cent in 2010.

Overall inequality: The Gini coefficient for household per capita expenditure in 2011–2012 was 34 per cent (series 1 from National Bureau of Statistics 2009, table 7.4; series 2 from National Bureau of Statistics 2014, table 7.8).

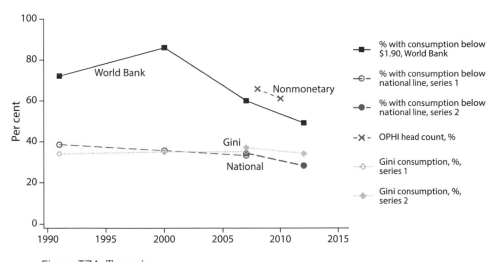

Figure TZA. Tanzania

The United Republic of Tanzania was formed in 1964 from the merger of Tanganyika and Zanzibar. (Zanzibar consists of islands lying off the coast in the Indian Ocean.) Tanzania is a low-income country according to the World Bank classification, with GNI per capita in 2015 of $910 (Atlas method) and $2,620 (PPP) and a population in that year of 53.5 million people.

TUNISIA

Poverty lines:

Poverty today: The World Bank estimates for 2010–2011 show that 2.0 per cent of the population were living in households with consumption per head below $1.90 a day and that the poverty gap was 0.4 per cent.

Who is poor?

Change over time:

Nonmonetary poverty: The OPHI Global MPI head count, based on deprivation according to a third or more of the weighted indicators, shows that 1.2 per cent of the population were in poor households in 2011–2012 (estimate based on MICS data). Split by rural and urban subpopulations, the rates were 3.2 and 0.1 per cent, respectively.

Overall inequality:

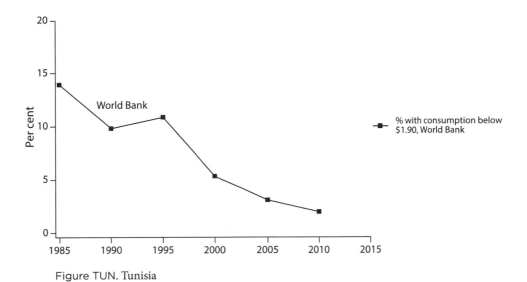

Figure TUN. Tunisia

Tunisia is a lower-middle-income country according to the World Bank classification, with GNI per capita in 2015 of $3,930 (Atlas method) and $11,060 (PPP) and a population in that year of 11.1 million people.

UGANDA

Poverty lines: National poverty estimates are made with information on household expenditure per adult equivalent contained in the Integrated Household Survey (IHS) of 1992–1993 and the Uganda National Household Survey (UNHS) for 1999–2000, 2002–2003, 2005–2006, 2009–2010, 2012–2013, and 2016–2017. The 2016–2017 survey saw inclusion of some new food items (food expenditure is measured by recall over seven days) and a change in recall periods for some nonfood items from one month to seven days (Uganda Bureau of Statistics 2017, pp. 79–80). The series shown is from Ministry of Finance (2014, table 2.1) and Uganda Bureau of Statistics (2017, table 7.6a). A national poverty line was established based on patterns of consumption recorded in a 1993 survey (not the IHS) and has since been updated in line with movements in consumer prices. A food basket yielding 3,000 Cal per day is costed where items in the basket are consumed in the same proportion as in a reference group taken as the bottom half of the distribution of expenditure per adult equivalent (the basket is adjusted for the age of the individual), and the poverty line is calculated as the cost of the food basket divided by the mean food share of households close to the food poverty line (Appleton 1999). In 1993, the year for which the line was first calculated, the poverty line was 16,443 Uganda shillings per adult equivalent per month; expressed per adult and per day, it corresponded to PPP\$1.13 per person per day. (Van Campenhout, Sekabira, and Aduayom [2016] provide poverty estimates for 1992–1993 to 2012–2013 using an alternative set of poverty lines.)

Poverty today: The World Bank estimates show that in 2012–2013 the proportion of the population living in households with consumption per head below \$1.90 a day was 35.9 per cent and that the poverty gap was 10.8 per cent. The national estimate of the poverty rate for the same year was 19.7 per cent, while the figure for 2016–2017 was 27.0 per cent.

Who is poor?

• The poverty rate in 2012–2013, according to national estimates, was 30.8 per cent in rural areas, compared with 15.2 per cent in urban areas.

• At the level of the region, poverty rates varied from 5.9 per cent in Kampala, which includes the capital, to 42.7 per cent in the Eastern region.

• For households with (small-scale) crop farming as the primary source of income, 35.8 per cent were below the poverty line, compared with 21.6 per cent and 23.0 per cent where the primary source was (small-scale) livestock farming and wage employment, respectively.

(Uganda Bureau of Statistics 2017, tables 7.6a and 7.12a)

Change over time: The national estimates show that there was a fall in poverty considerably in excess of one-half: from 56.4 per cent in 1992–1993 to 19.7 per cent in 2012–2013. But this was followed by a rise of 7.3 percentage points to 2016–2017.

Nonmonetary poverty: The OPHI Global MPI head count, based on deprivation according to a third or more of the weighted indicators, shows that 69.9 per cent of the population were in poor households in 2011 (estimate based on DHS data). Split by rural and urban subpopulations, the rates were 77.1 and 29.2 per cent, respectively. The harmonised time series of the head count (see editors' note) shows a decline in the national rate, from 77.9 per cent in 2006 to 66.8 per cent in 2011. There is also an official Multidimensional Poverty Index, with twelve indicators covering education, health, access to public utilities and housing conditions, and access to information. In 2012–2013, 53.8 per cent of households were deprived on at least four of the twelve indicators, a figure lower than the 63.9 per cent in 2009–2010 (Ministry of Finance 2014, p. 28).

Overall inequality: The Gini coefficient for household income per adult equivalent in 2012–2013 was 39.5 per cent. (It is not fully clear whether the data refer to income or expenditure.) This was three percentage points higher than thirty years earlier (Ministry of Finance 2014, p. v). The report of the 2016–2017 UNHS gives a Gini coefficient of 37.1 per cent; one table gives the same figures for earlier years as found in the Ministry of Finance report; another gives somewhat higher figures (Uganda Bureau of Statistics 2017, tables 7.9, 7.10).

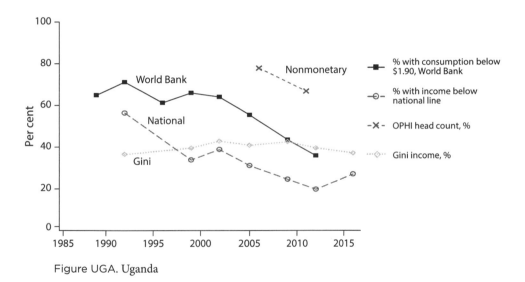

Figure UGA. Uganda

Uganda is a landlocked country in East Africa. It is a low-income country according to the World Bank classification, with GNI per capita in 2015 of $670 (Atlas method) and $1,780 (PPP) and a population in that year of 39.0 million people.

ZAMBIA

Poverty lines: The national line is based on a basic needs approach, which starts from the cost of a food basket (the food or "extreme" poverty line) established in 1991 and updated in line with December item-specific prices. The calorie requirements were 2,600 Cal for adult women and 2,750 for adult men. Nonfood requirements were calculated up to 2006 using a fixed food share ("about 70 per cent"); from 2006 the share is based on households whose per adult equivalent food expenditure was within 30 per cent of the food poverty line (Central Statistical Office 2012, p. 178). In 2010, the resulting poverty line corresponded to PPP$2.20 per person per day. Estimates of poverty (based on household expenditure per adult equivalent) were made with Priority Surveys (PSs) in 1991 and 1993 and Living Conditions Monitoring Surveys (LCMSs) in 1996, 1998, 2002–2003, 2004, 2006, 2010, and 2015. The equivalence scale adjusts for age: ages zero to three count as 0.36 adults, ages four to six as 0.62, ages seven to nine as 0.76, ages ten to twelve as 0.78, and ages thirteen and older as 1.0 (Central Statistical Office 2016, table 21.1). Series 1 is from Central Statistical Office (2005, table 12.7); the same publication warns (p. 129) that results from the 2002–2003 survey may not be comparable with those from other surveys (an expenditure diary was used rather than collecting information by recall), and the table concerned includes no figure for that year. Series 2 and 3 are from Central Statistical Office (2012, p. 181; 2016, figure 12.23). (There are some questions over the comparability of the figures for 2006 and 2010; see World Bank [2012], box 0.1.) The 2015 survey saw changes in methods (for example, the exclusion of remittances, hospital fees, and funeral expenses, a change in the treatment of durable goods, and a change in the calculation of the nonfood component of the poverty line), and the Central Statistical Office warns that "2015 poverty estimates are not directly comparable to the 2010 official poverty estimates" (2016, p. 104). Therefore, the 2015 figure is shown here separately as series 3.

Poverty today: The World Bank estimates show that in 2015 the proportion of the population living in households with consumption per head below $1.90 a day was 57.5 per cent and that the poverty gap was 29.5 per cent. In the same year, 54.4 per cent of the population were estimated to be below the national poverty line (series 3), and in 2010 the figure was 60.5 per cent (series 2). Subjectively, 40.7 per cent of the population in 2015 regarded themselves as "very poor" and 43.8 per cent as "moderately poor" (Central Statistical Office 2016, p. 113).

Who is poor?

- The poverty rate in 2015, according to the national poverty line, was 76.6 per cent in rural areas, compared with 23.4 per cent in urban areas.

- The poverty rate for female-headed households in 2015 was 56.7 per cent, compared with 53.8 per cent for male-headed households.

- In 2010, the poverty rate was 82.4 per cent where the household head was a farmer, compared with 25.3 per cent for wage-earners.

- In 2010, the poverty rate was 30.2 per cent for households with one or two members and 69.4 per cent for households of nine or more.

- In 2010, the poverty rate was 83.5 per cent where the household head had no education and 48.8 per cent where the head had secondary education.

(Central Statistical Office 2012, 2016)

Change over time: The national estimates show that the poverty rate was essentially stationary from 1991 to 2004. There was a fall of eight percentage points between 2006 and 2015, however, though the figure for 2015 is not directly comparable with those for earlier years. (There is a break in the series between 2004 and 2006, since the earlier years used a fixed food share ratio, while later years used year-specific ratios; see above.)

Nonmonetary poverty: The OPHI Global MPI head count, based on deprivation according to three or more indicators, shows that 56.6 per cent of the population were in poor households in 2013–2014 (estimate based on DHS data). Split by rural and urban subpopulations, the rates were 74.2 and 29.5 per cent, respectively. The harmonised time series of the head count (see editors' note) shows a decline in the national rate, from 72.0 per cent in 2001–2002 to 64.8 per cent in 2007.

Overall inequality: The Gini coefficient for household per capita income in 2015 was 69 per cent. This was nine percentage points higher than in 2006 (Central Statistical Office 2012, p. 151; 2016, figure 10.6.).

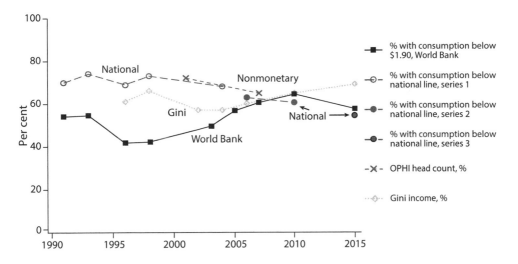

Figure ZMB. Zambia

Zambia is a landlocked sub-Saharan country. It is a lower-middle-income country according to the World Bank classification, with GNI per capita in 2015 of $1,560 (Atlas method) and $3,660 (PPP) and a population in that year of 16.2 million people.

National poverty reports for chapter 8

BOLIVIA

Poverty line: There are two national lines: an "extreme" poverty line (an income just sufficient to afford a food basket of minimum caloric intake) and a "moderate" poverty line (an income just sufficient to cover both that food basket and basic nonfood expenditures). (The methods for deriving the lines are described in, for example, UDAPE 2004.) At the end of 2012, the extreme line was set at Bs 365.50 per person per month in urban areas and Bs 298.63 in rural areas; the moderate line was set at Bs 693.20 and Bs 523.90, respectively. (Differences in prices are one reason for the line varying between urban and rural areas.) In terms of international dollars, the extreme poverty line was PPP$3.76 in urban areas and PPP$3.07 in rural areas; the moderate poverty line was PPP$7.12 in urban areas and PPP$5.38 in rural areas. Poverty is estimated using a national household survey, the Encuesta Continua de Hogares. The SEDLAC guide to methods reports that "in 2003–04 the survey was modified to record incomes over the whole year. That change implies serious comparability problems with previous years" (CEDLAS and World Bank 2014, p. 5). For this reason the national estimates of poverty rates—series 1 ("moderate") and series 2 ("extreme")—and Gini coefficients are shown with a break. These estimates are taken from the *Dossier de estadísticas sociales y económisas* on the website of Unidad de Análisis de Políticas Sociales y Económicas (UDAPE) (table 7.6.1 from dossier 24, downloaded in October 2016, and dossier 27, downloaded in December 2017).

Poverty today: The World Bank estimates for 2016 show that 7.1 per cent of the population were living in households with incomes per head below $1.90 a day and that the poverty gap was 3.0 per cent. The national extreme poverty line is set at between 60 and 100 per cent higher, so a higher national estimate of the poverty head-count rate is to be expected: 21.6 per cent in 2012, when the World Bank figure was 8.2 per cent. With the national moderate poverty line, the poverty head count for this year was 43.3 per cent.

Who is poor?

- For men and women, the extreme poverty rates in 2012 were close to identical: 21.1 per cent for men and 22.1 per cent for women.

- The extreme poverty rate in 2012 for those aged under twenty-five was 24.3 per cent, compared with 21.6 per cent for all age groups.

- In 2012, the extreme poverty rate for the indigenous population was 36.7 per cent, compared with 12.0 for the non-indigenous population.

- In 2012, the extreme poverty rate was 12.2 per cent in urban areas and 40.9 per cent in rural areas.

- The extreme poverty rate in 2012 was 48.5 per cent for those engaged in agriculture, forestry, fishing, or hunting.

Change over time: The World Bank estimates show a rise in the poverty rate in the 1990s, but then a fall from 2000, the poverty head count falling by 2014 to a quarter of its 2000 value. The national extreme poverty (and moderate poverty) rates confirm the fall in the twenty-first century, as does the more limited evidence for nonmonetary poverty. The World Bank series shows a slight rise over 2014 to 2016.

Nonmonetary poverty: The OPHI Global MPI head count, based on deprivation according to a third or more of the weighted indicators, shows that 20.5 per cent of the population were in poor households in 2008 (estimate based on DHS data). Split by rural and urban subpopulations, the rates were 43.0 and 4.9 per cent, respectively. The harmonised time series of the head count (see editors' note) shows a decline in the national rate, from 36.3 per cent in 2003 to 20.5 per cent in 2008. Alternative estimates based on five non-income dimensions for a rather longer period, 1999 to 2011, are given by Villarroel and Hernani-Limarino (2013).

Overall inequality: The Gini coefficient for income inequality was broadly stable between 1996 and 2006, but then fell from 59.0 per cent to 47 per cent in 2011 and remained at this level or a little higher until 2015. This is a major reduction in inequality. Eid and Aguirre, who analyse trends in both income and consumption inequality over 1999 to 2011, conclude that Bolivia was "the top performer in the Latin American region regarding income inequality reduction" during this period (Eid and Aguirre 2013, p. 75).

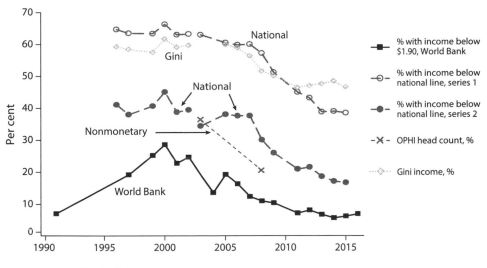

Figure BOL. Bolivia

The Plurinational State of Bolivia is a landlocked country in South America. Over a third of the population is classified as indigenous, and the name of the country was changed to reflect this in the new constitution of 2009. It is a lower-middle-income country according to the World Bank classification, with GNI per capita in 2015 of $3,000 (Atlas method) and $6,840 (PPP) and a population in that year of 10.7 million people.

BRAZIL

Poverty lines: The Instituto de Pesquisa Econômica Aplicada (IPEA) provides estimates of poverty in Brazil based on data for per capita household income from the long-running household survey Pesquisa Nacional por Amostra de Domicílios (PNAD). These figures, taken here from the IPEA website, are also included in the SEDLAC database. Series 1 relates to a "moderate" poverty line that is "twice the extreme poverty line, an estimate based on FAO and WHO recommendations" (www.ipeadata.gov.br, Proporção de pobres (P0)—Linha de Pobreza Baseada em Necessidades Calóricas) with different values of the line for twenty-four regions. Series 2 stems from the Brasil Sem Miseria (Brazil without Poverty) plan launched by the federal government in 2011, which uses cutoff points of R$70 income per capita to define families living in extreme poverty and R$140 to define those living in "moderate" poverty (the series shown in the graph). These two lines "are applied in all regions of Brazil and therefore do not take into account the existing differences in poverty between rural and urban areas, metropolitan and non-metropolitan regions . . . [the] values are not corrected annually: there is no established rule for updating the lines and they are not indexed to any type of variable, such as the minimum wage or the inflation rate" (Tronco and Ramos 2017, p. 295). The graph also shows a series from the SEDLAC database for the percentage of persons in households with income per capita beneath 50 per cent of the median (linked at 2004 to the "New PNAD" data series and linked at 1993 to the earlier PNAD series, on the assumption of no change between 1990 and 1992; see Atkinson et al. 2017, p. 14).

Poverty today: The World Bank estimates for 2015 show that 3.4 per cent of the population were living in households with incomes per head below $1.90 a day and that the poverty gap was 1.2 per cent. The national estimates show poverty rates of 15.1 per cent (series 1) and 9.0 per cent (series 2) for 2013, when the World Bank figure was 3.8 per cent.

Who is poor?

• Regional poverty rates in 2013 according to the official poverty line (series 1) show the country split into two halves: 6.7 per cent in the Centre-East, 6.9 per cent in the South, and 7.8 per cent in the South-East, but 25.8 per cent in the North and 28.8 per cent in the North-East.

Change over time:

Nonmonetary poverty: The OPHI Global MPI head count, based on deprivation according to a third or more of the weighted indicators, shows that 5.3 per cent of the population were in poor households in 2014 (estimate based on PNAD data). Split by rural and urban subpopulations, the rates were 12.0 and 4.1 per cent, respectively.

Overall inequality: The Gini coefficient for household equivalised income is from the SEDLAC database, linked at 2004 to the New PNAD data series, linked at 1993 to the earlier PNAD series, on the assumption of no change between 1990 and 1993 (see Atkinson et al. 2017, p. 14).

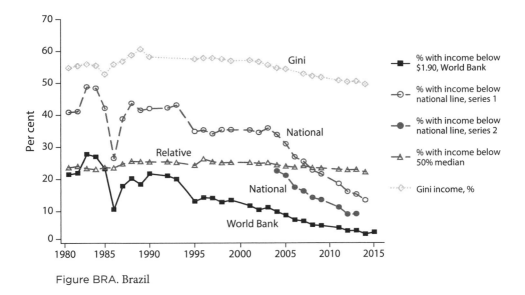

Figure BRA. Brazil

Brazil is an upper-middle-income country according to the World Bank classification, with GNI per capita in 2015 of $10,080 (Atlas method) and $15,020 (PPP) and a population in that year of 207.8 million people.

COLOMBIA

Poverty lines: National estimates of poverty are made by the Departamento Administrativo Nacional de Estadística (DANE), using an "extreme" poverty line that is the value of the basic food basket and a "moderate" poverty line taking into account in addition nonfood items based on the food share method. The moderate poverty line is updated annually with the consumer price index (CPI) relating to low-income households, and the extreme poverty line is adjusted with the CPI of just the food items for these households (DANE 2017). The "moderate" series is shown in the graph (taken from DANE 2017, p. 5; the same figures are given in the SEDLAC database). The welfare measure is income per capita as measured in the Gran Encuesta Integrada de Hogares (in 2002–2005 the Encuesta Continua de Hogares and before that the Encuesta Nacional de Hogares-Fuerza de Trabajo; see CEDLAS and World Bank 2014, p. 6). Relative poverty rates, not shown in the graph, are also given in the SEDLAC database.

Poverty today: The World Bank estimates for 2016 show that 4.5 per cent of the population were living in households with incomes per head below $1.90 a day and that the poverty gap was 1.8 per cent. The national estimates for the same year were 28.5 per cent for moderate poverty and 8.5 per cent for extreme poverty (DANE 2017, pp. 5 and 8).

Who is poor?

- For males, the poverty rate in 2016 according to the official poverty line (for "moderate" poverty) was 26.6 per cent; for females, it was 30.9 per cent.

- The poverty rate was 24.9 per cent for urban areas and 38.6 for rural areas.

Change over time:

Nonmonetary poverty: The OPHI Global MPI head count, based on deprivation according to a third or more of the weighted indicators, shows that 5.4 per cent of the population were in poor households in 2010 (estimate based on DHS data). Split by rural and urban subpopulations, the rates were 14.4 and 2.3 per cent, respectively. The harmonised time series of the head count (see editors' note) shows a decline in the national rate from 9.0 per cent in 2005 to 5.7 per cent in 2010. The graph also shows the national estimate of the nonmonetary poverty rate to be 17.8 per cent in 2016, compared to 30.4 per cent in 2010. (The estimates come from the SEDLAC database, "Official Poverty Estimates"; the same figures for 1997–2010 are in Salazar, Díaz, and Pinzón 2013, table 4; for 2010 onwards, see DANE 2017, p. 24). The measure is based on five dimensions (educational conditions of the home, conditions of childhood and youth, health, work, and access to home public services and housing conditions) involving fifteen indicators, and households with deprivation in at least a third of the weighted indicators are considered poor. The data used come from the Encuesta Nacional de Calidad de Vida.

Overall inequality: The Gini coefficient for income inequality has fallen modestly, from 56 per cent in 2002 to 51 per cent in 2012–2014.

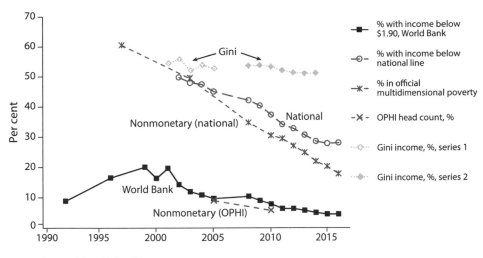

Figure COL. Colombia

Colombia is an upper-middle-income country according to the World Bank classification, with GNI per capita in 2015 of $7,130 (Atlas method) and $13,520 (PPP) and a population in that year of 48.2 million people.

DOMINICAN REPUBLIC

Poverty lines: Official poverty lines were calculated by the Ministerio de Economía, Planificación, y Desarrollo (MEPyD) and the Oficina Nacional de Estadística (ONE), following dissatisfaction with a variety of lines that had previously been used (MEPyD and ONE 2012), and are the basis for the poverty rate series estimated by ONE that start in 2000. (The SEDLAC database contains rates for 1992 and 1998 as well as those now estimated by ONE.) There are two poverty lines: an "extreme" line (series 1) and a "general" line (series 2). In 2015, the extreme poverty line (averaging March and September values) was RD$2,097.40 per person per month (equivalent to PPP$3.41 per person per day), and the general line was RD$4,555.80. Different poverty lines are set for urban and rural areas; for example, the extreme line in 2015 (average March and September values) was RD$2,125.90 in urban areas and RD$2,036.90 in rural areas (MEPyD and ONE 2015, figure A.4). The lines are adjusted using the Banco Central index of consumer prices. The lines were set using, in part, information collected in the 2007 survey Encuesta Nacional de Ingresos y Gastos de los Hogares. The extreme line represents the money needed to acquire a food basket providing 2,115 Cal in urban areas and 2,242 Cal in rural areas. The general line also takes into account the cost of nonfood goods and services considered essential, such as clothing and footwear, housing, home care, health, education, and transportation (see also the description in Aristy-Escuder 2017.) Poverty is measured using household disposable per capita income. The poverty rates shown in the graph are averages of rates for April and October taken from the ONE website in October 2016, which differ slightly from the rates for March and September given in MEPyD and ONE (2015, figure A.2); the rates are estimated with the Encuesta Nacional de Fuerza de Trabajo conducted by the Banco Central.

Poverty today: The World Bank estimates for 2016 show that 1.6 per cent of the population were living in households with incomes per head below $1.90 a day and that the poverty gap was 0.4 per cent. The poverty rate in 2015 according to the national extreme poverty line was 5.3 per cent (and 31.8 per cent according to the general line), when the World Bank figure was 1.9 per cent, reflecting the higher level of the national threshold.

Who is poor?

• The poverty rate in 2015 (average of March and September estimates) according to the "general" poverty line was 28.5 per cent in urban areas and 40.4 per cent in rural areas.

Change over time: A sharp rise in monetary poverty over 2002–2004 was associated with a surge in the inflation rate at a time of banking crisis (Aristy-Escuder 2017).

Nonmonetary poverty: The OPHI Global MPI head count, based on deprivation according to a third or more of the weighted indicators, shows that 8.8 per cent of the population were in poor households in 2014 (estimate based on MICS data). Split by rural and urban subpopulations, the rates were 11.7 and 7.9 per cent, respectively. The harmonised time series of the head count (see editors' note) shows a decline in the national rate, from 9.3 per cent in 2002 to 5.1 per cent in 2007.

Overall inequality: The Gini coefficient for household per capita income in 2015 was 45.6 per cent (averages of rates for March and September) (MEPyD and ONE 2015, figure A.3).

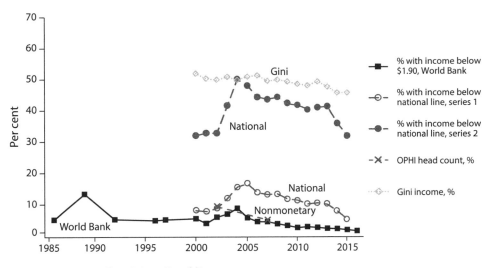

Figure DOM. Dominican Republic

The Dominican Republic occupies the eastern, and larger, part of the island of Hispaniola in the Caribbean. (The western part is occupied by Haiti.) It is the largest economy in the Caribbean. It is an upper-middle-income country according to the World Bank classification, with GNI per capita in 2015 of $6,240 (Atlas method) and $13,570 (PPP) and a population in that year of 10.5 million people.

GUATEMALA

Poverty lines:

Poverty today: The World Bank estimates for 2014 show that 8.7 per cent were living in households with incomes per head below $1.90 a day and that the poverty gap was 2.5 per cent.

Who is poor?

Change over time:

Nonmonetary poverty: The OPHI Global MPI head count, based on deprivation according to a third or more of the weighted indicators, shows that 24.8 per cent of the population were in poor households in 2014–2015 (estimate based on DHS data). Split by rural and urban subpopulations, the rates were 35.1 and 10.7 per cent, respectively.

Overall inequality:

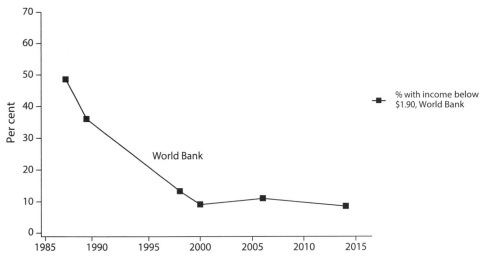

Figure GTM. Guatemala

Guatemala is a lower-middle-income country according to the World Bank classification, with GNI per capita in 2015 of $3,610 (Atlas method) and $7,510 (PPP) and a population in that year of 16.3 million people.

JAMAICA

Poverty lines: In 1988 the Planning Institute of Jamaica (PIOJ), together with the Ministry of Health, defined an official poverty line based on a minimum nutritional requirement of 11,225 Cal per day for a family of five, composed of one adult male, one adult female, an infant, a teenager, and a preteen child (Salmon 2002). The PIOJ constructs and costs a food basket for each of the three regions—the Kingston Metropolitan Area, other towns, and rural areas—to account for variation in prices across regions; this results in a food poverty line. Nonfood needs are incorporated into the overall poverty line by applying a multiplier (the reciprocal of the food share of quintile groups 1 and 2) to the food basket to arrive at the total poverty line for the family of five, which is then converted into a per adult equivalent poverty line to allow for differing needs based on gender and age (PIOJ 2011). (An adult male has a weight of 1.0, but an adult female has a weight of 0.74.) Poverty is measured with the Jamaica Survey of Living Conditions (JSLC), which is a subset of the Labour Force Survey, with household expenditure taken as the measure of welfare. The JSLC began in 1988, and estimates of poverty are available each year from 1990 (except in 2011, when the JSLC was not conducted); the series shown is taken from Ministry of Economic Growth and Job Creation (2016, appendix 7) and for 2013–2015 from the Statistical Institute of Jamaica website ("Living Conditions and Poverty" tables, downloaded July 2018). (The same figures, to 2012, are given in the SEDLAC database.)

Poverty today: The (dated) World Bank estimates for 2004 showed that 1.7 per cent of the population were living in households with consumption per head below $1.90 a day and that the poverty gap was 0.4 per cent. According to the national poverty line, 16.9 per cent of the population were poor in that year. The national estimate for 2015 was a poverty rate of 21.2 per cent. In 2012, when the overall poverty rate was 19.9 per cent, the rate of food poverty (household consumption beneath the food poverty line) was 7.5 per cent.

Who is poor?

- In 2015, the poverty rate according to the official poverty line was 14.3 per cent in the Kingston metropolitan area, 14.7 per cent in other towns, and 28.5 per cent in rural areas.

(Statistical Institute of Jamaica website).

Change over time: Poverty fell, according to the national estimate, from 19.7 per cent in 2002 to 9.9 per cent in 2007 before climbing back to 19.9 per cent in 2012. The rate has since remained at 20.0 per cent or higher.

Nonmonetary poverty: The OPHI Global MPI head count, based on deprivation according to a third or more of the weighted indicators, shows that 1.8 per cent of the population were in poor households in 2012 (estimate based on JSLC data). Split by rural and urban subpopulations, the rates were 2.5 and 1.1 per cent, respectively.

Overall inequality: The Gini coefficient for household per capita income was 59.9 per cent in 2002 (series taken from the SEDLAC database). The SEDLAC methods guide notes that "zero income report is a particularly relevant problem in Jamaica" (CEDLAS and World Bank 2014, p. 9).

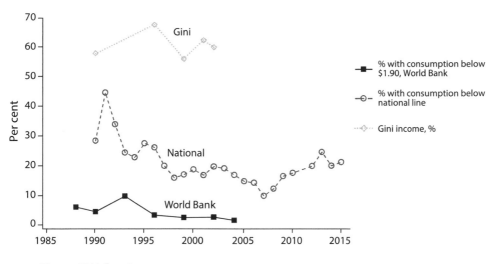

Figure JAM. Jamaica

Jamaica is an upper-middle-income country according to the World Bank classification, with GNI per capita in 2015 of $4,730 (Atlas method) and $8,860 (PPP) and a population in that year of 2.7 million people.

MEXICO

Poverty lines:

Poverty today: The World Bank estimates for 2016 show that 2.2 per cent of the population were living in households with income per head below $1.90 a day and that the poverty gap was 0.7 per cent. (Figures are also given in PovcalNet based on household consumption per head; see figure 8.3 in chapter 8.)

Who is poor?

Change over time:

Nonmonetary poverty: The OPHI Global MPI head count, based on deprivation according to a third or more of the weighted indicators, shows that 1.2 per cent of the population were in poor households in 2015 (estimate based on MICS data). Split by rural and urban subpopulations, the rates were 3.4 and 0.5 per cent, respectively.

Overall inequality:

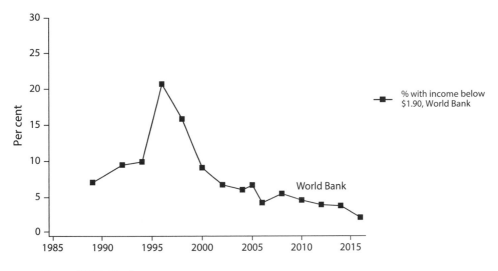

Figure MEX. Mexico

Mexico is an upper-middle-income country according to the World Bank classification, with GNI per capita in 2015 of $9,830 (Atlas method) and $17,150 (PPP) and a population in that year of 127.0 million people.

PANAMA

Poverty lines:

Poverty today: The World Bank estimates for 2016 show that 2.2 per cent of the population were living in households with incomes per head below $1.90 a day and that the poverty gap was 0.5 per cent.

Who is poor?

Change over time:

Nonmonetary poverty: Panama is not included in the countries covered by OPHI.

Overall inequality:

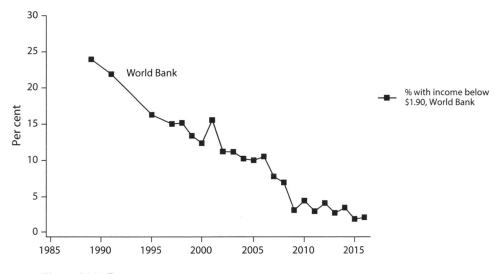

Figure PAN. Panama

Panama is an upper-middle-income country according to the World Bank classification with GNI per capita in 2015 of $11,730 (Atlas method) and $20,710 (PPP) and a population in that year of 3.9 million people.

PERU

Poverty line:

Poverty today: The World Bank estimates for 2016 show that 3.5 per cent of the population were living in households with incomes per head below $1.90 a day and that the poverty gap was 0.9 per cent.

Who is poor?

Change over time:

Nonmonetary poverty: The OPHI Global MPI head count, based on deprivation according to a third or more of the weighted indicators, shows that 10.5 per cent of the population were in poor households in 2012 (estimate based on the Continuous DHS data [see Rutstein and Way 2014]). Split by rural and urban subpopulations, the rates were 27.1 and 2.9 per cent, respectively. The harmonised time series of the head count (see editors' note) shows a decline in the national rate, from 19.5 per cent in 2005 to 10.5 per cent in 2012.

Overall inequality:

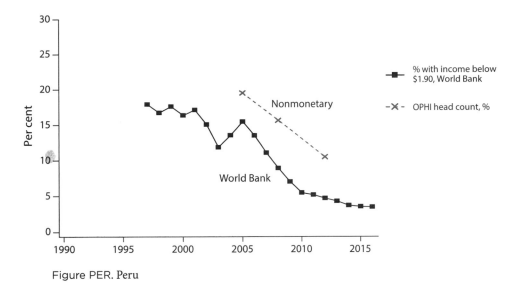

Figure PER. Peru

Peru is an upper-middle-income country according to the World Bank classification, with GNI per capita in 2015 of $6,150 (Atlas method) and $11,960 (PPP) and a population in that year of 31.4 million people.

TRINIDAD AND TOBAGO

Poverty lines:

Poverty today: The most recent World Bank estimate available is for 1992, which shows that 3.4 per cent of the population were living in households with incomes per head below $1.90 a day and that the poverty gap was 0.9 per cent.

Who is poor?

Change over time:

Nonmonetary poverty: The OPHI Global MPI head count, based on deprivation according to a third or more of the weighted indicators, shows that 5.6 per cent of the population were in poor households in 2006 (estimate based on MICS data). Split by rural and urban subpopulations, the rates were 5.7 and 5.4 per cent, respectively.

Overall inequality:

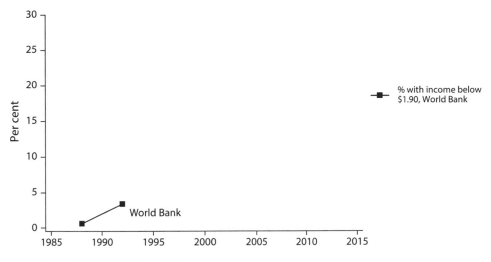

Figure TTO. Trinidad and Tobago

Trinidad and Tobago is a high-income country according to the World Bank classification, with GNI per capita in 2015 of $17,640 (Atlas method) and $29,630 (PPP) and a population in that year of 1.4 million people.

URUGUAY

Poverty lines:

Poverty today: The World Bank estimates for 2016 show that 0.1 per cent of the population were living in households with incomes per head below $1.90 a day and that the poverty gap was less than 0.1 per cent.

Who is poor?

Change over time:

Nonmonetary poverty: Uruguay is not included in the countries covered by OPHI.

Overall inequality:

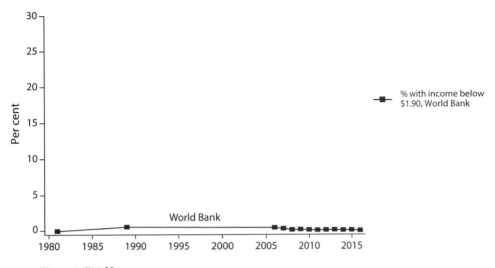

Figure URY. Uruguay

Uruguay is a high-income country according to the World Bank classification, with GNI per capita in 2015 of $15,830 (Atlas method) and $20,360 (PPP) and a population in that year of 3.4 million people.

National poverty reports for chapter 9

AUSTRALIA

Poverty lines: Australia does not have an official poverty line, but a basic needs standard was established in 1973 by the official Henderson inquiry (1975), and this is regularly updated by the Melbourne Institute of Applied Economic and Social Research (2016). For March 2016, the standard for a benchmark family of a couple (one working) and two dependent children was PPP$23.63 per day per person. Use is made of relative poverty lines—see Australian Council of Social Service (ACOSS) (2013)—such as 40 or 60 per cent of median household equivalised disposable income. In 2010, the 40 per cent of the median standard corresponded to PPP$30.64.

Poverty today: World Bank estimates show that in 2010, 0.4 per cent of the population were living in households with incomes per head below $1.90 a day and that the poverty gap was 0.3 per cent. In terms of relative poverty, the LIS Key Figures show that in that year 5.9 per cent were living in households with equivalised disposable income less than 40 per cent of the median, and 21.2 per cent below 60 per cent of the median. The LIS data are obtained from the Survey of Income and Housing, now conducted every two years, combined in 2010 with the Household Expenditure Survey.

Who is poor?

- The poverty rate is higher for children (7.0 per cent were living in households below 40 per cent of the median in 2010) and for the elderly (the corresponding figure was 8.0 per cent) (LIS Key Figures).

- For the disabled (those with a core activity restriction), the proportion living in households below 60 per cent of the median in 2012 was 44.5 per cent, compared with 19.7 per cent for the population aged fifteen and over (ACOSS 2013, table 4).

- According to ACOSS, "Aboriginal and Torres Strait Islander people were more likely to experience poverty than other Australians, with 19.3% of Aboriginal and Torres Strait Islander people living below the poverty line, compared with 12.4% of other Australians" (ACOSS 2013, p. 44, based on data from the Household, Income, and Labour Dynamics in Australia [HILDA] Survey).

- In 2010, "adults born in countries where English is not the main language faced a much higher risk of poverty (15.8% using the 50% poverty line) than those born in Australia (10.6%), or in an English speaking country (11.7%)" (ACOSS 2013, p. 44).

Change over time: The proportion below 40 per cent in 2010 was fractionally higher than thirty years earlier, and the proportion below 60 per cent of the median was 2.9 percentage points higher.

Nonmonetary poverty: A survey of multiple deprivation, the Poverty and Exclusion in Modern Australia (PEMA) survey, measured the proportion of households lacking items which a majority considered essential and also reported that they could not afford. In 2010, 15 per cent of households reported deprivation in at least three of the twenty-four items (ACOSS 2013, p. 52).

Overall inequality: Over the past thirty years, there has been a rise in the inequality of equivalised disposable household income as measured by the Gini coefficient. This followed a period from 1950 to 1978 when income inequality, measured by taxable and, later, gross income, had been falling. (Data are from the Australian Bureau of Statistics website [downloaded 10 October 2016], table 1.1, series 6523.0, where account has been taken of the change in methodology in 2007–2008 [see Wilkins 2014] by calculating a figure for that year based on the change in the estimates obtained on the "former basis" [1.2 percentage points] from table A7 of the 2007–2008 report, and then subtracting the difference (one percentage point) from the estimates for subsequent years; it has been linked at 1995 to series from LIS Key Figures. The series for gross income, which is not comparable, is from Hancock (1971, table 4).

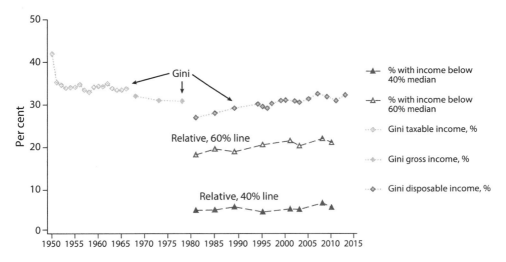

Figure AUS. Australia

Australia is a high-income country according to the World Bank classification, with GNI per capita in 2015 of $60,180 (Atlas method) and $44,570 (PPP) and a population in that year of 23.8 million people.

CANADA

Poverty lines: Canada does not have an official poverty line. Statistics Canada has published since 1967 low-income cut-offs (LICOs), based on the income threshold at which family spending on food, shelter, and clothing is more than 20 per cent higher than that of the average family. In 2014, the resulting cutoffs for a family of four adjusted by a square root equivalence scale (the square root of household size) varied from PPP$27.77 in rural areas to PPP$42.45 in cities of over 500,000 (calculated from table 206-0094, Statistics Canada CANSIM website). In addition, there is the market basket measure (MBM) developed by Employment and Social Development Canada (ESDC), first published for the 2000 reference year, representing a modest, basic standard of living for a reference family of two adults and two children (Hatfield, Pyper, and Gustajtis 2010). In 2014, the amount varied according to location from PPP$35.72 to PPP$44.16 (calculated from Statistics Canada, table 206-0093). Since 1991, Statistics Canada has published low-income statistics (LIM) showing the number of persons living in households which have equivalised (using the square root scale) household income below 50 per cent of the median adjusted income. In 2014, the amount for a household of four, equivalised by the square root scale, was PPP$48.50 per person per day (calculated from Statistics Canada, table 206-0091). The graph shows series for LICO and LIM but not for MBM.

Poverty today: World Bank estimates show that in 2013, 0.3 per cent of the population were living in households with incomes per head below $1.90 a day and that the poverty gap was 0.2 per cent. In terms of the different poverty standards described above, in 2014 there were 8.8 per cent of the population living in families below the LICOs, and 13.0 per cent were living in households with equivalised disposable income less than 50 per cent of the median (LIM). (The data are obtained from the Canadian Income Survey, previously the Survey of Labour and Income Dynamics, and the Survey of Consumer Finances.)

Who is poor?

- According to the LIM data, the poverty rate in 2014 was higher for those under eighteen years, being 14.7 per cent, compared with 12.6 per cent for those aged eighteen to sixty-four years and 12.5 per cent for those aged sixty-five and over. With the lower LICO standard, in contrast, the poverty rate in 2014 was 8.5 per cent for those aged under eighteen years, compared with 10.0 per cent for those aged eighteen to sixty-four years; the rate for those aged sixty-five years and over was 3.9 per cent.

- "The short-term variations in the low-income rates appeared to follow business cycles closely" (Murphy, Dionne, and Zhang 2012, p. 14).

- "The low-income rate among new immigrants was relatively low in the 1970s. It had tripled by the mid 1990s and declined substantially since then. In more recent years, however, the low-income rate for new immigrants started an upward trend" (Murphy, Dionne, and Zhang 2012, p. 36).

- In 2006, the census shows for all children a poverty rate (LIM measure) of 17 per cent, but 40 per cent among indigenous children, rising to 50 per cent for First Nations children (Macdonald and Wilson 2013, p. 13).

Change over time: The proportion below the LICO standard in 2014 was 8.8 per cent, compared with 13.0 per cent in 1976, so that there had been a definite reduction. In contrast, the proportion below the LIM (50 per cent of the median) in 2014 showed no change compared with 1976. Under both LICO and LIM, "dramatic declines in low-income rates for seniors occurred from the late 1970s to the mid 1990s" (Murphy, Dionne, and Zhang 2012, p. 29).

Nonmonetary poverty:

Overall inequality: Over the postwar period, from 1950 to 1995, there was no evident trend in inequality of equivalised disposable household income as measured by the Gini coefficient. There followed a rise, and the Gini coefficient in 2014 is some two percentage points higher than twenty years earlier (Statistics Canada, table 206-0033, for 1976 to 2014 [series 1]; Wolfson 1986, table 3, for Gini coefficient for equivalised gross family income for 1965 to 1983 [series 2]; Love 1979, table A.3, for Gini coefficient for gross family income restricted to nonfarm families for 1959–1971[series 3]).

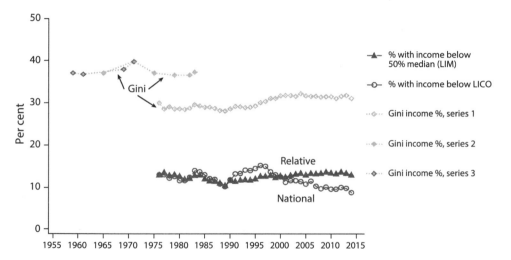

Figure CAN. Canada

Canada is a high-income country according to the World Bank classification, with GNI per capita in 2015 of $47,270 (Atlas method) and $43,970 (PPP) and a population in that year of 35.9 million people.

FINLAND

Poverty lines: Persons are classified as being at-risk-of-poverty when the household's equivalised (using modified OECD scale) disposable monetary income per consumption unit is below 60 per cent of the national median. In 2014, this was €14,300 annual income for a single person, which corresponded to PPP$42.42 per day per person.

Poverty today: World Bank estimates show that in 2015 fewer than 0.1 per cent of persons were living in households with incomes per head below $1.90 a day. In terms of the national definition, in 2014, 12.5 per cent were living in households with equivalised disposable income (OECD modified equivalence scale) less than 60 per cent of the median, and 2.3 per cent below 40 per cent of the median (Statistics Finland website, table 281_tjt_tau_052.xlsx [downloaded 26 October 2016]).

Who is poor?

• The poverty rate is lower for children, with 10.0 per cent living in households below 60 per cent of the median in 2014, and the elderly, for whom the corresponding figures were 8.0 per cent (aged sixty-five to seventy-four) and 22.2 per cent (aged seventy-five and over).

• In 2014, 12.8 per cent of women were living in households below 60 per cent of the median, compared to 12.2 per cent of men.

Change over time: The proportion below 60 per cent of the median has risen since 1993: in 2014 the poverty rate was five percentage points higher than twenty years earlier. This followed a period from 1971 to 1993 when the poverty rate fell by fourteen percentage points.

Nonmonetary poverty: The Eurostat indicator shows that 2.2 per cent of persons were suffering severe material deprivation (four or more items out of nine) in 2016 and 8.3 per cent were suffering deprivation (three or more items out of nine) (the series shown in the graph). In 2014, according to Statistics Finland, 2.5 per cent of persons lived in households that reported that they could make ends meet only "with great difficulty," and a total of 24.2 per cent reported at least "some difficulty" doing so (that is, the total that reported having "great difficulty," "difficulty," or "some difficulty" making ends meet) (Statistics Finland website, "Quality report: Income distribution statistics").

Overall inequality: Inequality of equivalised disposable household income as measured by the Gini coefficient rose by five percentage points between 1987 and 2000. This followed a period from 1966 to 1987 when income inequality had been falling. (Gini coefficient of equivalised [OECD modified scale] household disposable cash income from 1966 is from Statistics Finland, "Income and consumption: Income distribution statistics"; the figures for 1966–1981, 1987–1992, and 1993 are not fully comparable, and the figures prior to 2002 use the OECD equivalence scale. From 2011 onwards, Statistics Finland uses households' disposable money income as the main concept. Imputed income from owner-occupied dwellings and taxable realised capital gains are excluded.)

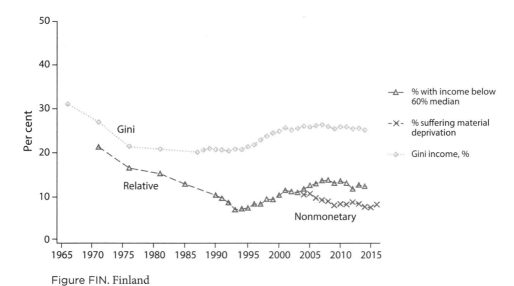

Figure FIN. Finland

Finland is a high-income country according to the World Bank classification, with GNI per capita in 2015 of $46,530 (Atlas method) and $40,840 (PPP) and a population in that year of 5.5 million people.

FRANCE

Poverty lines: The monetary line in France is expressed as a percentage (40, 50, and 60 per cent) of median household equivalised (using the modified OECD scale) disposable income. In 2014, 50 per cent of the median equivalised disposable income was €840 per month, or PPP$33.73 per person per day.

Poverty today: World Bank estimates show that in 2015 fewer than 0.1 per cent of the population were living in households with incomes per head below $1.90 a day. In 2014, 14.1 per cent of the population were living in households below 60 per cent of the median. (Observatoire des inégalités website, downloaded 1 October 2016; figures recalculated to allow for the changes in methodology in 2010 and 2012).

Who is poor?

- In 2013, 19.6 per cent of children younger than eighteen years were living in households below 60 per cent of the median, compared with 14.0 per cent for the population as a whole.

- In 2013, 7.9 per cent of pensioners were living in households below 60 per cent of the median, compared with 10.5 per cent for the active population aged eighteen and over.

- In 2014, 14.7 per cent of women were living in households below 60 per cent of the median, compared with 13.4 per cent of men.

- In 2014, 35.9 per cent of those living in single-parent families were below 60 per cent of the median.

Change over time: The percentage living in households below 60 per cent of the median fell from 1970 to the mid-1980s, but since then there is no apparent trend.

Nonmonetary poverty: The Eurostat indicator shows that 4.4 per cent of persons were suffering severe material deprivation (four or more items out of nine) in 2016, and 11.0 per cent were suffering material deprivation (three or more items out of nine) (the series shown in the graph). The national indicator showed that in 2012, 11.9 per cent of the population were suffering material deprivation.

Overall inequality: The Gini coefficient of equivalised (modified OECD scale) disposable household income in 2014 was 29.3 per cent. The Gini coefficient fell by five percentage points from 1970 to 1990, but has shown no sign of falling since that time (Observatoire des inégalités website, downloaded 5 October 2016).

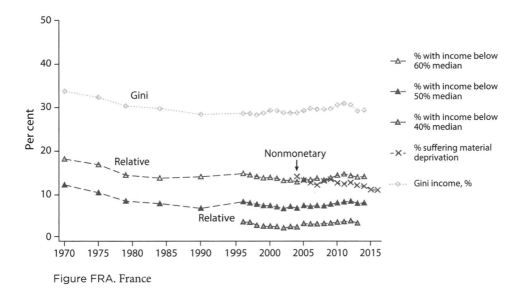

Figure FRA. France

France is a high-income country according to the World Bank classification, with GNI per capita in 2015 of $40,730 (Atlas method) and $40,470 (PPP) and a population in that year of 66.8 million people.

GERMANY

Poverty lines: The relative poverty line is set at 60 per cent of median household equiv-alised monthly disposable income. In 2013, the 60 per cent standard was PPP$37.24.

Poverty today: The World Bank estimates show that in 2015 fewer than 0.1 per cent of persons were living in households with incomes per head below $1.90 a day per per-son. In terms of relative poverty, the national Deutsche Institut für Wirtschaftsforsc-hung (DIW) figures show that in 2013, 14.2 per cent of persons were living in house-holds with equivalised (modified OECD scale) monthly disposable income less than 60 per cent of the median (this is the series shown in figure DEU). The Eurostat figures based on European Statistics on Income and Living Conditions (EU-SILC) show that 16.5 per cent of persons were living in 2015 in households with equivalised (modified OECD scale) disposable income less than 60 per cent of the median. (DIW figures for all Germany [West Germany from 1984 to 1990] are from SOEP Group 2015, p. 88, linked at 1983 via data on poverty in previous year to series from Becker [1997, table 2] for percentage of individuals in households with equivalised [original OECD scale] dis-posable household income below 50 per cent of the mean for all persons of German nationality in private households for West Germany; EU-SILC figures are from Euro-stat website, series tessi010, downloaded 1 July 2018.)

Who is poor?

- According to the EU-SILC estimates, in 2015 the poverty rate for children was 15.4 per cent and the rate for persons aged sixty-five and over was 17.6 per cent; the rate for those aged eighteen to sixty-four was 16.4 per cent.

- The EU-SILC data for 2015 show that 17.8 per cent of women were living in households below 60 per cent of the median, compared with 15.2 per cent of men.

Change over time: The proportion below 60 per cent of the median in 2013 was two percentage points higher than thirty years earlier.

Nonmonetary poverty: The Eurostat indicator shows that 3.7 per cent of persons were suffering severe material deprivation (four or more items out of nine) in 2016, and 9.7 per cent were suffering deprivation (three or more items out of nine) (the series shown in the graph).

Overall inequality: Income inequality as measured by the Gini coefficient was fall-ing from 1950 to the early 1970s, and then stabilised. From 2001, the Gini coefficient began to rise and today is some three percentage points higher than at the start of the century. (In series 1, the Gini coefficient of equivalised [modified OECD scale] monthly disposable household income for all persons in private households for all Germany [West Germany until 1990] is from SOEP Group 2015, p. 80; in series 2, data from the Income and Expenditure Survey [EVS] for West Germany are from Becker [1997], table 1, and Hauser and Becker [2001], p. 89.)

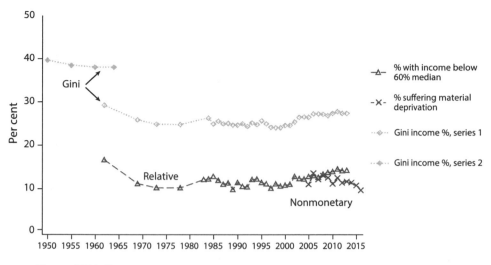

Figure DEU. Germany

Germany is a high-income country according to the World Bank classification, with GNI per capita in 2015 of $45,790 (Atlas method) and $48,260 (PPP) and a population in that year of 81.4 million people.

GREECE

Poverty lines: The poverty line applied in Greece is the EU standard set at 60 per cent of median household equivalised (using the modified OECD scale) disposable income. In 2014, the threshold was €4,512 per person per year, or PPP$20.31 per person per day.

Poverty today: The World Bank estimates for 2015 show that 1.5 per cent of the population were living in households with incomes per head below $1.90 a day, and that the poverty gap was 0.8 per cent. The Eurostat figures based on EU-SILC show that in 2016, 20.2 per cent were living in households with equivalised (modified OECD scale) disposable income less than 60 per cent of the median.

Who is poor?

- According to EU-SILC estimates, the proportion of women living in households below 60 per cent of the median in 2016 was equal to the proportion of men, at 20.2 per cent.

- In 2016 the poverty rate for children was 24.5 per cent, almost double that amongst persons aged sixty-five and over (12.5 per cent); the poverty rate for those aged eighteen to sixty-four was 21.7 per cent.

- The poverty rate for single-parent families in 2016 was 30.5 per cent.

- For the unemployed, the poverty rate in 2016 was 45.6 per cent.

Changes over time: The poverty rate fell, unevenly, from 1974 to the mid-2000s, but after the economic crisis in 2008 the poverty rate rose by three percentage points. The percentage suffering material deprivation more than doubled after 2008 (series 1 [monetary poverty]: Mitrakos and Tsakoglou 2012; series 2: Eurostat website, series tessi010, downloaded 1 July 2018).

Nonmonetary poverty: The Eurostat indicator shows that 39.0 per cent of persons were suffering material deprivation in 2016 (three or more items out of nine) and that 22.4 per cent were suffering severe material deprivation (four or more items out of nine).

Overall inequality: Measured by Gini coefficient, income inequality fell from 1974 to 1982, after which there was no evident trend (series 1: Mitrakos and Tsakoglou 2012; series 2 and 3: Eurostat website).

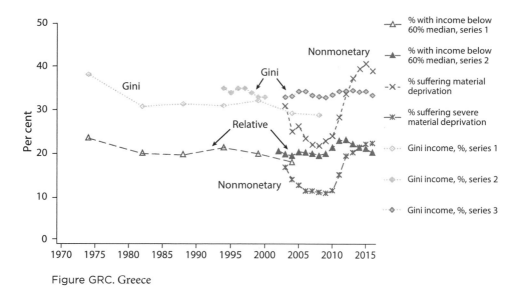

Figure GRC. Greece

Greece is a high-income country according to the World Bank classification, with GNI per capita in 2015 of $20,270 (Atlas method) and $26,790 (PPP) and a population in that year of 10.8 million people.

IRELAND

Poverty lines: The monetary line in Ireland calculated by the Central Statistical Office (CSO) is expressed as 60 per cent of median household equivalised (using the modified OECD scale) disposable income. In 2014, 60 per cent of the median equivalised disposable income was €10,926 per year, or PPP$36.10 per person per day. The CSO calculates the proportion of people living in households suffering multiple deprivation, defined as the enforced lack of two or more items from a list of eleven indicators. The monetary and nonmonetary indicators are combined in a measure of "consistent" poverty that determines the proportion of the population living in households both materially deprived and below the monetary poverty line; this is the official measure of poverty in Ireland. The CSO also calculates monetary poverty rates based on anchored relative poverty lines, and the graph shows the series for the percentage of persons living in households with equivalised disposable income below 60 per cent of the 2004 median.

Poverty today: World Bank estimates for 2014 show that 0.5 per cent of the population were living in households with incomes per head below $1.90 a day and that the poverty gap was 0.3 per cent. In the same year, 16.3 per cent of the population lived in households with equivalised disposable income less than 60 per cent of the median (data from EU-SILC, downloaded from the CSO website, October 2016 and August 2018; augmented from Nolan et al. 2014, table 15.3).

Who is poor?

- According to all three measures, the poverty rate in 2014 was higher for those under eighteen years of age, being 18.6 per cent for monetary poverty, 36.1 per cent for material deprivation, and 11.2 per cent for consistent poverty.

- The poverty rate for those aged sixty-five years and over was lower for all three measures, being 10.3 per cent for monetary poverty, 14.3 per cent for material deprivation, and 2.1 per cent for consistent poverty.

- Monetary poverty rate in 2014 was higher in rural areas (19.1 per cent) than in urban areas (14.6 per cent).

- Monetary poverty rate in 2014 was much higher where the head of household was unemployed (35.9 per cent).

Change over time: The monetary poverty rate in the 2000s fell significantly (by seven percentage points) during the period of rapid growth before the 2008 crisis, and this was mirrored in the consistent poverty measure. The fall came to an end after 2008. Relative monetary poverty remained broadly stable, but median incomes were falling, and poverty measured at an anchored threshold rose. Declining living standards were reflected in the sharp rise in the proportion living in households suffering material deprivation, leading to a doubling of consistent poverty.

Nonmonetary poverty: The Eurostat indicator shows that 15.5 per cent of persons were suffering material deprivation in 2016 (three or more items out of nine) and that 6.5 per cent were suffering severe material deprivation (four or more items out of nine). The national estimates (the series in the graph) show that the multiple deprivation rate in 2014 was higher than the monetary poverty rate at 29.0 per cent, and the intersection of the two in the consistent poverty rate was 8.0 per cent.

Overall inequality: Measured by Gini coefficient of equivalised (modified OECD scale) disposable household income from the CSO website and Nolan et al. (2014, table 15.1). Overall income inequality has fluctuated, but was little different in 2014 from twenty years earlier.

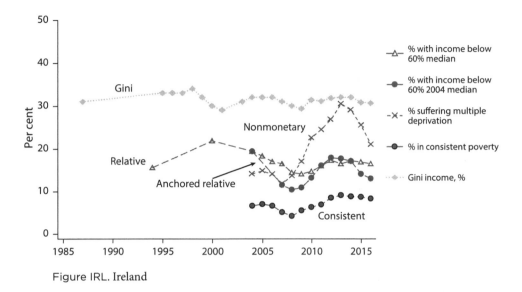

Figure IRL. Ireland

The Republic of Ireland covers five-sixths of the island of Ireland. (The remainder of the island, Northern Ireland, is part of the United Kingdom.) It is a high-income country according to the World Bank classification, with GNI per capita in 2015 of $51,630 (Atlas method) and $46,410 (PPP) and a population in that year of 4.6 million people.

ITALY

Poverty lines: Italy is an exception among high-income countries in that traditionally it estimates poverty using consumption. Since the 1980s, the national statistical office (Istat) computes a relative line, taking per capita expenditure (total expenditure divided by total sample size of persons) as the threshold for a childless couple (following Beckerman 1980). Thresholds for other households are derived with an equivalence scale (Carbonaro 1985) that assigns 0.60 to a single-member household, 1.33 to three-member households, 1.63 to four-member households, 1.90 to five-member households, 2.16 to six-member households, and 2.40 to households with seven or more members. Since 1997, Istat has also computed an absolute line set to the cost of a socially necessary basket of goods; currently, this varies by household size, members' ages, municipality size, and location (Istat 2009) and is adjusted over time using price indices specific for the main components of the basket and location. Both relative and absolute measures are based on the Household Budget Survey. Its revision in 2014 led to considerable falls in poverty rates (see chapter 4); Istat's backward estimation accounting for the revision gives rates for earlier years shown in the graph. Relative poverty rates are also estimated from household incomes by both Istat (EU-SILC and the former European Community Household Panel [ECHP], series 1) and the Bank of Italy (Survey of Household Income and Wealth [SHIW], series 2) with a threshold of 60 per cent of median household disposable income equivalised with the modified OECD scale. (The Bank of Italy includes respondents' estimates of imputed rents on owner-occupied homes; Istat does not.) In 2016, the lines for a single person were €637 per month for the relative expenditure measure; between €492 for an old person in a small town in the South and €818 for a young person in a city in the North for the absolute expenditure measure; €812 for the Istat income measure (in 2015); and €829 for the Bank of Italy income measure in 2016 (there was no survey in 2015). There is no official poverty line, but the absolute poverty rate is one of twelve equitable and sustainable well-being indicators that after 2018 are to be evaluated together with GDP by the Ministry of Economy and Finance in its economic planning.

Poverty today: The World Bank estimates show that in 2014, 1.2 per cent of persons were living in households with income below $1.90 a day per person, with a poverty gap of 0.9 per cent. National estimates range widely due to differences in source, methodology, and focus (consumption or income). In 2016 the poverty rate was 7.9 per cent with the consumption-based absolute line and 14.0 per cent with the consumption-based relative line. With an income-based relative line, the rate rises to 20.6 per cent with the EU-SILC data (2015) and to 22.9 per cent with the SHIW data (Istat and Eurostat websites, downloaded 4 March 2018; Banca d'Italia 2018, based on SHIW Historical Archive, v.10.0).

Who is poor? According to expenditure-based estimates, the recent rise in poverty mainly concerned households with children. In 2016 the absolute poverty rate for children was 12.5 per cent and that for persons aged sixty-five and over was 3.8 per cent, with rates of 10.0 per cent for those aged eighteen to thirty-four and 7.3 per cent for those aged thirty-five to sixty-four, reversing the relative positions of ten years earlier. Rates are much higher for households with foreigners (25.7 per cent for all-foreigner households, 27.4 per cent for mixed households) than for households of natives (4.4 per cent) (Istat website, downloaded 4 March 2018).

Change over time: The consumption-based estimates show modest variations from the mid-1990s to the Great Recession of 2008–2009. Despite the collapse in output and family incomes, the recession had little effect on poverty. The subsequent sovereign debt crisis in 2011–2012 caused instead a sharp and persistent rise, especially in absolute poverty. Variation over time is more limited for income-based estimates, but the picture is qualitatively similar. With all measures, the proportion of poor people in 2016 was two to three percentage points higher than twenty years earlier.

Nonmonetary poverty: The Eurostat indicator shows 12.1 per cent of the population suffering severe material deprivation (four or more items out of nine) in 2016; 20.6 per cent were suffering deprivation (three or more items out of nine) (the series in the graph), down almost five percentage points from the peak in 2012. The sharp increase between 2010 and 2011 was mostly driven by the fact that households already facing difficulties in paying for unexpected expenses or going on a one-week holiday away from home or keeping their home adequately warm also found it difficult to afford to eat meat, fish, or a protein equivalent as often as every second day (Istat 2012 and 2013).

Overall inequality: The Gini coefficient for income in the SHIW fell from the 1970s to reach a historical low in the early 1980s (Brandolini and Vecchi 2013). The Gini (series 2) rose abruptly between 1991 and 1993 and then oscillated during the next two decades (Brandolini, Gambacorta, and Rosolia 2018). Figures from EU-SILC are broadly in line (series 1) (Eurostat and Bank of Italy websites, downloaded 12 March 2018).

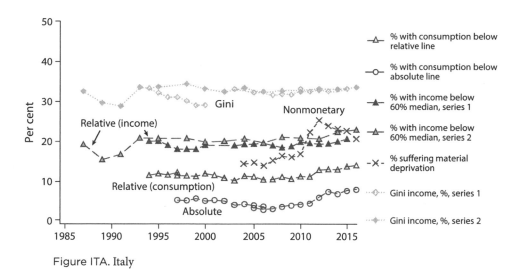

Figure ITA. Italy

Italy is a high-income country according to the World Bank classification, with GNI per capita in 2015 of $32,970 (Atlas method) and $35,850 (PPP) and a population in that year of 60.8 million people.

JAPAN

Poverty lines: Japan had no official poverty line for many years, but since 2009 government reports have provided estimates of relative poverty based on data from the Comprehensive Survey of Living Conditions (Noda 2015).

Poverty today: The World Bank estimates for 2008 show that 0.35 per cent of the population were living in households with incomes per head below $1.90 a day, and that the poverty gap was 0.17 per cent. There were 16.1 per cent of the population living in households below 50 per cent of equivalised post–tax and transfer median income in 2012 (equivalising by the square root of the number of household members). The series on this basis in the graph is from the online OECD database, OECD. Stat (downloaded March 2018), and, for 1988, 1991, and 1997, from Noda (2015, figure 1), who draws on reports of the Ministry of Health, Labour, and Welfare. (Noda shows the OECD's figure for 1995 as relating to 1994.) Three of the same estimates are given in OECD (2008, annex table 5.A2.1) and OECD (2015, table 1.A1.1), although the years to which the estimates refer differ in the latter publication. The series for the percentage under 60 per cent of the median is from OECD.Stat.

Who is poor?

- The relative poverty rate (those living in households below 50 per cent of the median) in 2012 was 16.3 per cent for children (aged zero to seventeen), 19.7 per cent for adults aged eighteen to twenty-five, 12.9 per cent for adults aged twenty-six to forty, 14.1 per cent for adults aged forty-one to fifty, 14.4 per cent for adults aged fifty-one to sixty-five, 17.0 per cent for adults aged sixty-six to seventy-five, and 21.3 per cent for adults aged seventy-six and over (OECD.Stat).

- In 2012, the rate on the same basis for "the working generation with children was 15.1%, within which the rate for households with one adult was 54.6% whereas that for households with two or more adults was 12.4%" (Noda 2015, p. 14).

Change over time: The proportion below 50 per cent of the median in 2012 was 16.1 per cent, four percentage points higher than in 1985.

Nonmonetary poverty: Estimates of multidimensional poverty for households with two or more persons have been made by Matsuyama (2016, table 6), following the Alkire-Foster method and using the National Survey of Family Income and Expenditure for 1989, 1994, 1999, and 2004. The dimensions considered are consumption, wealth, and dwelling environment, measured by four indicators (nondurable expenditure, possession of ten different items, level of savings, and living space). The dimensions include monetary indicators, and the resulting estimates are not therefore of nonmonetary poverty alone. The series in the graph is the proportion of persons (in households with two or more people) deprived in one or more indicators, and it falls from 16.6 per cent in 1989 to 9.2 per cent in 2004.

Overall inequality: In series 1, the Gini coefficient for equivalised disposable household income from 1981 is taken from the research of Lise et al. (2014), using data from the Family Income and Expenditure Survey (FIES), linked at 1981 to series from Tachibanaki (2005, table 1.1) that are based on the Income Redistribution Survey. In series 2, the Gini coefficient for equivalised disposable household income is from Fukawa (2006, table 1). In series 3, the Gini coefficient for equivalised disposable household income is from OECD (2015, table 1.A1.1) and OECD (2011, table A.1).

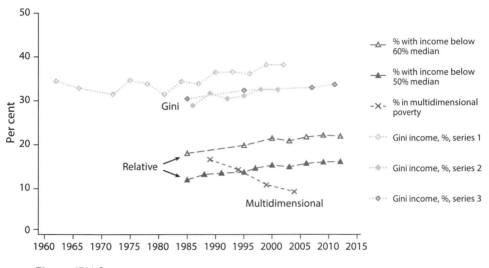

Figure JPN. Japan

Japan is a high-income country according to the World Bank classification, with GNI per capita in 2015 of $38,780 (Atlas method) and $38,870 (PPP) and a population in that year of 127.0 million people.

KOREA

Poverty lines:

Poverty today: The World Bank estimates for 2012 show that 0.3 per cent of the population were living in households with incomes per head below $1.90 a day, and that the poverty gap was 0.1 per cent.

Who is poor?

Change over time:

Nonmonetary poverty:

Overall inequality:

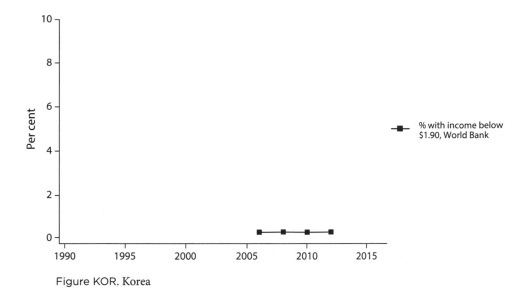

Figure KOR. Korea

The Republic of Korea (South Korea) is a high-income country according to the World Bank classification, with GNI per capita in 2015 of $27,250 (Atlas method) and $34,700 (PPP) and a population in that year of 50.6 million people.

NEW ZEALAND

Poverty lines: New Zealand does not have an official poverty line, but publications of the Ministry of Social Development have made use of measures based on the number of people in households below a specified percentage of median equivalised income, either the contemporary median or the median anchored at a point in time (Perry 2015). In 2014, the standard of 60 per cent of the median for a household of a couple and two dependent children was PPP$22.53 per day per person. The equivalence scale used is the "1988 Revised Jensen Scale" (Perry 2016, p. 12), which is close to the modified OECD scale.

Poverty today: The official estimates for 2015 show that 18 per cent of the population were living in households with equivalised disposable income less than 60 per cent of the median, and 10 per cent below 50 per cent of the median. The data are obtained from the Household Economic Survey. The series shown in the graph is for the percentage of the population below 60 per cent of the contemporary median before housing costs (Perry 2016, table F.3, which also gives figures based on 50 per cent of the contemporary median and on both bases for the median anchored in 2007).

Who is poor?

- The poverty rate, measured in terms of income, is a little higher for children: in 2015, 21 per cent were living in households below 60 per cent of the median.

- "Poverty rates for those in the Maori and Pacific ethnic groups are consistently higher than for those in the European/Pakeha ethnic group (roughly double), whatever measure is used" (Perry 2015, p. 112).

- "One third of those in the low-income group have post-school non-degree qualifications, even though the low-income rate for this group is much lower than that for the group with no formal qualifications, now a relatively small group" (Perry 2015, p. 113).

Change over time: In 2015, the proportion below 60 per cent of the median was four percentage points higher than thirty years earlier.

Nonmonetary poverty: The Ministry of Social Development publishes estimates of the extent of nonmonetary deprivation, based on the Material Well-being Index (Perry 2016a). These show that the proportion of the population in households in "less severe" deprivation (equivalent to seven or more deprivations out of seventeen) rose between 2007–2008 and 2011, from 10 per cent to 13 per cent, and then fell to 8 per cent in 2014–2015. The corresponding figures for "more severe" (nine or more deprivations out of seventeen) are 4 per cent, 6 per cent, and 5 per cent (Ministry of Social Development 2016, p. 5).

Overall inequality: Over the past thirty years, there has been a seven-percentage-point rise in the inequality of equivalised disposable household income as measured by the Gini coefficient (Perry 2016, table D.8, before housing cost series). For discussion as to whether the recent rise in the Gini coefficient is attributable to sampling fluctuations, see Perry (2016, p. 83). This does not affect the rise that took place largely before 2000. In the postwar years, the Gini coefficient for individual taxable income was declining (Easton 1983, table 10.7, figures after the introduction of PAYE).

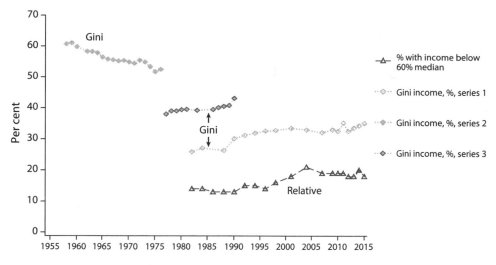

Figure NZL. New Zealand

New Zealand (Aotearoa in Maori) is a high-income country according to the World Bank classification, with GNI per capita in 2015 of $40,250 (Atlas method) and $35,680 (PPP) and a population in that year of 4.6 million people.

NORWAY

Poverty lines: Statistics Norway measures the number of people with low income, defined in terms of having equivalised (using the modified OECD scale) disposable income below 60 per cent of the median. For 2014, the standard for a couple and two children was PPP$31.93 per day per person.

Poverty today: The World Bank estimates for 2015 show that 0.2 per cent of the population were living in households with incomes per head below $1.90 a day, and that the poverty gap was less than 0.1 per cent. The national low-income figures show that 10.8 per cent of the population (excluding students) in 2014 were living in households with equivalised disposable income less than 60 per cent of the median, a figure that rose to 12.5 per cent if students were included (Statistics Norway website, data since 2005 from "Income statistics for households: Particular groups," table 5, and from Rapporter 32/2013, table 3.2, and from 1996 to 2004 from "Personal economy and housing conditions," table 06801, linked backwards at 1994 to earlier series from Income Distribution Survey 2005, table 5, and linked at 1986 to earlier series for 50 per cent of the median).

Who is poor?

- The poverty rate for those aged under eighteen was 11.5 per cent, compared with 10.8 per cent for the total population (excluding students).

- The poverty rate for immigrants from Western Europe, North America, or Oceania in 2014 was 15.6 per cent; the rate for immigrants from Eastern Europe, Asia, Africa, or Latin America was 36.4 per cent; for those born in Norway but whose parents were immigrants from Eastern Europe, Asia, Africa, or Latin America, the rate was 20.3 per cent.

- Statistics Norway (2013) found in a study of the period 1993 to 2011 that the poverty rates of immigrants declined the longer they had been in the country, and that for several groups the poverty rates were cut in half over the first five years of their residence in Norway. After the first five years, the poverty rates stabilise at around 12 to 20 per cent for immigrants from Asia, Africa, and South America, around 5 to 10 per cent for immigrants from Eastern Europe, and around 3 to 5 per cent for immigrants from Western Europe, North America, and Oceania.

Change over time: The proportion below 60 per cent of the median has risen by between one and two percentage points since 2001. Over the past thirty years as a whole, the poverty rate has remained broadly stable.

Nonmonetary poverty: The Eurostat indicator shows that 2.0 per cent of people were suffering severe material deprivation (four or more items out of nine) in 2016 and 4.1 per cent were suffering material deprivation (three or more items out of nine) (the series shown in the graph).

Overall inequality: Income inequality as measured by the Gini coefficient has risen over the past thirty years: in 2014 the coefficient was 4.6 percentage points higher than in 1986. This followed a period from 1950 to 1980 when income inequality was declining. (In series 1, the Gini coefficient of gross family income not equivalised is from

Aaberge, Atkinson, and Modalsli [2016], table A1, average of upper and lower bounds; in series 2, the Gini coefficient of equivalised (modified OECD scale) disposable household income is from the Statistics Norway website, "Income statistics for households: Distribution of income," total population.)

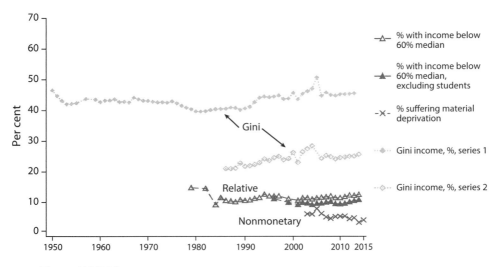

Figure NOR. Norway

Norway is a high-income country according to the World Bank classification, with GNI per capita in 2015 of $93,830 (Atlas method) and $64,590 (PPP) and a population in that year of 5.2 million people.

POLAND

Poverty lines: An extreme poverty rate based on the subsistence minimum calculated by the Institute of Labour and Social Affairs (Instytut Pracy i Spraw Socjalnych, IPiSS) is estimated by the Central Statistical Office (Główny Urząd Statystyczny, GUS) using the information on household expenditures recorded in the annual Household Budget Survey. The IPiSS minimum "includes only those needs whose satisfaction cannot be postponed and consumption below this level leads to biological destruction" (GUS 2017, p. 7). The poverty line and estimates based on it embody an equivalence scale that assigns a weight of 1.0 to the first person in the household, 0.7 for other persons aged fourteen or over, and 0.5 for every child under the age of fourteen (which corresponds to the original OECD scale) (GUS 2011, table 2; 2017a, chart 1; IPiSS website for 1996–1999, accessed December 2017). The IPiSS has calculated minima for many years (Atkinson and Micklewright 1992), and it is the higher social minimum that featured in several estimates of poverty in Poland in the 1980s and 1990s: series 1 is from Milanovic (1992, based on interpolation), and series 2 is from OECD (1996, table 14); both use income as the measure of household welfare. Szulc (2006, 2008) questions the methods used by the IPiSS in the 1990s, arguing that the rise in the social minimum and hence poverty is overstated. GUS also publishes estimates of relative poverty and of the percentage of people below a social assistance line (not shown here, same sources as above). The coverage of the Household Budget Survey was extended in 1992 to include households of the non-agricultural self-employed (Kordos 1996; Flemming and Micklewright 2000).

Poverty today: The World Bank estimates for 2015 show that 0.5 per cent of the population were living in households with incomes per head below $1.90 a day, and that the poverty gap was 0.2 per cent. In 2016, 4.6 per cent of the population was in extreme poverty as measured by the subsistence minimum calculated by the IPiSS (GUS 2017, p. 6).

Who is poor?

Change over time:

Nonmonetary poverty: The Eurostat indicator shows that 6.7 per cent of the population were suffering severe material deprivation (four or more items out of nine) in 2016, and 15.0 per cent were suffering material deprivation (three or more items out of nine), the series shown in the graph. (There is a break in the series for material deprivation in 2008.)

Overall inequality: In series 1, the Gini coefficient of individual distribution of household net per capita income, 1989–2001, is from UNICEF (2003, annex table 10.11), linked at 1989 to 1974–1988 from Atkinson and Micklewright (1992, tables PI1 and PI4, all households 1983–1988 linked at 1983 to series for worker households 1974–1982); in series 2, the Gini coefficient for equivalised income for 2004–2014 is from Eurostat (downloaded August 2018).

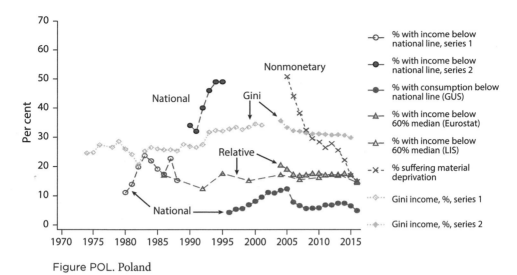

Figure POL. Poland

Poland is a high-income country according to the World Bank classification, with GNI per capita in 2015 of $13,340 (Atlas method) and $25,400 (PPP) and a population in that year of 38.0 million people.

PORTUGAL

Poverty lines: The official poverty line is set at 60 per cent of the median household equivalised (using the modified OECD scale) disposable income. In 2014, this was €13.87 per adult equivalent per day, or PPP$23.91.

Poverty today: The World Bank estimates for 2015 show that 0.5 per cent of the population were living in households with incomes per head below $1.90 a day, and that the poverty gap was 0.3 per cent. Estimates according to the national poverty line for 2015 show that 19.0 per cent were living in households with equivalised disposable income less than 60 per cent of the median (percentage of individuals living in households with equivalised [EU scale] disposable income below 60 per cent of the median: series 1 from Rodrigues [2005], series 2 from Rodrigues, Figueiras, and Junqueira [2011, figure 10] up to 2000 and from EU-SILC, Eurostat website, after 2000).

Who is poor?

- In 2014, 20.1 per cent of women were living in households below 60 per cent of the median, compared with 18.8 per cent of men.

- In 2014, 24.8 per cent of those aged under eighteen were living in households below 60 per cent of the median, as were 17.0 per cent of those aged sixty-five and over.

- The poverty rate for two-parent families in 2014 increased with the number of children: from 13.7 per cent for one-child families, to 20.5 for two-child families and 37.7 per cent for families with three or more children.

- Single-parent families in 2014 had a poverty rate of 34.6 per cent.

Change over time: The proportion below 60 per cent fell by five percentage points between 1994 and 2008; it then stabilised, before rising from 2011 to 2014 by 1.6 percentage points.

Nonmonetary poverty: The Eurostat indicator shows that 19.5 per cent of the population were suffering material deprivation (three or more items out of nine), and 8.4 per cent were suffering severe material deprivation (four or more items out of nine) in 2016. Applying an earlier measure of material deprivation, in 2008 just over 2.4 million people (23.0 per cent of the population) were deprived, of whom 900,000 were also income-poor (2007 incomes); this latter group constituted the "consistent poor" (Rodrigues and Andrade 2012).

Overall inequality: Income inequality as measured by the Gini coefficient fell from 1973 to the mid-1990s. It then rose from 1999 to 2004, after which there was a fall of four percentage points up to 2009. (The Gini coefficient of equivalised [modified OECD scale] disposable household income is from Rodrigues, Figueiras, and Junqueira 2012, figure 18 [series 1], figure 16 [series 2], and figure 14 [series 3]; series 1 is based on data from the European Community Household Panel and EU-SILC; data from 2009 are from EU-SILC, downloaded from the Eurostat website, "Income and Living Conditions in Europe.")

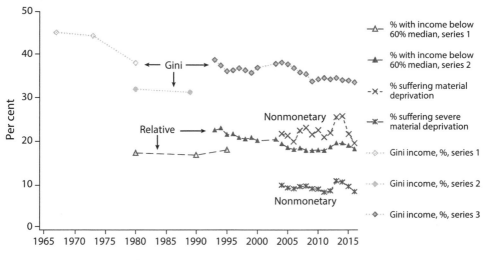

Figure PRT. Portugal

Portugal is a high-income country according to the World Bank classification, with GNI per capita in 2015 of $20,440 (Atlas method) and $28,590 (PPP) and a population in that year of 10.3 million people.

SWEDEN

Poverty lines:

Poverty today: The World Bank estimates for 2015 show that 0.5 per cent of the population were living in households with income per head below $1.90 a day, and that the poverty gap was 0.3 per cent. The Eurostat figures based on EU-SILC show that in 2015, 16.2 per cent were living in households with equivalised (modified OECD scale) disposable income less than 60 per cent of the median.

Who is poor?

Change over time:

Nonmonetary poverty: The Eurostat indicator shows that 3.7 per cent of the population were suffering material deprivation (three or more items out of nine), and 0.8 per cent were suffering severe material deprivation (four or more items out of nine) in 2016.

Overall inequality: The Gini coefficient for equivalised household income in 2015 was 27.6 per cent, compared to 21 per cent in 1996.

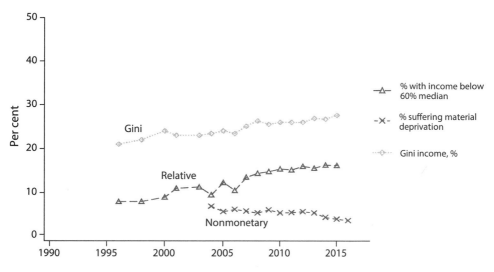

Figure SWE. Sweden

Sweden is a high-income country according to the World Bank classification, with GNI per capita in 2015 of $57,760 (Atlas method) and $48,410 (PPP) and a population in that year of 9.8 million people.

UNITED KINGDOM

Poverty lines: The official statistical publication, *Households Below Average Incomes* (*HBAI*) (Department for Work and Pensions 2016), contains estimates of the number of people living in "low income" households, where the "headline" definition is those with equivalised incomes below 60 per cent of the contemporary median (using the modified OECD equivalence scale). Figures are also given for other percentages of the median and for thresholds anchored in constant price terms. The Child Poverty Act 2010 set four targets that involved the headline indicator for children, an anchored low-income measure, a measure of combined low income and material deprivation, and a persistent poverty indicator. In 2014–2015, the 60 per cent standard was PPP$38.92 per person per day; a 40 per cent standard would be PPP$25.95.

Poverty today: The World Bank estimates for 2015 show that 0.2 per cent of the population were living in households with incomes per head below $1.90 a day, and that the poverty gap was 0.1 per cent. In terms of the national headline standard set at 60 per cent of the median, relative poverty in 2015–2016 was 16.3 per cent. With a lower line at 40 per cent of the median, the poverty rate was 5.0 per cent. (The estimates presented here are from the Institute for Fiscal Studies website [see Belfield et al. 2016], using data similar to the *HBAI* from the Family Resources Survey [previously the Family Expenditure Survey], augmented by information on top incomes from income tax records; definition "before housing costs.")

Who is poor?

- The poverty rate in 2014–2015 with the headline poverty standard was higher for children, with 18.8 per cent living in households below 60 per cent of the median, compared with an overall figure of 15.9 per cent.

- The headline rate for pensioners was slightly higher at 16.3 per cent, but fewer (3.8 per cent) were below 40 per cent of the median.

- Disabled people are identified as those who report any physical or mental health conditions or illnesses that last or are expected to last twelve months or more and that limit their ability to carry out day-to-day activities. The poverty rate in 2014–2015 with the headline standard was 18 per cent for disabled people, compared with 14 per cent for those living in households where no one reported a disability.

- In 2013–2014, individuals living in households headed by someone from an ethnic minority were more likely to have low income; this was particularly the case for households headed by someone of Pakistani or Bangladeshi ethnic origin.

Change over time: The proportion below the headline standard of 60 per cent of the contemporary median rose sharply over the 1980s, reaching a peak of 22 per cent in 1990, and has since declined to around 15 per cent. It remains, however, higher than the average for the 1960s and 1970s. The proportion below 40 per cent of the median, in contrast, has not declined since 1990 and is more than double the average for 1961 to 1979.

Nonmonetary poverty: The Eurostat indicator shows that 5.2 per cent of the population were suffering severe material deprivation (four or more items out of nine) in 2016 and that 12.5 per cent were suffering from material deprivation (three or more items out of nine) (the series shown in the graph). The Child Poverty Act 2010 set a target for the proportion of children who are in material deprivation and live in households where income is less than 70 per cent of median household income. Material deprivation in this national measurement is defined in terms of the enforced lack of twenty-one items, where the responses are weighted according to the prevalence of the item in the population and deprivation is defined as a score of 25 or more (where 100 is the maximum). In 2013–2014, 13 per cent of children lived in households experiencing low income (70 per cent standard) and material deprivation. There is a break in the material deprivation series in 2012.

Overall inequality: Over the 1980s, inequality of equivalised disposable household income as measured by the Gini coefficient rose by around ten percentage points, and there is no sign of a decline since 1990. (In series 1 [1949–1976], the Gini coefficient of after-tax income, not equivalised, among tax units ["Blue Book series"] is from Atkinson and Micklewright [1992], table BI1. In series 2 [1961–2014], the Gini coefficient of equivalised (modified OECD scale) disposable household income for all persons in the United Kingdom [Great Britain up to 2001–2002] is from the Institute for Fiscal Studies website, "Living Standards, Inequality, and Poverty" spreadsheet [before housing costs (BHC)], downloaded October 2016; the data are from the Family Expenditure Survey from 1961 up to financial year 1993–1994 [calendar years up to 1992], thereafter from the Family Resources Survey.)

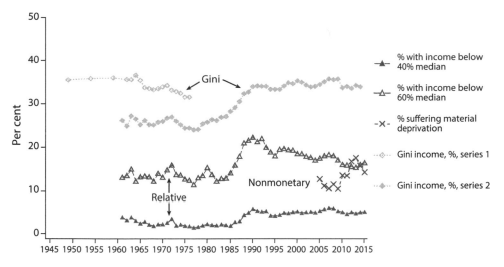

Figure GBR. United Kingdom

The United Kingdom consists of England, Wales, Scotland, and Northern Ireland. Great Britain refers to the United Kingdom apart from Northern Ireland. It is a high-income country according to the World Bank classification, with GNI per capita in 2015 of $43,720 (Atlas method) and $40,550 (PPP) and a population in that year of 65.1 million people.

UNITED STATES

Poverty lines: The United States has had an official poverty line since 1965. The threshold is set at three times the cost of a minimum food diet in 1963, updated annually for inflation using the consumer price index. It takes account of family size, composition, and age of householder. In 2015, the threshold for a single person was PPP$33.10 per day, and for a family of four it was PPP$16.61 per person per day. The Census Bureau also publishes figures for a supplemental poverty measure (SPM) that incorporates in the income definition "deductions such as tax payments, work expenses, and medical costs in its family resource estimates as well as additions to reflect noncash resource transfers, such as housing subsidies and food assistance programs." The thresholds for this measure are derived using "data on spending for basic necessities (food, shelter, clothing, and utilities) and are adjusted for geographic differences in the cost of housing" (US Census Bureau 2016, p. 4). The measure incorporates regular changes in the consumption basket taken to represent basic needs. (This series is not shown in the graph.)

Poverty today: The World Bank estimates for 2016 show that 1.3 per cent of the population were living in households with incomes per head below $1.90 a day, and that the poverty gap was 1.0 per cent. In the same year, 12.7 per cent of persons were living in households below the official US poverty line. (The official poverty estimates are drawn from the Current Population Survey Annual Social and Economic Supplement [CPS ASEC].) In terms of relative poverty, the LIS Key Figures for 2016 show that 10.8 per cent were living in households with equivalised disposable income less than 40 per cent of the median and 24.3 per cent lived below 60 per cent of the median.

Who is poor?

- The poverty rate in 2016, according to the official poverty line, was 11.3 per cent for males and 14.0 per cent for females.

- The poverty rate for those aged under eighteen was 18.0 per cent; for those aged sixty-five and over, it was 9.3 per cent.

- The poverty rate was 11.0 per cent for whites, 10.1 per cent for Asians, 19.4 per cent for Hispanics, and 22.0 per cent for blacks.

- The poverty rate was 15.9 per cent inside principal cities, 10.0 per cent in metropolitan areas outside principal cities, and 15.8 per cent outside metropolitan areas.

- For foreign-born naturalized citizens, the poverty rate was 10.0 per cent; for foreign-born noncitizens, the rate was 19.5 per cent.

- For those with no high school diploma, the poverty rate was 24.8 per cent; for those with a bachelor's degree or higher, the rate was 4.5 per cent.

- For those reporting a disability, the poverty rate was 26.8 per cent, compared with 10.3 per cent for those with no disability.

- Those aged eighteen to sixty-four who did not work at least one week per year had a poverty rate of 30.5 per cent; those who worked full-time year-round had a rate of 2.2 per cent.

(US Census Bureau 2017, table 3)

Change over time: The proportion below the official poverty line has varied cyclically, peaking in 1982–1983, 1993, and 2010–2012, but the long-run downward trend from 1948 came to an end in the early 1970s. The poverty rate in 2016 was little different from that thirty-five years earlier. The relative poverty measure for 2016 shows that the proportion below 60 per cent of the median was 1.8 percentage points lower in 2016 than in 1979. (The proportion of the population below the official poverty line before 1959 is from Fisher [1986]; the proportion after 1959 is from the US Census Bureau website, "Historical Poverty Tables" [table 2], and from US Census Bureau [2016, table B-1]. No adjustment is made for the revision of the series in 2013 or for earlier revisions. The proportion living in households with disposable income below 50 per cent of the median is from Meyer and Sullivan [2010, appendix table 7], updated by linking forward to OECD iLibrary. Other relative poverty measures are from LIS Key Figures.)

Nonmonetary poverty: An indicator of multiple deprivation constructed by Mitra and Brucker (2015, measure 2) for 2012, with four components for self-reported health status, educational attainment, employment status, and insecurity (absence of health insurance), found 8.8 per cent of persons to be deprived on two or more dimensions. The overlap with income poverty was 3.3 per cent.

Overall inequality: Over the past thirty-five years, there has been an increase of eight percentage points in the inequality of equivalised gross household income as measured by the Gini coefficient. (US Census Bureau 2017, table A-3, adjusted for the break in 1993 on the assumption that half of the recorded change between 1992 and 1993 was due to the change in methods, linked backwards at 1967 to the series from 1945 given by Budd [1970, table 6], where it should be noted that the series before 1967 excludes those living alone or with unrelated individuals.)

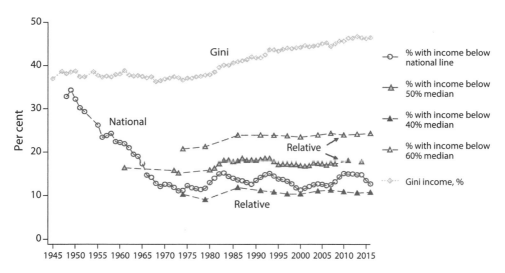

Figure USA. United States

The United States of America is a high-income country according to the World Bank classification, with GNI per capita in 2015 of $56,290 (Atlas method) and $56,430 (PPP) and a population in that year of 321.4 million people.

NATIONAL REPORT REFERENCES

NATIONAL POVERTY REPORTS FOR CHAPTER 6

BANGLADESH

Begum, S. S., Q. Deng, and B. Gustafsson. 2011. "Economic growth and child poverty in Bangladesh and China." IZA Discussion Paper 5929. IZA, Bonn.

Khan, A. R. 2005. "Measuring inequality and poverty in Bangladesh: An assessment of the survey data." *Bangladesh Development Studies* 31 (3/4): 1–34.

Khan, A. R., and B. Sen. 2006. "The structure and distribution of personal income and poverty reduction: A case study of Bangladesh during the 1990s." In J. K. Boyce, S. Cullenberg, P. K. Pattanaik, and R. Pollin, eds., *Human development in the age of globalization: Essays in honour of Keith B. Griffin*. Edward Elgar, Cheltenham.

Ministry of Finance. 2015. *Poverty and inequality in Bangladesh: Journey towards progress (2014–15)*. Macroeconomic Wing, Ministry of Finance, Government of the People's Republic of Bangladesh.

World Bank. 2013. *Bangladesh poverty assessment: A decade of progress in reducing poverty, 2000–2010*. World Bank, Washington, DC.

CAMBODIA

Asian Development Bank. 2014. *Cambodia: Country poverty analysis 2014*. Asian Development Bank, Mandaluyong City, Philippines.

Gibson, J. 2005. "Statistical tools and estimation methods for poverty measures based on cross-sectional household surveys." Chapter 5 in *Handbook on poverty statistics: Concepts, methods, and policy use*. United Nations Statistics Division, New York.

Krongkaew, M., and H. M. Z. Ragayah. 2006. "Income distribution and sustainable economic development in East Asia: A comparative analysis." Paper available from EADN Network.

Ministry of Planning. 2013. *Poverty in Cambodia—A new approach: Redefining the poverty line*. Royal Government of Cambodia, Phnom Penh.

World Bank. 2014. *Where have all the poor gone? Cambodia Poverty Assessment 2013*, 2nd ed. World Bank, Washington, DC.

World Bank. 2016. "Poverty and shared prosperity at a glance." Sheet for Cambodia, April. World Bank, Washington, DC.

CHINA

Alkire, S., and Y. Shen. 2017. "Exploring multidimensional poverty in China: 2010 to 2014." *Research on Economic Inequality* 25: 161–228.

Alston, P. 2016. "End-of-mission statement on China, by Professor Philip Alston, United Nations special rapporteur on extreme poverty and human rights." Office of the UN High Commissioner for Human Rights, Geneva.

Gao, Q. 2017. *Welfare, work, and poverty: Social assistance in China.* Oxford University Press, Oxford.

Gustafsson, B., and S. Ding. 2016. "Unequal growth: How household incomes and poverty in urban China has developed since 1988." Working Paper 55. China Institute for Income Distribution, Beijing Normal University.

Gustafsson, B., and S. Ding. 2017. "Unequal growth: How household incomes and poverty in urban China have developed since 1988, with an emphasis on the period from 2007 to 2013." Working Paper 2017–18. Centre for Human Capital and Productivity, Department of Economics, Western University, Ontario.

Gustafsson, B., S. Li, and H. Sato. 2014. "Data for studying earnings, the distribution of household income, and poverty in China." Discussion Paper 8244. IZA, Bonn.

Khan, A. R. 1998. "Poverty in China in the period of globalization: New evidence on trend and pattern." Issues in Development Discussion Paper 22. International Labour Office, Geneva.

Khan, A. R. 2004. "Growth, inequality, and poverty." Issues in Employment and Poverty Discussion Paper 15. International Labour Organization, Geneva.

Li, S. 2001. "Changes in poverty profile in China." WIDER Discussion Paper 2001/21. UNU-WIDER, Helsinki.

Li, S. 2013. "Changes in income inequality in China in the last three decades." Paper presented at the Third Conference on Chinese Capital Market, NYU Center on US–China Relations, 6 December, New York University, New York.

Li, S. 2016. "Income inequality and economic growth in China in the last three decades." *The Round Table: The Commonwealth Journal of International Affairs* 105(6): 641–665.

Li, S., H. Sato, and T. Sicular. 2013. *Rising inequality in China.* Cambridge University Press, Cambridge.

National Bureau of Statistics (NBS). 2004. "Poverty Statistics in China." Rural Survey Organisation, National Bureau of Statistics, Beijing.

National Bureau of Statistics (NBS). 2015. *Poverty monitoring report of Rural China.* China Statistics Press, Beijing.

National Bureau of Statistics (NBS). 2017. *Poverty monitoring report of Rural China.* China Statistics Press, Beijing.

National Bureau of Statistics (NBS). 2018. "Statistical Communiqué of the People's Republic of China on the 2017 National Economic and Social Development." Press release, 28 February. NBS, Beijing.

Wang, X., H. Feng, Q. Xia, and S. Alkire. 2016. "On the relationship between income poverty and multidimensional poverty in China." OPHI Working Paper 101. University of Oxford.

World Bank. 2009. *China: From poor areas to poor people: China's evolving poverty reduction agenda: An assessment of poverty and inequality in China.* Report 47349-CN. World Bank, Washington, DC.

Zhang, Y., and R. Wang. 2011. "The main approach of proposed integrated household survey of China." Wye City Group on Statistics on Rural Development and Agricultural Household Income, Fourth meeting, Rio de Janeiro, 9–11 November.

FIJI

Fiji Bureau of Statistics (FBoS). 2015. *2013–14 Household Income and Expenditure Survey Preliminary Findings—Release 1.* FBoS Release 98, 31 December. Fiji Bureau of Statistics, Suva.

Narsey, W. 2006. *Report on the 2002–03 Household Income and Expenditure Survey.* Fiji Islands Bureau of Statistics, Suva.

Narsey, W. 2008. *The quantitative analysis of poverty in Fiji.* Fiji Islands Bureau of Statistics, Suva, Fiji, and School of Economics, University of the South Pacific, Suva, Fiji.

Narsey, W. 2011. *Report on the 2008–09 Household Income and Expenditure Survey for Fiji.* Fiji Bureau of Statistics, Suva.

Narsey, W. 2012. *Poverty in Fiji: Changes 2002–03 to 2008–09 and policy implications.* Fiji Bureau of Statistics, Suva.

Narsey, W., T. Raikoti, and E. Waqavonovono. 2010. *Preliminary report: Poverty and household incomes in Fiji in 2008–09 (based on the 2008–09 Household Income and Expenditure Survey).* Fiji Bureau of Statistics, Suva.

GEORGIA

Atkinson, A. B., and J. Micklewright. 1992. *Economic transformation in Eastern Europe and the distribution of income.* Cambridge University Press, Cambridge.

Geostat. 2017. "Subsistence minimum calculation methodology for working age male." Tbilisi (downloaded 7 August 2017).

World Bank. 1999. *Georgia poverty and income distribution*, vol. 2, *Technical papers.* Report 19348-GE. World Bank, Washington, DC.

World Bank. 2002. *Georgia poverty update.* Report 22350-GE. World Bank, Washington, DC.

World Bank. 2009. *Georgia poverty assessment.* Report 44400-GE. World Bank, Washington, DC.

INDIA

Asian Development Bank, 2007. *Key indicators 2007.* Asian Development Bank, Manila.

Alkire, S., and S. Seth. 2015. "Multidimensional poverty reduction in India between 1999 and 2006: Where and how?" *World Development* 72: 93–108.

Alkire, S., C. Oldiges, and U. Kanagaratnam. 2018. "Multidimensional poverty reduction in India 2005/6–2015/16: Still a long way to go but the poorest are catching up." OPHI Research in Progress 54a. University of Oxford, Oxford.

Deaton, A., and J. Drèze. 2014. "Squaring the poverty circle." *The Hindu*, 25 July.

Deaton, A., and V. Kozel. 2005. "Data and dogma: The great Indian poverty debate." *World Bank Research Observer* 20(2): 177–199.

Majumdar, D. 2010. "Decreasing poverty and increasing inequality in India." In OECD, *Tackling inequalities in Brazil, China, India, and South Africa.* OECD, Paris.

More, S., and N. Singh. 2015. "Poverty in India: Concepts, measurement, and status." Munich Personal RePEc Archive MPRA Paper 62400.

Planning Commission. 2013. *Poverty estimates for 2011–2012.* Government of India, Press Information Bureau.

Planning Commission. 2014. *Data-book compiled for use of Planning Commission.* 22 December. Planning Commission, New Delhi.

Rangarajan, C. 2014. *Report of the expert group to review the methodology for measurement of poverty.* Planning Commission, New Delhi.

Vanneman, R., and A. Dubey. 2013. "Horizontal and vertical inequalities in India." In J. C. Gornick and M. Jäntti, eds., *Income inequality: Economic disparities and the middle class in affluent countries.* Stanford University Press, Stanford, CA.

INDONESIA

Asra, A. 1989. "Inequality trends in Indonesia, 1969–1981: A re-examination." *Bulletin of Indonesian Economic Studies* 25: 100–110.

Asra, A. 2000. "Poverty and inequality in Indonesia." *Journal of the Asia Pacific Economy* 5: 91–111.

Booth, A. 1993. "Counting the poor in Indonesia." *Bulletin of Indonesian Economic Studies* 29: 53–83.

Booth, A. 2000. "Poverty and inequality in the Soeharto era: An assessment." *Bulletin of Indonesian Economic Studies* 36: 73–104.

Booth, A. 2016. *Economic change in modern Indonesia.* Cambridge University Press, Cambridge.

Krongkaew, M., and H. M. Z. Ragayah. 2006. "Income distribution and sustainable economic development in East Asia: A comparative analysis." Paper available from EADN Network.

Miranti, R. 2010. "Poverty in Indonesia 1984–2002: The impact of growth and changes in inequality." *Bulletin of Indonesian Economic Studies* 46: 79–97.

Priebe, J. 2014. "Official poverty measurement in Indonesia since 1984: A methodological review." *Bulletin of Indonesian Economic Studies* 50: 185–205.

Sundrum, R. M. 1979. "Income distribution, 1970–76." *Bulletin of Indonesian Economic Studies* 15: 137–141.

MALAYSIA

Department of Statistics Malaysia. 2009. *Household Income and Basic Amenities Survey report.* Department of Statistics Malaysia, Putrajaya.

Department of Statistics Malaysia. 2012. *Household Income and Basic Amenities Survey report.* Department of Statistics Malaysia, Putrajaya.

Department of Statistics Malaysia. 2014. *Household Income and Basic Amenities Survey report.* Department of Statistics Malaysia, Putrajaya.

Krongkaew, M., and H. M. Z. Ragayah. 2006. "Income distribution and sustainable economic development in East Asia: A comparative analysis." Paper available from EADN Network.

Mok, T. Y. 2009. "Poverty lines, household economies of scale, and urban poverty in Malaysia." PhD thesis, Lincoln University.

Ragayah, H. M. Z. 2008. "Income inequality in Malaysia." *Asian Economic Policy Review* 3: 114–132.

Snodgrass, D. R. 2002. "Economic growth and income inequality: The Malaysian experience." In M. G. Asher, D. Newman, and T. P. Snyder, eds., *Public policy in Asia.* Quorum Books, Westport, CT.

UNDP. 2007. *Malaysia: Measuring and monitoring poverty and inequality.* UNDP Malaysia, Kuala Lumpur.

NEPAL

Acharya, S. 2004. "Measuring and analysing poverty (with particular reference to the case of Nepal)." *European Journal of Comparative Economics* 1: 195–215.

"CBS view on poverty in Nepal." Downloaded October 2017.

Central Bureau of Statistics. 2004. "Poverty trends in Nepal (1995–96 and 2003–04)." National Planning Commission, Kathmandu.

National Planning Commission and OPHI. 2018. *Nepal Multidimensional Poverty Index: Analysis towards action.* Government of Nepal, Kathmandu.

Prennushi, G. 1999. "Nepal: Poverty at the turn of the twenty-first century." IP Report 174. World Bank, Washington, DC.

Uematsu, H., A. R. Shidiq, and S. Tiwari. 2016. "Trends and drivers of poverty reduction in Nepal: A historical perspective." Policy Research Working Paper 7830. World Bank, Washington, DC.

World Bank. 2006. "Nepal: Resilience amidst conflict." Report 34834-NP. Washington, DC.

SOLOMON ISLANDS

Solomon Islands National Statistics Office/UNDP. 2008. *Analysis of the 2005/06 Household Income and Expenditure Survey.* Department of Finance, Honiara.

Solomon Islands National Statistics Office. 2015. *Solomon Islands poverty profile based on the 2012/13 Household Income and Expenditure Survey.* Ministry of Finance and Treasury, Honiara.

Solomon Islands National Statistics Office. 2015a. *Household Income and Expenditure Survey 2012/13: National analytical report,* vol. 1. Ministry of Finance and Treasury, Honiara.

SRI LANKA

Sri Lanka Department of Census and Statistics. 2004. *Announcement of the official poverty line.* Sri Lanka Department of Census and Statistics, Colombo.

Sri Lanka Department of Census and Statistics. 2008. *Household Income and Expenditure Survey—2006/07 Final Report.* Sri Lanka Department of Census and Statistics, Colombo.

Sri Lanka Department of Census and Statistics. 2017. *Poverty indicators—Household Income and Expenditure Survey 2016*. Sri Lanka Department of Census and Statistics, Colombo.

Weerahewa, J., and J. Wickramasinghe. 2005. "Adjusting monetary measures of poverty to non-monetary aspects: An analysis based on Sri Lankan data." Paper presented at the American Agricultural Economic Association annual meeting, Providence, RI, 24–27 July.

THAILAND

Krongkaew, M., and H. M. Z. Ragayah. 2006. "Income distribution and sustainable economic development in East Asia: A comparative analysis." Paper available from EADN Network.

VIETNAM

Baulch, B., and E. Masset. 2003. "Do monetary and nonmonetary indicators tell the same story about chronic poverty? A study of Vietnam in the 1990s." *World Development* 31(3): 441–453.

Benjamin, D., L. Brandt, and B. McCaig. 2016. "Growth with equity: Income inequality in Vietnam, 2002–14." Discussion paper 10392. IZA, Bonn.

Krongkaew, M., and H. M. Z. Ragayah. 2006. "Income distribution and sustainable economic development in East Asia: A comparative analysis." Paper available from EADN Network.

Tran, V. Q., S. Alkire, and S. Klasen. 2015. "Static and dynamic disparities between monetary and multidimensional poverty measurement: Evidence from Vietnam." OPHI Working Paper 97. University of Oxford.

NATIONAL POVERTY REPORTS FOR CHAPTER 7

CÔTE D'IVOIRE

Cogneau, D., K. Houngbedji, and S. Mesplé-Somps. 2014. "The fall of the elephant: Two decades of poverty increase in Côte d'Ivoire (1988–2008)." WIDER Working Paper 2014/144. UNU-WIDER, Helsinki.

Cogneau, D., K. Houngbedji, and S. Mesplé-Somps. 2016. "The fall of the elephant: Two decades of poverty increase in Côte d'Ivoire, 1988–2008." In C. Arndt, A. McKay, and F. Tarp, eds., *Growth and poverty in Sub-Saharan Africa*. Oxford University Press, Oxford.

Dabalen, A., and S. Paul. 2013. "Recovering comparable poverty estimates in Côte D'Ivoire." *Journal of Development Studies* 49: 1412–1426.

Institut National de la Statistique. 2008. *Enquête sur le niveau de vie des ménages*. République de Côte D'Ivoire, Abidjan.

Institut National de la Statistique. 2015. *Enquête sur le niveau de vie des ménages en Côte d'Ivoire (ENV 2015): Profil de pauvreté*. République de Côte D'Ivoire, Abidjan.

Kakwani, N. 1993. "Poverty and economic growth with application to Côte d'Ivoire." *Review of Income and Wealth*, series 39: 121–139.

GHANA

Coulombe, H., and A. McKay. 1995. "An assessment of trends in poverty in Ghana 1988–1992." PSP Discussion Paper Series 81. World Bank, Washington, DC.

Ghana Statistical Service (GSS). 2000. *Poverty trends in Ghana in the 1990s*. GSS, Accra.

Ghana Statistical Service. 2007. *Patterns and trends of poverty in Ghana 1991–2006*. GLSS5. GSS, Accra.

Ghana Statistical Service. 2013. *Non-monetary poverty in Ghana: 2010 population and housing census report*. GSS, Accra.

Ghana Statistical Service. 2014. *Poverty profile in Ghana (2005–2013)*. GSS, Accra.

McKay, A., J. Pirttilä, and F. Tarp. 2015. "Ghana: Poverty reduction over thirty years." WIDER Working Paper 2015/052. World Institute for Development Economics Research, Helsinki.

KENYA

Bigsten, A. 1986. "Welfare and economic growth in Kenya, 1914–76." *World Development* 14(9): 1151–1160.

Bigsten, A. 1987. *Income distribution and growth in a dual economy: Kenya 1914–1976*. Department of Economics Memorandum 101. Gothenburg University.

Bigsten, A., D. K. Manda, G. Mwabu, and A. Wambugo. 2016. "Incomes, inequality, and poverty in Kenya." In C. Arndt, A. McKay, and F. Tarp, eds., *Growth and poverty in Sub-Saharan Africa*. Oxford University Press, Oxford.

Kabubo-Mariara, J., and G. Ndeng'e. 2004. "Measuring and monitoring poverty: The case of Kenya." Paper presented at the Poverty Analysis and Data Initiative (PADI) Workshop on Measuring and Monitoring Poverty, May 7th–8th, Mombasa.

Kenya National Bureau of Statistics. 2007. *Basic report on well-being in Kenya*. Nairobi.

Kenya National Bureau of Statistics. 2018. *Basic report on well-being in Kenya*. Nairobi.

MAURITIUS

Central Statistics Office. 2005. *Household Budget Survey 2001/02: Analytical report*. Ministry of Finance and Corporate Affairs, Port Louis.

Statistics Mauritius. 2015. *Poverty analysis 2012*. Ministry of Finance and Economic Development, Port Louis.

Statistics Mauritius. 2018. *Household Budget Survey 2017—Preliminary results*. Ministry of Finance and Economic Development, Port Louis.

Subramanian, A. 2001. "Mauritius: A case study." *Finance and Development* 38(4): 1–7.

MOZAMBIQUE

Alfani, F., C. Azzarri, M. d'Errico, and C. Molini. 2012. "Poverty in Mozambique: New evidence from recent household surveys." Policy Research Working Paper 6217. World Bank, Washington, DC.

Arndt, C., S. Jones, K. Mahrt, V. Salvucci, and F. Tarp. 2017. "A review of consumption poverty estimation for Mozambique." In C. Arndt and F. Tarp, eds., *Measuring poverty and well-being in developing countries*. Oxford University Press, Oxford.

Arndt, C., and K. Mahrt. 2017. "Estimation in practice." In C. Arndt and F. Tarp, eds., *Measuring poverty and well-being in developing countries*. Oxford University Press, Oxford.

Ministério de Economia e Finanças. 2016. *Pobreza e bem-estar em Moçambique: Quarta avaliação nacional (IOF 2014/15)*. Ministério de Economia e Finanças, Maputo.

Ministry of Economics and Finance. 2016. *Poverty and well-being in Mozambique: Fourth national poverty assessment (IOF 2014/15)*. Executive summary. Ministry of Economics and Finance, Maputo.

Ministry of Planning and Development. 2010. *Poverty and well-being in Mozambique: Third national poverty assessment*. Ministry of Planning and Development, Maputo.

Van den Boom, B. 2011. "Analysis of poverty in Mozambique: Household poverty status, child malnutrition, and other indicators, 1997, 2003, 2009." Report for the G19 bilateral donors. Centre for World Food Studies, VU University, Amsterdam.

NIGER

Institut National de la Statistique. 2008. *Tendances, profil, et déterminants de la pauvreté au Niger 2005–2007/08*. Ministère de l'Economie et des Finances, Niamey.

Institut National de la Statistique. 2013. *Profil et déterminants de la pauvreté au Niger en 2011: Premiers resultats de l'Enquête Nationale sur les Conditions de Vie des Ménages et l'Agriculture au Niger (ECVMA)*. Ministère de l'Economie et des Finances, Niamey.

UN Economic Commission for Africa (Nations Unies Commission Économique pour l'Afrique). 2016. *Profil de pays 2015—Niger*. UN Economic Commission for Africa, Addis-Ababa.

World Bank. 2014. *Republic of Niger: Trends in poverty, inequality, and growth, 2005–2011*. Report 89837-NE. World Bank, Washington, DC.

World Bank. 2015. *Republic of Niger: Measuring poverty trends: Methodological and analytical issues*. Report 89838-NE. World Bank, Washington, DC.

SOUTH AFRICA

Beegle, K., L. Christiaensen, A. Dabalen, and I. Gaddis. 2016. *Poverty in a rising Africa*, vols. 1 and 2. World Bank, Washington, DC.

Budlender, J., M. Leibbrandt, and I. Woolard. 2015. "South African poverty lines: A review and two new money-metric thresholds." Southern Africa Labour and Development Research Unit Working Paper 151. University of Cape Town, Cape Town.

Leibbrandt, M., I. Woolard, A. Finn, and J. Argent. 2010. "Trends in South African income distribution and poverty since the fall of apartheid." OECD Social, Employment and Migration Working Papers 101. OECD, Paris.

Leibbrandt, M., I. Woolard, H. McEwen, and C. Koep. 2010a. "Better employment to reduce inequality further in South Africa." In OECD, *Tackling inequalities in Brazil, China, India, and South Africa*. OECD, Paris.

Statistics South Africa. 2008. *Measuring poverty in South Africa: Methodological report on the development of the poverty lines for statistical reporting*. Technical Report D0300. Statistics South Africa, Pretoria.

Statistics South Africa. 2014. *Poverty trends in South Africa: An examination of absolute poverty between 2006 and 2011*. Statistics South Africa, Pretoria.

Statistics South Africa. 2017. *Poverty trends in South Africa: An examination of absolute poverty between 2006 and 2015*. Statistics South Africa, Pretoria.

Van der Berg, S., and M. Louw. 2004. "Changing patterns of South African income distribution: Towards time series estimates of distribution and poverty." *South African Journal of Economics* 72: 546–572.

Whiteford, A. C., and D. E. van Seventer. 2000. "South Africa's changing income distribution in the 1990s." *Studies in Economics and Econometrics* 24: 7–30.

TANZANIA

Arndt, C., L. Demery, A. McKay, and F. Tarp. 2016. "Growth and poverty reduction in Tanzania." In C. Arndt, A. McKay, and F. Tarp, eds., *Growth and poverty in Sub-Saharan Africa*. Oxford University Press, Oxford.

Atkinson, A. B., and M. A. Lugo. 2010. "Growth, poverty, and distribution in Tanzania." IGC Working Paper 10/0831. London School of Economics, London.

Economic and Social Research Foundation. 2015. *Tanzania Human Development Report 2014*. Economic and Social Research Foundation, Dar es Salaam.

National Bureau of Statistics. 2009. *Household Budget Survey, 2007: Tanzania Mainland*. National Bureau of Statistics, Dar es Salaam.

National Bureau of Statistics. 2014. *Tanzania mainland: Household Budget Survey main report, 2011/12*. National Bureau of Statistics, Dar es Salaam.

Office of Chief Government Statistician–Zanzibar. 2012. *Household Budget Survey 2009/10 final report*. Office of Chief Government Statistician, Zanzibar City.

World Bank. 2015. *Tanzania mainland poverty assessment*. World Bank, Washington, DC.

World Bank. 2017. *Zanzibar poverty assessment*. World Bank, Washington, DC.

UGANDA

Appleton, S. 1999. "Changes in poverty in Uganda, 1992–1997." Centre for the Study of African Economies Discussion Paper 99.22. University of Oxford.

Ministry of Finance. 2014. *Poverty status report 2014*. Economic Development Policy and Research Department, Ministry of Finance, Kampala.

Uganda Bureau of Statistics. 2017. *Uganda National Household Survey 2016/17*. Uganda Bureau of Statistics, Kampala.

Van Campenhout, B., H. Sekabira, and D. H. Aduayom. 2016. "Poverty and its dynamics in Uganda: Explorations using a new set of poverty lines." In C. Arndt, A. McKay, and F. Tarp, eds., *Growth and poverty in Sub-Saharan Africa*. Oxford University Press, Oxford.

ZAMBIA

Central Statistical Office. 1997. "The evolution of poverty in Zambia 1991–1996." Central Statistical Office, Lusaka.

Central Statistical Office. 2005. *Living Conditions Monitoring Survey report 2004*. Central Statistical Office, Lusaka.

Central Statistical Office. 2012. *Living Conditions Monitoring Survey report 2006 and 2010*. Central Statistical Office, Lusaka.

Central Statistical Office. 2016. *2015 Living Conditions Monitoring Survey report*. Central Statistical Office, Lusaka.

Masumbu, G., and K. Mahrt. 2016. "Assessing progress in welfare improvements in Zambia." In C. Arndt, A. McKay, and F. Tarp, eds., *Growth and poverty in Sub-Saharan Africa*. Oxford University Press, Oxford.

World Bank. 2012. *Zambia poverty assessment*. Report 81001-ZM. World Bank, Washington, DC.

NATIONAL POVERTY REPORTS FOR CHAPTER 8

BOLIVIA

CEDLAS and World Bank. 2014. "A guide to SEDLAC Socio-Economic Database for Latin America and the Caribbean." CEDLAS and World Bank, Buenos Aires and Washington, DC.

Eid, A., and R. Aguirre. 2013. "Trends in income and consumption inequality in Bolivia: A *fairy* tale of growing dwarfs and shrinking giants." *Revista Latinoamericana de Desarrollo Económico/Latin American Journal of Economic Development* 20: 75–110.

Unidad de Análisis de Políticas Sociales y Económicas (UDAPE). 2004. "Informe técnico cálculo de las líneas de pobreza." 13° Taller Regional sobre la Construcción de Líneas de Pobreza en América Latina, Lima.

Villarroel, P., and W. Hernani-Limarino. 2013. "La evolución de la pobreza en Bolivia: Un enfoque multidimensional." *Revista Latinoamericana de Desarrollo Económico/ Latin American Journal of Economic Development* 20: 7–74.

BRAZIL

Atkinson A. B., J. Hasell, S. Morelli, and M. Roser. 2017. *The chartbook of economic inequality*. INET, Oxford Martin School, University of Oxford.

Gasparini, L., G. Cruces, and R. Tornarolli. 2011. "Recent trends in income inequality in Latin America." *Economia* 11: 147–190.

Instituto de Pesquisa Econômica Aplicada (IPEA). 2013. "Duas décadas de desigualdede e pobreza no Brasil medidas pela Pnad/IBGE." Communica do IPEA 159.

Tronco, G. B., and M. P. Ramos. 2017. "Poverty lines in the Brasil Sem Miséria lan: A review and proposed alternatives in poverty measurement according to the methodology of Sonia Rocha." *Revista de Administração Pública* 51(2): 294–311.

COLOMBIA

CEDLAS and World Bank. 2014. "A guide to SEDLAC Socio-Economic Database for Latin America and the Caribbean." CEDLAS and World Bank, Buenos Aires and Washington, DC.

Departamento Administrativo Nacional de Estadística (DANE). 2017. *Pobreza monetaria y multidimensional en Colombia 2016*. Technical bulletin, 22 March. DANE, Bogotá.

Salazar, R. A., B. Y. Díaz, and R. D. Pinzón. 2013. "Multidimensional poverty in Colombia, 1997–2010." ISER Working Paper Series 2013-03. Institute for Social and Economic Research, University of Essex.

DOMINICAN REPUBLIC

Aristy-Escuder, J. 2017. "Income definition, price indexes, and the poverty headcount in the Dominican Republic." In F. G. Carneiro and S. Sirtaine, eds., *When growth is not enough: Explaining the rigidity of poverty in the Dominican Republic*. World Bank Group, Washington, DC.

Gasparini, L., G. Cruces, and L. Tornarolli. 2016. "Chronicle of a deceleration foretold: Income inequality in Latin America in the 2010s." Working Paper 198. CEDLAS, Universidad Nacional de la Plata, La Plata.

Ministerio de Economía, Planificación y Desarrollo (MEPyD) and Oficina Nacional de Estadística (ONE). 2012. *Metodología para el cálculo de la medición oficial de la pobreza monetaria en la República Dominicana*. MEPyD and ONE, Santo Domingo.

MEPyD and ONE. 2015. *Buletín de estacísticas officiales de pobreza monetara* 1(2, October). MEPyD and ONE, Santo Domingo.

Morillo Pérez, A. 2008. "Medición de la pobreza monetaria mediante las Encuestas de Fuerza de Trabajo (EFT) del Banco Central de la República Dominicana: Propuesta metodológica y resultados 2000–2008." Ministerio de Economía, Planificación, y Desarrollo—Unidad Asesora de Análisis Económico y Social (UAAES).

JAMAICA

CEDLAS and World Bank. 2014. "A guide to SEDLAC Socio-Economic Database for Latin America and the Caribbean." CEDLAS and World Bank, Buenos Aires and Washington, DC.

Ministry of Economic Growth and Job Creation. 2016. *National policy on poverty: National Poverty Reduction Programme*. Green paper. Government of Jamaica, Kingston.

Planning Institute of Jamaica (PIOJ). 2011. "Alternative approaches to the measurement of poverty in Jamaica: Comparing the estimates of the Planning Institute of Jamaica and the International Monetary Fund." Technical Note TN-2001-11-04. PIOJ, Kingston.

Salmon, J. 2002. "Poverty eradication: The Jamaican experience." *Social and Economic Studies* 51(4): 63–94.

PERU

Rutstein, S., and A. Way. 2014. *The Peru Continuous DHS experience*. DHS Occasional Paper 8. ICF, Rockville, MD.

NATIONAL POVERTY REPORTS FOR CHAPTER 9

AUSTRALIA

Australian Council of Social Service (ACOSS). 2013. *Poverty in Australia 2012*, 3rd ed. ACOSS, Strawberry Hills.

Hancock, K. 1971. "The economics of social welfare in the 1970s." In H. Weir, ed., *Social welfare in the 1970s*. Australian Council of Social Service, Sydney.

Henderson, R. F., chair. 1975. *Poverty in Australia*. Commission of Inquiry into Poverty, Canberra.

Melbourne Institute of Applied Economic and Social Research. 2016. *Poverty lines: Australia, March quarter 2016*. University of Melbourne, Melbourne.

Saunders, P. 1993. "Longer run changes in the distribution of income in Australia." *Economic Record* 69: 353–366.

Saunders, P., Y. Naidoo, and M. Griffiths. 2008. "Towards new indicators of disadvantage: Deprivation and social exclusion in Australia." *Australian Journal of Social Issues* 43(2): 175–194.

Saunders, P., and M. Wong. 2012. "Promoting inclusion and combating deprivation: Recent changes in social disadvantage in Australia." Social Policy Research Centre, University of New South Wales.

Wilkins, R. 2014. "Evaluating the evidence on income inequality in Australia in the 2000s." *Economic Record* 90: 63–89.

CANADA

Hatfield, M., W. Pyper, and B. Gustajtis. 2010. "First comprehensive review of the market basket measure of low income." Applied Research Branch paper. Human Resources and Skills Development Canada.

Love, R. 1979. *Income distribution and inequality in Canada*. Ministry of Supply and Services, Ottawa.

Macdonald, D., and D. Wilson. 2013. *Poverty or prosperity: Indigenous children in Canada*. Canadian Centre for Policy Alternatives, Ottawa.

Murphy, B., C. Dionne, and X. Zhang. 2012. "Low income in Canada: A multi-line and multi-index perspective." Income Research Paper Series 75F0002M. Statistics Canada, Ottawa.

Murphy, B., X. Zhang, and C. Dionne. 2010. "Revising Statistics Canada's Low Income Measure (LIM)." 75F0002M, June. Statistics Canada, Ottawa.

Osberg, L. 2001. "Poverty among senior citizens: A Canadian success story." In P. Grady and A. Sharpe, eds., *The state of economics in Canada: Festschrift in honour of David Slater.* McGill-Queen's University Press, Montreal.

Wolfson, M. C. 1986. "Stasis amid change: Income inequality in Canada 1965–1983." *Review of Income and Wealth* 32: 337–369.

Zhang, X. 2010. "Low income measurement in Canada: What do different lines and indexes tell us?" Income Research Paper Series, Statistics Canada, Ottawa.

FINLAND

Berglund, M., M. Jäntti, L. Parkatti, and C. Sundqvist. 1998. "Long-run trends in the distribution of income in Finland 1920–1992." Åbo Akademi University.

Blomgren, J., H. Hiilamo, O. Kangas, and M. Niemalä. 2014. "Finland: Growing inequality with contested consequences." In B. Nolan, W. Salverda, D. Checchi, I. Marx, A. McKnight, I. G. Tóth, and H. van de Werfhorst, eds., *Changing inequalities and societal impacts in rich countries.* Oxford University Press, Oxford.

Riihelä, M., R. Sullström, and M. Tuomala. 2003. "On recent trends in economic poverty in Finland." Tampere Economic Working Paper 23. Department of Economics, University of Tampere.

FRANCE

Boiron, A., J. Labarthe, L. Richet-Mastain, and M. Z. Bonnin. 2015. "Les niveaux de vie en 2013." *Insee Première 1566.* INSEE, Paris.

Concialdi, P. 1997. "Income distribution in France: The mid-1980s turning point." In P. Gottschalk, B. Gustafsson, and E. Palmer, eds., *Changing patterns in the distribution of economic welfare: An international perspective.* Cambridge University Press, Cambridge.

Godefroy, P., J. Pujol, E. Raynaud, and M. Tomasini. 2010. "Inégalités de niveau de vie et mesures de la pauvreté en 2006." INSEE (website), Paris.

GERMANY

Becker, I. 1997. "Die Entwicklung der Einkommensverteilung und der Einkommensarmut in den alten Bundesländern von 1962 bis 1988." In I. Becker and R. Hauser, eds., *Einkommensverteilung und armut.* Campus, Frankfurt.

Deutsche Institut für Wirtschaftsforschung (DIW). 1973. "Einkommensverteilung und Schichtung der privaten Haushalte in der Bundesrepublik Deutschland 1950 bis 1970." Wochenbericht 25, Berlin.

Frick, J. R., M. M. Grabka, and R. Hauser. 2010. *Die Verteilung der Vermögen in Deutschland.* Edition Sigma, Berlin.
Hauser, R., and I. Becker. 2001. "Einkommensverteilung im Querschnitt und im Zeitverlauf 1973–1998." Bundesministerium für Arbeit und Sozialordnung, Bonn.
SOEP Group. 2015. "SOEP 2013—SOEPmonitor Individuals 1984–2013 (SOEP v30)." SOEP Survey Papers 284: Series E. DIW/SOEP, Berlin.

GREECE

ELSTAT. 2016. "2015 Survey on Income and Living Conditions." Press release. Piraeus.
Kaplanoglou, G., and V. T. Rapanos. 2015. "Evolutions in consumption inequality and poverty in Greece: The impact of the crisis and austerity policies." Department of Economics Discussion Report. University of Athens.
Katsimi, M., T. Moutos, G. Pagoulatos, and D. Sotiropoulos. 2014. "Greece: The (eventual) social hardship of soft budget constraints." In B. Nolan, W. Salverda, D. Checchi, I. Marx, A. McKnight, I. G. Tóth, and H. van de Werfhorst, eds., *Changing inequalities and societal impacts in rich countries.* Oxford University Press, Oxford.
Mitrakos, T. 2013. "Inequality, poverty, and living conditions in Greece: Recent developments and prospects." *Social Cohesion and Development* 8: 37–58.
Mitrakos, T., and P. Tsakloglou. 2012. "Inequality and poverty in Greece: Myths, realities, and the crisis." In O. Anastasakis and D. Singh, eds., *Reforming Greece: Sisyphean Task or Herculean Challenge?* South East European Studies at Oxford, European Studies Centre, St. Antony's College, University of Oxford.
Papatheodorou, C., and Y. Dafermos. 2010. "Structure and trends of the economic inequality and the poverty in Greece and the EU, 1995–2008." Observatory of Economic and Social Changes Report 2. Labour Institute, Greek General Confederation of Labour (in Greek).

IRELAND

Nolan, B., and C. T. Whelan. 2011. *Poverty and deprivation.* Oxford University Press, Oxford.
Nolan, B., C. T. Whelan, E. Calvert, T. Fahey, D. Healy, A. Mulcahy, B. Maître, M. Norris, I. O'Donnell, and N. Winston. 2014. "Ireland: Inequality and its impacts in boom and bust." In B. Nolan, W. Salverda, D. Checchi, I. Marx, A. McKnight, I. G. Tóth, and H. van de Werfhorst, eds., *Changing inequalities and societal impacts in rich countries.* Oxford University Press, Oxford.

ITALY

Banca d'Italia. 2018. *Survey on Household Income and Wealth—2016.* Banca d'Italia, Rome.
Beckermann, W. 1980. "Stime della povertà in Italia nel 1975." *Rivista Internazionale di Scienze Sociali* 88(2): 220–249.
Brandolini, A., R. Gambacorta, and A. Rosolia. 2018. "Inequality amid stagnation: Italy over the last quarter of a century." In B. Nolan, ed., *Inequality and inclusive growth*

in rich countries: Shared challenges and contrasting fortunes. Oxford University Press, Oxford.

Brandolini, A., and G. Vecchi. 2013. "Standards of living." In G. Toniolo, ed., *The Oxford handbook of the Italian economy since unification.* Oxford University Press, Oxford.

Carbonaro, G. 1985. "Nota sulle scale di equivalenza." In Commissione d'indagine sulla povertà, ed., *La povertà in Italia.* Istituto Poligrafico dello Stato, Rome.

Istat. 2009. *La misura della povertà assoluta.* Methods and norms 39. Istituto nazionale di statistica, Rome.

Istat. 2012. *Reddito e condizioni di vita—anno 2011.* Statistical report. Istituto nazionale di statistica, Rome.

Istat. 2013. *Reddito e condizioni di vita—anno 2012.* Statistical report. Istituto nazionale di statistica, Rome.

Istat. 2017. *Poverty in Italy.* http://www.istat.it/en/archive/202342.

Ministero dell'Economia e delle Finanze (MEF). 2017. *Comitato per gli indicatori di benessere equo e sostenibile.* http://www.mef.gov.it/ministero/comitati/CBES/.

JAPAN

Fukawa, T. 2006. "Income distribution in Japan based on IRS 1987–2002." *Japanese Journal of Social Security Policy* 5: 27–34.

Kohara, M., and F. Ohtake. 2014. "Rising inequality in Japan: A challenge caused by population ageing and drastic changes in employment." In B. Nolan, W. Salverda, D. Checchi, I. Marx, A. McKnight, I. G. Tóth, and H. van de Werfhorst, eds., *Changing inequalities and societal impacts in rich countries.* Oxford University Press, Oxford.

Lise, J., N. Sudo, M. Suzuki, K. Yamada, and T. Yamada. 2014. "Wage, income, and consumption inequality in Japan, 1981–2008: From boom to lost decades." *Review of Economic Dynamics* 17: 582–612 (supplementary materials).

Matsuyama, J. 2016. "Measuring poverty in Japan from a multidimensional perspective." Faculty of Economics, University of Toyama.

Noda, H. 2015. "How does the Japanese government measure and announce its official poverty rates?" Department of Welfare Science, Aichi Prefectural University.

Organisation for Economic Cooperation and Development (OECD). 2008. *Growing unequal? Income distribution and poverty in OECD countries.* OECD, Paris.

OECD. 2011. *Divided we stand: Why inequality keeps rising.* OECD, Paris.

OECD. 2015. *In it together: Why less inequality benefits all.* OECD, Paris.

Tachibanaki, T. 2005. *Confronting income inequality in Japan.* MIT Press, Cambridge, MA.

NEW ZEALAND

Easton, B. 1983. *Income distribution in New Zealand.* New Zealand Institute of Economic Research, Wellington.

Ministry of Social Development. 2016. *The 2016 household incomes report and the companion report using non-income measures (the NIMs report): Summary.* Ministry of Social Development, Wellington.

Perry, B. 2015. *Household incomes in New Zealand: Trends in indicators of inequality and hardship 1982 to 2014.* Ministry of Social Development, Wellington.

Perry, B. 2016. *Household incomes in New Zealand: Trends in indicators of inequality and hardship 1982 to 2015.* Ministry of Social Development, Wellington.

Perry, B. 2016a. *The material wellbeing of New Zealand households: Trends and relativities using non-income measures, with international comparisons.* Ministry of Social Development, Wellington.

NORWAY

Aaberge, R., A. B. Atkinson, and J. Modalsli. 2016. "The long-run distribution of income in Norway." Statistics Norway, Oslo.

Statistics Norway. 2013. "Immigrant poverty dynamics." Report 2013/40. Statistics Norway, Oslo.

POLAND

Atkinson, A. B., and J. Micklewright. 1992. *Economic transformation in Eastern Europe and the distribution of income.* Cambridge University Press, Cambridge.

Central Statistical Office (GUS). 2011. *Ubóstwo w Polsce w 2010 r.* GUS, Warsaw.

Central Statistical Office (GUS). 2017. *Quality of life in Poland.* GUS, Warsaw.

Central Statistical Office (GUS). 2017a. *Zasięg ubóstwa ekonomicznego w Polsce w 2016 r.* GUS, Warsaw.

Flemming, J., and J. Micklewright. 2000. "Income distribution, economic systems, and transition." In A. B. Atkinson and F. Bourguignon, eds., *Handbook of income distribution*, vol. 1. Elsevier Science BV, Amsterdam.

Kordos, J. 1991. "Poverty measurement in Poland." GUS, Warsaw.

Kordos, J. 1996. "Forty years of the household budget surveys in Poland." *Statistics in Transition* 2: 1119–1138.

Milanovic, B. 1992. "Poverty in Poland: 1978–88." *Review of Income and Wealth* 38(3): 329–340.

Organisation for Economic Cooperation and Development (OECD). 1996. *OECD Economic Surveys: Poland 1997.* OECD, Paris.

Szulc, A. 2006. "Poverty in Poland during the 1990s: Are the results robust?" *Review of Income and Wealth* 52(3): 423–448.

Szulc, A. 2008. "Checking the consistency of poverty in Poland: 1997–2003 evidence." *Post-Communist Economies* 20(1): 33–55.

UNICEF. 2003. *Social Monitor.* Innocenti Research Centre, Florence.

PORTUGAL

Instituto Nacional de Estatística. 2016. *Portugal—30 Years European Integration.* Instituto Nacional de Estatística, Lisbon.

Rodrigues, C. F. 2005. "Distribuição do rendimento, desigualdade e pobreza." PhD thesis, Universidade Technica de Lisboa.

Rodrigues, C. F., coordinator. 2016. *Desigualdade do rendimento e pobreza em Portugal.* Fundação Francisco Manuel dos Santos, Lisbon.

Rodrigues, C. F., and I. Andrade. 2012. "Monetary poverty, material deprivation, and consistent poverty in Portugal." *Notas Económicas* 35: 21–39.

Rodrigues, C. F., R. Figueiras, and V. Junqueira. 2011. "Portugal: Um pais profundamente desigual." Instituto Superior de Economia e Gestão, Lisbon.

Rodrigues, C. F., R. Figueiras, and V. Junqueira. 2012. *Desigualdade económica em Portugal.* Fundação Francisco Manuel dos Santos, Lisbon.

UNITED KINGDOM

Atkinson, A. B., and J. Micklewright. 1992. *Economic transformation in Eastern Europe and the distribution of income.* Cambridge University Press, Cambridge.

Belfield, C., J. Cribb, A. Hood, and R. Joyce. 2016. *Living standards, poverty, and inequality in the UK: 2016.* Institute for Fiscal Studies, London.

Department for Work and Pensions. 2016. *Households below average income, 1994/95 to 2014/15.* Department for Work and Pensions, London.

Waldfogel, J. 2013. *Britain's war on poverty.* Russell Sage Foundation, New York.

UNITED STATES

Budd, E. C. 1970. "Postwar changes in the size distribution of income in the US." *American Economic Review: Papers and Proceedings* 60: 247–260.

Fisher, G. 1986. "Estimates of the poverty population under the current official definition for years before 1959." Office of the Assistant Secretary for Planning and Evaluation, US Department of Health and Human Services, Washington, DC.

Meyer, B. D., and J. S. Sullivan. 2010. "Five decades of consumption and income poverty." National Bureau of Economic Research Working Paper 14827. Published as "Consumption and income poverty in the US," in P. N. Jefferson, ed., *The Oxford handbook of the economics of poverty.* Oxford University Press, Oxford, 2012.

Mitra, S., and D. L. Brucker. 2015. "Income poverty and multiple deprivations in a high income country: The case of the United States." Department of Economics Discussion Paper 2014-05 (revised). Fordham University, New York.

US Census Bureau. 2016. *Income, poverty, and health insurance coverage in the United States: 2015.* US Government Printing Office, Washington, DC.

US Census Bureau. 2017. *Income, poverty, and health insurance coverage in the United States: 2016.* US Government Printing Office, Washington, DC.

BIBLIOGRAPHY

Aaberge, R., F. Bourguignon, A. Brandolini, F. Ferreira, J. Gornick, J. Hills, M. Jäntti, S. P. Jenkins, E. Marlier, J. Micklewright, B. Nolan, T. Piketty, W. J. Radermacher, T. M. Smeeding, N. H. Stern, J. Stiglitz, and H. Sutherland. 2017. "Tony Atkinson and his legacy." *Review of Income and Wealth* 63(3): 411–444.

Aaberge, R., and A. Brandolini. 2015. "Multidimensional poverty and inequality." In A. B. Atkinson and F. Bourguignon, eds., *Handbook of income distribution*, vol. 2A. Elsevier, Amsterdam.

Aaberge, R., A. Langørgen, and P. Lindgren. 2010. "The impact of basic public services on the distribution of income in European countries." In A. B. Atkinson and E. Marlier, eds., *Income and living conditions in Europe*. Publications Office of the European Union, Luxembourg.

Abel-Smith, B., and P. Townsend. 1965. *The Poor and the poorest*. LSE Occasional Papers on Social Administration 17. G. Bell and Sons, London.

Acemoglu, D., and J. A. Robinson. 2010. "Why is Africa poor?" *Economic History of Developing Regions* 25(1): 21–50.

Acharya, S. 2004. "Measuring and analysing poverty (with particular reference to the case of Nepal)." *European Journal of Comparative Economics* 1: 195–215.

Aden, N. 2016. "The roads to decoupling: 21 countries are reducing carbon emissions while growing GDP." Blog post. World Resources Institute, Washington, DC.

Ahluwalia, M. S. 1974. "Income inequality: Some dimensions of the problem." In H. B. Chenery, M. S. Ahluwalia, C. L. G. Bell, J. H. Duloy, and R. Jolly, eds., *Redistribution with growth*. Oxford University Press, London.

Ahluwalia, M. S., N. G. Carter, and H. B. Chenery. 1979. "Growth and poverty in developing countries." *Journal of Development Economics* 6: 299–341.

Akumu, O., and B. Frouws. 2017. "Drought: A contributing or limiting factor in migration?" ReliefWeb, UN Office for the Coordination of Humanitarian Affairs, New York.

Alesina, A., and D. Rodrik. 1994. "Distributive politics and economic growth." *Quarterly Journal of Economics* 109(2): 465–490.

Alkire, S. 2018. "The research agenda on multidimensional poverty measurement: Important and as-yet unanswered questions." OPHI Working Paper 119. University of Oxford, Oxford.

Alkire, S., and M. Apablaza. 2017. "Multidimensional poverty in Europe 2006–2012: Illustrating a methodology." In A. B. Atkinson, A.-C. Guio, and E. Marlier, eds., *Monitoring social inclusion in Europe*. Publications Office of the European Union, Luxembourg.

Alkire, S., and J. Foster. 2011. "Counting and multidimensional poverty measurement." *Journal of Public Economics* 95: 476–487.

Alkire, S., J. Foster, S. Seth, M. E. Santos, J. M. Roche, and P. Ballon. 2015. *Multidimensional poverty measurement and analysis*. Oxford University Press, Oxford.

Alkire, S., and S. Jahan. 2018. "The new Global MPI 2018: Aligning with the Sustainable Development Goals." OPHI Working Paper 121. University of Oxford, Oxford.

Alkire, S., U. Kanagaratnam, and N. Suppa. 2018. "The Global Multidimensional Poverty Index (MPI): 2018 revision." MPI Methodological Notes 46. OPHI, University of Oxford, Oxford.

Alkire, S., C. Oldiges, and U. Kanagaratnam. 2018. "Multidimensional poverty reduction in India 2005/6–2015/16: Still a long way to go but the poorest are catching up." OPHI Research in Progress 54a. University of Oxford, Oxford.

Alkire, S., and G. Robles. 2017. "Multidimensional Poverty Index—Summer 2017: Brief methodological note and results." MPI Methodological Notes 44. OPHI, University of Oxford, Oxford.

Alkire, S., J. M. Roche, and A. Vaz. 2017. "Changes over time in multidimensional poverty: Methodology and results for 34 countries." *World Development* 94: 232–249.

Alkire, S., and M. E. Santos. 2014. "Measuring acute poverty in the developing world: Robustness and scope of the multidimensional poverty index." *World Development* 59: 251–274.

Alkire, S., and S. Seth. 2015. "Multidimensional poverty reduction in India between 1999 and 2006: Where and how?" *World Development* 72: 93–108.

Allen, R. C. 2013. "Poverty lines in history, theory, and current international practice." Nuffield College, Oxford.

Allen, R. C. 2016. "Absolute poverty: When necessity displaces desire." Discussion Paper in Economic and Social History 141. University of Oxford.

Allen, R. C. 2017. "Absolute poverty: When necessity displaces desire." *American Economic Review* 107(12): 3690–3721.

Almås, I., T. Beatty, and T. Crossley. 2018. "Lost in translation: What do Engel curves tell us about the cost of living?" IFS Working Paper W18/04. Institute for Fiscal Studies, London.

Alston, P. 2017. "Statement on visit to the USA, by Professor Philip Alston, United Nations Special Rapporteur on extreme poverty and human rights." Office of the UN High Commissioner for Human Rights, Geneva.

Alston, P. 2018. *Report of the Special Rapporteur on extreme poverty and human rights on his mission to the United States of America.* Human Rights Council, Thirty-Eighth Session, 18 June–6 July, UN General Assembly, New York.

Alston, P. 2018a. "Statement on visit to the United Kingdom, by Professor Philip Alston, United Nations special rapporteur on extreme poverty and human rights." Office of the UN High Commissioner for Human Rights, Geneva.

Altimir, O. 1987. "Income distribution statistics in Latin America and their reliability." *Review of Income and Wealth* 33(2): 111–155.

Alvaredo, F., and A. B. Atkinson. 2016. "Top incomes in South Africa over a century 1903–2013." INET Oxford Working Paper 2016–06. Institute for New Economic Thinking at the Oxford Martin School, University of Oxford.

Arndt, C., A. McKay, and F. Tarp, eds. 2016. *Growth and poverty in sub-Saharan Africa.* Oxford University Press, Oxford.

Arndt, C., and J. Volkert. 2011. "The capability approach: A framework for official German poverty and wealth reports." *Journal of Human Development and Capabilities* 12(3): 311–337.

Arrow, K. J. 2006. "Freedom and social choice: Notes in the margin." *Utilitas* 18: 52–60.

Asian Development Bank (ADB). 2008. *Research study on poverty-specific purchasing power parities for selected countries in Asia and the Pacific.* Asian Development Bank, Manila.

ATD Fourth World. 2015. Submission to the Commission on Global Poverty.

Atkinson, A. B. 1969. *Poverty in Britain and the reform of social security.* Cambridge University Press, Cambridge.

Atkinson, A. B. 1970. "On the measurement of inequality." *Journal of Economic Theory* 2: 244–263.

Atkinson, A. B. 1975. *The economics of inequality,* 1st ed. Oxford University Press, Oxford.

Atkinson, A. B. 1987. "On the measurement of poverty." *Econometrica* 55: 749–764.

Atkinson, A. B. 1990. "Public economics and the economic public." *European Economic Review* 34: 225–248.

Atkinson, A. B. 1997. "Bringing income distribution in from the cold." *Economic Journal* 107: 297–321.

Atkinson, A. B. 1998. *Poverty in Europe.* Blackwell Publishers, Oxford.

Atkinson, A. B. 1999. *The economic consequences of rolling back the welfare state.* MIT Press, Cambridge, MA.

Atkinson, A. B., ed. 2005. *New sources of development finance.* Oxford University Press, Oxford.

Atkinson, A. B. 2008. *The changing distribution of earnings in OECD countries.* Oxford University Press, Oxford.

Atkinson, A. B. 2013. "Ensuring social inclusion in changing labour and capital markets." Economic Papers 481. Directorate-General for Economic and Financial Affairs, European Commission, Brussels.

Atkinson, A. B. 2014. "The colonial legacy: Income inequality in former British African colonies." WIDER Working Paper 2014/045. UN University World Institute for Development Economics Research, Helsinki.

Atkinson, A. B. 2014a. *Public economics in an age of austerity.* Routledge, London and New York.

Atkinson, A. B. 2015. *Inequality: What can be done?* Harvard University Press, Cambridge, MA.

Atkinson, A. B., and F. Bourguignon. 2000. "Pauvreté et inclusion dans une perspective mondiale." *Revue d'économie du développement* 8: 13–32 (English version published as "Inclusion from a world perspective" in *Governance, equity, and global markets,* La Documentation Française, 179–192).

Atkinson, A. B., and F. Bourguignon. 2001. "Poverty and inclusion in a world perspective." In J. Stiglitz and P.-A. Muet, eds., *Governance, equity, and global markets,* Oxford University Press, Oxford.

Atkinson, A. B., and A. Brandolini. 2001. "Promise and pitfalls in the use of 'secondary' data-sets: Income inequality in OECD countries as a case study." *Journal of Economic Literature* 39(3): 771–799.

Atkinson, A. B., and A. Brandolini. 2010. "On analyzing the world distribution of income." *World Bank Economic Review* 24: 1–37.

Atkinson, A. B., B. Cantillon, E. Marlier, and B. Nolan. 2002. *Social indicators: The EU and social inclusion.* Oxford University Press, Oxford.

Atkinson, A. B., A.-C. Guio, and E. Marlier, eds. 2017. *Monitoring social inclusion in Europe.* Publications Office of the European Union, Luxembourg.

Atkinson, A. B., A.-C. Guio, and E. Marlier. 2017a. "Monitoring the evolution of income poverty and real incomes over time." In A. B. Atkinson, A.-C. Guio, and E. Marlier, eds., *Monitoring social inclusion in Europe.* Publications Office of the European Union, Luxembourg.

Atkinson, A. B., J. Hasell, S. Morelli, and M. Roser. 2017. *The chartbook of economic inequality.* Institute for New Economic Thinking at the Oxford Martin School, University of Oxford, Oxford.

Atkinson, A. B., and E. Marlier. 2010. *Analysing and measuring social inclusion in a global context.* Department of Economic and Social Affairs, United Nations, New York.

Atkinson, A. B., and E. Marlier. 2011. "Human development and indicators of poverty and social exclusion as part of the policy process." *Indian Journal of Human Development* 5: 293–320.

Atkinson, A. B., and J. Micklewright. 1983. "On the reliability of income data in the Family Expenditure Survey, 1970–1977." *Journal of the Royal Statistical Society: Series A* 146(1): 33–61.

Atkinson, A. B., and J. Micklewright. 1992. *Economic transformation in Eastern Europe and the distribution of income.* Cambridge University Press, Cambridge.

Atkinson, A. B., and T. Piketty, eds. 2007. *Top incomes over the twentieth century: A contrast between continental European and English-speaking countries.* Oxford University Press, Oxford.

Atkinson, A. B., and T. Piketty, eds. 2010. *Top incomes: A global perspective.* Oxford University Press, Oxford.

Atkinson, A. B., L. Rainwater, T. M. Smeeding. 1995. *Income distribution in OECD countries: The evidence from the Luxembourg Income Study.* OECD, Paris.

Atkinson, A. B., and N. H. Stern. 2017. "Tony Atkinson on poverty, inequality, and public policy: The work and life of a great economist." *Annual Review of Economics* 9: 1–20.

Atkinson, A. B., and J. E. Stiglitz. 1969. "A new view of technological change." *Economic Journal* 79: 573–578.

Austin, G. 2010. "African economic development and colonial legacies." *International Development Policy/Revue internationale de politique de développement* 1: 11–32.

Austin, G. 2015. "The economics of colonialism in Africa." In C. Monga and J. Y. Lin, eds., *The Oxford handbook of Africa and economics,* vol. 1, *Context and concepts.* Oxford University Press, Oxford.

Australian Agency for International Development (AusAID). 2009. *Tracking development and governance in the Pacific.* AusAID, Canberra.

Baldwin, E., Y. Cai, and K. Kuralbayeva. 2018. "To build or not to build? Capital stocks and climate policy." Working Paper 290. Grantham Research Institute on Climate Change and the Environment, London.

Bane, M. J., and D. T. Ellwood. 1986. "Slipping in and out of poverty." *Journal of Human Resources* 21: 1–23.

Banerjee, A. 2011. "Draw the right line." *Hindustan Times,* October 24.

Basu, K. 2006. "Gender and say: A model of household behaviour with endogenously determined balance of power." *Economic Journal* 116: 558–580.

Basu, K., and J. E. Foster. 1998. "On measuring literacy." *Economic Journal* 108: 1733–1749.

Batana, Y., M. Bussolo, and J. Cockburn. 2013. "Global extreme poverty rates for children, adults, and the elderly." *Economics Letters* 120: 405–407.

Beegle, K., L. Christiaensen, A. Dabalen, and I. Gaddis. 2016. *Poverty in a rising Africa*, vols. 1 and 2. World Bank, Washington, DC.

Bell, E. T. 1953. *Men of mathematics*, vol. 2. Pelican Books, London.

Bhagat, R. B. 2005. "Rural-urban classification and municipal governance in India." *Singapore Journal of Tropical Geography* 26(1): 61–73.

Bhagwati, J. N. 2004. *In defense of globalization*. Oxford University Press, Oxford.

Bhalla, A. S., and P. McCormick. 2009. *Poverty among immigrant children in Europe*. Palgrave-Macmillan, Basingstoke.

Bigsten, A. 1986. "Welfare and economic growth in Kenya, 1914–76." *World Development* 14: 1151–1160.

Bigsten, A. 1987. "Income distribution and growth in a dual economy: Kenya 1914–1976." Department of Economics, University of Gothenburg.

Blank, R. M. 2008. "How to improve poverty measurement in the United States." *Journal of Policy Analysis and Management* 27: 233–254.

Blow, L., and A. Leicester. 2012. "Do the poor pay more? An investigation of British grocery purchase prices." Institute for Fiscal Studies, London.

Boskin, M. J., E. R. Dulberger, R. J. Gordon, Z. Griliches, and D. W. Jorgenson. 1996. *Final report of the Commission to Study the Consumer Price Index*. US Senate Committee on Finance, US Government Printing Office, Washington, DC.

Boskin, M. J., E. R. Dulberger, R. J. Gordon, Z. Griliches, and D. W. Jorgenson. 1998. "Consumer prices in the Consumer Price Index and the cost of living." *Journal of Economic Perspectives* 12(1): 3–26.

Bossuroy, T., and D. Cogneau. 2013. "Social mobility and colonial legacy in five African countries." *Review of Income and Wealth* 59(S1): S84–S110.

Bourguignon, F. 2003. "The growth elasticity of poverty reduction: Explaining heterogeneity across countries and time periods." In T. Eicher and S. Turnovsky, eds., *Inequality and growth: Theory and policy implications*. MIT Press, Cambridge, MA.

Bourguignon, F. 2015. "Appraising income inequality databases in Latin America." *Journal of Economic Inequality* 13: 557–578.

Bourguignon, F., A. Bénassy-Quéré, S. Dercon, A. Estache, J. W. Gunning, R. Kanbur, S. Klasen, S. Maxwell, J.-P. Platteau, and A. Spadaro. 2010. "The Millennium Development Goals: An assessment." In R. Kanbur and M. Spence, eds., *Equity and growth in a globalizing world*. World Bank Publications, New York.

Bowden, S., B. Chiripanhura, and P. Mosley. 2008. "Measuring and explaining poverty in six African countries: A long-period approach." *Journal of International Development* 20: 1049–1079.

Bradbury, B., S. P. Jenkins, and J. Micklewright. 2001. "Conceptual and measurement issues." In B. Bradbury, S. P. Jenkins, and J. Micklewright, eds., *The dynamics of child poverty in industrialised countries*. Cambridge University Press, Cambridge.

Bradshaw, J., and E. Mayhew. 2011. *The measurement of extreme poverty in the European Union*. European Commission, DG Employment, Social Affairs and Inclusion, Brussels.

Brandolini, A., and F. Carta. 2016. "Some reflections on the social welfare bases of the measurement of global income inequality." *Journal of Globalization and Development* 7: 1–15.

Brandolini, A., and P. Cipollone. 2003. "Urban poverty in developed countries." In Y. Amiel and J. A. Bishop, eds., *Research on economic inequality,* vol. 9, *Inequality, welfare, and poverty: Theory and measurement.* Elsevier Science, Oxford.

Brown, C., M. Ravallion, and D. van de Walle. 2017. "Are poor individuals mainly found in poor households? Evidence using nutrition data for Africa." Policy Research Working Paper 8001. World Bank, Washington D C.

Browning, M., P.-A. Chiappori, and Y. Weiss. 2014. *Family economics.* Cambridge University Press, New York.

Buhmann, B., L. Rainwater, G. Schmaus, and T. Smeeding. 1988. "Equivalence scales, well-being, inequality, and poverty: Sensitivity estimates across ten countries using the Luxembourg Income Study (LIS) database." *Review of Income and Wealth* 34: 115–142.

Bundesregierung. 2017. *Lebenslagen in Deutschland: Der fünfte Armuts- und Reichtumsbericht der Bundesregierung.* Bundesregierung, Berlin.

Calvo-González, O. 2016. "Why are indigenous peoples more likely to be poor?" *The Data Blog,* 17 February. World Bank, Washington, DC.

Caplovitz, D. 1968. *The poor pay more: Consumer practices of low-income families.* Free Press, New York.

Carr-Hill, R. 2013. "Missing millions and measuring development progress." *World Development* 46: 30–44.

Carr-Hill, R. 2015. "Non-household populations: Implications for measurements of poverty globally and in the UK." *Journal of Social Policy* 44: 255–275.

Case, A., and A. Deaton. 2015. "Rising morbidity and mortality in midlife among white non-Hispanic Americans in the 21st century." *PNAS* 112: 15078–15083.

Casley, D. J., and D. A. Lury. 1987. *Data collection in developing countries,* 2nd ed. Oxford University Press, Oxford.

Castleman, T., J. Foster, and S. C. Smith. 2015. "Person equivalent headcount measures of poverty." Institute for International Economic Policy Working Paper Series 2015–10. George Washington University, Washington, DC.

Centro de Estudios Distributivos, Laborales, y Sociales (CEDLAS), and World Bank. 2014. "A Guide to SEDLAC Socio-Economic Database for Latin America and the Caribbean." CEDLAS and World Bank, Buenos Aires and Washington, DC.

Chakravarty, S. R. 2009. *Inequality, polarization, and poverty.* Springer, New York.

Chance, W. 1966. "A note on the origins of index numbers." *Review of Economics and Statistics* 48(1): 108–110.

Chandy, L., and C. Smith. 2014. "How poor are America's poorest? U.S. $2 a day poverty in a global context." Policy Paper 2014-03. Brookings Institution, Washington, DC.

Channon, A., S. Padmadas, and J. McDonald. 2011. "Measuring birth weight in developing countries: Does the method of reporting in retrospective surveys matter?" *Maternal and Child Health Journal* 15(1): 12–18.

Chediak, M. 2017. "The latest bull case for electric cars: The cheapest batteries ever." 5 December. Bloomberg New Energy Finance, London.

Chen, S., and M. Ravallion. 2004. "How have the world's poorest fared since the early 1980s?" *World Bank Research Observer* 19: 141–170.

Chen, S., and M. Ravallion. 2010. "The developing world is poorer than we thought, but no less successful in the fight against poverty." *Quarterly Journal of Economics* 125: 1577–1625.

Chen, S., and M. Ravallion. 2013. "More relatively-poor people in a less absolutely-poor world." *Review of Income and Wealth* 59(1): 1–28.

Cherchye, L., B. De Rockz, A. Lewbel, and F. Vermeulen. 2015. "Sharing rule identification for general collective consumption models." *Econometrica* 83: 2001–2041.

Chiappori, P.-A., and C. Meghir. 2015. "Intrahousehold inequality." In A. B. Atkinson and F. Bourguignon, eds., *Handbook of income distribution*, vol. 2B, Elsevier, Amsterdam.

Chūbachi, M., and K. Taira. 1976. "Poverty in modern Japan: Perceptions and realities." In H. T. Patrick, ed., *Japanese industrialization and its social consequences.* University of California Press, Berkeley.

Citro, C. F., and R. T. Michael, eds. 1995. *Measuring poverty: A new approach.* National Academies Press, Washington, DC.

Cogneau, D., K. Houngbedji, and S. Mesplé-Somps. 2016. "The fall of the elephant: Two decades of poverty increase in Côte d'Ivoire, 1988–2008." In C. Arndt, A. McKay, and F. Tarp, eds., *Growth and poverty in Sub-Saharan Africa.* Oxford University Press, Oxford.

Collier, P. 2007. *The bottom billion.* Oxford University Press, Oxford.

Consejo Nacional para la Evaluacion de la Politica de Desarrolo Social (CONEVAL). 2010. *Methodology for multidimensional poverty measurement in Mexico.* CONEVAL, Mexico City.

Corsi, M., F. Botti, and C. D'Ippoliti. 2016. "The gendered nature of poverty in the EU: Individualized versus collective poverty measures." *Feminist Economics* 22(4): 82–100.

Côte d'Ivoire Institut National de la Statistique. 2008. *Enquete sur le niveau de vie des menages (ENV2008): Rapport définitif.* Institut National de la Statistique, Abidjan.

Coulter, F. A. E., F. A. Cowell, and S. P. Jenkins. 1992. "Equivalence scale relativities and the extent of inequality and poverty." *Economic Journal* 102(414): 1067–1082.

Dabalen, A., E. Graham, K. Himelein, and R. Mungaim. 2014. "Estimating poverty in the absence of consumption data: The case of Liberia." Policy Research Working Paper 7024. World Bank, Washington, DC.

Dabalen, A. L., I. Gaddis, and N. T. V. Nguyen. 2016. "CPI bias and its implications for poverty reduction in Africa." Policy Research Working Paper 7907. World Bank, Washington, DC.

Datt, G., and M. Ravallion. 1992. "Growth and redistribution components of changes in poverty measures: A decomposition with applications to Brazil and India in the 1980s." *Journal of Development Economics* 38(2): 275–295.

Deaton, A. 1997. *The analysis of household surveys.* Johns Hopkins University Press, Baltimore.

Deaton, A. 1998. "Getting prices right: What should be done?" *Journal of Economic Perspectives* 12(1): 37–46.

Deaton, A. 2005. "Measuring poverty in a growing world (or measuring growth in a poor world)." *Review of Economics and Statistics* 87: 1–19.

Deaton, A. 2010. "Price indexes, inequality, and the measurement of world poverty." *American Economic Review* 100: 5–34.

Deaton, A. 2013. *The great escape: Health, wealth, and the origins of inequality.* Princeton University Press, Princeton, NJ, and Oxford.

Deaton, A., and B. Aten. 2017. "Trying to understand the PPPs in ICP 2011: Why are the results so different?" *American Economic Journal: Macroeconomics* 9(1): 243–264.

Deaton, A., and J. Drèze. 2009. "Food and nutrition in India: Facts and interpretations." *Economic and Political Weekly* 44 (7): 42–65.

Deaton, A., and O. Dupriez. 2011. "Purchasing power parity exchange rates for the global poor." *American Economic Journal: Applied Economics* 3: 137–166.

Deaton, A., and A. Heston. 2010. "Understanding PPPs and PPP-based national accounts." *American Economic Journal: Macroeconomics* 2(4): 1–35.

Deaton, A., and V. Kozel. 2005. "Data and dogma: The great Indian poverty debate." *World Bank Research Observer* 20(2): 177–199.

Decancq, K., and M. A. Lugo. 2012. "Weights in multidimensional indices of well-being: An overview." *Econometric Reviews* 32: 7–34.

Decerf, B. 2015. "A new index combining the absolute and relative aspects of income poverty: Theory and application." CORE Discussion Paper 2015/50. Center for Operations Research and Econometrics, Louvain-la-Neuve.

Dell'Aglio, D., W. Cunningham, S. Koller, V. C. Borges, and J. S. Leon. 2007. "Youth well-being in Brazil: An index for cross-regional comparisons." World Bank Policy Research Working Paper 4189. World Bank, Washington, DC.

Demery, L., and C. Grootaert. 1993. "Correcting for sampling bias in the measurement of welfare and poverty in the Côte d'Ivoire Living Standards Survey." *World Bank Economic Review* 7: 263–292.

Deming, E. 1944. "On errors in surveys." *American Sociological Review* 9: 359–369.

Devarajan, S. 2013. "Africa's statistical tragedy." *Review of Income and Wealth* (series 59, special issue): S9–S15.

Diewert, W. E. 1998. "Index number issues in the consumer price index." *Journal of Economic Perspectives* 12(1): 47–58.

Di Meglio, E., D. Dupré, F. Montaigne, and P. Wolff. 2017. "Investing in statistics: EU-SILC." In A. B. Atkinson, A.-C. Guio, and E. Marlier, eds., *Monitoring social inclusion in Europe*. Publications Office of the European Union, Luxembourg.

Dollar, D., and A. Kraay. 2002. "Growth is good for the poor." *Journal of Economic Growth* 7(3): 195–225.

Dollar, D., T. Kleineberg, and A. Kraay. 2016. "Growth is still good for the poor." *European Economic Review* 81: 68–85.

Dominican Republic. 2012. *Metodología para el cálculo de la medición oficial de la pobreza monetaria en la República Dominicana*. Ministerio de Economía, Planificación y Desarrollo (MEPyD) and Oficina Nacional de Estadística (ONE), Santo Domingo.

Dorfman, R., P. A. Samuelson, and R. M. Solow. 1958. *Linear programming and economic analysis*. McGraw-Hill, New York.

Drèze, J., and A. Sen. 2013. *An uncertain glory: India and its contradictions*. Allen Lane, London.

Duclos, J.-Y., and A. Araar. 2006. *Poverty and equity*. Springer, Ottawa.

Dykstra, S., C. Kenny, and J. Sandefur. 2014. "Global absolute poverty fell by almost half on Tuesday." Blog, 2 May. Center for Global Development, Washington, DC.

Easterly, W., and S. Rebelo. 1993. "Marginal income tax rates and economic growth in developing countries." *European Economic Review* 37(2–3): 409–417.

Economic Commission for Latin America and the Caribbean (ECLAC). 2018. *Social Panorama of Latin America, 2017.* LC/PUB.2018/1-P. Santiago.

The Economist. 2017. "The Big Mac index full data-set." Accessed 10 November 2017.

Edgeworth, F. Y. 1881. *Mathematical psychics.* C. Kegan Paul and Co., London.

Edin, K. J., and H. L. Shaefer. 2015. *$2.00 a day: Living on almost nothing in America.* Houghton Mifflin Harcourt, Boston.

Ehrhart, C. 2009. "The effects of inequality on growth: A survey of the theoretical and empirical literature." ECINEQ Working Paper 107. Society for the Study of Economic Inequality, Palma de Mallorca.

Equality Trust. 2016. "The spirit level." Downloaded 2 December 2016.

Erikson, R. 1993. "Descriptions of inequality: The Swedish approach to welfare research." In M. Nussbaum and A. Sen, eds., *The quality of life.* Clarendon Press, Oxford.

European Commission. 2017. *Social Protection Committee annual report 2017.* Publications Office of the European Union, Luxembourg.

Eurostat. 2017. *Persistent at-risk-of-poverty rates.* Online database accessed August 2017.

Expert Centre. 1995. "Technical report on results of anthropometric measurements in Uzbekistan." Expert Centre, Tashkent.

Feenstra, R. C., R. Inklaar, and M. P. Timmer. 2015. "The next generation of the Penn World Table." *American Economic Review* 105(10): 3150–3182.

Fellegi, I. P. 1997. "On poverty and low income." 13F0027XIE, September. Statistics Canada, Ottawa, Ontario.

Ferreira, F. H. G. 2017. "Global poverty today, the 1908 winter in St. Petersburg, and 'controversy bias.'" *Let's Talk Development* blog, 12 November. World Bank, Washington, DC.

Ferreira, F. H. G., S. Chen, A. L. Dabalen, Y. M. Dikhanov, N. Hamadeh, D. M. Jolliffe, A. Narayan, E. B. Prydz, A. L. Revenga, P. Sangraula, U. Serajuddin, and N. Yoshida. 2015. "A global count of the extreme poor in 2012: Data issues, methodology, and initial results." Policy Research Working Paper 7432. World Bank, Washington, DC.

Ferreira, F. H. G., S. Chen, A. L. Dabalen, Y. M. Dikhanov, N. Hamadeh, D. M. Jolliffe, A. Narayan, E. B. Prydz, A. L. Revenga, P. Sangraula, U. Serajuddin, and N. Yoshida. 2016. "A global count of the extreme poor in 2012: Data issues, methodology, and initial results." *Journal of Economic Inequality* 14: 141–172.

Ferreira, F. H. G, and M. A. Lugo. 2013. "Multidimensional poverty analysis: Looking for a middle ground." *World Bank Research Observer* 2: 220–235.

Ferreira, F. H. G., and N. Lustig. 2015. "Appraising cross-national income inequality databases: An introduction." *Journal of Economic Inequality* 13(4): 497–526.

Ferreira, F. H. G., and M. Ravallion. 2009. "Poverty and inequality: The global context." In W. Salverda, B. Nolan, and T. M. Smeeding, eds., *The Oxford handbook of economic inequality.* Oxford University Press, Oxford.

Fesseau, M., F. Wolff, and M. L. Mattonetti. 2013. "A cross-country comparison of household income, consumption, and wealth between micro sources and national accounts aggregates." OECD Statistics Working Paper 2013/03. OECD, Paris.

Fisher, G. M. 1992. "The development and history of the poverty thresholds." *Social Security Bulletin* 55(4): 3–14.

Fisher, J., D. S. Johnson, and T. M. Smeeding. 2015. "Inequality of income and consumption in the US: Measuring the trends in inequality from 1984 to 2011 for the same individuals." *Review of Income and Wealth* 61: 630–650.

Flemming, J., and J. Micklewright. 2000. "Income distribution, economic systems, and transition." In Atkinson, A. B. and F. Bourguignon, eds., *Handbook of income distribution*, vol. 1. Elsevier, Amsterdam.

Folbre, N. 1986. "Hearts and spades: Paradigms of household economics." *World Development* 14: 245–255.

Food and Agriculture Organization (FAO). 2001. *Human energy requirements*. Food and Nutrition Technical Report 1. FAO, Rome.

Foster, J. E. 1998. "Absolute versus relative poverty." *American Economic Review Papers and Proceedings* 88: 335–341.

Foster, J., J. Greer, and E. Thorbecke. 1984. "A class of decomposable poverty measure." *Econometrica* 52: 761–776.

Frankel, S. H. 1942. "World economic solidarity." *South African Journal of Economics* 10: 169–192.

Frazer, H., A.-C. Guio, E. Marlier, B. Vanhercke, and T. Ward. 2014. "Putting the fight against poverty and social exclusion at the heart of the EU agenda: A contribution to the Mid-Term Review of the Europe 2020 Strategy." OSE Paper Series, Research Paper 15. European Social Observatory (OSE), Brussels.

Fusco, A., A.-C. Guio, and E. Marlier. 2010. "Characterising the income poor and the materially deprived in European countries." In A. B. Atkinson and E. Marlier, eds., *Income and living conditions in Europe*. Eurostat, Luxembourg.

Gallup, J. L. 2013. "Is there a Kuznets curve?" Working paper. Portland University, Portland, OR.

Garner, T., D. Johnson, and M. Kokoski. 1996. "An experimental consumer price index for the poor." *Monthly Labour Review* (September): 32–42.

Garroway, C., and J. R. de Laiglesia. 2012. "On the relevance of relative poverty for developing countries." OECD Development Centre Working Paper 314. OECD, Paris.

Gazdar, H. 2003. "A review of migration issues in Pakistan." Refugee and Migratory Movements Research Unit, University of Dhaka, Dhaka.

Gentilini, U., and A. Sumner. 2012. "What do national poverty lines tell us about global poverty?" IDS Working Paper 392. Institute of Development Studies, Brighton.

Ghana Statistical Service. 2014. *Ghana Living Standards Survey round 6 (GLSS 6) main report*. Ghana Statistical Service, Accra.

Gibson, J. 2005. "Statistical tools and estimation methods for poverty measures based on cross-sectional household surveys." Chapter 5 in *Handbook on poverty statistics: Concepts, methods, and policy use*. United Nations Statistics Division, New York.

Gibson, J., K. Beegle, J. De Weerdt, and J. Friedman. 2015. "What does variation in survey design reveal about the nature of measurement errors in household consumption?" *Oxford Bulletin of Economics and Statistics* 77(3): 466–474.

Giménez, L., and D. Jolliffe. 2014. "Inflation for the poor in Bangladesh: A comparison of CPI and household survey data." *Bangladesh Development Studies* 37: 57–81.

Global Coalition to End Child Poverty. 2015. Submission to the Commission on Global Poverty.

Goedemé, T., B. Storms, T. Penne, and K. Van den Bosch, eds. 2015. *The development of a methodology for comparable reference budgets in Europe—Final report of the pilot project*. Publications Office of the European Union, Luxembourg.

Goldin, I., G. Cameron, and M. Balarajan. 2011. *Exceptional people: How migration shaped our world and will define our future*. Princeton University Press, Princeton, NJ, and Oxford.

Goldstein, S. 1990. "Urbanization in China, 1982–87: Effects of migration and reclassification." *Population and Development Review* 16: 673–701.

Greenberg, J. 2014. "Meet the 'zombie stat' that just won't die." PunditFact, 3 July.

Greenstein, J., U. Gentilini, and A. Sumner. 2014. "National or international poverty lines or both? Setting goals for income poverty after 2015." *Journal of Human Development and Capabilities* 15 (2–3): 132–146.

Grootaert, C., and R. Kanbur. 1994. "A new regional price index for Côte d'Ivoire using data from the International Comparisons Project." *Journal of African Economies* 3: 114–141.

Groves, R. M., F. Fowler, M. Couper, E. Singer, and R. Tourangeau. 2004. *Survey methodology*. Wiley, New York.

Groves, R. M., and L. Lyberg. 2010. "Total survey error: Past, present, and future." *Public Opinion Quarterly* 74: 849–879.

Guio, A.-C., D. Gordon, and E. Marlier. 2012. "Measuring material deprivation in the EU: Indicators for the whole population and child-specific indicators." Eurostat Methodologies and Working Papers. Office for Official Publications of the European Communities, Luxembourg.

Guio, A.-C., D. Gordon, and E. Marlier. 2017. "Measuring child material deprivation in the EU." In A. B. Atkinson, A.-C. Guio, and E. Marlier, eds., *Monitoring social inclusion in Europe*. Publications Office of the European Union, Luxembourg.

Guio, A.-C., D. Gordon, E. Marlier, H. Najera, and M. Pomati. 2018. "Towards an EU measure of child deprivation." *Child Indicators Research* 11(3): 835–860.

Guio, A.-C., D. Gordon, H. Najera, and M. Pomati. 2017. "Revising the EU material deprivation variables." Eurostat Statistical Working Papers. Publications Office of the European Union, Luxembourg.

Guio, A.-C., and E. Marlier. 2017. "Amending the EU material deprivation indicator: Impact on the size and composition of the deprived population." In A. B. Atkinson, A.-C. Guio, and E. Marlier, eds., *Monitoring social inclusion in Europe*. Publications Office of the European Union, Luxembourg.

Guio, A.-C., and K. Van den Bosch. 2018. "Deprivation among couples: Sharing or unequal division?" 2018 Net-SILC3 International Conference on Comparative EU Statistics on Income and Living Conditions, Athens.

Gustafsson, B., and S. Ding. 2016. "Unequal growth: How household incomes and poverty in urban China have developed since 1988." Working Paper 55. China Institute for Income Distribution, Beijing Normal University.

Gustafsson, B., and S. Ding. 2017. "Unequal growth: How household incomes and poverty in urban China have developed since 1988, with an emphasis on the period from 2007 to 2013." Working Paper 2017–18. Centre for Human Capital and Productivity, Department of Economics, Western University, Ontario.

Haddad, L. J., and S. R. Kanbur. 1990. "How serious is the neglect of intra-household inequality?" *Economic Journal* 100: 866–881.

Hallegatte, S., M. Bangalore, L. Bonzanigo, M. Fay, T. Kane, U. Narloch, J. Rozenberg, D. Treguer, and A. Vogt-Schilb. 2016. *Shock waves: Managing the impacts of climate change on poverty.* Climate Change and Development Series, World Bank, Washington, DC.

Hallegatte, S., F. Henriet, A. Patwardhan, K. Narayanan, S. Ghosh, S. Karmakar, U. Patnaik, A. Abhayankar, S. Pohit, J. Corfee-Morlot, C. Herweijer, N. Ranger, S. Bhattacharya, M. Bachu, S. Priya, K. Dhore, F. Rafique, P. Mathur, and N. Naville. 2010. *Flood risks, climate change impacts and adaptation benefits in Mumbai: An initial assessment of socioeconomic consequences of present and climate change induced flood risks and of possible adaptation options.* OECD, Paris.

Harrington, M. 1962. *The other America.* Macmillan, New York.

Havinga, I., G. Kamanou, and V. Q. Viet. 2010. "A note on the mis(use) of national accounts for estimation of household final consumption expenditures for poverty measures." In S. Anand, P. Segal, and J. E. Stiglitz, eds., *Debates on the measurement of global poverty.* Oxford University Press, Oxford.

Howes, S. 1993. "Income inequality in urban China in the 1980s: Levels, trends, and determinants." Development Economics Research Programme, Discussion Paper EF 3. London School of Economics, London.

Hulme, D. 2016. *Should rich nations help the poor?* Polity Press, Cambridge.

Hungarian Central Statistical Office. 1975. *Hungarian survey on relative income differences.* KSH, Budapest.

Hussain, A. 2003. "Urban poverty in China: Measurement, patterns and policies." International Labour Office, Geneva.

Ibañez, A. M. 2008. *Desplazamiento forzoso en Colombia: Un camino sin retorno hacia la Pobreza.* Ediciones Uniandes, Bogotá.

Intergovernmental Panel on Climate Change (IPCC). 2013. *Climate change, 2013: The physical science basis: Contribution of working group I to the fifth assessment report of the Intergovernmental Panel on Climate Change,* edited by T. F. Stocker, D. Qin, G.-K. Plattner, M. Tignor, S. K. Allen, J. Boschung, A. Nauels, Y. Xia, V. Bex, and P. M. Midgley. Cambridge University Press, Cambridge.

International Energy Agency (IEA). 2017. *Tracking clean energy innovation progress.* OECD/IEA, Paris.

International Fund for Agricultural Development (IFAD). 2011. *Rural poverty report 2011.* IFAD, Rome.

International Labour Organization (ILO). 2013. *Methodologies of compiling consumer price indices: 2012 ILO survey of country practices: Preliminary results.* ILO, Geneva.

International Labour Organization, IMF, OECD, UNECE, Eurostat, and World Bank. 2004. *Consumer price index manual: Theory and practice.* ILO, Geneva.

International Obesity Task Force. 2005. "Obesity in Europe." Briefing Paper, EU Platform on Diet, Physical Activity, and Health. International Obesity Task Force, London.

International Renewable Energy Agency (IRENA). 2018. *Renewable power generation costs in 2017.* IRENA, Abu Dhabi.

Istat. 2009. *La misura della povertà assoluta.* Metodi e norme 39. Istat, Rome.

Istat. 2015. *La nuova indagine sulle spese per consumi in Italia.* Methods: Statistical readings. Istat, Rome.

Istat. 2016. *Income and living conditions: Year 2015.* Istat, Rome.

Istat. 2017. "Spese per consumi delle famiglie." Anno 2016, Statistiche, 6 July. Istat, Rome.

Instituto Nacional de Estatística. 2014. *Resultados preliminares do recenseamento geral da população e habitação de Angola 2014.* INE, Luanda.

Instituto Nacional de Estatística. 2016. *Resultados definitivos do recenseamento geral da população e habitação de Angola 2014.* INE, Luanda.

Jencks, C. 2016. "Why the very poor have become poorer." *New York Review of Books,* 9 June.

Jenkins, R. 2001. *Churchill.* Macmillan, London.

Jenkins, S. P. 1991. "Poverty measurement and the within-household distribution: agenda for action." *Journal of Social Policy* 20(4): 457–483.

Jenkins, S. P. 2011. *Changing fortunes: Income mobility and poverty dynamics in Britain.* Oxford University Press, Oxford.

Jenkins, S. P. 2015. "World income inequality databases: An assessment of WIID and SWIID." *Journal of Economic Inequality* 13(4): 629–671.

Jenkins, S. P., A. Brandolini, J. Micklewright, and B. Nolan, eds. 2013. *The Great Recession and the distribution of household income.* Oxford University Press, Oxford.

Johnson, P., and S. Webb. 1989. "Counting people with low incomes: The impact of recent changes in official statistics." *Fiscal Studies* 10: 66–82.

Jolliffe, D. M., and E. B. Prydz. 2017. "Societal poverty: A relative and relevant measure." Policy Research Working Paper 8073. World Bank, Washington, DC.

Jolly, R. 2012. "Foreword: UNICEF, children, and child poverty." In A. Minujin and S. Nandy, eds., *Global child poverty and well-being: Measurement, concepts, policy, and action.* Policy Press, Bristol.

Kaldor, N. 1955. "Alternative theories of distribution." *Review of Economic Studies* 23(2): 83–100.

Kamanou, G., M. Ward, and I. Havinga. 2005. "Statistical issues in measuring poverty from non-survey sources." Chapter VI in *Handbook on poverty statistics: Concepts, methods, and policy use.* Statistics Division, United Nations, New York.

Kelley, C. P., S. Mohtadi, M. A. Cane, R. Seager, and Y. Kushnir. 2015. "Climate change in the Fertile Crescent and implications of the recent Syrian drought." *PNAS* 112(11): 3241–3246.

Kenya National Bureau of Statistics. 2007. *Basic report on well-being in Kenya.* Nairobi, Kenya.

Kilic, T., U. Serajuddin, H. Uematsu, and N. Yoshida. 2017. "Costing household surveys for monitoring progress toward ending extreme poverty and boosting shared prosperity." Policy Research Working Paper 7951. World Bank, Washington, DC.

Khan, A. R. 1998. "Poverty in China in the period of globalization: New evidence on trend and pattern." Issues in Development Discussion Paper 22. International Labour Office, Geneva.

Khan, A. R. 2004. "Growth, inequality, and poverty." Issues in Employment and Poverty Discussion Paper 15. International Labour Organization, Geneva.

Khan, R., O. Morrissey, and P. Mosley. 2016. "Colonial legacy and poverty reduction in Sub-Saharan Africa." CREDIT Research Paper 16/01. Centre for Research in Economic Development and International Trade, University of Nottingham.

Kirsch, T. D., C. Wadhwani, L. Sauer, S. Doocy, and C. Catlett. 2012. "Impact of the 2010 Pakistan floods on rural and urban populations at six months." *PLOS Currents Disasters* (22 August).

Klavus, J. 1999. "Health care and economic well-being: Estimating equivalence scales for public health care utilization." *Health Economics* 8(7): 613–625.

Koen, V. 1997. "Price measurement and mismeasurement in Central Asia." In J. Falkingham, J. Klugman, S. Marnie, and J. Micklewright, eds. *Household welfare in Central Asia*. Macmillan Press, Basingstoke.

Kohara, M., and F. Ohtake. 2014. "Rising inequality in Japan: A challenge caused by population ageing and drastic changes in employment." In B. Nolan, W. Salverda, D. Checchi, I. Marx, A. McKnight, I. G. Tóth, and H. van de Werfhorst, eds., *Changing inequalities and societal impacts in rich countries*. Oxford University Press, Oxford.

Kordos, J. 1991. "Poverty measurement in Poland." Central Statistical Office, Warsaw.

Kordos, J. 2005. "Household surveys in transition countries." In United Nations, *Household sample surveys in developing and transition countries*. Studies in Methods Series F 96. Department of Economic and Social Affairs, Statistics Division, United Nations, New York.

Kostermans, K. 1994. "Assessing the quality of anthropometric data: Background and illustrated guidelines for survey managers." LSMS Working Paper 101. World Bank, Washington, DC.

Krause, E., and R. E. Reeves. 2017. *Hurricanes hit the poor the hardest*. Social Mobility Memos, 18 September. Brookings Institution, Washington, DC.

Kuklys, W. 2005. *Amartya Sen's capability approach: Theoretical insights and empirical applications*. Springer, Berlin.

Kulshrestha, A. C., and A. Kar. 2005. "Consumer expenditure from the national accounts and national sample survey." In A. Deaton and V. Kozel, eds., *The great Indian poverty debate*. Macmillan, New Delhi.

Kuznets, S. 1955. "Economic growth and income inequality." *American Economic Review* 45: 1–28.

Li, S. 2016. "Income inequality and economic growth in China in the last three decades." *The Round Table: The Commonwealth Journal of International Affairs* 105(6): 641–666.

Li, S., H. Sato, and T. Sicular. 2013. *Rising inequality in China*. Cambridge University Press, Cambridge.

Liberia Institute of Statistics and Geo-Information Services (LISGIS). 2016. *Household Income and Expenditure Survey 2014: Statistical abstract*. LISGIS, Monrovia.

Lindert, P. 2004. *Growing public: Social spending and economic growth since the eighteenth century*. Cambridge University Press, Cambridge.

Lise, J., and S. Seitz. 2011. "Consumption inequality and intra-household allocations." *Review of Economic Studies* 78: 328–355.

Lise, J., N. Sudo, M. Suzuki, K. Yamada, and T. Yamada. 2014. "Wage, income, and consumption inequality in Japan, 1981–2008: From boom to lost decades." *Review of Income Dynamics* 17: 582–612.

Logan, T. 2009. "Are Engel curve estimates of CPI bias biased?" *Historical Methods* 42(3): 97–109.

Lustig, N. 2015. "The redistributive impact of government spending on education and health: Evidence from thirteen developing countries in the Commitment to Equity project." In S. Gupta, M. Keen, B. J. Clements, and R. A. de Mooij, eds., *Inequality and fiscal policy*. International Monetary Fund, Washington, DC.

Lyons-Amos, M., and T. Stones. 2017. "Trends in Demographic and Health Survey data quality: An analysis of age heaping over time in 34 countries in Sub Saharan Africa between 1987 and 2015." *BMC Research Note* 10: 760.

Macdonald, D., and D. Wilson. 2013. *Poverty or prosperity: Indigenous children in Canada*. Canadian Centre for Policy Alternatives, Ottawa.

Mack, J., and S. Lansley. 1985. *Poor Britain*. Allen and Unwin, London.

Maddison, A. 2001. *The world economy: A millennial perspective*. OECD, Paris.

Marlier, E., and A. B. Atkinson. 2010. "Indicators of poverty and social exclusion in a global context." *Journal of Policy Analysis and Management* 29: 285–304.

Marlier, E., A. B. Atkinson, B. Cantillon, and B. Nolan. 2007. *The EU and social inclusion: Facing the challenges*. Policy Press, Bristol.

Matthews, M. 1986. *Poverty in the Soviet Union*. Cambridge University Press, Cambridge.

McAuley, A. 1979. *Economic welfare in the Soviet Union: Poverty, living standards, and inequality*. George Allen and Unwin, Hemel Hempstead, and University of Wisconsin Press, Madison.

McKay, A., J. Pirttilä, and F. Tarp. 2015. "Ghana: Poverty reduction over thirty years." WIDER Working Paper 2015/052. World Institute for Development Economics Research, Helsinki.

Meyer, B. D., and J. X. Sullivan. 2017. "Consumption and income inequality in the US since the 1960s." NBER Working Paper 23655. National Bureau of Economic Research, Cambridge, MA.

Micklewright, J. 2001. "Should the UK government measure poverty and social exclusion with a composite index?" In CASE, *Indicators of progress: A discussion of approaches to monitor the government's strategy to tackle poverty and social exclusion*, CASE Report 13. Centre for Analysis of Social Exclusion, London School of Economics and Political Science, London.

Micklewright, J. 2002. "Social exclusion and children: A European view for a US debate." CASE paper 51. Centre for Analysis of Social Exclusion, London School of Economics and Political Science, London.

Micklewright, J., and S. Ismail. 2001. "What can child anthropometry reveal about living standards and public policy? An illustration from Central Asia." *Review of Income and Wealth* 47(1): 65–80.

Milanovic, B. 1990. "Poverty in Poland, 1978–88." Background paper for the *World Development Report 1990*. World Bank, Washington, DC.

Milasi, S., and R. J. Waldmann. 2018. "Top marginal taxation and economic growth." *Applied Economics* 50(19): 2156–2170.

Ministero dell'Economia e delle Finanze. 2018. "Documento di economia e finanza 2018: Allegato: Indicatori di benessere equo e sostenibile." Ministero dell'Economia e delle Finanze, Rome.

Mitra, S. 2006. "The capability approach and disability." *Journal of Disability Policy Studies* 16(4): 236–247.

Mitra, S., A. Posarac, and B. Vick. 2013. "Disability and poverty in developing countries: A multidimensional study." *World Development* 41: 1–18.

Mitrakos, T. 2013. "Inequality, poverty, and living conditions in Greece: Recent developments and prospects." *Social Cohesion and Development* 8: 37–58.

Morciano, M., R. Hancock, and S. Pudney. 2015. "Disability costs and equivalence scales in the older population." *Review of Income and Wealth* 61(3): 494–514.

Morduch, J., and R. Schneider. 2017. *The Financial Diaries: How American families cope in a world of uncertainty.* Princeton University Press, Princeton, NJ.

Morelli, S., T. M. Smeeding, and J. P. Thompson. 2015. "Post-1970 trends in within-country inequality and poverty: Rich and middle income countries." In A. B. Atkinson and F. Bourguignon, eds., *Handbook of income distribution,* vol 2A, Elsevier, Amsterdam.

Moyo, D. 2010. *Dead aid: Why aid is not working and how there is another way for Africa.* Penguin Press, London.

Mozambique Ministry of Economics and Finance. 2016. *Poverty and well-being in Mozambique: Fourth national poverty assessment (IOF 2014/15).* Executive summary. Ministry of Economics and Finance, Maputo.

Muellbauer, J. N. J. 1977. "Community preferences and the representative consumer." *Econometrica* 44: 979–999.

Mugambe, K. 2009. "The Poverty Eradication Action Plan." In F. Kuteesa, E. Tumusiime-Mutebile, A. Whitworth, and T. Williamson, eds., *Uganda's economic reforms: Insider accounts.* Oxford University Press, Oxford.

Murphy, B., X. Zhang, and C. Dionne. 2010. "Low income in Canada: A multi-line and multi-index perspective." Income Research Paper Series catalog 75F0002M—no. 001. Statistics Canada, Ottawa.

Murphy, E., and E. Garvey. 2004. "A consumer price index for low-income households in Ireland (1989–2001)." Working Paper 04/03. Combat Poverty Agency, Dublin.

Nandy, S., and D. Gordon. 2015. "Policy relevant measurement of poverty in low, middle and high income countries." In E. Braathen, J. May, and G. Wright, eds., *Poverty and inequality in middle income countries: Policy achievements, political obstacles.* Zed Books, London.

Naoroji, D. 1901. *Poverty and un-British rule in India.* S. Sonnenschein & Co., London.

Narayan, D., R. Chambers, M. K. Shah, and P. Petesch. 2000. *Voices of the poor: Crying out for change.* Oxford University Press, New York.

Narayan, D., with R. Patel, K. Schafft, A. Rademacher, and S. Koch-Schulte. 2000a. *Voices of the poor: Can anyone hear us?* Oxford University Press, New York.

Narayan, D., and P. Petesch. 2002. *Voices of the poor: From many lands.* Oxford University Press, New York.

National Research Council. 2000. *Beyond six billion: Forecasting the world's population.* National Academies Press, Washington, DC.

Nepal Central Bureau of Statistics. 2005. *Poverty trends in Nepal (1995–96 and 2003–04).* National Planning Commission, Kathmandu.

Nepal Central Bureau of Statistics. 2011. *Poverty in Nepal 2010/11.* Central Bureau of Statistics, Kathmandu.

Nepal Central Bureau of Statistics. 2016. *Annual Household Survey 2014/15 (major findings).* Central Bureau of Statistics, Kathmandu.

Newhouse, D., P. Suarez-Becerra, and M. Evans. 2016. "New estimates of extreme poverty for children." Policy Research Working Paper 7845. World Bank, Washington, DC.

Nickel, J. W. 2014. "What future for human rights?" *Ethics and International Affairs* 28: 213–223.

Nussbaum, M. 1988. "Nature, function, and capability: Aristotle on political distribution." *Oxford Studies in Ancient Philosophy* (suppl.): 145–184.

Nussbaum, M. 2000. *Women and human development: The capabilities approach*. Cambridge University Press, New York.

Nussbaum, M. 2000a. *Sex and social justice*. Oxford University Press, Oxford.

Nussbaum, M. 2003. "Capabilities as fundamental entitlements: Sen and social justice." *Feminist Economics* 9: 33–59.

Nussbaum, M., and J. Glover, eds. 1995. *Women, culture, and development: A study of human capabilities*. Clarendon Press, Oxford.

Okun, A. M. 1975. *Equality and efficiency: The big tradeoff*. Brookings Institution, Washington, DC.

Organisation for Economic Cooperation and Development (OECD). 1996. *Economic Survey of Poland 1997*. OECD, Paris.

OECD. 2008. *Growing unequal?* OECD, Paris.

OECD. 2015. *In it together*. OECD, Paris.

O'Higgins, M., and S. P. Jenkins. 1990. "Poverty in the EC: Estimates for 1975, 1980, and 1985." In R. Teekens and B. M. S. Van Praag, eds., *Analysing poverty in the European Community*. Eurostat, Luxembourg.

Olinto, P., K. Beegle, C. Sobrado, and H. Uematsu. 2013. "The state of the poor: Where are the poor, where is extreme poverty harder to end, and what is the current profile of the world's poor?" *Economic Premise* 125(October). World Bank, Washington, DC.

Oreskes, N., and E. Conway. 2010. *Merchants of doubt*. Bloomsbury Press, London.

Orshansky, M. 1965. "Counting the poor: Another look at the poverty profile." *Social Security Bulletin* 28: 3–29.

Ostry, J. D., A. Berg, and C. G. Tsangarides. 2014. "Redistribution, inequality, and growth." IMF Staff Discussion Note SDN/14/02. International Monetary Fund, Washington, DC.

Overseas Development Institute (ODI). 2015. *Exclusion in household surveys: Causes, impacts, and ways forward*. ODI, London.

Pahl, J. 1989. *Money and marriage*. Macmillan, London.

Pan Ké Shon, J.-L. 2015. "Pourquoi l'indicateur de pauvreté en conditions de vie baisse malgré la crise économique ouverte en 2008?" Document de travail de la Direction des Statistiques Démographiques et Sociales F1502. Institut National de la Statistique et des Études Économiques, Paris.

Parker, M. 2011. *The sugar barons*. Windmill Books, London.

Paukert, F. 1973. "Income distribution at different levels of development: A survey of the evidence." *International Labor Review* 108: 97–125.

Pemberton, S., D. Gordon, S. Nandy, C. Pantazis, and P. Townsend. 2007. "Child rights and child poverty: Can the international framework of children's rights be used to improve child survival rates?" *PLOS Medicine* 4: e307.

Perkins, D. H. 1988. "Reforming China's economic system." *Journal of Economic Literature* 26: 601–645.

Perry, B. 2016. *Household incomes in New Zealand: Trends in indicators of inequality and hardship, 1982 to 2015*. Ministry of Social Development, Wellington.

Persson, T., and G. Tabellini. 1994. "Is inequality harmful for growth?" *American Economic Review* 84(3): 600–621.

Pettersson, H., and P. Silva. 2005. "Analysis of design effects for surveys in developing countries." In United Nations, *Household sample surveys in developing and transition countries*. Studies in Methods Series F 96. Department of Economic and Social Affairs, Statistics Division, United Nations, New York.

Pfeiffer, A., R. Millar, C. Hepburn, and E. Beinhocker. 2016. "The '2° C capital stock' for electricity generation: Committed cumulative carbon emissions from the electricity generation sector and the transition to a green economy." *Applied Energy* 179: 1395–1408.

Piketty, T. 2014. *Capital in the Twenty-First Century*. Harvard University Press, Cambridge, MA.

Pincus, J., and J. Sender. 2008. "Quantifying poverty in Viet Nam: Who counts?" *Journal of Vietnamese Studies* 3: 108–150.

Planning Institute of Jamaica. 2007. "The poverty-environment nexus: Establishing an approach for determining Special Development Areas in Jamaica."

Platt Boustan, L., M. E. Kahn, P. W. Rhode, and M. L. Yanguas. 2017. "The effect of natural disasters on economic activity in US counties: A century of data." NBER Working Paper 23410. National Bureau of Economic Research, Cambridge, MA.

Ponthieux, S. 2013. "Income pooling and equal sharing within the household—What can we learn from the 2010 EU-SILC module?" Eurostat Methodologies and Working Papers. Publications Office of the European Union, Luxembourg.

Ponthieux, S. 2017. "Intra-household pooling and sharing of resources: A tentative 'modified' equivalised income." In A. B. Atkinson, A.-C. Guio, and E. Marlier, eds., *Monitoring social inclusion in Europe*. Publications Office of the European Union, Luxembourg.

Prais, S. J. 1959. "Whose cost of living?" *Review of Economic Studies* 26: 126–134.

Prennushi, G. 1999. "Nepal: Poverty at the turn of the twenty-first century: Main report and background studies." South Asia Region Report IDP 174. World Bank, Washington, DC.

Pullum, T., S. Assaf, and S. Staveteig. 2017. "Comparisons of DHS estimates of fertility and mortality with other estimates." DHS Methodological Reports 2. ICF, Rockville, MD.

Rangarajan, C. 2014. *Report of the Expert Group to review the methodology for measurement of poverty*. Planning Commission, New Delhi.

Ranger, N., S. Hallegatte, S. Bhattacharya, M. Bachu, S. Priya, K. Dhore, F. Rafique, P. Mathur, N. Naville, F. Henriet, C. Herweijer, S. Pohit, and J. Corfee-Morlot. 2011. "An assessment of the potential impact of climate change on flood risk in Mumbai." *Climate Change* 104: 139–167.

Ravallion, M. 1988. "Expected poverty under risk-induced welfare variability." *Economic Journal* 98: 1171–1182.

Ravallion, M. 2001. "Growth, inequality, and poverty: Looking beyond averages." *World Development* 29(11): 1803–1815.

Ravallion, M. 2003. "Measuring aggregate welfare in developing countries: How well do national accounts and surveys agree?" *Review of Economics and Statistics* 85: 645–652.

Ravallion, M. 2007. "Inequality *is* bad for the poor." In S. Jenkins and J. Micklewright, eds., *Inequality and poverty re-examined*. Oxford University Press, Oxford.

Ravallion, M. 2011. "On multidimensional indices of poverty." *Journal of Economic Inequality* 9: 235–248.

Ravallion, M. 2012. "Mashup indices of development." *World Bank Research Observer* 27: 1–32.

Ravallion, M. 2015. "On testing the scale sensitivity of poverty measures." *Economics Letters* 137: 88–90.

Ravallion, M. 2016. *The economics of poverty: History, measurement, and policy.* Oxford University Press, Oxford.

Ravallion, M. 2017. "An interesting step backwards in measuring global poverty." Department of Economics, Georgetown University.

Ravallion, M., and S. Chen. 2011. "Weakly relative poverty." *Review of Economics and Statistics* 93: 1251–1261.

Ravallion, M., and S. Chen. 2013. "A proposal for truly global poverty measures." *Global Policy* 4: 258–265.

Ravallion, M., S. Chen, and P. Sangraula. 2007. "New evidence on the globalization of urban poverty." *Population and Development Review* 33: 667–702.

Ravallion, M., S. Chen, and P. Sangraula. 2009. "Dollar a day revisited." *World Bank Economic Review* 23: 163–184.

Ravallion, M., G. Datt, and D. van de Walle. 1991. "Quantifying absolute poverty in the developing world." *Review of Income and Wealth*, series 37: 345–361.

Ravallion, M., G. Datt, D. van de Walle, and E. Chan. 1991. "Quantifying the magnitude and severity of absolute poverty in the developing world in the mid-1980s." PRE Working Paper 587. World Bank, Washington, DC.

Rawls, J. 1971. *A theory of justice.* Harvard University Press, Cambridge, MA.

Reddy, S. G., and T. W. Pogge. 2010. "How *not* to count the poor." In S. Anand, P. Segal, and J. E. Stiglitz, eds., *Debates on the measurement of global poverty.* Oxford University Press, Oxford.

Renwick, T., and L. Fox. 2016. "The supplemental poverty measure: 2015." *Current Population Report* P60-258 (revised). US Census Bureau, Washington, DC.

Ridley, M. 2015. "My life as a climate change lukewarmer." *The Times [of London]*, 19 January.

Ringius, L., P. Frederiksen, and K. Birr-Pedersen. 2002. *Burden sharing in the context of global climate change: A North-South perspective.* Technical Report 424. National Environmental Research Institute, Denmark.

Riskin, C., and Q. Gao. 2009. "The changing nature of urban poverty in China." Initiative for Policy Dialogue Working Paper Series. Columbia University, New York.

Robertson, D. H. 1954. "Utility and all what?" *Economic Journal* 64: 665–678.

Robinson, M. 2002. Statement at the World Summit on Sustainable Development Plenary Session, Johannesburg, 29 August.

Rowntree, B. S. 1901. *Poverty: A study of town life.* Longmans, Green and Co., London.

Rowntree, B. S. 1902. *Poverty: A study of town life,* 2nd ed. Macmillan and Co., London.

Sahn, D. E., and D. C. Stifel. 2003. "Urban-rural inequality in living standards in Africa." *Journal of African Economics* 12(4): 564–597.

Sala-i-Martin, X., and M. Pinkovskiy. 2010. "African poverty is falling . . . much faster than you think!" Working Paper 15775. National Bureau of Economic Research, Cambridge, MA.

Salazar, R. A., B. Y. Díaz, and R. P. Pinzón. 2013. "Multidimensional poverty in Colombia, 1997–2010." ISER Working Paper Series 2013-03. Institute for Social and Economic Research, University of Essex.

Santos, M. E., and P. Villatoro. 2018. "A multidimensional poverty index for Latin America." *Review of Income and Wealth*, series 64(1): 52–82.

Satz, D. 2003. "International economic justice." In H. LaFollette, ed., *The Oxford handbook of practical ethics*. Oxford University Press, Oxford.

Scott, K., D. Steele, and T. Temesgen. 2005. "Living Standards Measurement Study Surveys." In United Nations, *Household sample surveys in developing and transition countries*. Studies in Methods Series F 96. Department of Economic and Social Affairs, Statistics Division, United Nations, New York.

Secretariat of the Pacific Community. 2015. "2020 World Round of Population and Housing Censuses—Pacific Island countries' census planning meeting: International recommendations/standards, contemporary technologies and regional cooperation." Pacific 2020 Census Round Planning Meeting/Working Paper 2a.

Sen, A. K. 1976. "Poverty: An ordinal approach to measurement." *Econometrica* 44: 219–231.

Sen, A. K. 1985. *Commodities and capabilities*. North-Holland, Amsterdam.

Sen, A. K. 1990. "Gender and cooperative conflicts." In I. Tinker, ed., *Persistent inequalities*, Oxford University Press, Oxford.

Sen, A. K. 1992. *Markets and governments*. Institute for Economic Development, Boston University.

Sen, A. K. 1992a. *Inequality reexamined*. Harvard University Press, Cambridge, MA.

Sen, A. K. 1993. "Capability and well-being." In M. C. Nussbaum and A. K. Sen, eds., *The quality of life*. Clarendon Press, Oxford.

Sen, A. K. 2009. *The idea of justice*. Allen Lane, London.

Shaefer, H. L., and K. Edin. 2013. "Rising extreme poverty in the United States and the response of federal means-tested transfers." *Social Service Review* 87: 250–268.

Shorrocks, A. F. 1995. "Revisiting the Sen poverty index." *Econometrica* 63: 1225–1230.

Shue, H. 1996. *Basic rights*, 2nd ed. Princeton University Press, Princeton, NJ.

Singer, P. 1972. "Famine, affluence, and morality." *Philosophy and Public Affairs* 1: 229–243.

Smeeding, T. M., and L. Rainwater. 2004. "Comparing living standards across nations: Real incomes at the top, the bottom, and the middle." In E. N. Wolff, ed., *What has happened to the quality of life in the advanced industrialized nations?* Elgar, Northampton, MA.

Smeeding, T. M, P. Saunders, J. Coder, S. Jenkins, J. Fritzell, A. J. M. Hagenaars, R. Hauser, and M. Wolfson. 1993. "Poverty, inequality, and family living standards impacts across seven nations: The effect of noncash subsidies for health, education, and housing." *Review of Income and Wealth* 39: 229–256.

Smith. A. 1776. *An inquiry into the nature and causes of the wealth of nations*. W. Strahan and T. Cadell, London.

Smith, L. C., O. Dupriez, and N. Troubat. 2014. "Assessment of the reliability and relevance of the food data collected in national household consumption and expenditure surveys." IHSN Working Paper 008. International Household Survey Network.

Social Protection Committee Indicators Sub-Group. 2015. Portfolio of EU Social Indicators for the monitoring of progress towards the EU objectives for social protection and social inclusion (2015 update). European Commission, Brussels.

Solomon Islands Statistics Office. 2006. *Household Income and Expenditure Survey 2005/6: National report*, part 1. Department of Finance and Treasury, Honiara.

Solomon Islands National Statistical Office. 2015. *Solomon Islands 2012/13 Household Income and Expenditure Survey National Analytical Report*, vol. 1. Ministry of Finance and Treasury, Honiara.

Solomon Islands National Statistical Office. 2015a. *Solomon Islands poverty profile based on the 2012/13 household income and expenditure survey*. Ministry of Finance and Treasury, Honiara.

Solomon Islands National Statistical Office and UNDP Pacific Centre. 2008. *Analysis of the 2005/06 household income and expenditure survey*. Ministry of Finance and Treasury, Honiara.

Solt, F. 2009. "Standardizing the World Income Inequality Database." *Social Science Quarterly* 90(2): 231–242.

Solt, F. 2015. "On the assessment and use of cross-national income inequality datasets." *Journal of Economic Inequality* 13(4): 683–691.

Solt, F. 2016. "The Standardized World Income Inequality Database." *Social Science Quarterly* 97(5): 1267–1281.

Spinoni, J., G. Naumann, H. Carrao, P. Barbosa, and J. Vogt. 2013. "World drought frequency, duration, and severity for 1951–2010." *International Journal of Climatology* 34: 2792–2804.

Sri Lanka Department of Census and Statistics. 2011. *Poverty indicators: Household income and expenditure survey, 2009/10*, Ministry of Finance and Planning, Colombo.

Statistics Canada. 2016. *Low income lines: What they are and how they are created*. Income Research Paper Series 75F0002M—no. 002. Statistics Canada, Ottawa, Ontario.

Statistics Mauritius. 2015. *Poverty analysis 2012*. Ministry of Finance and Economic Development, Port Louis.

Steckel, R. H. 1995. "Stature and the standard of living." *Journal of Economic Literature* 33: 1903–1940.

Stern, N. H. 2009. *A blueprint for a safer planet*. Bodley Head, London.

Stern, N. H. 2018. "Public economics as if time matters: Climate change and the dynamics of policy." *Journal of Public Economics* 162: 4–17.

Stigler, G. J. 1945. "The cost of subsistence." *Journal of Farm Economics* 27: 303–314.

Stiglitz, J. E. 2012. *The price of inequality*. W. W. Norton, New York.

Storms, B., T. Goedemé, K. Van den Bosch, and K. Devuyst. 2013. "Towards a common framework for developing cross-nationally comparable reference budgets in Europe." ImPRovE Methodological Paper 13/02. Poverty Reduction in Europe: Social Policy and Innovation (ImPRovE), Antwerp.

Subramanian, S. 2009. "'How many poor in the world?': A critique of Ravallion's reply." *Economic and Political Weekly* 44(5): 67–71.

Sukhatme, P. V. 1961. "The world's hunger and future needs in food supplies." *Journal of the Royal Statistical Society: Series A* 124: 463–525.

Szulc, A. 1990. "Aggregate poverty measures for Poland, 1980–1989 evidence." Third Polish British Seminar on Social Policy, Madralin/Warsaw.

Tandel, V., K. Hiranandani, and M. Kapoor. 2016. "What's in a definition? A study on implications and suitability of urban definitions in India through its Employment Guarantee Programme." Working Paper 1. IDFC Institute, Mumbai.

Tanzania National Bureau of Statistics. 2014. *Household Budget Survey main report 2011/12*. Ministry of Finance, Dar es Salaam.

Thane, P., and R. Davidson. 2016. *The Child Poverty Action Group 1965 to 2015*. CPAG, London.

Tobin, J. 1970. "On limiting the domain of inequality." *Journal of Law and Economics* 13: 263–277.

Törmälehto, V.-M., and H. Sauli. 2017. "The distributional impact of imputed rent in EU-SILC 2007–2012." In A. B. Atkinson, A.-C. Guio, and E. Marlier, eds., *Monitoring social inclusion in Europe*. Eurostat, Luxembourg.

Townsend, P. 1962. "The meaning of poverty." *British Journal of Sociology* 13(3): 210–227.

Townsend, P. 1979. *Poverty in the United Kingdom: A survey of household resources and standards of living*. Allen Lane, Harmondsworth.

Tresoldi, J. C. 2013. "How are urban and rural areas determined in census cartography in Latin America?" January 23. POPClimate, United Nations Population Fund.

Uematsu, H., A. R. Shidiq, and S. Tiwari. 2016. "Trends and drivers of poverty reduction in Nepal: A historical perspective." Policy Research Working Paper 7830. World Bank, Washington, DC.

Uganda Bureau of Statistics. 2014. *Uganda National Household Survey 2012/2013*. Uganda Bureau of Statistics, Kampala.

Uganda Ministry of Finance. 2014. *Poverty status report 2014*. Economic Development Policy and Research Department, Ministry of Finance, Kampala.

United Nations. 1954. *International definition and measurement of standards and levels of living*. United Nations Publications, New York.

United Nations. 2011. "World marriage patterns." *Population Facts*. Department of Economic and Social Affairs, Population Division, United Nations, New York.

United Nations. 2012. *Final draft of the guiding principles on extreme poverty and human rights*. United Nations, New York.

United Nations. 2014. *A world that counts*. Report by the Independent Expert Advisory Group on a Data Revolution for Sustainable Development, United Nations, New York.

United Nations. 2017. "Universal Declaration of Human Rights: History of the Document." United Nations website.

United Nations. 2017a. "Household size and composition around the world." *Population Facts*. Department of Economic and Social Affairs, Population Division, United Nations, New York.

United Nations. 2017b. *Principles and recommendations for population and housing censuses*, 3rd revision. Department of Economic and Social Affairs, United Nations, New York.

United Nations. 2018. *Tier classification for global SDG indicators.* 11 May. Department of Economic and Social Affairs, United Nations, New York.

United Nations Development Programme (UNDP). 1990. *Human Development Report 1990.* Oxford University Press, New York.

UNDP. 1999. *Human Development Report 1999.* Oxford University Press, New York.

UNDP. 2007. *Malaysia: Measuring and monitoring poverty and inequality.* UNDP Malaysia, Kuala Lumpur.

UNDP. 2016. *Human Development Report 2016.* UND, New York.

UNDP and Institute of National Planning. 2010. *Egypt Human Development Report 2010. Youth in Egypt: Building our future.* UNDP and Institute of National Planning, Cairo.

United Nations Environment Programme (UNEP). 2017. *The Emissions Gap Report 2017.* UNEP, Nairobi.

United Nations Permanent Forum on Indigenous Issues (UNPFII). 2016. "Indigenous peoples: Conflict, peace, and resolution." Fifteenth Session, New York.

United Nations Research Institute for Social Development (UNRISD). 2016. "Editorial—2016 flagship report published: Policy innovations for transformative change." *UNRISD eBulletin* 31(November).

US Agency for International Development (USAID). 2013. "Consumer price indices for the poor in Indonesia." USAID, Washington, DC.

US Department of Commerce. 2012. "Census coverage measurement estimation report: Summary of estimates of coverage for persons in the United States." Memorandum from Patrick J. Cantwell to David C. Whitford, prepared by Thomas Mule, DSSD 2010 Census Coverage Measurement Memorandum Series 2010-G-01, 22 May. US Government Printing Office, Washington, DC.

Van Ginneken, W., and J. Park. 1984. *Generating internationally comparable income distribution estimates.* International Labour Office, Geneva.

Vassen, M., M. Thiam, and T. Lê. 2005. "The Demographic and Health Surveys." In United Nations, *Household Sample Surveys in Developing and Transition Countries.* Studies in Methods Series F 96. Department of Economic and Social Affairs, Statistics Division, United Nations, New York.

Villarroel, P., and W. Hernani-Limarino. 2013. "La evolución de la pobreza en Bolivia: Un enfoque multidimensional." *Revista Latinoamericana de Desarrollo Económico/ Latin American Journal of Economic Development* 20: 7–74.

Walzer, M. 1983. *Spheres of justice: A defense of pluralism and equality.* Basic Books, New York.

Wambile, A., A. Dabalen, J. Mistiaen, and P. Gubbins. 2016. "The effect of survey design on household expenditure estimates and poverty: Case of diary versus recall from Kenya." November.

Wang, X., H. Feng, Q. Xia, and S. Alkire. 2016. "On the relationship between income poverty and multidimensional poverty in China." OPHI Working Paper 101. University of Oxford, Oxford.

Webb, J. 2002. "Always with us? The evolution of poverty in Britain, 1886–2002." DPhil. thesis, Nuffield College, University of Oxford.

Weisbrod, B. A, W. L. Hansen. 1968. "An income–net worth approach to measuring economic welfare." *American Economic Review* 58: 1315–1329.

Whelan, C. T., B. Nolan, and B. Maître. 2014. "Multidimensional poverty measurement in Europe: An application of the adjusted headcount approach." *Journal of European Social Policy* 24(2): 183–197.

Wilkinson, R. G., and K. Pickett. 2009. *The spirit level.* Allen Lane, London.

Winsemius, H. C., B. Jongmam, T. Veldkamp, and S. Hallegatte. 2018. "Disaster risk, climate change, and poverty: Assessing the global exposure of poor people to floods and droughts." *Environment and Development Economics* 3(special issue 3, "Poverty and Climate Change"): 328–348.

Wittenberg, M. 2015. "Problems with SWIID: The case of South Africa." *Journal of Economic Inequality* 13(4): 673–677.

Woolley, F., and J. Marshall. 1994. "Measuring inequality within the household." *Review of Income and Wealth*, series 40: 415–431.

World Bank. 1978. *World Development Report 1978.* World Bank, Washington, DC.

World Bank. 1990. *World Development Report 1990: Poverty.* Oxford University Press, New York.

World Bank. 1999. *Georgia poverty and income distribution*, vol. 1, *Main report.* Report 19348-GE. World Bank, Washington, DC.

World Bank. 1999a. *Vietnam Development Report 2000: Attacking poverty.* Country Economic Memorandum, Report 19914-VN. World Bank, Washington, DC.

World Bank. 2001. *World Development Report 2000/2001: Attacking poverty.* Oxford University Press, New York.

World Bank. 2005. *World Development Report 2006: Equity and development.* Oxford University Press, New York.

World Bank. 2006. "Nepal: Resilience among conflict: An assessment of poverty in Nepal, 1995–96 and 2004–04." Report 34834-NP. World Bank, Washington, DC.

World Bank. 2009. *China: From poor areas to poor people: China's evolving poverty reduction agenda: An assessment of poverty and inequality in China.* Report 47349-CN. World Bank, Washington, DC.

World Bank. 2012. "Liberia poverty note: Tracking the dimensions of poverty." Report 69979-LR. World Bank, Washington DC.

World Bank. 2013. *Bangladesh poverty assessment: Assessing a decade of progress in reducing poverty, 2000–2010.* Bangladesh Development Series Paper 31. World Bank, Washington, DC.

World Bank. 2014. *Summary of results and findings of the 2011 International Comparison Program.* World Bank, Washington, DC.

World Bank. 2014a. *Where have all the poor gone? Cambodia Poverty Assessment 2013*, 2nd ed. World Bank, Washington, DC.

World Bank. 2015. *A measured approach to ending poverty and boosting shared prosperity: Concepts, data, and the twin goals.* Policy research report. World Bank, Washington, DC.

World Bank. 2015a. "World Bank's new end-poverty tool: Surveys in poorest countries." Press release, 15 October. World Bank, Washington, DC.

World Bank. 2016. *Poverty and shared prosperity 2016: Taking on inequality.* World Bank, Washington, DC.

World Bank. 2016a. *Indigenous Latin America in the twenty-first century: The first decade.* World Bank, Washington, DC.

World Bank. 2016b. "Monitoring global poverty: A cover note to the report of the Commission on Global Poverty, chaired by Prof. Sir Anthony B. Atkinson." 18 October. World Bank, Washington DC.

World Bank. 2017. *Monitoring global poverty: Report of the Commission on Global Poverty*. World Bank, Washington, DC.

World Bank. 2018. *Poverty and shared prosperity 2018: Piecing together the poverty puzzle*. World Bank, Washington, DC.

World Bank Group. 2016. *Global Monitoring Report 2015/2016: Development goals in an era of demographic change*. World Bank, Washington, DC.

Xu, X. 2015. *Study on statistics issues of China's income distribution* (in Chinese). Peking University Press, Beijing.

Zambia Central Statistical Office. 2012. *Living Conditions Monitoring Survey report 2006 and 2010*. Lusaka, Zambia.

Zambia Central Statistical Office. 2016. *2015 Living Conditions Monitoring Survey: Key findings*. Central Statistics Office, Lusaka.

Zhang, Y., and R. Wang. 2011. "The main approach of proposed integrated household survey of China." Wye City Group on Statistics on Rural Development and Agricultural Household Income, Fourth meeting, Rio de Janeiro, 9–11 November.

Zhu, L. 2015. "Poverty measures taken in China." Submission to the Commission on Global Poverty.

INDEX OF NAMES

Index excludes national reports beginning at page 247. Page numbers in *italics* refer to figures, tables, and boxes.

INDEX OF SUBJECTS

Index excludes national reports beginning at page 247. Page numbers in *italics* refer to figures, tables, and boxes.